Speculative Television and the Doing and Undoing of Religion

This book explores the concept that, as participation in traditional religion declines, the complex and fantastical worlds of speculative television have become the place where theological questions and issues are negotiated, understood, and formed.

From bodies, robots, and souls to purgatories and post-apocalyptic scenarios and new forms of digital scripture, the shows examined—from *Buffy the Vampire Slayer* to *Westworld*—invite their viewers and fans to engage with and imagine concepts traditionally reserved for religious spaces. Informed by recent trends in both fan studies and religious studies, and with an emphasis on practice as well as belief, the thematically focused narrative posits that it is through the intersections of these shows that we find the reframing and rethinking of religious ideas.

This truly interdisciplinary work will resonate with scholars and upper-level students in the areas of religion, television studies, popular culture, fan studies, media studies, and philosophy.

Gregory Erickson is Professor at The Gallatin School of New York University, USA.

Routledge Advances in Television Studies

15 A European Television Fiction Renaissance
Premium Production Models and Transnational Circulation
Edited by Luca Barra and Massimo Scaglioni

16 Difficult Women on Television Drama
The Gender Politics of Complex Women in Serial Narratives
Isabel C. Pinedo

17 Global Trafficking Networks on Film and Television
Hollywood's Cartel Wars
César Albarrán-Torres

18 Cognition, Emotion, and Aesthetics in Contemporary Serial Television
Edited by Ted Nannicelli and Héctor J. Pérez

19 Children, Youth, and International Television
Edited by Debbie Olson and Adrian Schober

20 Quality Telefantasy
How US Quality TV Brought Zombies, Dragons and Androids into the Mainstream
Andrew Lynch

21 Speculative Television and the Doing and Undoing of Religion
Gregory Erickson

Speculative Television and the Doing and Undoing of Religion

Gregory Erickson

LONDON AND NEW YORK

First published 2023
by Routledge
4 Park Square, Milton Park, Abingdon, Oxon OX14 4RN

and by Routledge
605 Third Avenue, New York, NY 10158

Routledge is an imprint of the Taylor & Francis Group, an informa business

© 2023 Gregory Erickson

The right of Gregory Erickson to be identified as author of this work, and
of Rachel Sowers for her contribution to Chapter 3, of Colleigh Stein
for her contribution to Chapters 7, 8 and 10, and of Cathryn Piwinski
for her contribution to Chapter 8, has been asserted in accordance with
sections 77 and 78 of the Copyright, Designs and Patents Act 1988.

All rights reserved. No part of this book may be reprinted or reproduced
or utilised in any form or by any electronic, mechanical, or other
means, now known or hereafter invented, including photocopying and
recording, or in any information storage or retrieval system, without
permission in writing from the publishers.

Trademark notice: Product or corporate names may be trademarks
or registered trademarks, and are used only for identification and
explanation without intent to infringe.

British Library Cataloguing-in-Publication Data
A catalogue record for this book is available from the British Library

Library of Congress Cataloging-in-Publication Data
A catalog record has been requested for this book

ISBN: 9781032123615 (hbk)
ISBN: 9781032129631 (pbk)
ISBN: 9781003227045 (ebk)

DOI: 10.4324/9781003227045

Typeset in Baskerville
by codeMantra

To every person I have ever watched or talked about television with,
   starting with my father, who watched
   Star Trek's "Amok Time" with me in the late 60s,
   my very first memory of television

Contents

Alternative Table of Contents	ix
List of Images	xi
Preface	xiii
Acknowledgments	xix

Introduction: television's religious imaginations	1

PART I
Beyond human   23

  1 **Aliens: science fiction and otherworldly religions**   25

  2 **Vampires: the undead challenge to religion**   53

  3 **Zombies: alternative resurrections**   76
    WITH A CONTRIBUTION BY RACHEL SOWERS

PART II
Beyond borders   95

  4 **Ghosts and bodies: borders of the real**   97

  5 **Cyborgs and androids: borders of the soul**   118

  6 **Gods and monsters: borders of the knowable**   149

viii *Contents*

PART III
Beyond time 167

7 **The material past: books, libraries, and scripture** 169
WITH A CONTRIBUTION BY COLLEIGH STEIN

8 **The digital present: fans, participatory culture, and**
virtual congregations 194
WITH CONTRIBUTIONS BY CATHRYN PIWINSKI
AND COLLEIGH STEIN

9 **The future nothing: believing in the impossible or the**
impossibility of belief 215

10 **Endings and re-enchanted time: what comes after** 234
WITH A CONTRIBUTION BY COLLEIGH STEIN

Bibliography 251
Index 263

Alternative Table of Contents

A Game of Thrones	*149-152, 180-190, 205-212*
Battlestar Galactica	*31-37, 171-172*
Buffy the Vampire Slayer	*57-64, 108-110, 175-176, 200-205, 216-218*
Dracula (Netflix)	*70-74*
Doctor Who	*17-19, 44-52, 90-93, 98-99, 110-112, 127-134, 156-159, 176-180, 222-223, 228-229, 239-241, 243-245*
Dollhouse	*136-141, 238-239*
Firefly	*37-44, 159-162, 221-222*
Good Omens	*230-233*
The Leftovers	*112-114*
Manifest	*100-101*
Once Upon a Time	*172-172*
Outlander	*242-243*
True Blood	*19-20, 64-70, 106-108, 162-164, 218-219*
Sense8	*224-228*
Warrior Nun	*164-165*
Westworld	*118-122, 141-147*

Images

1.1	"Are you alive?" (*Battlestar Galactica*, "Miniseries")	33
1.2	Jayne's fallen statue (*Firefly*, "Jaynestown")	43
2.1	Dracula in 2020 BBC's *Dracula* ("The Dark Compass")	54
2.2	Dracula in 1931 *Dracula*	54
2.3	Buffy's cross (*Buffy the Vampire Slayer*, "Welcome to the Hellmouth")	58
2.4	Jew stabbing the host, from the Museu Nacional d'Arte de Catalunya	67
2.5	Dracula faces the sun in BBC's *Dracula* ("The Dark Compass")	73
3.1	Medieval church painting of the Last Judgment, from St. Thomas-Salisbury, from 1470–1500	77
3.2	Baptist Church in *The Walking Dead* ("What Lies Ahead")	83
3.3	Zombies in church (*The Walking Dead*, "What Lies Ahead")	83
3.4	Concluding shot of "Welcome to the Tombs" (*The Walking Dead*)	88
5.1	Cyborg dying on a cross (*Doctor Who*, "Deep Breath")	129
5.2	Headless Monks (*Doctor Who*, "A Good Man Goes to War")	132
6.1	Satan on the Impossible Planet (*Doctor Who*, "Satan Pit")	158
7.1	Sunnydale High Library (*Buffy the Vampire Slayer*, "The Harvest")	176
7.2	Citadel Library (*Game of Thrones*, "The Winds of Winter")	181
7.3	Sam seeing the Citadel Library (*Game of Thrones*, "The Winds of Winter")	181
7.4	Henry's broken glasses (*The Twilight Zone*, "Time Enough at Last")	192
9.1	River stares into space (*Firefly*, "Bushwhacked")	221
9.2	Crucifixion in *Good Omens* ("Hard Times")	231
9.3	Aziraphale and Crowley watch the crucifixion (*Good Omens*, "Hard Times")	232
10.1	"Church Cancelled" due to COVID	247

Preface

In one version of the story, this book has a specific beginning. In the late 1990s, I was a graduate student in English Literature, living in Brooklyn, NY, and just beginning to think about my dissertation on modernist literature and what I was calling the "absence of God." Throughout much of this span of time, I (proudly) did not own a television. Yet, by 2005, I was a professor at New York University teaching courses on popular culture, television, and media and religion; by 2008, I had published a book on popular culture and several articles on television, and by 2015, I was beginning this book on television and religion. One logical way for me to frame this preface would be to point to a cause of my seemingly dramatic shift in academic interests leading to this book. Although, as will become clear, I am not a big believer in the truth of origin stories, I do believe that we all still have and need these stories. This book's origin story began on May 19, 1998, a time when my days were spent reading James Joyce, Virginia Woolf, and Samuel Beckett, as well as reading and grading first-year composition essays. At some point, on that particular Tuesday night, I had given up on productivity, and I turned on my newly acquired television (large, used, carried home on the subway). May 19 was the air date of the season two finale of *Buffy the Vampire Slayer*, "Becoming (Part 2)." I had seen a couple of the early *Buffy* episodes, but my distracted (and, to be honest, judgmental) viewing had revealed nothing out of the ordinary, just something to have on in the background. But, throughout the episode, I was drawn more and more into the plot and finally—my ungraded papers forgotten on the floor—into its dramatic ending. Somewhere in those seconds between when Angel, Buffy's vampire-lover-turned-evil, suddenly recovered his soul and Buffy's realization that she is still morally obligated to kill him, I started using television to think with.

I spent the next months catching up on the first two seasons of *Buffy* by watching home-recorded VCR tapes purchased on eBay and waiting for season three. The following years found me presenting on *Buffy* at a popular culture conference, incorporating it into the concluding chapter of my PhD dissertation, and writing an essay for a collection of scholarly works on *Buffy*, the seminal *Fighting the Forces* edited by Rhonda Wilcox and David Lavery. In the next decade, I taught and wrote about *Buffy*, *Firefly*, and *Dollhouse*, as well as other speculative television such as *True Blood*, *Battlestar Galactica*, and *Doctor Who*. In each case, I

xiv *Preface*

first found elements in television that I could use to help me think through the ideas I was working on in my more traditional scholarly work on religion and literature.

A decade later, in the winter and spring of 2015, I was engaged in (or overcommitted to) four competing activities that, in retrospect, form intersecting arcs of how I now define this topic's importance. During those deliriously busy months, I was working on writing the first sections of this book: watching television, taking notes, reading articles, looking over my previous writings, and working with my undergraduate research assistant, Colleigh Stein (now finished with graduate school and still helping me with this book). At the same time, I was also writing and researching a second project on the history of religious heresy and modernist literature. As part of my research for this second book, I was commuting to Washington, D.C. every weekend to participate in a seminar at the Folger Shakespeare Library on defining the human soul in Renaissance and Reformation thought. Finally, in my professional life, I was teaching an interdisciplinary seminar at NYU on different approaches to reading and representing James Joyce's impossibly difficult final novel, *Finnegans Wake*. It was a time when my scholarly imagination was in contradiction. On the one hand, during long hours at the Folger Shakespeare Library and solitary writing retreats in rural Pennsylvania, I sought what Rousseau described as "lengthy and peaceful meditations that are incompatible with the commotion of life in society." But, on the other hand, to truly capture the interaction of television, fan cultures, lived religion, and vernacular theory that forms this book, I felt the need to enter into and try to learn from and represent this rich and productive commotion. It was when these radically different experiences—in concert with my everyday activities as an NYU faculty member—started to merge, that the overall concept of this book began to come together. Somewhere between perusing *Doctor Who* fan sites, reading Erasmus from a fifteenth-century edition, brainstorming with my class over how to depict an indecipherable *Finnegans Wake* passage, and studying competing interpretations of the presence of the host in the medieval Catholic Mass, my ideas came into focus. Among the dusty, fragile manuscripts at the Folger Library and the collaborative Google Docs that were the beginnings of this book, lay the spaces of this new world of religious exploration I wanted to capture. My realization was that this book needed to be about how speculative television *and* institutional, popular, and lived forms of religion are all part of a tension between old and new models of knowledge and of reading and writing.

Like *Westworld*'s Dolores in the futuristic, cyber-storage Forge or *Game of Thrones*' Samwell Tarley in the medievalist Citadel, I found myself in a new kind of library, making connections with stories past, present, and future and imagining new possibilities of meaning making. Readers of this book will find evidence of these interchanges woven throughout the chapters. References to a text from Martin Luther may very well be part of a discussion of the largest library in the universe, the reference is equal parts Folger Library and *Doctor Who*—and the interpretation may very well be expressed through the radical theological concepts of Thomas Altizer, the invented languages of James Joyce, or a quote from a fan

Preface xv

blog. New types of knowledge and new ways of thinking require new structures and new languages and new modes of reading and writing. It was this realization that inspired me to create a less-centralized style of writing that was constructed collaboratively between friends, students, colleagues, scholars, fans, and myself. A type of writing that, as much as possible, both captured and analyzed the intellectual echoes that these shows are setting off in the real world.

What a television drama can offer is a more open, discursive web that includes the shows and their multiple interpretations and meanings across fans, critics, and academics, but also includes viewing devices, blogs, communities, spin-offs, video games, fan fictions, university platforms, and viewing practices. My interest is in how this unique web is part of the process through which these texts become more than just a demonstration of thinking about religion; it becomes the language of and even a realization of these ideas. A television show is not an argument or a finished narrative; it is a trip without a destination and an opening for speculative thinking.

Television and its discursive worlds are both marginal and mainstream, and are part of intellectual conversations and activities that bind young and old, scholars and fans. Although serious discussions around speculative television have been going on for several decades—we can look to *The Twilight Zone*, *Star Trek*, and *Twin Peaks* as early examples—this interaction continues to change and grow in its influence. In the academic world, the intellectually engaged portions of informal faculty gatherings often become discussion of television shows: no one really understood each other's research projects, but everyone had ideas about *The Wire*, *Mad Men*, or *Game of Thrones*. While these conclusions are mostly anecdotal, I find that the active fans of the shows I am writing about—the ones creating blogs, wikis, and study guides—are not the nerdy *Star Trek* fans that were parodied on *Saturday Night Live* in the 1980s or the stereotypically socially challenged scientists on the more recent *Big Bang Theory*.

Mainstream media as well has become more aware of the power speculative television has to push the boundaries of thinking. A 2008 *New Yorker* reviewer wrote that "*Battlestar Galactica* comments on contemporary culture by imagining dystopic alternatives and by doing so it invites the viewer to interrogate notions of self, nations, and belief that are often taken to be nonnegotiable both on television and in our living rooms." At its best, speculative television moves beyond belief and disbelief, and examines deeper issues of how we understand and process our surroundings, how we understand our fears, our beginnings, and our endings. In other words, unlike Fox News' interviewing Richard Dawkins about his atheism, or Bill Maher urging intolerance against all religions on HBO, in texts like *Battlestar Galactica*, these issues of belief are allowed to be earnestly questioned and explored. A television drama can stretch ambiguity and questioning out over years, encouraging loyal viewers to watch and re-watch, speculate and debate—to force viewers to imagine possibilities and points of view that are outside of their acquired belief systems. Shows like *Battlestar Galactica* are positioned as both complex texts and as centers of fan activity—it is online discussion groups, podcasts, fan fiction, and scholarly collections, as well as the shows themselves that

xvi   *Preface*

create these networks of religious interrogation that I will attempt to study in the pages that follow.

The basic premise for the book has been in my mind for many years. Starting with pieces I had previously written on the role of religion in the television of Joss Whedon and then moving into more recent dramas, I wanted to show how themes traditionally confined to religion or discussions of religion were now being negotiated within television dramas, particularly those of science fiction and fantasy. I had first considered writing one chapter on *Buffy*, one on *The Walking Dead*, and so on. This was how the project started—and frankly it would have been much easier (and probably finished long ago). The more I thought about it, however, the more convinced I was that this is not how people think about and, more importantly, think *with* television anymore. If I really wanted to understand how we think religiously through the television we watch and talk about, it was clear to me that the experiences and the conversations were never about any one show. Rather than offer specific readings of individual shows—analysis already done better by other scholars, journalists, and fans, many of whom I cite—I instead want to call attention to a conversation that I see happening among and across these shows. It seems to me that one of the more significant emerging discursive patterns of the twenty-first century is the practice of placing popular culture texts into dialogue with each other. Although I will touch on many different television shows, I will focus on six as my main texts: *Battlestar Galactica*, *True Blood*, *Buffy the Vampire Slayer*, *Firefly*, *The Walking Dead*, and *Doctor Who*. I will also occasionally refer to or offer sections on other shows that are part of this larger conversation: *Dollhouse*, *Game of Thrones*, *Lost*, *The Leftovers*, *Stranger Things*, *Orphan Black*, *Sense8*, *Once Upon a Time*, *Westworld*, *Altered Carbon*, and others. Some shows will appear in several different chapters, while others make only one appearance. I will introduce each show in detail the first time I refer to it and, in general, I will start this introduction with the pilot, the first episode, or the first season. After that first mention, my use of episodes and seasons will be more random; with the shows that I focus on most, I try to more or less move through the series chronologically as I move through the book. That being said, I have no expectation of readers reading the chapters in order, and I have included an alternative table of contents and a detailed index for readers who are interested in following a specific show through the book.

* * *

I finished writing this book in 2020–2021, much of the year socially distanced due to the COVID virus, teaching classes remotely, and occasionally leaving my apartment to meet friends in the park or join in the Black Lives Matter protests, literally taking place outside my front door. Teaching, meetings, writing workshops, and happy hours all happened online through the same device where I watched much of my television. Suddenly I was living in what felt like a speculative world of floating heads, empty cities, conspiracy theories, and pandemics. During the 2021 spring semester, I taught a seminar on the science and the

Preface xvii

literature of time travel, and what had seemed like a fun topic in the planning, now turned into a serious exploration of what it feels like to wake up one day in a futuristic world that you do not recognize, or what it is to realize that time and space are now being experienced differently than before. At the same time, people forced to quarantine, work from home, and shelter in place, turned to television for comfort. I had students and friends engage in *Buffy* re-watches together; videos were released featuring actors from *Doctor Who* and other shows encouraging people to stay brave and take care of one another. As we try to comprehend our world in crisis, speculative television—like religion—seemed to offer both instruction and catharsis as well as familiar rituals and fresh perspective.

* * *

While most of this book is previously unpublished, versions of some sections have appeared in earlier articles and chapters. Like the monsters and gods in this book, they have been completely revised, broken apart, and reinscribed into a new context. Antecedent versions of these sections can be found in the following publications:

"Old Heresies and Future Paradigms: Joss Whedon on Body and Soul" *Reading Joss Whedon,* eds. Rhonda Wilcox et al. Syracuse University Press, 2014.

"Drink in Remembrance of Me: Blood, Bodies, and Divine Absence in *True Blood*" in *True Blood: Investigating Southern Gothic,* ed. Brigid Cherry. I.B. Tauris, 2013.

"Bodies and Narrative in Crisis: Figures of Rupture and Chaos in Season 6 and 7" in *Buffy Goes Dark: Essays on the Final Two Seasons of Buffy the Vampire Slayer on Television,* eds. Lynn Edwards, Elizabeth Rambo, James South. McFarland, 2008. With Jennifer Lemberg.

"Humanity in a 'Space of Nothin': Morality, Religion, Atheism, and Possibility in *Firefly*" in *Investigating Firefly and Serenity: Joss Whedon's Further Worlds,* eds. Rhonda Wilcox and Tanya Cochran. I.B. Tauris, 2008.

"Revisiting *Buffy*'s (A)Theology: Religion: 'Freaky' or just 'A Bunch of Men Who Died'" in *Slayage: The International Journal of Buffy+* 13/14, 2004

Acknowledgments

I am a different person now than I was when I started this book. I like to think that I am a better person, a better teacher, and a better colleague. If that is true, then the communal experience of writing this book has been part of those changes. Much of this material in this book was first presented at conferences: the Popular Culture Association, the Society for Heresy Studies, the American Academy of Religion, and the Fan Studies Network. Thank you to my amazing students at New York University's Gallatin School of Individualized Study, especially those students in the seminars I taught on "Religion and Popular Culture," "Imagining the Library," "Time Travel: Science, Fiction, and the Western Imagination," and "TV and Participatory Fan Culture." Many of these students are still a big part of my life and still inspire me every day. Also, a big thank you to Susanne Wofford and the Gallatin School for the generous support I have received over my years of teaching and research.

I would like to thank two people who were involved with this book in every way: brainstorming, workshopping, researching, editing, and contributing their own sections in the later chapters. Colleigh Stein and Cathryn (Catie) Piwinski were both students of mine, first as undergraduate and then graduate students. Since then, they have become colleagues and friends. Colleigh was my research assistant as an undergraduate and a graduate student and for the years in between. She commented on early drafts, read and annotated dozens of books and articles, watched and took notes on episodes, and helped me organize communal viewing sessions. She introduced me to fan studies, and her expertise on *Game of Thrones* and fan communities (the subject of her Master's thesis) made many sections of this book possible. Catie was also my research assistant for a different project, but our working relationship spilled over into this book. She also edited this whole book. Her editing helped these chapters take some sort of shape as she continually asked me: "what is this doing here?" or "what's the point of this?" We also spent many hours watching and re-watching many of the shows in this book. Thank you both; this book would not exist without you.

There are so many other people who made this book possible. Thanks to Jennifer Lemberg, with whom I talked and wrote about *Buffy the Vampire Slayer* when we were in grad school together. I am pretty sure a few of the sentences in here are yours. Thanks to Richard Santana, my co-author of the first book I wrote

xx   *Acknowledgments*

on popular culture and religion. Thanks to Jennifer, Richard, Tanya Radford, and Eugene Vydrin, for workshopping sections along the way. Thanks to Sasha Sharova, Eleanor Weeks, Rachel Stern, Martha Stevens, Eugene, Catie, and Colleigh for participating in watching and brainstorming sessions. Thanks to Jacob Ford for helping with the images. Thanks to John McKone and Sue Mennicke who were my *Doctor Who* watching partners in the 1980s. Thanks to David Lavery and Rhonda Wilcox for getting me into *Buffy* studies. Lauren Greenspan for teaching me the scientific side of time travel. Ross Edwards for philosophical conversation that found their way into some of my arguments. Adrianna Borgia for thinking about vampires and chaos monsters with me. Olivia Warschaw for hanging out with me at the UK Fan Network conference. Thanks to Charles Mathews and Kurtis Schaeffer who led a summer NEH seminar on the study of religion that introduced me to new patterns of thinking and writing that I am still processing. And Andy Romig, Erin Templeton, Sarah Barry, Rachel Sowers, Kofi Opam, Jamie Denburg, Lori Ungemah, Kate Loxtercamp, Scott Thornton, and Tim McCarthy. Thanks to Angelina for everything (and for doing the bibliography!). And my kitties Ñoñita and Mittens who sat on my lap and watched a lot of television (Ñoñita likes *The Walking Dead*, Mittens prefers *Outlander*). And so many others, I am sorry for not getting you all in here.

I decided somewhere along the line that if I was going to write scholarly books, then I was going to do it communally. The names on this page are some of my best friends, and some of the best people and scholars I know. It has been, for the most part, a joyful (dare I say religious?) experience, and I hope some of that comes through in the reading.

Introduction

Television's religious imaginations

Perhaps someday in the not so distant future, on some outpost light years from Earth, or in some subterranean shelter deep below the Earth's contaminated and flooded surface, conversations will be had or scriptures will be read that tell the stories of Earth's twenty-first century. The stories will be of a society that learned (or failed to learn) to confront a series of emerging problems and issues facing the human race: new plagues, environmental disasters, digital and pharmaceutical enhancements, artificial intelligence, the discovery of extraterrestrial life forms, and the possibility of extreme life extension or post-biological immortality. Innovations (and technological disruptions) in each of these categories—it will be imperfectly remembered—threatened to unravel the fabric of human culture. If the human past is any indicator, these stories will be told as part of religious traditions that weave together the old and the new, the historical and the fictional, the realistic and the magical. These traditions will perhaps still be expressed through sacred texts, art, and ritual, and may trace their radical changes back to a twenty-first century that redefined the concepts of scripture, body, mind, and reality upon which previous religious traditions had been constructed. Perhaps the twenty-first century will be remembered as a second axial age—like the eighth to third centuries BCE—a culture of innovation and destruction that spawned new ways of thinking, praying, and dying, and that produced new legends and new paradigms of spiritual practice and belief.

Writing from the point of view of 2022, we can predict that scientists who are already born today will continue to create more intelligent machines; they will manufacture pills to make people smarter; they may download a person's consciousness for storage, and they may prolong human life beyond our current limits of imagination. These are pretty standard predictions of the human future, and no doubt other developments will arise that have not yet been envisioned. But whatever the future has in store for us, it is today's stories and today's art that will begin to shape and determine how we will react to and treat these new emerging creations. My book is based on the idea that this art does not hang in museums, and the stories that will make up new scriptures and religions are not expressed in the sermons, tracts, and stained glass of traditional religious practices. Instead, this art—the images, ideas, and stories that people will argue and obsess over, will grow up with and pass on—is found in peoples' homes and in

DOI: 10.4324/9781003227045-1

2 Television's religious imaginations

their pockets. The stories that will determine what the constantly changing and fluid concepts like "human," "other," "real," "soul," and "death" mean in the future, can be found on the internet and on our portable devices. These stories are on television.

While its platforms, dissemination, and presentation have changed radically, television—in some form or another—has been the dominant medium of American popular culture for over half a century. Because of its flexible programming nature—from *The Twilight Zone* and Watergate to the Kardashians and live coverage of January 6—television has maintained a constantly shifting, but influential role in documenting and shaping the changing landscapes of culture, aesthetic taste, politics, technology, and belief. In this role of producing, commenting on, and reflecting the ideas, events, and narratives that make up the webs of intersecting culture that humans spin, television necessarily has religious significance. If, as I claim here and elsewhere, popular culture and religion necessarily intersect, mirror, and influence each other, then the position of television in this relationship is central.[1] Much of this is not a particularly original claim. For several decades now, thinkers have pointed to the importance of media narrative in communicating and negotiating our moral, philosophical, or religious futures. Theologian Elaine Graham, for example, points to the centrality of texts of popular culture as "supplying Western culture with exemplary and normative representations of what humanity might become" (221). The influential scholar of religion J.Z. Smith writes, "television has become our national text, it holds pride of place in our nation's canon, having an authority matched only by the Bible in earlier times" (16). And while reality television, documentaries, news networks, and TV evangelists all offer useful lenses to study these influences, it is speculative fiction, I argue, that most effectively pushes the human imagination in new directions. Throughout this book, I will demonstrate how television science fiction and fantasy dramas have the potential to create intense experiences of perceiving, questioning, and debating philosophical and religious issues outside of institutional control.

The actual subject of my analysis will be a series of fantasy, science fiction, and speculative dramas from about 1997 to 2021, essentially from the beginning of *Buffy the Vampire Slayer* to season three of *Westworld* and the end of *Game of Thrones*; almost the exact period that television scholar Jason Mittell labels the "era of complex television" and an "era of narrative experimentation and innovation, challenging the norms of what the medium can do" (31). Television has also become more diffuse. As shows have moved away from what critics call "monoculture," the importance of any single show has declined. Traditional television has been greatly replaced by streaming services, nonlinear viewing, and binge watching, with more shows to keep up with and smaller viewing audiences. We are not all talking about the same shows anymore. This same period also saw much discussed shifts in the nature of religious belief and practice, particularly among younger generations. Data from the Public Religion Research Institute show that over the two decades from *Buffy* to *Westworld*, the number of Americans identifying as religiously unaffiliated went from 5% to 25%, And although younger generations have historically been less traditionally religious than their parents, today's younger generation (a large part of the viewing audience I am talking about) is at least two and a half times more religiously unaffiliated than any generation in the history of the United States.[2] Furthermore, these "nones," as they are often called, are not made up exclusively of atheists and agnostics; many of them are what we might call "unattached believers" and often identify as "religious" but not attached to a specific religious tradition. They also have been more open about identifying with new hybrid forms of spirituality, unselfconsciously combining, for example, Christian mysticism or Orthodox Judaism with magic, witchcraft, and polyamory and considering it all part of their religious identity.

As the same time that these shifts in our religious beliefs have opened up new possible questions, definitions, and practices, shows like *Buffy*, *Firefly*, *Battlestar Galactica*, *Doctor Who*, *True Blood*, *Game of Thrones*, *The Leftovers*, *Sense8*, *Westworld*, *The Handmaid's Tale*, and *Altered Carbon* have explored and continue to explore questions that echo and retrace paths of religion: who we are, what we are becoming, how we tell and preserve our stories, and how we imagine our past and future. These are shows that do not establish themselves clearly within any kind of religious orientation, and stage alternative realities that allow them to recreate religious speculation in ways that imply important questions and comments on actual belief and practice.

As philosophers like Mark C. Taylor often insist, religion is most interesting where it is the least obvious.[3] Another way of saying this is that our understandings of what religion is and does are so culturally and historically constructed that the only way to provide an analysis beneath these layers of received knowledge is to look for indirect paths through and around. The actual "religion" that is portrayed in speculative television is often superficially one-dimensional—religion is good and God is benevolent, or religious "cults" are creepy and manipulative, or religious rituals and texts are mysterious links to magical and ancient sources of power long forgotten by humankind. Further discussions of the shows, however, by both fans and scholars, often reveal complex negotiations of theological issues and concepts less explicitly identified as religion. It is for this reason that I will often choose not to study "actual" religion as depicted in, for example, the multiple faiths of *Game of Thrones*, the complicated mythologies of *Battlestar Galactica*, the fringe movements of *The Leftovers*, or the Christ-like resonances in the sacrifices of characters on *Buffy*, *Doctor Who*, and *The Walking Dead*. Another way of saying this might be that I am not looking for "religion," but instead for the "religious." Even within these speculative dramas, religion *as* religion, whether presented by the show itself or identified by fans and critics, tends to follow a conservative set of rules in which religion is about retreating to the safety of unquestioned and provided answers and reductive definitions of concepts like "God," "scripture," and "faith." But, as many philosophers past and present have argued, religion is more truly about chaos and disruption than it is about unchanging truth, and, in this book, I am therefore looking for ways that television causes us to reexamine and question these solidified and accepted concepts.

4 *Television's religious imaginations*

By placing complex issues within fictional and fantastical contexts, these shows create a freedom of exploration that exceeds questions allowed within most religious communities or on mainstream news and documentaries; television communities (scholarly and popular) are more open and encouraging of creative dispute and debate. Often what is most interesting are the underlying implied questions rather than those directly connected to main plot points. These questions may not be addressed or worked out during the show itself, but instead plant themselves in viewers' imaginations to be addressed in the context of popular culture conferences, fan discussions, blog posts, and in dialogue with other shows. Shows like *Buffy* and *The Walking Dead* implicitly ask us whether supernatural powers can exist in a world without God; *Battlestar Galactica* and *Westworld* ask if there is such a thing as sentience or transcendence outside of the human experience; *Doctor Who* asks us what existed before the universe and if we have a responsibility for what happens after humans are gone forever; *True Blood* and *Game of Thrones* force us to reexamine the borders we draw between science, religion, and magic; fan activities such as viewing parties, participatory blogs, and comic cons encourage us to think about new rituals and communal practices, textual interpretation, and fluid identities. These are issues rarely addressed from a pulpit or in a classroom, yet they are increasingly and inescapably part of the religious experience of living in the modern world and imagining and shaping the one to come.

* * *

This book is built on the premise that two of the most crucial philosophical and intellectual challenges in the first half of the twenty-first century will be theorizing the surprising (to some) persistence of religious practice and defining what it means to be "human." These two issues are in many ways closely related, and cannot be understood apart from each other. Religious practices and beliefs, as they exist in popular, institutional, and intellectual thought, were widely predicted to be disappearing in the mid-twentieth century, but have instead emerged as still influential (if changing) forces in the twenty-first century. On the other hand, the understanding of what constitutes the human or "posthuman" is now, as many theorists and philosophers predict, the most important ethical, medical, and technological question for the new century. As advances in molecular biology, pharmacology, genetics, and artificial intelligence have changed our understanding of "human nature," theorists have grappled with the new problem of defining the human. Twentieth-century theorists such as Michel Foucault introduced the idea that the pathological, the marginal, and the abject were necessary factors in defining the shifting concept of the human that we think of as "normal." These problems and questions, however, are not just for academics; they are also issues that humanity as a whole increasingly needs to grapple with. As we realize how inescapably our religious thought affects our epistemological and ontological assumptions, it is obvious that, regardless of our confessed belief, religion and theology will continue to define what it means to be human, and thus, what it means to be "inhuman." We may not, however, always recognize these ways of thinking or the texts that explore them as "religious."

Theorists such as Elaine Graham, J.Z. Smith, Henry Jenkins, and others who will appear throughout this book, have pointed to popular culture in general, and science fiction and fantasy narratives in particular, as the texts through which issues such as these are negotiated and defined. For Graham, texts of monsters and aliens can help us understand human nature by delineating boundaries, rather than attempting to describe some sort of human *essence*. The loosening of an unquestioned normativity and exceptionalism of the human is one of the most significant shifts in the last half-century; one need only to compare the original *Star Trek* model, which consistently celebrates "humanness," with the rebooted *Battlestar Galactica*, where one of the main themes is the blurred physical and ethical boundaries that separate the humans from the "human-form" Cylons. Another example would be to compare the original 1973 *Westworld* film to the HBO series (2018–present), in which the newer version offers a much more morally ambiguous space between human and machine, therefore complicating the idea of free will, the nature of freedom, and explicitly asking if the Hosts are perhaps more free, more real, or more alive than the humans.

None of these ideas are unique to television of course, or even to recent times. Henry James wrote about a parallel universe in his 1908 short story "The Jolly Corner." *The Wizard of Oz* showed us a parallel universe in color in 1939. H.G. Wells gave us a time machine and a traveler who journeyed to a future world after the end of humanity a decade before anyone had heard of Einstein or the theory of relativity. The *Terminator* movies question ideas of the human, and science fiction novels have performed this kind of speculative work for decades. But unlike films or novels, which are usually presented as a finished product and a complete narrative, television dramas produce dialectical conversation and interaction as an ongoing process that includes issues of communal experience and practice not nearly as prevalent in other speculative media. One of my main fascinations with this subject has been the dialogue between fans, scholars, and writers that occurs within the unfinished, in-process, semi-canonical, and fragmented narratives that television can give us.

While early television studies, especially in America, were either from the world of cultural studies or based on models of literary criticism, recent scholars like Jason Mittell have looked more closely at TV's narratological possibilities:

> Television's narrative complexity is predicted on specific facets of storytelling that seem uniquely suited to the television series structure apart from film and literature and that distinguish it from conventional modes of episodic and serial forms. (18)

A television series allows viewers to discuss or think through issues deep within their religious experiences that are rarely brought into question. Few Christians (or atheists, for that matter) are willing or encouraged to publicly question what they mean by "faith" or "morality," but within the context of the *X-Files, Battlestar*

6   *Television's religious imaginations*

Galactica, Firefly, Doctor Who, or *Altered Carbon*, these becomes central debates. The speculative nature of these shows creates a defamiliarization to debates over belief than more "realistic" shows like *Bones* or *House*, which engage in similar questions of religious belief and skepticism, but their familiar worlds leave less room for questions and explorations. When these religious and philosophical issues exist in a fantastical or futuristic setting, viewers are often destabilized from their core beliefs and may be surprised to find the moral or philosophical positions that they are taking, a space of confusion that is the beginning of speculative thought. Television, in the words of Diana Winston:

> converts social concerns, cultural conundrums, and metaphysical questions into stories that explore and even shape notions of identity and destiny—the building blocks of religious speculation. (2)

Perhaps the Doctor's desire to wipe out the evil Daleks is actually a reprehensible and genocidal impulse. Maybe the humans on *Battlestar Galactica* do not deserve to survive. Maybe the "extinction event" on *The Walking Dead* is natural biological evolution. These moments of doubt are then worked out by fans, critics, and academics in practices ranging from research and teaching, to writing blogs, reviews, and fan fiction.

Definitions and methodology

For both academic scholars and the general population, defining the words "religion" and "television" has recently become more difficult. Asking what television *is*, or what religion *is*, is to also realize that we are actually in the middle of a debate over definitions. For much of the second half of the twentieth century, the answers to these two questions would have seemed pretty clear to most people. A television was a piece of furniture and a telecommunication medium or device used for transmitting and receiving moving images and sounds, particularly entertainment, advertising, and news. Religion, at least in the West, was generally considered a set of beliefs, texts, and doctrines related to a supernatural being and an institution. It is one of the points of this book that the movements away from these commonly understood definitions of television and religion are related. The increase in young people that define their religious identification as "none" or "spiritual but not religious" is rooted in more fluid definitions of religion, but can also be connected to changes in television-viewing. The decentered television cultures of today have not only moved away for the television as a central object of furniture in the home—but new viewing practices, participatory fan interactions, and speculative themes all indicate new ways of understanding the boundaries around concepts, such as time, the posthuman, and extinction and apocalypse that have traditionally been defined as "religious" thinking.

In the 1950s, television became arguably the primary medium for transmitting information and molding public opinion. Most homes had one large television set and this piece of furniture served as a gathering place for families in the evening.

Daniel Boorstin compared the family gathering around the television with the cave dweller's fire that drew people together for "warmth and safety and togetherness" (36). By the late twentieth century, however, this scenario of the television as a center of activity was no longer true; most homes had multiple televisions and videocassette recorders that allowed for more private viewing experiences, and the individualization and diffusion has only increased since then. While viewing now happens on laptops, tablets, and phones, it is also just as likely to happen in coffee shops, on buses and trains, and in offices as it is in the home. Televisions and television-viewing have very literally become decentered, moving out of the center of the family living room and the center of their shared evening activities. Television can no longer accurately be depicted as the "flow" that Raymond Williams influentially described in *Television: Technology and Cultural Form* over 40 years ago. Twenty-first-century viewers can now choose not to be subject to this "flow" of "uninterrupted, unpunctuated stream of programmes, advertisements, announcements and logos," described by cultural studies scholar Simon During (118), but to instead program their own viewing experiences. In the first decades of the twenty-first century, even the word "television" has become an ambiguous term. With the rise of internet streaming platforms such as Hulu, Prime, Netflix, and Apple TV+, and as more and more "television" viewing is done on computers, laptops, phones, and tablets, the definition of what constitutes television has changed. Is television a genre, an object, or a viewing platform? Furthermore, as we will explore throughout this book, the act of "watching" now includes various virtual, and physical communal gatherings and social interactions.

It is significant that these shifts have led to more isolated and private viewing at the same time that new kinds of communal viewing have emerged. It is also important that this tension between more isolated experiences and new experiments in social interaction mirror movements in religious and spiritual practices (a process only radically accelerated by the COVID-19 pandemic). Social and deeply ritualistic gatherings around the final *Game of Thrones* episodes or the screening of certain TV episodes in movie theaters, such as the *Doctor Who* 50th Anniversary Special, offers a different kind of interactive fan activity and further expands our definition of "television" and "religion."

Martha Stevens writes about the ritualistic potential of *Doctor Who*, focusing on an event around the show's 50th Anniversary event in London that featured a *Doctor Who*-themed wedding ceremony for 50 couples. As she writes, "despite the fact that stated in his words in 'Blink' the Doctor is 'rubbish' at weddings, he seems to have created a market for them." She concludes her analysis:

> Dressing up like the Tenth Doctor or walking down the aisle to "Sad Man With a Box" has become the same as wearing a veil and singing "Here I am Lord" to represent a connection to God. *NuWho* forged this creative space for a religious and romantic ideology that is as tantalizing as it is marketable. Couples may consider this mass wedding as the ultimate act of fandom and fan loyalty but it becomes convoluted when one considers the consumer magic involved in these events. Overall this mass wedding may have been a

8   *Television's religious imaginations*

visual spectacle of Tardis dresses and Time Lord officiants but the most interesting thing about it is the layered expression of society's perceptions and expectations of both fandoms and weddings that one can find upon closer inspection.

As Stevens' analysis points out, events like these look forward to new understandings and practices of ritual, lived religion, magic, and the sacred in ways inseparable from television and television fandom.

The same period of time that saw television move from a family-centered activity in the living room to our phones and laptops has also seen our concept of religion develop and change in contradictory and unexpected ways. Shows like *Doctor Who*, *Westworld*, and *Sense8* point to a future of implied religions, and experimental viewing practices; future churches, like future of television will involve various forms of virtual reality systems and participatory platforms we have yet to imagine. For most Americans, at least, religion has traditionally been defined by what one believes. Although religious studies scholars have recently challenged these definitions—identifying them as stemming from a Protestant-influenced ideology that tends to privilege belief over actions, practice, and identity—it still dominates the popular conception of what religion is or is not.

By the early 1950s, at the same time that superstar evangelist Billy Graham was filling Madison Square Garden (significantly, with nationally televised sermons) and "in God We Trust" was adopted as the US official motto, many scholars were predicting that "religion"—beliefs in gods, and afterlives, and resurrections—would slowly decline and disappear. Building on Enlightenment thinkers and mid-twentieth-century figures from Freud to Durkheim, this idea is summarized by sociologist C. Wright Mills in his 1959 work, *The Sociological Imagination*:

> Once the world was filled with the sacred—in thought, practice, and institutional form. After the Reformation and the Renaissance, the forces of modernization swept across the globe and secularization, a corollary historical process, loosened the dominance of the sacred. In due course, the sacred shall disappear altogether. (32–33)

For most scholars and for a growing segment of the general public, this "secularization thesis" seems to have been short sighted. Religion, it is clear, has not gone away, and both scholars and journalists have pointed to various "returns" of religion. Peter Berger, an early advocate of the secularization thesis, famously recanted his earlier prediction of an inevitable secularization:

> The world today, with some exceptions… is as furiously religious as it ever was, and in some places more so than ever. This means that a whole body of literature by historians and social scientists loosely labeled "secularization theory" is essentially mistaken. (*Desecularization* 2)

Television's religious imaginations 9

While the term "secularization" as understood by twentieth-century thinkers no longer seems right, much evidence does suggest that much of the West is rapidly becoming less traditionally religious. Studies and polls, while they do show a decline in traditional and mainstream religious identification, show a wider acceptance of different practices labeled "religious." The past several decades of television dramas are one way to see this, as shown through the various alternative practices formerly not identified as religion. Examples of these expanded definitions of religion include the Pagan or Wiccan practices on *Buffy* or *The Chilling Adventures of Sabrina*, the blurring of religion and magic in *Game of Thrones*, or of religion and technology in *The Leftovers*, and new modes of creating alternative spiritual communities from the psychic community of "sensates" on *Sense8* to the telepathic song of the alien Ood on *Doctor Who.*

We also find in television, a way to shift away from narrow, American, and Protestant-influenced, definitions of religion that neglect the actual experiences of people. Focusing more on what people *do* in the name of religion—rather than what they believe or what their particular sect believes—allows us to examine practices outside of traditional faiths. Robert Orsi, an important religious studies scholar of what is called "lived religion," writes that practices often assumed to be outside of accepted religions "constitute a powerful alternative experience of the modern—not in reaction to the modern… but as another way of being in the world" (*Madonna of 115th Street* xx). Religion, in other words, is as much about what we do as it is about what we believe. Even ideas of religious practice have been greatly expanded as in, for example, the idea that coffee hour after church is perhaps as much a religious practice as communion, or that the drinking rituals that follow a funeral in a small German Catholic town are as much a part of the religion as the scripted funeral practices in the church or the cemetery. Part of my purpose in this book is to try to use television and television-viewing to both interrogate ways of defining religion and to move beyond them. One of my underlying tenets throughout this book is that we should not assume that there is such a thing as an unquestioned and inherently "religious experience." Rather, there are only experiences we chose to *characterize* as religious, whether they occur in a cathedral, a spinning class, or in front of the television. Religion, as religious studies scholar Graham Harvey writes, "should mean the acts and lives of religionists, including what they declare and share about their imaginations" (24). In other words, humans—through their actions and interactions—continuously create the definition of religion; it is not handed down to us on stone tablets, or given to us through the mystical and miraculous. As the influential religious studies scholar Russell McCutcheon writes, "it is only when we start out with the presumption that religious behaviors are ordinary social behaviors—and not extraordinary private experiences—that we will come to understand them" (14–15). It is my intention in this book to bring these different perspectives on religion to the study of television and its viewers. Science fiction and fantasy often pose scenarios that implicitly question these concepts in ways that push us against these inherited borders. Just what is "religion" on *Buffy*, or *Game of Thrones*, or *True Blood*, or *Doctor Who*? While each of these shows has organizations or beliefs

10   *Television's religious imaginations*

or practices that are referred to as religion, the main characters tend to draw on rituals, practices, and powers that they call something else. What these shows are dramatizing—as we will continually see throughout this book—are the tensions between new and traditional forms of constructing meaning, recording and transmitting history, and asserting truth claims: all central roles of Western, text-based religions and religious scripture.

Critics writing about the relationship of religion to a literary or media text often write about religion within the limited confines of the traditional definition given by Mircea Eliade: religion as a sacred cosmic order against the chaos. But religious texts and practices—although they tend to define our concepts of truth and solid meaning—have always been nomadic and fragmented, and rooted in doubt as much as truth. These themes of absence will run throughout this book, and I will continually point to ways that television provides paths out of reductive definitions of concepts, such as God, faith, and scripture, and creates new models of meaning-making. Thinking about religion in this way leads us into forms of "radical theology," a type of thinking that recognizes the religious desires, structures, and organization of our world, but that also embraces that profound doubt in divinity, miracles, and grace that most religious positions avoid. Relegated to the fringes of theological or philosophical thought, such radical theological movements as the "Death of God" theology or "Christian atheism" provide a lens through which to view many of the television shows I will be discussing and offer new ways to understand shifts in religious practices that are built upon doubt and skepticism. In working out these ideas, we will visit the empty churches of *The Walking Dead*, the Godless beginnings and endings in *Doctor Who*, the white-clothed, chain-smoking nihilists of *The Leftovers*, the religious atheism of *Firefly* and *Buffy*, or the literal death-of-god that concludes season three of *Westworld*. The path to a form of sacred—these shows seem to suggest—may be through experiencing a negation of the divine.

For many people, these experiences are best described or dramatized by the television they watch and talk about. If religion has been about institutions and mediation, what do we call these experiences? Do we still call this "religion"? Berger asks the provocative question: "How can the nocturnal voices of the angels be remembered in the sobering daytime of ordinary life"? The history of religion, he claims, gives us the answer: "by incorporating the memory in traditions claiming social authority" (45). For Berger, this is a way of affirming religious tradition in a modern world, but he also acknowledges that this makes the "memory fragile and vulnerable to social change." Yet for him, "there is no other way for the insights of religious experience to survive in time" (45). I will argue in this book that television presents one such "other way." Television narratives—especially complex serial narratives of the surreal, the fantastic, and the speculative—are important parts of how we as a species will construct, deconstruct, and reconstruct religious meaning to fit our future. This book will look at human practices and human-made creative texts, and whether they are prayer or Comic Con, *Battlestar Galactica*, or the Book of Genesis does not influence my methodology. There are all social practices surrounding texts and stories, all meaning-making by humans.

We are, of course, both more and less religious than we were when Berger wrote *Desecularization* in 1972. We are more plural, more posthuman: our virtual avatars and Zoom relationships have made us more acclimated to experiences not rooted in the body, whereas other practices (queering identities, tattoos, yoga) have made us more aware of our bodies. Where television may help us in moving beyond Berger, is in demonstrating just how much pressure our popular narratives have put on his central terminology. I will look across the past twenty-some years of speculative television dramas to find scenes, episodes, and fan practices that resemble what religious studies scholars such as Berger speak of as "moments of rupture" in the "massively real world of ordinary existence" (36). These moments, which have always both challenged and supported orthodox religions, can exist on the borderline between sleep and wakefulness, during extreme physical pain or pleasure, or from drug-induced states, but one can also argue that these states can be achieved through the experience of imaginative and speculative narrative. We might think here of the Doctor showing a human companion (and us) the very edges and end of the universe or the spiritual and sexual ecstasy we see in the virtual, psychic orgies on *Sense8*. Another kind of example, and perhaps a similar feeling, is found in attending Comic Con with a group of people or writing collaborative fan fiction to physically and emotionally imagine a world outside of your own humanity and everyday life. For many of the television fans we are talking about, especially those who define themselves as having no religious affiliation or as being "spiritual but not religious," these shows provide alternative worlds and viewing experiences that are both intensely modern and yet somehow "re-enchanted" outside of traditional religion.

Like the church in season one of *Westworld*, which is both a fictional simulacra of a nineteenth-century rural church and an entrance into a futuristic laboratory, the role of religion in contemporary American culture sits at an uneasy place between the real and virtual, between analog and digital, between material and imaginary, and between an imperfectly remembered past and an uncertain future. No longer exclusively a living room experience at 9:00 p.m., the non-locatable time and space of television mirrors contemporary religious experiences. Dramas from *The Walking Dead* to *Game of Thrones* to *True Blood* to *The Handmaid's Tale* ask us to what extent we can rely on old narratives and where we might look for new ones. Americans, for the most part, still believe in the supernatural power of an ancient book and in an ancient prophet, but at the same time, might "attend" church online and claim their primary spiritual fulfillment in an expensive exercise studio or from a meditation app. Most of the 40% of young Americans who claim no religious affiliation are still open to various beliefs and religious practices. While they may not ponder the tensions or contradictions within these practices, they might also spend an evening watching the quest for a supernatural "Washington's Bible" on *Sleepy Hollow*, the construction of a virtual church on *Westworld*, or the desperate attempt to find solace in what seems like another meaningless death in *The Walking Dead*. In each case, we observe the tension of

12   *Television's religious imaginations*

"religious" practice or belief in worlds without any obvious god. To understand Western religion in the twenty-first century is to understand the tension and relationship between the textual, the digital, and the lived; or, to put it another way, the book, the internet, and practice. What interests me are the tensions between ontological shifts in television, the definitional instability of contemporary popular religion, and the shift in the discursive spaces of both. These tensions are exactly what the shows I am writing about often dramatize, and these science fiction and fantasy narratives become a part of how we understand these conflicting pressures, shifts, and gaps.

New viewing practices

Jason Mittell writes while "all viewing starts with the core act of comprehension," the recent trend of serial dramas has "increased the medium's tolerance for viewers to be confused" (164). While Mittell and other television scholars focus on such techniques as flashbacks, flash forwards, recaps, and fan practices such as binging, spoiling, and re-watching, what is often neglected in these studies is the fact that the viewer navigating this confusion is very rarely singular. Although shows may be watched alone, the understanding of them is almost always communal. Just as many recent studies of religion have turned more toward practice, communal interaction, and the resulting processes of creating meaning and telling stories, in many ways, the study of popular culture has gone through a similar shift. If we are to make statements about a show's "meaning," and particularly its religious meaning, such constructions cannot be *found* within the text of the show, but are instead *produced* in the interactions between fan, writer, critic, actor, and showrunner. It is in these intersections of television drama, fan communities, amateur criticism, and scholarly activity that have grown up around select television shows where we can best find examples of how popular culture has re-invented and re-scripted traditional religious faith and activity. While much of this book will still be focused on the content of television dramas, I am also concerned with the ways that fans produce their own content: creating blogs, posting original artwork, writing fan fiction, and otherwise remixing online content. Increasingly, these creations are viewed and, in turn, engaged with by a public. In the case of television, as we will explore in later chapters, this content has begun to cross over into "canonical" material, even challenging the concept of what it is to be "canonical." Fan material and fan platforms influence writing and casting decisions: they are used in promotional materials and even placed into the actual shows and plotlines. The BBC may control the content of *Doctor Who*, but they have much less control over the growing community of bloggers and fan fiction writers that are part of that show's appeal.

Through creating their own fictional content and critical platforms, fan-produced materials ultimately play a role in the reception and perception of the show, and even in the decisions of producers and showrunners. Perhaps the most obvious example here would be *Game of Thrones* and the interplay between books and television, authors and showrunners, and an intense fan community

Television's religious imaginations   13

full of alternative versions, story lines, and complicated theories. The growing awareness of these kinds of fan/show interactions have chipped away at the still too common perception of the television-viewing experience as essentially passive, uncritical, and uncreative. Critics, viewers, scholars, and—with stubborn exceptions—the popular media now take television and the active and participatory nature of the viewing experience more seriously as a potentially critical and creative intellectual experience. The most common, although incomplete, explanation for these shifts points to new technology. Through DVDs, DVRs, downloaded episodes, podcast commentaries, streaming sites, and online blogs, wikis, and fan sites, viewers can now study every episode and every scene, review dialogue that they missed or found especially interesting or ambiguous, stop and examine an interesting image, and discuss themes and minutiae immediately with like-minded viewers in online communities.

As a way to think about the shifts in viewing practices across a twenty-year period, we can compare watching *Buffy the Vampire Slayer* in 1997 with watching *The Walking Dead* in 2017. Along with the slightly earlier *X-Files*, *Buffy* was one of the first shows to find its audience growth tied to the rise of the internet, as fan communities, fan fiction, websites, and even a peer-reviewed academic website (*Slayage*) devoted to the show developed during its seven-season run. The show also spawned a publishing industry of paperback novels and comic books—not a new phenomenon (*Star Trek*, etc.), but newly complicated by the fact that *Buffy* creator Joss Whedon became involved in the comic books, even carrying on the plot of the show after its television conclusion. Yet, despite this plural presence, the show itself remained central to the discourse and the majority of viewers from 1993 to 2003 (even with the rise of video recording technology) would have experienced the show on their living room television set, each Monday night at 9:00 p.m.

Fans of *The Walking Dead* in 2017, however, might have watched the show on a television, a computer, a tablet, or a smartphone, whenever and wherever they wished, and as many times as they wanted. There really was no such thing as "missing" an episode, technically speaking, as there were multiple ways of accessing past episodes. If viewers did watch the show in "real" time, they might have shared comments with friends online whom they had never met face to face; they might have participated in AMC's "Two Screen Experience," which offered participatory activities, such as polls with other fans; they could have stopped the show and rewound to repeat a line of dialogue or examine an image more closely, and they might have also watched the *Talking Dead* afterward, a talk show featuring interviews, analyses, and highlights related to the just-aired episode. After finishing the show, they might have immediately gone to their favorite blogs to read other interpretations of the episode and, while there, perhaps left their own comments. Fans could have debated an element of the plot ("Is Glenn really dead?") or a more abstract question ("Should there be a moral distinction between how we treat walkers and how we treat dangerous animals?"). They might have compared the episode to the original comics or the digital comics; they might have chosen to re-watch the AMC-presented black and white version;

14 *Television's religious imaginations*

they might have supplemented their viewing with the AMC-produced webisodes, they might have participated in a rewriting or remixing of the episode themselves, content which they then might have shared with their online community for further commenting, creating, and editing.[4] As Rachel Wagner writes, "our fascination with fluidity results in a transformation from stories as fixed texts to stories as fictional worlds" (17). As we will explore throughout this book, speculative television dramas examine this fascination with the book and the magic of the written word, and the tension between the idea of its permanence and its potential to be rewritten, erased, or altered.

As thinkers like Foucault have taught us, discourse does not simply describe, it also creates, and for prominent media and fan studies scholar Henry Jenkins, "Fandom is one of those spaces where people are learning to live and collaborate within a knowledge community" (134). The discursive space that these television shows, critics, fans, and theorists enter into is one where texts and critical platforms have expanded and deepened beyond traditional or finite definition. Popular television dramas of the early-twenty-first century (*Lost, The Leftovers, Game of Thrones,* and *Westworld* are just four of many examples) required a collective intelligence for fans to truly appreciate all the intricate details. No one viewer watching the series a single time (or even multiple times) could hope to catch all the complexities. No scholar would (or should) dare to attempt an analysis of such a show without relying on these fan-driven platforms. In many cases, a full understanding not only relies upon fan-based scholarship of the show (early examples include the massive "Lostpedia," which launched in 2005, or Westeros. org in 1999), but also on experiencing the surrounding material such as podcasts and short webisodes. As Jenkins writes, we do not yet have good "criteria for evaluating works that play themselves out across multiple media" (99), and traditional critics of television shows such as *Lost* or *Game of Thrones* rarely take the time to study the surrounding apparatuses, which for many viewers are essential to a full experience. Although, as evidenced by the increasing number of conferences and publications, professional scholars are part of a trend toward thinking philosophically through television and popular culture, this impulse is primarily driven (economically and textually) by a highly literate general audience hungry to share and test its knowledge and ideas about their popular texts. Discussions about television drama in newspaper reviews, scholarly monographs, online journals, informational wikis, and comments section of blogs represent new hybrid types of scholarship about complex texts. Even a publication as associated with traditional, static consumption as *The New York Times* now offers extensive, fan-driven discussions of its regular television summaries in the online edition and features such as a spring 2019 re-watch of *Game of Thrones* to prepare fans for the final season. While theoretical books and articles about television shows are still predominantly written by professional academics, they are commonly read and commented on within the fan communities, and, increasingly, scholars likewise draw on fan discussion platforms for their research, often quoting blogs with the same confidence that they would quote an article from a peer-reviewed journal.

Television's religious imaginations   15

My methodology in this book therefore includes more than the traditional practice of watching television, taking notes, reading scholarly monographs on related subjects, and working through current theories of religion and media. To represent the central discursive space of speculative television and religion, I also studied fan sites, read—and quoted—student essays, and organized brainstorming and viewing sessions to discuss specific ideas, shows, and episodes. The interactive intelligence of the television fan community (which includes, but is not limited to, professional scholars, professors, and college students) is truly awe-inspiring, and exploring this resource was one of the joys of this project. In an attempt to capture some of that communal energy, several chapters in this book will involve multiple authorial voices and co-authored sections. The quotations that readers will encounter will not always obviously belong to a category of scholar, fan, theorist, student, or youth; if an undergraduate said something to me that I think puts them into conversation with a tenured media theorist, I may place them on the same page without marking their credentials or privileging one over the other.

***

Although boundaries blur and categories overlap, there are, broadly speaking, four main areas of analysis in this book. First, I will be pointing to ways that themes and scenes in speculative television dramas provide alternatives to traditional religious understandings and concerns. The television that I am writing about in this book explores—sometimes implicitly and sometimes explicitly— questions of identity (what makes me who I am and not someone else?), of human definition (and is that definition changing?), of reality, and of the relationship between body and mind. They ask what the role of religious faith, narrative, and ritual will be in a world where hopes and dreams are impossible or constantly manipulated. They interrogate what it means to create life and to be created, and they imagine a confrontation with an absolute Other, and what it is like to think about morality and ethics and death in a world without religious faith. Shows from *Battlestar Galactica* to *The Walking Dead* to *Doctor Who* continually force us to reimagine these issues: what does it mean to encounter a religion that has been forgotten? What does it mean for a culture to dismiss its origin myths? If religion represents hopes, emotions, and dreams, what does it mean if these are no longer applicable or even recognizable?

These kinds of questions have traditionally, in the West at least, been addressed in sacred texts, and my second area of analysis explores ways that television depicts our changing relationship to understanding, interpreting, and creating these sacred texts or scripture. For many believers, sacred texts are often assumed to be perfect copies of a heavenly original. But, as the history of writing (and the final episodes of *Game of Thrones*) teaches us, texts are always in flux: in their content, their creation, and in how they are read. As writing technologies change, the ways we communicate our stories change. When religious texts moved from scroll to codex, it changed how they were read: now it was possible

16 *Television's religious imaginations*

to flip back and forth between pages, finding connections and repetitions not legible before. The use of Bibles, Torahs, and Qurans online and on phone apps will change meanings in ways that print-based thinkers fail to understand. These digital texts are searchable and malleable in ways not previously envisaged. The human relationship with scripture then becomes even more interactive and creative. Televisions will play an important role in learning to negotiate this rapidly changing world of digital scripture. From the book of fairy tales in *Once Upon a Time*, the Fillory books in *The Magicians*, and the prophecies of *Battlestar Galactica* and *Good Omens*, to the school library in *Buffy*, the Citadel library in *Game of Thrones*, and an entire library planet on *Doctor Who*, issues of canonicity, the power of the book, and questions about who and what gets to control knowledge and claim a text as scripture, are, as we shall see, negotiated throughout speculative television dramas.

My third area of analysis lies in thinking about what the future of religion might look like. Science fiction and fantasy, of course, have their own traditions of imagining religion, and shows like *Firefly*, *Battlestar Galactica*, and *Game of Thrones* offer variations on these themes. A trend that I see many of these shows participating in is the moving and blurring of the lines between religion, magic, and science. As Randall Styers writes, "one strategy Western culture has continually used to define modern notions of religion, is to contrast them with 'nonrational' forms of magic" (71), and television shows such as *Lost*, *Game of Thrones*, and *Doctor Who* present evidence of where these lines are shifting. Perhaps even more importantly, as our new century sees an expanded interest by both scholars and practitioners in new religious movements, television is strategically poised to offer multiple perspectives on this issue, as it can variously influence the future, attempt to depict it, and, perhaps most radically, actually become part of the future of religion.

Thinking about television *as* religion brings me to the fourth area: the lived experiences of viewing television. Watching television, like prayer, is simultaneously a deeply private and deeply social activity. Serious viewers of television dramas, like practitioners of much American religion, create their own texts, and, in collaboration with more official readings, create their own theories and interpretations. Television serial drama creates a community around a continuous story—and also through loyalty, interpretations and predictions, and around celebrity figures—much like a religious community or congregation. Like much of American Christianity, fan-based theorizing operates outside of and is defined against institutional and legitimated modes of thought.

Absent faith or faith in absence?

Let us return to our opening future community of humanoid creatures telling stories of a distantly remembered twenty-first century. Does TV help us understand the kind of world these stories or new scriptures might narrate? Would they be tales of a humanity existing in small pockets, wandering through the wreckage of our current world like on *The Walking Dead*? Will they be hurtling precariously

Television's religious imaginations   17

through space on an outdated ship surrounded by an unidentifiable, but superior species that they have created like on *Battlestar Galactica*? Or will they take place in a world that looks and functions the same but where all the rules have suddenly changed as on *The Leftovers* or *True Blood*?

In the third season of the rebooted *Doctor Who*, there is an episode set in the year 5-billion-53, when the Doctor and his twenty-first-century companion travel to a new Earth, the "second home of mankind" and the fifteenth iteration of "New York." The episode, "Gridlock," presents this Earth as an almost-dead planet with the whole population stuck forever in perpetual gridlock on the enclosed motorway, spending year after year living in their hover vans, driving a few meters at a time, and finding only closed exits. Their only connections to any official institution involve being repeatedly placed on hold by the police, hearing regular recorded traffic reports, and a "daily contemplation," during which all the drivers and passengers sing a Christian hymn together.

The metaphorical and existential possibilities of perpetual gridlock are obvious and the episode explores them fully: Is life just a never-ending journey through gridlock? Is there anything else beyond it? Is there a destination, an exit, anyone to help you if there is trouble or danger? The drivers and passengers of New Earth are a clear representation of the human condition, yet they seem unaware of these questions as they look for a way to the faster lanes, wait endlessly on hold for the police, hope for an exit ramp some day in the future, sing hymns, make love, have babies, and ignore the ominous monstrous sounds from below. The religious resonances of the episode are fleshed out in multiple ways. The only two characters left alive on the Earth's upper city are the "Face of Boe"—a recurring God-like character who is giving the last of his life energy to keep the population alive—and Novice Hame, a nun (who is also part-cat). While each of these two characters offers some recognizable form of what it means to be "religious," the episode is most usefully seen as a commentary on, rather than a demonstration of, belief or faith.

As the Doctor's new companion, Martha Jones, faces a desperate moment trapped in one of the vehicles, she says to the original occupants, "you've got your faith, you've got your songs and your hymns. And I've got the Doctor." It is interesting that Martha, a new companion, can so easily compare Christian faith to her faith in the Doctor, and, by so doing, sets up the episode to interrogate faith as a human desire. The Doctor challenges one of the drivers: "What if there's nothing? Just the motorway with the cars going 'round and 'round and 'round and 'round. Never stopping forever." Just after the Doctor says this, the recorded voice announces the "daily contemplation" and there is an extended scene where we witness drivers and passengers sing the hymn "The Old Rugged Cross." One possible way to read this scene is to see "religion" here as a Marxist opiate, giving people false hope of a better life, where there may very well just be "nothing." But it can be read in more affirming ways as well, and the episode was indeed initially viewed positively by several Christian fan communities.

The presence of a Christian hymn whose words emphasize the physical cross is particularly provocative and—like the crosses in *True Blood* and *The Walking*

18 *Television's religious imaginations*

Dead—can suggest a form of religion even in an atheistic world, a type of radical theology of negation. While the cross is generally understood by both Christians and non-Christians as representing suffering and resurrection, some contemporary theologians have advanced a counter reading: the cross and the moment of the death of Christ instead represents the absence of a God—no Father, no Son, we are on our own. Yet—and here is where it is still a "Christian" reading—we need the crucifixion to continually remind ourselves of our isolation. In other words, we need the Christian myth, but partly to establish and remind us of its own fictionality. Read this way, the singing of the "Old Rugged Cross" resonates differently. It still has a religious and even a "Christian" resonance, but one that emphasizes the absence of divinity more than its presence. The ending of the episode, as the Face of Boe appears to die, giving one last bit of his energy to save Earth's population, is yet another echo of the crucifixion myth. Even though the episode ends on the singing of another hymn ("Lord with me Abide"), and even though Martha has indeed been rescued by her Doctor-savior, the people of Earth are now on their own. At the end, the Doctor tells Martha a story of his actions in a great Time War and the total destruction of his people and his planet, a story that gives a dark shadow to the Doctor's upbeat personality through the following years of the series. Throughout this book, we will continually explore this idea of the dark side of the divinity or the act of worshipping a figure that disappoints us.

The complicated religious tensions in this episode were played out in real-life events surrounding the episode in 2008, when it was nominated for an Epiphany Award, an honor given by the conservative Christian media organization, Movieguide. The Epiphany prizes "seek to create a deeper spiritual awareness in mankind and increase man's love and understanding of God" (movieguide.org). The nomination was apparently withdrawn when the prize committee realized that writer Russell T. Davies' intentions and sexual orientation (i.e. atheist, gay) were not in line with their values. What is interesting for our purposes is that both sides were right and wrong. The episode, on some level, *is* a way of increasing an understanding of God, even if it is a way of understanding the tension between faith and divine absence. And when Davies writes that, in the episode, the Doctor "realises that no one is going to help them. There is no higher authority," it is a form of religious thought that would be recognized by some Christian-identified radical theologians, who look to the moment between the crucifixion and the resurrection as the most profound Christian moment—one of anticipation and hope, but one lacking the miraculous or the supernatural ending. This Christianity—like the original Gospel of Mark—is one without a resurrection at the end; it is instead a Christianity aimed at personal and communal responsibility rather than a magical savior who rises from the dead. This moment of an Easter Saturday rather than Sunday—a space of religious doubt or spiritual atheism—is one we will explore in the coming chapters. As we will see throughout this book, *Doctor Who*, *Buffy*, *The Walking Dead*, *Lost*, and *Battlestar Galactica* are all examples of shows that are both disenchanted and re-enchanted: they are post-religious and post-secular, worlds of science *and* ghosts, of rationality *and* magic.

We find many of these same ideas dramatized in a much different way in a first season episode of HBO's vampire drama *True Blood* ("Cold Ground"). After the main character, Sookie, has fallen in love with a two-hundred-year-old vampire and Civil War veteran named Bill, her beloved grandmother is violently murdered. At the funeral, overwhelmed by telepathically overhearing the judgmental thoughts of people who disapprove of her relationship with a vampire, she yells at everyone to "shut the fuck up." Upon leaving, Sookie finds Bill's grave. This moment, presented without any editorial comment via music, image, or words, forces the viewer to fill in the blanks—perhaps like Sookie, questioning or doubting the role of death, gods, and Christian burials. The image of Sookie, at first in the cemetery for her grandmother's funeral, but now looking at the grave of the man she is dating, embodies the complexity of the image of the cross. Sookie is surrounded by crosses whose representation has suddenly been radically destabilized. Bill's grave—like the surrounding crosses or like *the* Cross—seems to represent an ending and a beginning, a presence and an absence. Sookie knows that no body lies beneath that stone—but then Christianity, too, begins with an empty grave. After the emergence of the reality of vampires, it is not that graves and crosses have lost their meaning, but their meaning is now somehow different. This scene occupies the dialectical tension between belief and nonbelief and between essence and imagination—a space where negation and affirmation are inseparable.

Both of these episodes—different genres and set centuries apart—go to the heart of contemporary questions of religious meaning-making and -unmaking. Whether it is the purgatories of *Sleepy Hollow* and *Supernatural*, the timeless landscapes of *Doctor Who*, the post-apocalyptic nihilism of *The Walking Dead* and *The Leftovers*, the enchanted science of *Lost* and *Fringe*, or the virtual, post-biological dystopias of *Westworld*, *Dollhouse*, and *Altered Carbon*, we, as viewers, fans, and scholars, are forced to exist in ongoing, in-between spaces that continually ask us who we are, where we are going, and how we will continue to tell our religious stories that shape our pasts and determine our futures. These tensions speak to our modern human condition, our own existential "gridlock." As we work our way through the themes and sections of this book, the theme of simultaneous presence and absence and belief and doubt will occupy much of the analysis. We will find it in the agnosticism of a crucifix-wielding vampire Slayer, in a monotheistic cyborg who does not know she is a creation of humans, and in the irrational optimism of a time-traveling, regenerating alien, who has seen the birth and death of thousands of civilizations.

Chapter summaries

Chapter One, "Aliens: science fiction and otherworldly religion," looks at television science fiction since the original *Star Trek* and the role it has played in imagining the future of human religion and, at the same time, how it has cast a critical eye at current practice and beliefs. The chapter then looks specifically at three shows—*Battlestar Galactica*, *Firefly*, and *Doctor Who*—and argues that

20 *Television's religious imaginations*

they challenge dominant narratives of inevitable secularization, and explore ideas of digital scriptures, posthuman souls, and scenarios of divine absence. From the monotheistic Cylons in *Battlestar Galactica*, to the religious atheism and bleakness of *Firefly*, to *Doctor Who's* redrawing of the borders between science, religion, and magic, each of these shows offers open-ended and ultimately *religious* spaces for fans to rethink their own received ideas and inherited beliefs.

Chapter Two, "Vampires: the undead challenge to religion," starts with *Dracula* and then moves on to two television vampire dramas from the turn of the twenty-first century: *Buffy the Vampire Slayer* and *True Blood*. Both shows acknowledge the power of traditional religious symbols, stories, and objects while simultaneously confirming the necessity of creating new forms of belief and meaning. This chapter examines television's vampires and how they blur the lines between religion and power, good and evil, belief and unbelief, and body and soul.

Chapter Three, "Zombies: alternative resurrections," turns to the other undead figure, the zombie. While televised vampires tended to be sexy and dangerous, but redeemable, televised zombies are presented in worlds that forced viewers to imagine a hopeless and unbearable future. This chapter explores the post-apocalyptic world of *The Walking Dead*, where beneath the background landscape of southern churches, priests, cemeteries, and crosses, we find a complicated set of questions surrounding the role of religion in a society undergoing radical change, particularly the themes of bodies, death, resurrection, and mercy in what seems to be a fallen and nihilistic world.

Chapter Four, "Ghosts and bodies: borders of the real," examines ideas of ghosts, death, and the "real," through episodes from *Buffy*, *Doctor Who*, *Westworld*, *True Blood*, and *The Leftovers*. The repetition of the themes of immortality and the insistence of ghosts, replicants, copies, and imitations that these shows present week after week ask us not only about our possible futures, but also about our religious pasts. These shows each present a version of what it means to die, what it means to quest for and perhaps achieve a form of afterlife, and where that fits into our worlds of science and magic.

Chapter Five, "Cyborgs and androids: borders of the soul," looks at episodes of *Battlestar Galactica*, *Doctor Who*, *Buffy*, *Westworld*, and other dramas to reframe a series of ancient questions revolving around the idea of the human soul. The Cylons on *Battlestar Galactica*, Actives on *Dollhouse*, Hosts on *Westworld*, and Gangers on *Doctor Who* all complicate the robot paranoia of earlier sci-fi periods and offer alternative, non-human perspectives and possibilities that challenge accepted narratives of a soulless technological future.

In Chapter Six, "Gods and monsters: borders of the knowable," I rethink the complex and constantly shifting relationship between gods and monsters. Contemporary reimaginings of ancient gods and monsters can reveal new paths of fear and desire, and can suggest how the lines between religion, magic, and science continue to shift in our current century. The chapter demonstrates how the dragons on *Game of Thrones*, a Satan figure on *Doctor Who*, the First Evil on *Buffy*,

Television's religious imaginations 21

and ambiguous monster figures on other shows all participate in the ongoing redefining of our concept of human, monstrous, and divine.

Chapters Seven through Ten turn to the idea of scripture, stories, memory, and time and how speculative television is changing how we think about their stability and ability to hold eternal truths. For many in the West, "religion" is unthinkable without a "book." Science fiction and fantasy shows have unsurprisingly been interested in sacred texts as well. In Chapter Seven, "The material past: books, libraries, and museums," I explore libraries and books in *Buffy*, *Game of Thrones*, *Westworld*, and *Doctor Who*, as well as the future of the book and the role of scripture in a digital world. Colleigh Stein contributes a section on the idea of "canon" and how speculative television and fan culture are changing our ideas of what that means. Ultimately, the chapter asks how our digital world has introduced the normalcy of flexible texts that can always be rewritten or altered, and how that changes our sense of "scripture" or religious "truth."

Like much modern religion, fan-based theorizing operates outside of institutional and legitimated modes of thought. Chapter Eight, "The digital present: fans, participatory culture, and virtual congregations," is a collaborative effort among myself, Colleigh, and Cathryn Piwinski, and it uses television and television fan cultures to think about the idea of civil and lived religion through communal and shared viewing practices. Traditional religion has often been based on "presence," or "hope," or on sacred places, objects, and practices. Can there be any kind of religion outside of these signifiers of certainty? While Chapter Seven focused on presence—physical books and actual libraries—Chapter Nine, "The future nothing: believing in the impossible or the impossibility of belief," turns to nothingness and absence. It then uses these ideas to explore larger ideas of divine absence and versions of a death-of-god theology. From an empty "heaven" on *Buffy*, to vast gaps of empty space on *Firefly* and *Battlestar Galactica*, to the radically unknowable yet familiar world on *The Leftovers*, this chapter asks how we continue to create a meaningful world as the abyss seems to widen.

The final chapter, "Endings and re-enchanted time: what comes after," ends the book with the nonlinear and chaotic elements of storytelling in the later seasons of *Buffy* and in the episodic confusion of *Dollhouse*. The chapter will also look at ideas of time, especially the concepts of sacred or enchanted time versus secular or disenchanted time, and the way that fan practices around time travel dramas like *Doctor Who* can be understood as a way of re-enchanting time and narrative. This kind of thinking leads to a reframing of religion and television-viewing as related lived practices rather than engagements with a coherent and unchanging set of texts. These new practices of imagining time and texts—at the intersection of science fiction, religion, fan culture, and speculative physics—offer new imaginative possibilities for thinking about human possibilities. Like the Doctor and his companion traveling to the future to watch the Earth explode, many of these dramas attempt to place us somewhere beyond our imagination. What we do with these impossible imaginings will determine the possibilities of our future.

Notes

1 See, for example, *Religion and Popular Culture: Rescripting the Sacred* (McFarland 2008; 2016), by Richard Santana and Gregory Erickson.
2 www.prri.org.
3 An important influence on this book, Mark C. Taylor's work has changed radically over the years. However, this idea of religion being most interesting where it is least obvious can be found across most of his work from *Erring* (1984) to *After God* (2009).
4 An interesting comparison can be found in the difference between the *Buffy* community after season five, after Buffy's death scene ended the show's run on the CW network and *The Walking Dead* fans post season six when social media was on fire with theories of who Negan had killed, and intense criticism of the way the season had ended. Both sets of fans had questions and concerns about the future of their show, both created various scenarios and theories, but the level and type of activity surrounding *The Walking Dead* was much more critical and interactive. The final season of *Game of Thrones*, of course, went to another level entirely, with many fans refusing to even accept it.

Part I

Beyond human

1 Aliens

Science fiction and otherworldly religions

Science fiction, television, and religion

One of the very first scenes in the twenty-first-century reimagined version of *Battlestar Galactica* takes place on the futuristic-looking planet of Caprica, where the scientist Gaius Baltar strolls with his lover: a young woman who we will soon find out is actually a cyborg (Cylon) known as model Number Six and who is using Baltar to gain the knowledge the Cylons need to destroy the planet. When Six comments, "God wanted me to help you," Baltar condescendingly asks, "He spoke to you?"

SIX: You don't have to mock my faith.
BALTAR: Sorry. I'm just not that religious.
SIX: Does it bother you that I am?
BALTAR: It puzzles me that an intelligent, attractive woman such as yourself should be taken in by all that mysticism and superstition.

This early scene sets up the beginning of competing positions that will be played out and then complicated and subverted throughout the series. What first appears as stereotypical gendered positions familiar to the most traditional science fiction—a male scientist stands for reason, logic, and, therefore, atheism, and his beautiful blonde female companion for irrationality, emotion, and religion—instead forces us to rethink our assumptions. This scene takes place just before the Cylon attack that almost wipes out humanity. Baltar will survive and will later apparently become one of the few human believers in monotheism—even becoming a charismatic religious leader—and he will be haunted by what appears to be the same young woman in these scenes. Many of the scenes in the reoccurring conversation between Baltar and the (perhaps) hallucinated Six take on a religious tone, as she claims that "God is love," and asks him questions such as: "What is it that drives you to blasphemy, Gaius?" At one point, when he insists that she is just a figment of his imagination, she says, "Have you considered the possibility that I can very well exist only in your head without being a hallucination?" This is an implicit comment on the blurred lines between religious belief or disbelief, irrationality and logic: in other words, if God is only in the human

DOI: 10.4324/9781003227045-3

26 *Beyond human*

imagination, does that mean he does not exist? As we will see, from the *Star Trek* franchise to *Firefly*, *Battlestar Galactica*, and *Doctor Who*, television can ask questions like these in fresh and complicated ways that embrace the history of science fiction, but also combine traditional tropes of speculative fiction with new models of digital texts, virtual reality, and participatory fan culture to reimagine the future of religion. In this chapter, I will look at how several recent television SF shows address, develop, and interact with ideas of the religious, specifically, how these dramas—and the surrounding critical and fan discourses—have played an important role in reimagining just what religion is, what it looks like, what it does, and what it might become.

Historical context: writing the future

This is not a particularly original claim. For Darko Suvin, one of the first literary critics to write seriously about science fiction, it is a "literary genre whose necessary and sufficient conditions are the presence and interaction of estrangement and cognition, and whose main formal device is an imaginative framework alternative to the author's empirical environment" (8). For theologian Elaine Graham, the cultural purpose of science fiction is to explore the "uncharted extremities of humanity, nature, and artifice" (60). What these two very different theorists (secularist and theologian) share with my project is in acknowledging that SF can be used to imagine new ways of living and thinking, of existing together with others, and as reimagining the self. The first English language science fiction novels—Mary Shelley's *Frankenstein* and H.G. Wells' *The Time Machine*—forced readers to think about current directions in scientific and social thought and, by radically extending these ideas, to ponder about questions as what makes us human, what is the future of the human species, and who gets to tell these stories. For theorist Fredric Jameson, science fiction's "emergence at the end of the nineteenth century signaled a kind of uneasy and even painful mutation in... the consciousness of the evolution of human society," and from their beginning in the nineteenth century, science fiction stories have been about speculative thinking, or more precisely, they have been a form of speculative thinking.

As science fiction moved from a genre that existed in pulp publications and B-movies to high-budget Hollywood productions, it often seemed to support the secularization thesis, which reinforced the belief that science and rationality were diametrically opposed to religious faith and practice. As Farah Mendelsohn claims in an essay on science fiction and religion, much SF posits as a given that "all advanced cultures are secularist" and sees religion "less as a mode of thought and more as a lack of thought." Throughout science fiction, "religion is repeatedly depicted as dangerous, diverting humans (and aliens) from the path of reason and true enlightenment" (266). In many of these examples, the message seems to be that "religion is not only dangerous and misleading, but that sentient beings are generally too weak-willed to reject it" (269). Mendelsohn divides the early genre science fiction into three categories: the incredible invention, the future war, and the fantastic journey. Then, and now, it is the fantastic journey that lends itself most to religious reflection (265). These journeys to other worlds often used religion as a way to make "strange," to emphasize the otherness of distant non-human civilizations. The rise of spiritualism, fundamentalism, apocalypticism, and new religious movements following the trauma of World War I offers another, and somewhat unexplored, layer to the origin of our modern models of science, religion, and literature. For the most part, however, the emerging science fiction world assumed it represented the voice of a secularist future and treated religion with, at best, polite contempt: religion was essentially of the "Other," the backward and the primitive, and its role in SF was either to be undermined or to indicate the level of civilization that any given alien race had achieved. And, as Mendelsohn writes, science fiction "is full of stories in which superstition is defeated by explanation" (265). For much science fiction, gods and miracles are ultimately just physics. The association of religion with the primitive or the uncivilized remained a common trope in the "Golden Age" of science fiction in the 1940s and 1950s. As Mendelsohn points out, an interesting new theme of narratives of this time (now influenced by the apocalyptic horrors of the Second World War) was the use of religious belief and ritual as an "indication of failure," in which SF writers saw civilization as destroying themselves over and over again and portrayed religion as a "point upon the curve through which humans, if separated from history and from civilization, would pass over and over again" (266).

Despite its reputation as a force for secularization, by the second-half of the twentieth century, science fiction stories (short stories, novels, and then films and television) often provided narratives through which to think about religion. In the 1960s, classic SF such as Frank Herbert's *Dune*, Walter Miller's *A Canticle for Leibowitz*, Robert Heinlein's *Stranger in a Strange Land*, and Stanley Kubrick's *2001* all used forms of religion as central plot devices. Miller's novel *A Canticle for Leibowitz*—which tells a story spanning thousands of years of a Catholic monastery after a devastating nuclear war, and the slow rebuilding of civilization itself—is the most well-known and complicated version of this trope. Later, twentieth-century novels, such as *Hyperion* and *Galatea 2.2*, and films, such as *Close Encounters of the Third Kind*, are examples that, on the one hand, seem to support the secularization thesis, but that, upon closer inspection, might be seen to complicate it, both by offering new models of faith and religious practice, and also by subverting and questioning the progress narrative of rationalism.

The original three *Star Wars* films (1977–1983) presented a loosely new age faith in "the force," and created new forms of "religious" practice among fans who developed their own *Star Wars* viewing rituals and also participated in detailed exegetical arguments over *Star Wars* scripture and canon. The argument could be made that *Star Wars*—which incorporated elements of both SF and fantasy— was a developmental force in influencing a media-savvy generation that went on to deeply challenge traditional religious institutions, expand the concept of "lived religion," and question the relationship of spiritual and religious. These phenomena can be seen in the emergence of the real-world practice of "Jediism," once dismissed as a joke, but now taken seriously as a form of religion by both practitioners and religious scholars.[1] In our post-*Star Wars* world, SF has moved

28 *Beyond human*

from the fringes, from the pulp, and from the eccentric, into a mainstream conversation about what might be and who we might become and what else is out there beyond our ability to perceive and understand.

But while *Star Wars* presented one new path of imagining and creating religious experience, twenty-first-century speculative television offers different narratives, different media, different viewing practices, different audiences, and has different kinds of impacts. The first question might be to ask what recent television SF contributes to our understanding of religion that is different from earlier SF genres and media. From the perspective of television history, but also the history of SF in the popular consciousness, the original *Star Trek* (1966–1969) is an important transitional moment. From a religious perspective, *Star Trek* fulfilled two functions. Commonly understood to be at least a-religious if not anti-religious, the original *Star Trek* seemed to go along with the secularization thesis that saw the future as evolving toward a more rational, and therefore less religious, society. The crew of the original series served on a ship with no clergy and no explicit practice of religion, and the more religious alien societies on the show tended toward the primitive, while the more secular (i.e. Vulcan) were more advanced.

While some critics have read the original *Star Trek* as an example of a deeply humanistic and secular view, others point to the ways it still contains a traditional view of the role of religion. As Andrew Copson writes, *Star Trek* "has a hopeful vision of the future: one in which mankind has united around shared human values, joined in a common endeavor to reach the stars, and happily left religion behind on the way." Although Copson writes to praise the show's humanistic core, when he writes that "all the phenomena encountered within it are investigated rationally and, though they may at first seem inexplicable, are understood in the end as susceptible to naturalistic explanations," we can see his—and the show's—belief that a kind of Enlightenment rationality and science will ultimately provide answers. Although some of this conceit was problematized in later spin-offs, the core secularism was still often reiterated, as when Captain Jean-Luc Picard, from *The Next Generation*, is mistaken for a god by an alien and he points to the rejection of religion as an evolutionary advance:

> Millennia ago, they abandoned their belief in the supernatural. Now you are asking me to sabotage that achievement, to send them back into the dark ages of superstition and ignorance and fear? ("Who Watches the Watchers?")

On the other hand, as James McGrath writes, "*Star Trek* had a 'theological' component to its discourse, and this was present from the very first episode to air" (473). These theological components are found in how the show held up the elements of a human Judeo-Christian culture as normative. For example, the show may have been too secularist to believe in a Christian afterlife, but it certainly elevated the human soul to something that transcended the biological, and the main theme could arguably be a quest by the emotional Captain Kirk to humanize the universe: a type of missionary project.

The first television alien to influence the popular religious imagination may have been *Star Trek's* Spock. Like *Star Trek* itself, Spock's "Live Long and Prosper" is about as human, or at least as American, as you can get, and sounds more like the twenty-first-century prosperity gospel of Joel Osteen than something from an alien Vulcan world. The phrase reinforces the neoliberal, normative, and humanistic values of longevity, individualism, and acquisitiveness. Scholars, critics, and fans have used Spock's character as a source of debate over definitions of religion or secularism, and recent fan commentary continues these debates online, demonstrating how *Star Trek* still plays a role in religious definition and activity long after its original run. A fan on a *Star Trek* subreddit recently wrote:

> Ironically, I think the most humanist species is the Vulcans. I think people make the mistake of believing that Vulcans are driven purely by logic. In fact, while logic guides them, they're actually in search of a kind of neoplatonic beauty and truth. That's why they're not just interested in utilitarian maximization (like the Borg) but instead they devote themselves to science and the arts.

Another fan argues that Spock and the Vulcans are atheists, and that they "shroud their practices in rituals that seem like religion because it's a coping mechanism." Yet another fan writes that Vulcans are a species that "quite literally worship logic [and] who can't seem to wrap their head around the fact that worship is an emotion." What is significant here, and across hundreds of other fan posts, is that the terms of the debate between fans are some of the very same issues that define twenty-first-century religion and religious studies. In both cases, definitions and interpretations are becoming less about institutions, doctrines, texts, and beliefs and more about lived practices and experiences.

Yet, we can nonetheless find some Christian writers who continue to look for a recognizable Gospel in *Star Trek* and who also turn to the character of Spock. In a 2016 piece, Chandra Johnson quotes Christian blogger Paul Asay:

> When you see Spock, you see someone who sees the whole universe for what it is: It operates by a set of rules, but at the same time, he doesn't shut out the possibility of remarkable things happening.

Asay's vision of Spock is just one example of how *Star Trek* gives Christians a model to live by in an increasingly scientific, secular world. He writes:

> Spock's mind is open to the amazing and when you approach life from a position of faith, that's what's required… You don't turn off your brain, but you remain open to the possibility of the miraculous. (Qtd in Johnson)

Current fans of *Star Trek*, though, are likely to see Vulcans not as a path to Christianity or to a perfect, rational, post-Enlightenment atheism, but as a species

30　*Beyond human*

that has developed a new blend of religious practice and mental discipline. One Reddit commentator wrote:

> Since the Vulcans are a very spiritual people and at one time were a very religious people it wasn't logical to completely abandon that part of their identity even if they do not hold the religious beliefs anymore. ("Does it seem strange that Vulcans have a religion?")

This series of posts and responses is a classic example of a fan-based conversation, taking place on a twenty-first-century digital platform, offering a more nuanced interpretation of religion on *Star Trek* than perhaps the show itself did, and certainly more than many scholars and critics have observed.

In this chapter and throughout this book, I follow the example of the Reddit commentator above in looking for more subversive and speculative spaces in which the shows and their fans question the standard received narratives of science, religion, and human exceptionalism. The three science fiction shows I examine in this chapter (and throughout the book)—*Firefly*, *Battlestar Galactica*, and *Doctor Who*—each present multiple narratives and contradictory ideas surrounding alien worlds and secularization, and offer challenging futuristic and extraterrestrial depictions of religious traditions, practices, and scriptures. Although, as many scholars and fans have noted, the shows (inevitably) contain elements of Christian and other world religions, they can offer us perspectives to view and even reframe these elements. More specifically, each of these shows provides material that fans and scholars can use to discuss topics such as the human soul, the material body, post-biological sentience, and alternative understandings of time, history, gender, desire, death, and divinity. Although science fiction as a genre is always about commenting on the present, the past, *and* the future, each of the three shows complicate this formula by self-consciously commenting on earlier models of science fiction as well.

Novelist James Morrow's assertion that "like cabbages and kings, theology and science fiction are not normally mentioned in the same breath" is perhaps no longer—if it ever was—true. Yet, it is still often in unpredictable places where we see television science fiction and fantasy creating a discourse that borrows from and explores the contradictions within religion. These perspectives can be found, for example, in *Battlestar Galactica*'s human and Cylon characters' desire to believe in a form of the sacred. Belief or faith on *Battlestar Galactica* exists differently from what it does in our Western Judeo-Christian world: it is neither good nor bad, neither right nor wrong, neither human nor alien, and it is rarely defined in opposition to rationality, science, or progress. Most of the series presents—without judgment or truth claims—various shades of faith, belief, and desire for an imagined divinity, a holy land, or a miraculous creation myth. Whether it is the "One God," or "the gods," or the prophecy of finding a semi/mythical "Earth," the show explores the nature of faith in ways that question its role outside an established referent. *Firefly*, on the other hand, presents a world of emptiness where the presence of transcendent divinities and prophesied endings would seem ridiculous. Yet, *Firefly* offers shades of faith within that nihilistic nothing-ness. In other words, while *Battlestar Galactica* leaves the idea of a divine presence ambiguous but possible, *Firefly* offers little hope beyond divine absence, but, as we will see, a divine absence that does not have to be anti-religious. *Doctor Who* offers a less consistent, or stable, thesis; with hundreds of episodes and multiple lead actors, show runners, genres, and platforms, it offers multiplicity and contra-diction rather than any definable positions or themes. This flexibility, however, is what gives it potential to present episodes and ideas that function as religious thought experiments on the nature of time, history, scripture, prophecy, science, and magic.

Battlestar Galactica: a posthuman desire for divinity

The twenty-first-century reboot of *Battlestar Galactica* (2004–2009) represented a significant moment in the shift toward a broader spectrum of fans, critics, and media scholars taking televised science fiction seriously, and *Battlestar Galactica* is still talked about as a breakthrough for televised science fiction drama. When it was awarded the title of Best Television Show of 2005 from *Time Magazine*, critic James Poniewozik introduced the show by saying, "Most of you probably think this entry has got to be a joke. The rest of you have actually watched the show." A remake of the 1978 series of the same name, the reimagined *Battlestar Galactica*, consists of a two-part miniseries followed by four seasons. The show centers on a futuristic universe where an endangered and radically reduced rem-nant of the human species flees a race of sentient machines known as Cylons, who the humans originally created and who rebelled and then destroyed human civilizations.

The original Cylons of the 1978 series were reptilian aliens who created a race of robots. These earlier robots eventually wiped out their leaders due to a programming error, a classic trope in artificial intelligence narratives. In the new, more politically charged, version of the show, the Cylons were originally created by humans as an android-work force and the series takes place years after a Human–Cylon war. These Cylons, however, "evolve" into biological human-looking creatures, seemingly driven by a religious fervor often opposed to the "false" religion of the colonial humans. These and other shifts in plot and tone, push the show much deeper into gray areas and blurred boundaries within its ethical, ontological, and religious universe. The show offers more complex and morally ambiguous narratives about Cylons who come in models that look just like humans, and it creates a world where Cylon *and* human characters face anxi-eties over creation, procreation, forgotten histories, and moral responsibility, and where the answers are never easy and the facts rarely stable. As Janice Leidl writes: "Cylons are both other and self, destroyers and preservers. They consider themselves to have evolved beyond humanity but face a limited future, replicat-ing only in exact duplicates of their few existing models" (190). Both humans and Cylons claim a common history and share a mythical past that they each think applies only to themselves, but the Cylons consider themselves the true

32 *Beyond human*

interpreters of the human scriptures. Like debates among early Christians, they disagree over who are the proper heirs of the scriptures and the prophecies; *whose* is the correct interpretation?

The miniseries begins with lines of text: "The Cylons were created by Man. / They were created to make life easier on the Twelve Colonies. / And then the day came when the Cylons decided to kill their masters" ("Night 1"). The original purpose of the Cylons was to serve mankind as a sentient, robotic labor-force that would not come with the complications and rights that human workers possess. The sentient Cylons refused to fulfill their ordained purpose as laborers and instead rebelled against the civilization that created them. Thus, *Battlestar Galactica* begins with one of the most basic fears repeated by the genre since Mary Shelley's *Frankenstein*: what happens if we can no longer control our technology? And what happens if we realize that our "technology" is alive and capable of fear, anger, suffering, and affection? *Battlestar Galactica*, like *Frankenstein*, is ultimately not about good humans versus evil monsters, but is instead about parental responsibility, racism, xenophobia, slavery, and competing religious practices, prophetic texts, and mythologies. The long arc of *Battlestar Galactica* frames these questions over a series of episodes and years that allows viewers and showrunners to gradually explore the contradictions and nuances involved in accepting a non-human, often antagonistic, species as deserving of empathy and understanding.

Most of the series takes place on a battleship known as Galactica. At the advent of the series, the ship is about to be decommissioned and turned into a museum. The ship is a throwback to a pre-digital era, and the set emphasizes telephones with cords, plastic charts, steering wheels, and joysticks. Within the context of the plot, it is the fact that the ship is not digital and is not online with the rest of the fleet that allows it to survive—it is only the old fighter jets that work against the more advanced technology of the Cylons. (Although significantly, as we will learn, Cylon technology is partly biological.) Thus, the show stages the tension between the digital, the material, and the biological, using it as a metaphor for understanding the difference between humans and machines, between brains and computers, between perhaps even sacred and secular (although that becomes complicated). The metaphor is an unstable one, however, and the somewhat conservative aesthetic of the miniseries episodes—anti-technology, pro-military, dualistic good and evil—will be radically complicated in the following episodes in ways that are not foreshadowed in the first hours of the show.

* * *

In the opening scene of the miniseries, a man sits alone in a room on a ship. A subtitle informs us that the human-made Cylon robots rebelled and that it is now 40 years after the Human–Cylon war. Humans and Cylons live on separate planets, and while they are scheduled to meet every year at this armistice station, the Cylons have never shown up. This time, however, the door opens and the man looks up in surprise. We first see two armored and metallic Cylon robots, similar

Aliens 33

Image 1.1 "Are you alive?" (*Battlestar Galactica*, "Miniseries").

to what viewers of the original series were used to (although, unlike the original 1970s series, where the Cylons were actors in outfits, these robots are fully computer generated). Then, through the door walks a woman, who we will come to know as the Cylon model Number Six. She speaks the first line of dialogue in the series: "Are you alive?"—then requests the man "prove" his affirmation by kissing him (Image 1.1). This first scene of the miniseries closes with the armistice station being blown up as the initial act of war from the Cylons.

This opening scene presents what appears to be two humans engaging in the very human activities of talking, kissing, and murdering, and it is only later that we realize that one of them was a Cylon. This sets up tensions that will drive the whole series, as the behavior of humans and Cylons is often indistinguishable to both characters and viewers. "Are you alive?" is a version of the question that both Cylon and human will grapple with throughout the series. The plot of the first miniseries episode begins with the Cylons launching a surprise nuclear attack intended to exterminate the human race. Virtually all of the population of the Twelve Colonies of humans are killed and the military is mostly destroyed in this attack made possible by a virus introduced into the computer network. Only the antiquated Galactica and a handful of commercial ships survive.

After the miniseries, the first few hours of the first season—which set up the plot of a "rag-tag" fleet of ships housing the remnants of humanity being pursued through space by the Cylons—also introduce various religiously themed questions that will be developed through the subsequent seasons. Cylons come in only twelve human flesh models known by their numbers, which means that there are many copies of each; every model has certain characteristic personality traits, although they also each have an individual personality. Most Cylons practice

34 *Beyond human*

monotheism, which plays a big role in the series, but which also perhaps clashes with their concept of being.

Anthropologists who study religion associate cultural monotheism with an emphasis on individuality, so the idea of one single God worshipped by a multitude of identical models introduces friction at the very roots of the Cylon concept of being. The humans, on the other hand, are either polytheistic or are strict non-believers. Sympathetic characters and moments occupy, at some points, each faith position. Atheist, religious, and fundamentalist leaders are each given positions of strength and insight, and appear, at least at times, to correctly perceive the human (or Cylon) condition. Sometimes the prophecies of the gods seem to come true, sometimes a determinate God seems to step in; sometimes the atheistic rationality of science seems to be the correct path. When Commander Adama says to the more religious president, for example, "These stories about Kobol, gods, the Arrow of Apollo, they're just stories, legends, myths. Don't let it blind you to the reality that you face" ("Kobol's Last Gleaming"), unlike most television dramas, it is not clear who holds the correct viewpoint. Although the president will later refer to him as "Admiral Atheist," they will also end the series as partners and lovers, learning to respect and accept each other's views. In the same way that the line between Cylon and human blurs, so does the border between belief and disbelief.

Viewers, despite themselves, and outside of their personal beliefs—conscious and unconscious—are brought into the debate, perhaps finding themselves sympathizing with a point of view they claim to refute in their own lives, and sometimes forced to confront theoretical arguments outside of their own practices. To look at just one example among many, one fan who identified as polytheist, wrote:

> [The] philosophical tension between [mono- and polytheism] has provided a phenomenal backdrop to the series as a whole, and has informed particular moments in the story arc in a way that a traditional western look at religion probably would not.

This fan goes on to explore the ideas of cyclical versus linear time that are expressed in the language of the show, as well as the idea that the Cylon monotheism is a "manifestation of their centralized computer society." They conclude by placing the show's meaning-making systems onto the practices and speculations of the viewers:

> Within this dark and gloomy exploration of the human psyche through the lens of a "refugee camp in space" we can examine some of the most basic preconceptions of what our religion—our total response to the universe— provides us in the face of personal and societal crisis. (dailykos.com/stories April 4, 2008)

Fans and critics commonly criticize the show's lack of a full exploration of these philosophical issues. The promising religious clashes and theological paradoxes

Aliens 35

set up in the early seasons are either forgotten, simplified, or muddled in the later seasons. Jennifer Stoy, while acknowledging that "theology and mythology... colours and motivates the entire show," also writes of the "incredible ignorance and carelessness of the theology and mythology within the show." For her, this is "extraordinarily problematic, given that religious concerns are a prominent and recurring theme on the show" (16). Ultimately for Stoy, in its later episodes, *Battlestar Galactica* fails to take the "ambiguities and irrationalities of religion seriously," and instead assumes a "cheery pluralistic way out" (18). But while critics and fans alike critiqued this aspect of the show, it is interesting to think about how and why *Battlestar Galactica* was unable to follow through on these themes. I argue that this is in large part because they exist *as* questions and by their very nature are not able to offer conclusion or closure. While I agree with Stoy's criticism of the show's presentation of religion, there are ways that we can see this "cheery pluralistic way out" as a common religious move in the face of theological complexity: "God works in mysterious ways" is perhaps the most obvious. Like shows from *Lost* to *Westworld*, *Battlestar Galactica* was better at setting up philosophical complexities than it was at fully developing them—but, in each case, these unresolved or underdeveloped subplots present voids for speculation and fan activity to fill. And perhaps these failures speak to our own time's inability to truly articulate complete responses to unanswerable speculation. While Jameson claims, science fiction has "largely evolved into the historical or historicist mode of consciousness," it is still largely constricted by the ideology of the time in which it was created; its power exists in challenging our present to recognize itself in the *process* of reimagining our future ("Radical Fantasy" 274).

* * *

In the pilot, Commander Adama—unaware of the nuclear destruction just beginning on the planet surfaces—speaks at the decommission ceremony for Galactica. Seeming to cut away from his prepared remarks, he instead ponders: "When we fought the Cylons, we did it to save ourselves from extinction. But we never answered the question, 'Why?'." He then asks a question relevant to many of the shows examined in this book: "Why are we as a people worth saving?" In his speech, Adama makes a common SF characterization of humanities' sins, especially the irresponsible creation of the Cylons, saying, "You cannot play God, then wash your hands of the things that you've created." These statements are more prophetic than he could know, and it is just a short time later that he gives another speech: as the fleet of beat-up ships and surviving humans flee their destroyed world and are pursued by the Cylons, Adama addresses the entire crew at a religious memorial for the dead. Surrounded by covered dead bodies, and speaking to a hopeless crew who have just lost their families and their homes, the atheist Adama creates a reason, imagines a goal, and returns to their creator, all in a few sentences by citing the old legend of a planet called Earth, the mythical home of a lost thirteenth colony. Earth, says Adama, is "not unknown. I know where it is! Earth—the most guarded secret we have" (Miniseries "Night

36   *Beyond human*

Two"). When President Roslin later challenges him on his claim, Adama admits privately, "You're right. There's no Earth. It's all a legend... You have to have something to live for. Let it be Earth." What Adama, the supposed atheist, is proposing here is a type of theology based not in the belief in a god, but in the desire for one—a theology in which the desire for or a search for the divine is more important than actual existence. As Jeff Robbins writes in his book on radical theology, the "idea of God and the desire for God outlive the death of God" (6). In the case of Adama, he hopes that the desire for a mythical Earth will provide hope that will survive the end of their civilization.

Adama's question (Do we as a species deserve to survive?) is later remembered by a fighter pilot who is revealed to be a Cylon; when Adama asks Lt. Sharon "Boomer" Valerii why the Cylons hate humanity so much, she answers:

> I don't know if "hate" is the right word... it's like you said at the ceremony... you said something that sounded like it wasn't the speech you had prepared. You said, "Man never asked itself why it should survive." Maybe you don't...

Of course, the idea that maybe humans don't deserve to survive was implied in Adama's speech. The idea of finitude and death, not only for an individual but for an entire species is a place where science fiction reaches out to touch religion, as both tend to imagine apocalyptic scenarios, impossible quests, and non-biological consciousness.

The Cylons have a different kind of faith, one that does not contain what feels like an impossible quest, but is instead more rooted in faith in a divine being. Yet, despite their belief in an existent, transcendent, and single God, the Cylons too have a version of radical or death-of-god theology. When Six says, "We're the children of humanity. That makes them our parents," another Cylon answers, "Parents have to die," thus repeating a narrative in myth and religion from the first Greek gods to the Book of Mormon in which parents die, are killed, or are overthrown in order for the next generation to create a new world.

On *Battlestar Galactica*, as Kieran Tranter writes, while "religion was a cynical space for politicking... the show was not cynical about the divine," in that, as we watch the series "plans of humans and machines became more understandable in accord with a divinely-instigated grand design." In other words, religious institutions in *Battlestar Galactica* are critiqued as political, but the "divine was represented seriously" and, more importantly, as "active" (Tranter 132). It is this word "active" that is worth thinking more about. *Battlestar Galactica*, for the most part, strikes a careful balance between a God (or gods) who plays an active role in history and the possibility that this is all just imagined. Themes and scenes of prayer, fate, prophecy, and God's plan (often, but not only, spoken of by the Cylons) still imply questions: Are prayers answered? Is there a divine plan? These kinds of questions are kept unanswered in the early seasons of the show and ambiguously answered in the later seasons. Perhaps most to this point are the conversations that ask questions of divine creation and destruction; of beginnings and endings. When a Cylon asks Adama, "what if God decided he made a mistake, and he decided to give souls to another creature, like the Cylons?" he answers "God didn't create the Cylons, man did. And I'm pretty sure we didn't include a soul in the programming" (Miniseries). Unlike many SF films, this opening definitive statement, one that sets up a clear us-versus-them scenario, is far from the final word on the subject, and, in fact, by the second season, even Adama has backtracked from both his humanistic assumptions and absolute atheism.

As in other shows in this book, I find much more generative religious thought and possibility in the areas of the drama that are not obviously framed as religion or religious. My analysis of *Battlestar Galactica* will move away from ideas of religious institutions and divinity and will focus instead on the shifting relationship of belief to doubt, presence with absence, and the real and the imagined. These dichotomies, stressed across Western religious texts and practices, are dramatically unstable throughout *Battlestar Galactica*. As the lines between human and Cylon, secular and spiritual, history and prophecy, scientific law and divine purpose, and past and future continue to blur, watching the show becomes a meditation on our own religious traditions and the radical doubts and beliefs that make up our religious pasts and futures.

Firefly and broken scriptures

While *Battlestar Galactica* borrowed themes from the classic narrative of the Westbound, utopia-seeking covered wagons, *Firefly* (2002–2003) made these implicit connections to the past more literal as it combined the cowboy western with futuristic science fiction. *Firefly* premiered on the Fox network on September 20, 2002, although, as we will see, it had a somewhat complicated and imprecise beginning in terms of both time and plot. Set in the year 2517, the show follows the adventures of a renegade crew on a small spaceship—a "Firefly" model. The series explores the lives of nine characters, some of whom fought on the losing side of a civil war, and all of whom now make a living on the fringes of society. Set in a future where the United States and China have fused to form one central federal government, the debates, images, and plotlines borrow freely from the American Western and pulp science fiction of the early- and mid-twentieth century.

The world of *Firefly* is, in many ways, a completely recognizable one. The show's depictions of abuse of power and the subjection and alienation of marginalized populations are only slightly more extreme examples of current human and social conditions, and unlike almost every other televised science fiction drama, there are only humans in *Firefly*. Religion, as well, appears to have changed very little in the years since the American twenty-first century. While there is some evidence of East/West fusion, we still see a largely Judeo-Christian sensibility that has a concept of sin and damnation, priests, monks and abbeys, the same definitive and canonical Bible, crosses, marginalized fundamentalist sects, and a masculine image of a monotheistic God. While these religious signifiers are generally presented without comment, much of the show's dramatic tension comes from characters balancing personal survival with their sense of ethical behavior

38 *Beyond human*

and loyalty to traditional religious practices and beliefs. In establishing extreme versions of familiar situations, and by constantly foregrounding conflicting views of ethical and faith systems, *Firefly* continually addresses contemporary questions: What is the relationship between religion and ethics? What is the point of ritual in an apparently meaningless world? Is there a future for the idea of a divinely inspired sacred text? Unlike earlier science fiction dramas like *Star Trek*, which tend to respond to ethical questions with solid and "logical" solutions based in an absolute sense of humanity and a clear right and wrong, *Firefly* problematizes all of these questions, demonstrating the impossibility of satisfactory answers. *Firefly* explores through misdirection, confusion, and paradox: there is never a clear path, an absolute answer.

Firefly, as one of the head writers, Jane Espenson, explains, is "about what it means to be human in a world where no obvious rewards await the virtuous" (2). Showrunner Joss Whedon described the show as "nine people looking into the blackness of space and seeing nine different things." As we will see throughout this book, this "blackness" is used to explore various shades of belief and disbelief, nihilism, and concepts of transcendence and nothingness. Whedon originally pitched the show to the Fox television network as "depression in space" (DVD commentary to "Serenity"). The word *space* here takes on a deeper meaning if we expand the definition beyond "outer space" to include the nothingness, emptiness, and atheism that occupies much of the show. Space suggests an empty container, a vacuum, or an emptiness that can be seen either as destruction or as possibility—as a black hole or an empty canvas. However, these empty, Godless spaces can also be spaces of meditation on spirituality and even on divinity.

Firefly is now mostly remembered as the paradigmatic example of a series canceled before it had time to fully develop its characters, plots, and themes. This status continually poses questions of incompletion, ambiguity, and fragmentation, and in the fans' conception of the show—despite the fan-supported film *Serenity*, which offered a limited sense of closure—*Firefly* is always incomplete. Although the film offered some short cut explanations, within the series, the major questions are all left hanging: we never really learn or know where the monstrous Reavers come from, River is always in the act of becoming, Shepherd Book's back story is only hinted at. In many ways, this ambiguity enhances some of the most important themes of the show and—while, years later, fans still speculate on where the show could and should have gone—its sparse structure gives a sense of the never-ending search for meaning within emptiness and incompletion that is central to the show itself.

* * *

As fans of the series know, *Firefly* had essentially two pilot episodes, two endings, and one non-broadcast episode that was central to the plot and to understanding the final episode. The complex "origin myth" of the series has become almost canonical among fan communities. The initial pilot episode, the two-hour "Serenity," was rejected by the network as too slow, too dark, and too depressing.

A second episode, "The Train Job" was then quickly written and had to function as a pilot, giving background information and introducing characters, all the while compromising the original concept by creating a more cheerful show and a "jollier" Malcolm (or as Whedon remarks on the DVD commentary, Mal's "uncompromising character... which we compromised on"). Fans love to complain about the evil Fox empire (and, in fact this interpretation has itself worked its way into TV as a running joke on shows such as *Big Bang Theory*), and, in many ways, the real Fox has joined the fictional Alliance as a villainous organization inside and outside the context of the show. One way of thinking about this issue is to point to how DVDs and then streaming services perhaps served to reassert some sense of authorial intent over network control. But, more importantly for our purposes, we can see how alternative reading strategies develop. Rather than just denouncing the evil network, or pointing to the quality difference or conceptual gaps between the two versions, we can see these two versions not as contradictory, but as portraying a more nuanced and plural story. In other words, like modern literary interpretation of contradictory versions of scripture, whatever the extenuating circumstances were that resulted in two somewhat incompatible beginnings, by acknowledging the complexity of separate sources and incompatible versions, we can arrive at a richer more complex text.

The Hebrew Bible offers two versions of the David story, one where David is introduced as a shy sensitive shepherd boy who plays music and a second where he is an arrogant charismatic leader who announces to Goliath "I will strike you down and cut off your head" before he slays him. Both Davids have survived in later versions of the story, and in our modern imagination, David needs to be *both* the sensitive artist and the future powerful leader. In *Firefly*, we can see the pilot episodes as presenting two different versions of Mal's personality and the show's aesthetic. Like the Gospels, which present a Christ crucified on both Passover (Mark) and the day before Passover (John), giving us a Jesus that can attend a last Passover supper and also symbolize the lambs killed in preparation for that very meal, the two pilots give us a Malcolm that is embittered and misanthropic and is also curmudgeonly charitable. *Firefly* is pessimistic *and* hopeful, depressing *and* uplifting, religious *and* atheistic. This logic of both/and rather than of either/or points to the theme of plurality and a type of mental organization whereby seemingly contradictory information works not to negate, but to present nonlinear, anti-narrative, non-metaphysical, and multiple positions.

The original pilot—an episode that begins with the loss of religious faith and life on a battlefield and ends with a prostitute blessing a monk—and "The Train Job" set up the ideological tensions of the series through presenting contesting and dialectical philosophical positions, most obviously represented by the contrast between the atheist Malcolm Reynolds and the faithful Shepherd Book. The ideological clash between Mal and Book points to the dichotomy of pragmatism versus faith, and, conversely, demonstrates how each view is limited. The original pilot presents the framework of the arc for both Book and Mal, arcs that entail personal confrontations with their belief systems and with their relationship to religion and ethics, neither of which, in the context of the show, can be shown

40 *Beyond human*

to offer a satisfactory path. In the opening scene—the tragic Battle of Serenity Valley—Mal represents the ideal charismatic, supportive, and spiritual leader: he exhorts his troops, "we've done the impossible and that makes us mighty"; he kisses a cross for luck; he tells a frightened soldier that they are "too pretty for God to let us die"; and he refers to their coming air support as "angels." When the support never comes, and they are advised to surrender, enemy Alliance ships descend into the valley, and a stunned Mal stares uncomprehendingly, not even noticing as the man standing next to him is killed. In this moment, Mal's vision of optimism and faith dissolves; his trust in humans and God disappears. In a version of the scene that was not used, Mal's second-in-command Zoe says, "are we really getting out? Thank God," to which Mal cynically responds, "God? Whose color is he flying?" Although expressing differently placed skepticism, both versions of the scene present first an embracing and then a rejection of God, a giving and taking away of any guarantee of meaningfulness. The speed with which Mal moves from belief to doubt suggests that the line between these paths is thin: they are opposite sides of the same coin, different points along the same continuum.

The next scene jumps forward six years and opens with the image of a space-walking, upside-down Malcolm setting charges to an abandoned ship to perform an illegal salvage operation. The abrupt cut to Mal upside-down, of course, symbolizes the state of his world since the end of the war. More suggestive, however, is realizing that there is no upside-down in space—no reference point, no ground, no horizon. It is only a matter of perspective. The rest of the episode emphasizes Mal's "fallenness" from any concept of God or divine nature, especially through a contrast to Shepherd Book, who has left an abbey (but not his faith) to board the ship. Book's first and last names represent two sides of Abrahamic religion: the need to root meaning in a single text and the wandering humble shepherd. Although Mal makes a point of respecting Shepherd's presence on the ship, he dismisses any religious role that Book might play, telling him, "If I'm your mission Shepherd, best give it up. You're welcome on my boat. God ain't" ("Train Job"). Yet even this characteristic dismissal raises provocative questions. Mal, as becomes clear throughout the series, believes in a strong code of right and wrong. But what standard of ethics does Mal believe in and where does it come from? What God is it who is not welcome on "his boat"? At the end of "The Train Job," as he and Zoe return much-needed stolen medical supplies, Mal insists there are certain moral situations when man doesn't have a choice; he must do what's "right." When a sheriff in "The Train Job" tells Mal that sometimes a man has a choice, Mal's answer implies a sense of absolute right and wrong: "I don't believe he does." The word *believe* is central here. Mal's ethical system seems to be both fluid and uncompromising, yet it comes from a belief, or at least a desire to believe, in *something*. Literally and metaphorically floating in space, Mal wants an anchor, wants to believe in a world that is either upside-down or right-side-up, wrong or right.

The opening and closing scenes of *Firefly* present images of a human searching for meaning in a cruel world seemingly devoid of direction or divine guidance. A full season and fourteen episodes later, the final shot of the series shows a defeated bounty hunter floating to his inevitable death in the vast emptiness of space, sardonically commenting to himself, "Well, here I am." The series is framed by these two defining moments—the first a realization of true hopelessness, and the last a recognition of what Heidegger calls the "throwness," or the random brute facticity of the human condition—and explores, through humor, drama, tragedy, irony, and imagery, multiple reactions to the meaninglessness of the human condition. But while the attempt to create meaning out of blackness or empty space may be an existential quest, it is not necessarily an atheistic or impossible one. Like the bounty hunter floating in space or Mal staring numbly at the descending Alliance ships, life on *Firefly* often appears as nothing but bleakness. However, as was obvious throughout the show, life does contain flickers of hope and meaning, moments that often paradoxically come flush up against (and often resist) ideas of the religious or the ethical, often through reinterpretations of the very idea of space as nothing.

Mal's paradoxical ways of seeing and creating meaning are revealed in two comments from the pilot. Early in the episode, he remarks that he likes complexities because "the woods are the only place I can see a clear path." Yet later when they have escaped a dangerous brush with Reavers, he announces to the crew "we're out of the woods." These directly contradicting statements suggest the ambiguity between the appearance of a clear, right path and the opposing idea of clarity only within multiplicity or chaos. The second idea sees plurality and chaos not as error but as a way to see "meaning" through misdirection and confusion. The metaphor of a "path" to meaning is perhaps a misleading one, as it suggests images of straight lines and clear vision, a clarity that is subverted by the visual style of the show. There are few straight lines, absolute boundaries, framed images, or black and white areas, visually, morally, or theologically. Mal's clear path through the woods is an apt description of the show's indirect approach to questions of understanding concepts like "right" and "God."

Although presented as philosophically in opposition, both Mal and Book are contained by linear and modern assumptions which still dominate our late/-post-Enlightenment reading strategies, and which survive, partly, because of the persistence of traditional monotheistic thinking even outside of belief. Mal may reject God, but it is a very specific God he denies, and in his denial, he still maintains the hierarchical structures of monotheism. Mal replaces God with human, but merely transfers the attributes of the divine to the human; he still insists on a strict moral good, free will, and the on a single coherent narrative of a clearly defined individual. He denies God, but fails to rewrite the book. Book, as well, perhaps fails to rewrite his text—a book that still has an end, that still progresses from Genesis to Apocalypse, from Fall to Paradise. If we can say with Jacques Derrida that the "idea of the book is the idea of a totality" (*Grammatology* 18), then the idea of a totally autonomous book represents a single unified God, and, as his name suggests, Book's faith also translates to the belief in a single definable and unified self. These are all assumptions of unity the show calls into question.

42 *Beyond human*

Firefly, like *Buffy*, *Dollhouse*, and *Doctor Who*, offers alternative models for connecting story, time, and possibility—models without clear origin or definitive endings. Of course, Jacques Derrida, the atheist, like Joss Whedon, the atheist, like Russel T. Davies, the atheist, are all trying something different from a pure denial of the "reality" of a transcendent god that must either exist or not. Derrida, as John Caputo writes, "is repeating religion with a difference, miming religious time nondogmatically, for this is a messianic time *sans* a Messiah, an apocalypse *sans* apocalypse, a religion *sans* religion" (Caputo 70–71). "Religion without religion" is a common phrase in theoretical writing in the current century, but applied to the television I am interested in, it is useful in thinking about the impossibility of a stable idea of the words and concepts of religion or religious.

* * *

The questions of the posthuman, the persistence of irrational faith, the possibility of a sacred text, and the relationship of religion to ethics are addressed directly in the episode "Jaynestown." The episode weaves together two plots: on the ship, the damaged young psychic, River, and the wandering preacher, Shepherd Book, engage in a conversation on faith and the Bible, while, on a small outer planet, the rest of the crew finds that the good-hearted outlaw Jayne has been made a legendary hero due to a misunderstanding of his actions on a previous visit. The episode opens with River "fixing" Book's Bible of its "contradictions" and "repetitions" by systematically tearing out pages. River (who previously described herself as "broken" in the episode "Safe") tells Book that his Bible is "broken" and attempts a solution:

> So we'll integrate non-progressional evolution theory with God's creation of Eden. Eleven inherent metaphoric parallels already there. Important number prime number. One goes into the house of 11, 11 times but always comes out one. ... Noah's ark is a problem...

Book tells her, "You don't fix the Bible," to which River responds, "It's broken. It doesn't make sense." Book then gives his fullest statement about faith: "It's not about making sense. It's about believing in something. And letting that belief be real enough to change your life. It's about faith. You don't fix faith. It fixes you." Although it appears that we as viewers are supposed to sympathize with the apparent wisdom of Book's comment that "you don't fix faith, it fixes you," we are not allowed to remain comfortable with this sentiment. It is immediately subverted when the scene then cuts to the planet where the workers, or "mudders," are literally singing the praises of Jayne. This direct juxtaposition of Book's justification of irrational belief with the praises of a slave-like caste for an undeserving, selfish criminal forces us to question Book's comments. It is worth thinking about to what extent the mudders' faith in Jayne has indeed "fixed" them. There is little difference between Book's faith in the Bible and the mudders' faith in

Aliens 43

Jayne, which are both based on stories or events that "don't make sense" and indeed are not, for the most part, factually "true." If the episode demonstrates (as it seems to) that faith in Jayne is the wrong kind of faith, then it, by implication, also questions the faith of (the) Book.

Book's comment that "you don't fix faith, it fixes you" is darkly parodied in this episode by the atheistic Captain Malcolm Reynolds when he says that "every man ever got a statue made of him was one kind of a son-of-a-bitch or another. Ain't about you, Jayne. It's about what they need." Mal would almost certainly affirm that Book's Judeo-Christian God is indeed a "son-of-a-bitch," yet a viewer might ask if Mal and Book are on opposite sides here or come to some sort of agreement. While Mal's humanist pragmatism, again, appears intentionally contrasted with Book's faith, *both* Mal's and Book's statements agree on the power of faith above and beyond any core essential presence of truth. They are both a form of thought that finds the divine not in presence or certainty, but in our desire for him/it. Jayne's tale, like the story of Noah's ark in the Bible, is only a "problem" if we focus on the misreading of flawed evidence that has been inaccurately reproduced and transmitted. The question is whether that matters or not. When, later in the episode, Jayne pushes his own statue down, it is a version of the "death of God" that Western culture experienced in the nineteenth and twentieth centuries (Image 1.2). Yet God continues to be an influential presence in the twenty-first (and evidently twenty-sixth) century. Even after hearing the "truth" about Jayne, a mudder sacrifices his life to save him. The obvious implied question is whether his sacrifice is noble or foolish, but there are deeper religious resonances as well. Woven into this plot line is the ancient cyclical myth of a god rising from the ashes of their own death. Adding an equally ancient but less

Image 1.2 Jayne's fallen statue (*Firefly*, "Jaynestown").

44 *Beyond human*

familiar interpretation, we offer the idea that ashes and death are a necessary part of divine experience.

There are two divergent ways of interpreting the events in this episode. Faith in the Bible, like faith in Jayne, while it may be pragmatic and may fix things, is often reductively labeled as, on some level, foolish, a "primitive" society relying on superstition. But a second, more nuanced reading is represented by River, who can perhaps be seen as not "broken" after all. Like plural interpretations of the Bible, she needs to be allowed (and to allow herself) to be multiple and nonlinear: she needs to have—to quote her own reading of Genesis in Book's Bible—a "non-progressional evolution." The ending of the episode, when River remarks wryly to Book to "just keep walking, preacher man," it is a humorous deflection from further debate, but also a suggestion from her nonlinear perspective that Book and his "book" have not found or provided an answer yet, but may still be necessary. As the credits start to roll, the background music is an instrumental version of the mudder's song "The Man they Call Jayne," suggesting that the hymn of praise will survive the "truth" and be shared across cultures and time.

As we have realized in our own time of Christian atheists and the "spiritual but not religious," faith can remain even when the story is broken. While faith may "fix," it is not always for the best, and faith certainly can never be "fixed"—that is, positioned in a stable and secure place—and neither can we. River's view of scripture resembles philosopher Mark C. Taylor's characterization of scripture as an act of "wandering." For Taylor, "instead of a finished product, the text [of scripture] is the social activity of countless co-producers. Productive readers infinitely… extend the text" (*Erring* 182). Taylor defines wandering, not as being lost, but as an act that "liberates the drifter from obsessive preoccupations with the past and the future" (157). In the same way that River takes the pages of Book's "broken" Bible out of order, she removes her "broken" self from the accepted human paths of time and causality. To "keep walking,"—to embrace an ever slippery, Protean, plural reality—is to actually only experience a trace of any sort of reality: to see "truth" as footsteps in the sand that will be erased by the next windstorm. As River seems to realize, neither Book nor Mal can fix, attach, or create any kind of stable meaning to a book, a myth, or an absolute sense of right and wrong. In the same way that Mal, who says he can "see most clearly in the woods" and yet feels morally compelled to lead his crew out of them, so also can faith or truth only exist nomadically; they are always on the move, and in the necessary search for them one can only "keep walking."

Doctor Who: religion, big history, and the impossible

Doctor Who began in 1963, the day after the JFK assassination, in the early days of civil rights, counterculture, and Vatican II, and in the year religious historian Callum Brown identified as the "death of Christian Britain." The long life of the show, as well as its multiple stars, showrunners, writers, and directors, has allowed it to adapt to changing horizons in politics, sexuality, and religion.

Aliens   45

Part melodrama, part fairy tale, part fantasy, and part classic science fiction, its flexible genres open up multiple possibilities for writers, and fans, to explore. Recent studies of fan and participatory culture have expanded and complicated the understanding of how ideas travel between media and viewer even further. *Doctor Who* embraces fan culture on an expansive scale, from conventions, comics, and audiobooks to the BBC's recent use of the series to explore new technologies, including mini-episodes, podcast commentaries, interactive adventures, video blogs, companion programming, and "fake" websites. In 2006, the BBC launched two spin-off series, *Torchwood* and *The Sarah Jane Smith Adventures*, followed by *Class* in 2017.

Like the "reimagined" *Battlestar Galactica*, it is in its twenty-first-century "regeneration" or "New Who" that the show became an important philosophical voice, partly through the ways in which it linked, borrowed from, parodied, and commented on the cultures surrounding its earlier version. On the other hand, the earlier roots of the show—particularly its challenging themes of time, narrative, and continuity—provide the contemporary creators of the show and its legions of fans/critics/scholars with an additional exegetical level to play with. In the early years of the original series, *Doctor Who* often seemed to unapologetically embrace the secularization thesis associated with mainstream science fiction. Episodes throughout the 70s and 80s often followed the intellect-conquers-faith model, and episodes focusing on the religious faith and practice of alien cultures emphasized a false belief or regressive character that could be uncovered through the Doctor's superior insight and perspective. As James McGrath points out, "in many of these early episodes the Doctor adopted a disdainful and condescending view of those simple-minded people who believed in magic and gods rather than science" (479). However, like much of *Star Trek* and much classic SF, even in its most anti-religious moments, *Doctor Who* retains a blind faith in reason, and, as McGrath also shows, *Doctor Who* "in the very attempt to replace superstition with science… finds itself affirming those traditional supernatural beliefs at the same time, albeit in new ways" (479). McGrath provides an example from an early *Doctor Who* episode that echoes the gendered exchange from *Battlestar Galactica* that I opened the chapter with:

DOCTOR: Everything that happens in life must have a scientific explanation. If you know where to look for it, that is…

JO: Yes, but suppose something was to happen and nobody knew the explanation. Well, nobody in the world, in the universe. Well, that would be magic, wouldn't it?

DOCTOR: You know, Jo, for a reasonably intelligent young lady, you do have the most absurd ideas. (479)

Jo's "absurd" question here is nonetheless an insightful one: What do we call something that happens that is beyond science? Is there a "scientific explanation" for what existed before the big bang? Or for the "reason" the big bang happened at all? As McGrath writes, "the introduction of a secular-scientific framework

46   *Beyond human*

results in the transformation of religion rather than its elimination" (481). The ambiguous space created by this "transformation" of religious language and ideas into scientific-sounding explanations is given more explicit attention after the 2005 revival, but throughout the series, as Andrew Crome points out, "*Doctor Who* has displayed a degree of ambiguity on religion that allows for both pro- and anti-religious readings" ("Heaven Sent" 112). In 1972, a British reverend wrote that the ultimate triumph of Good over Evil was the "most important connection between *Doctor Who* and religion" (qtd. in Crome, *Religion and Doctor Who* xviii), but this is a much harder claim to make 50 years later. The arcs of many of the shows discussed in this book—for example, *Buffy the Vampire Slayer* or *The Walking Dead*—move from an essentially good-versus-evil model in the early seasons to much more complex depictions of these positions. In the same way, while early Cold War *Doctor Who* perhaps presented a reductive moral organization, the *New Who* and the post-event, post-genocidal Doctor has established a much more complex relationship with religion and good and evil.

Despite continuing to be identified with a secular perspective, *Doctor Who*, as Crome writes, "has always contained a rich current of religious themes and ideas at its heart" (*Religion and Doctor Who* xii). Connections to religion in the show may take the form of seeing the Doctor (or the TARDIS) as a religious figure, imagining the future of human or non-human religions, exploring alternative sacred texts or ways of reading or preserving tribal knowledge and history, and imagining new ways of defining religion. Furthermore, online fan fiction features multiple stories linking the Doctor to Christ, and comparisons of the Doctor to Christ are common among critics and Christian commentators (Crome, *Religion and Doctor Who* xvii). Therefore, while many commentators still fall back on the secular nature of the show, others attempt to establish a more explicitly religious one.

In either case, the actual experiences of watching, thinking about, and participating in the discourse surrounding the show often cannot be reduced to such formulations. An example might be found in the two-part season three finale, which takes place in present-day London when the "Master"—a renegade Time Lord—has hypnotized the world with a network called Archangel, and is now prime minister of the United Kingdom. He takes over the world and takes the Doctor captive, but the Doctor's companion, Martha, manages to escape and travels the world for a year to gather support for the weakening Doctor. She implores everyone to think of one word—"Doctor"—just as the Master intends to launch his fleet, so that their combined thoughts, traveling through the network, are able to rejuvenate him. The Doctor, victorious again, says to the Master at the end: "I forgive you." Although the word "prayer" was not used, some viewers found this episode a testament to the power of prayer and to Christian forgiveness. On the other hand, the *Doctor Who* podcast *Run* represented a popular alternative view in finding the ending "stupid," and a "magic band aid plan," and concluding bluntly with "fuck this shit." The idea of all humanity thinking a word at the same time as an example of the power of prayer or language is simultaneously a weak plot point and a reductive concept of both prayer and magic; however, it is also an attempt to think beyond the individual human, to find power in the radically communal, a religious theme we find throughout speculative fiction.

Most critical analysis of *Doctor Who* has concentrated on the human/not-human time-traveling figure of the Doctor, especially in how they relate to the surrounding humans. The point of view of the Doctor is, as Crome writes, one in which "only he has truly experienced the mysteries of creation" (*Religion and Doctor Who* xii). Although fans are implicitly required to see this character as a unified one, the Doctor is, of course, created by multiple actors, writers, and visual styles, and—even within the context of the show—challenges the idea of a stable identity. Throughout the show, the concepts of what a Time Lord is, or what the TARDIS is, or what the rules of time are, are not consistent or even coherent. As writer and showrunner Steven Moffat said at ComicCon 2017, "What would *Doctor Who* continuity be without blatant and unresolvable contradictions?" To search for a meaning across these contradictions is part of the experience of watching *Doctor Who*. To be a regular viewer is to be aware of the balance between a desire to form the contradictions into a linear narrative and an embrace of the fragmentary. We, as fans, want the show to be consistent, we want to believe in the regeneration of the Doctor. Yet fans also delight in the continued debate about their favorite Doctor, offer critiques each time the actor changes, and complain about new writers and showrunners.

Although ostensibly aimed at a young audience, the show has continually, and increasingly in its current incarnation, challenged and addressed ideas about issues of trauma, memory, ethics, war, race, heteronormativity, and the value of human life. Like its approach to other familiar themes and questions (What is a human? What does it mean to die? Is genocide or slavery ever justifiable? What happens when history is forgotten?), the new revival of the show in 2005 created more complicated representations of religious themes in spite of (or, perhaps partly because of) the often-mentioned atheism of showrunners Russell T. Davies and Steven Moffat. The new show often questioned or expanded traditional ideas of religion, divinity, and ritual, as well as offering us a view of futurist nuns, prophets, angels, scripture, and a fifty-first-century Church of England.

* * *

The first few moments of the pilot episode "Rose" illustrate some of the themes that are most significant within this book. That the episode is named for the first companion already indicates a shift in the psychological core of the show—one that will be seen and negotiated more through the companion's eyes and through encounters with Earth than with the Doctor, Time Lords, and alien worlds. The opening image of this first episode immediately reminds us that we are now in the digital twenty-first century; the shot (which repeats as the opening of season two, and then three more times in the first five seasons) starts from a point of view in space that then quickly descends—Google Earth style—into modern day London, then to a digital alarm clock in Rose's bedroom. We see a quick montage

48 *Beyond human*

of Rose's working day as a shop girl until, at closing time, she descends into the basement where things quickly turn creepy. When store mannequins come to life and attack her, the Doctor appears and grabs her hand and utters his first words of the new series: "Run," followed shortly after with "I'm the Doctor, by the way… nice to meet you, Rose. Run for your life." Although companions are different in significant ways, their participation in the Doctor's narrative or timeline shares two vital aspects of religious identity: belief and practice. They must *believe* the impossible claims that the Doctor makes, and they must *act* in accordance with them. "Run" contains both of these concepts: it encompasses, for Rose and the others, a leap of faith—they must first accept premises previously thought impossible—and they must act; they must run. The very physical act of running as a theme in a show where time travel is real offers another visual commentary on the tension between the old and new, the material and digital. Despite its time-traveling alien main character, the show remains materially earth-bound. *Doctor Who*—like the religious/theological ideologies which we will be drawing comparisons with—is both earthly and cosmic, both immanent and transcendent. Perhaps the most transcendent idea in the show—the TARDIS itself—is also humorously material and comes with levers, knobs, and parking brakes from Earth circa 1960.

Rose, in a further effort to find out who the Doctor is, looks him up on the internet—a search that leads her to a man named Clive Finch. Finch is a stereotypical, introverted conspiracy theorist who has tracked the figures of the Doctor through history. In this first episode of the new *Doctor Who*, the Doctor's impossibility becomes visible through digital technology. Raphael Kiyani writes that the character of Clive works to "ground the world of *Doctor Who* to our world," a grounding that becomes a major theme in the new series. Twenty-first-century Google and the internet have become our trusted sources of knowledge and where we turn to make sense of the unknown. At the same time, the internet has become a space where truth and lies, fact and fiction, and explanation and conspiracy are intertwined and manipulated in ways never before experienced by humans. Religion—which has been built on innovations in the traveling of ideas on such subjects as truth, the real, and scripture—is constantly being reimagined through new technology from the book to the printing press to artificial intelligence. Our current religious imagination thinks simultaneously through, with, and against these technological beliefs, and, as we will see, speculative television and its fan cultures are powerful tools in thinking through these relationships.

For Clive Finch, the Doctor is a "legend woven throughout history… he brings a storm in his wake and he has only one constant companion… death." For Kiyani, "likening the Doctor to some sort of God/Death figure" suggests that "perhaps there's a darker streak behind the clownish smile," which becomes another important theme in this new series. Although Clive—who will soon die violently—has no idea, the following seasons will develop just how the Doctor is indeed "woven" and sometimes unwoven through history—and into and out of texts. The first few seasons are built on ideas of how history is made and unmade,

Aliens 49

recorded and forgotten, and to what extent it can be "unwoven." These questions of the reality and the ineffability of topics like death, time, and the future always exist on the edge of religious negotiations and our limited ability to imagine them—either visually, scripturally, or digitally.

Many of the most poignant moments to come will focus on how different companions—faced with new expanded perceptions of time, death, and the human—will go about making choices. Sometimes these are as familiar as leaving family and partner to travel to exotic places with an exotic stranger. But other times, it involves accepting a whole new view of the cosmos in a brief moment and then acting on that radical new belief—a conversion experience of sorts. These kinds of decisions are introduced at the end of this opening episode when Rose—as she tries to decide whether she should leave and travel with the Doctor—asks him, "Are you alien?" He replies, "Yes." Then she asks, "Is it always this dangerous?" He again responds, smiling, "Yes." When he assures her that the Box will not only "go anywhere in the universe free of charge," but also "travels in time," Rose *runs* into the TARDIS. "Run for your life," he told her, but now her running is about leaving the safety of twenty-first-century working class London for the alien, the dangerous, and the impossible: a true leap of faith into a new belief system with no guarantee of landing. The Doctor's companions—and, by extension, the viewers—are thrown into a world where they must imagine the possibility of millions of aliens, of infinite spaces, unstable histories, and parallel worlds. Rose makes the decision, as each companion will, to embrace the impossible, the danger, and the desire to be surprised.

The first real moment of somber introspection in the pilot centers on the ideas of the Doctor's identity and on what it means to live in a universe beyond our understanding. In it, Rose asks the Doctor, "Tell me. Who are you?" The Doctor responds:

> It's like when you're a kid, the first time they tell you that the world is turning and you just can't quite believe it 'cause everything looks like it's standing still. I can feel it… [he takes her hand] … the turn of the earth. The ground beneath our feet is spinning at a thousand miles an hour. The entire planet is hurtling around the sun at sixty-seven thousand miles an hour. And I can feel it. We're falling through space, you and me, clinging to the skin of this tiny little world. And, if we let go… [He releases her hand] …That's who I am. Now forget me, Rose Tyler. Go home.

This sense of both individual importance (the universe exists because I can perceive it), and insignificance ("clinging" to a "tiny little world") is another of the essentially existential and religious tensions in this pilot episode. We must imagine it and then think about how truly small we are, an overwhelming feeling that blurs the distinction between atheistic and religious. *Doctor Who* is a world that is both disenchanted and re-enchanted; a world of both rationality and science and of gods and ghosts and religion and magic. Regular viewers, just like

50   *Beyond human*

Rose, are not quite able to "go home" after watching. Instead, we get this sense of a world both larger and more mysterious than we can imagine.

The last two episodes of the first season ("Bad Wolf" and "The Parting of the Ways"), predictably gave fans the return of the Doctor's arch rival, the Daleks. The Daleks, presumably eliminated in the great Time War that left the Doctor alone and psychologically damaged, have returned, but with a difference. They have a great religious leader—the "God of all Daleks"—they have developed a "concept of blasphemy," and represent the dark side of religion. Not extinct, like the Doctor thought, the Daleks have gradually rebuilt themselves out of dying humans. Added to the Dalek vocabulary of "exterminate, exterminate" are now phrases such as "Worship him! Worship him!" and "Do not blaspheme! Do not blaspheme!" It is, in many ways, a traditional science fiction depiction of religion built on intolerance or insanity, and which leads to its own destruction: each Dalek contains at its core a hatred of the human flesh out of which they are made. It is, on the surface, both machine-versus-human and cultish intolerance-versus-humanistic rationalism. Each Dalek is both machine and flesh, and the human infrastructure they are attacking is a satellite functioning as a series of giant game shows. The ideas of the real-versus-the virtual and the post human-versus-the human are complicated here—just which figure is which? As the Doctor prepares to destroy all human and Dalek life, the God of the Daleks refers to him as the "Great Exterminator." Despite what seemed a battle of good versus evil between a savior and a power-hungry god-figure, suddenly the borders are very blurred.

Although the Doctor, intending to sacrifice both himself and his TARDIS, sends Rose away and back to her own time, she returns with the TARDIS and her own form of religious power gained by exposing herself to the "heart of the TARDIS." Her existential question over inferiority and her place in the universe is seemingly answered as she temporarily becomes the most powerful being, able to now say to the emperor of the Daleks: "You are tiny. I can see the whole of time and space."

> I can see everything.
> All that is.
> All that was.
> And all that ever could be.

Just for a moment, Rose is God. Each of the companions will have access to all of time and space, or at least more than can be comprehended from a human perspective. New companions, like Rose, are often taken to see the end of the Earth, the end of the universe, the end of time, and then are expected to return to an earth they have just seen obliterated and resume their mundane job and their human relationships. Rose cannot live a normal life with her boyfriend and mother knowing that the Doctor is fighting for his life and the survival of humankind thousands of years of the future—from her new perspective, all of this is simultaneous.

Aliens 51

ROSE: Two hundred thousand years in the future, he's dying, and there's nothing I can do.

ROSE'S MOM: Well, like you said two hundred thousand years. It's way off.

ROSE: But it's not. It's now. That fight is happening right now, and he's fighting for us, for the whole planet, and I'm just sitting here eating chips. ("The Parting of the Ways")

Rose, the Doctor, and the viewers of the show experience what scientists and historians of science call the "long address" of the human and "deep" or "big history." "Big History" is a view of, or approach to, history that "places human history within the context of cosmic history, from the beginnings of the universe up until life on Earth today" (Spier 1). This view of history also encourages speculative questions about the future, such as the human migration to other planets or the limits of human survival (Spier 202). Although scholars of big history identify themselves and their work within the field of history, they often trace their origins back to such speculative writers as H.G. Wells, whose *The Time Machine* is one of the first science fiction novels.[2] Seeing such a wide scope of history, while it may still necessarily be human-centered, also forces us to rethink our sense of importance and our place in the universe. It makes us ponder the long expanses of time before we existed and after we exist. This perspective is also the effect of traveling with the Doctor.

* * *

Science fiction, as we have seen, has historically been associated with secularism and anti-religious sentiments. *Doctor Who*, as well, is often seen, as anti-religious. This view, however, is a point of debate among fans, critics, and scholars. Kieran Tranter points to a series of reasons that support the claim that in *Doctor Who*, "religious organisations and religiosity are not to be trusted" (134). The Doctor rarely collaborates with religious leaders; humans and aliens who are religious are presented as dangerously naïve, and claims to be divine are inevitably an illusion or a deception; gods are usually revealed to be some sort of powerful aliens (134–135). Tranter contrasts *Doctor Who* with *Battlestar Galactica*, maintaining that while on *Battlestar Galactica*, religion is a "cynical space for politicking," but the divine is "represented seriously," on *Doctor Who* "not only is religion presented as a failed form of knowing and doing, but the divine is also presented as failure" (134). Tranter's "failure of the divine" sees the drama of this failure as a statement against any kind of religious thinking. Although he acknowledges religion and the divine are "all over" *Doctor Who*, he ultimately concludes that the religions that the Doctor comes across are "morally bankrupt" and that belief in the divine is "aligned with destiny, evil and death" (133–134). He contrasts these beliefs with a faith in the senses and in the material world.

"Divine failure" is, as we shall see, a deeply theological concept within schools of radical theology, and one that is part of many human religious traditions, including discussions of the Christian God's "weakness" and the moment of

52 *Beyond human*

failure inherent in Christ's crucifixion. *Doctor Who* can counterintuitively be seen to depict—in ways similar to claims by theologians across Judaism, Islam, and Christianity—that when we take our gods too literally, they tend to disappear. If we can truly name, describe, understand, or hear the words of a divine being, it brings that being down to our level and diminishes divinity. Thinking through, or at least alongside, these kinds of perspectives, changes the apparent opposition between theism and atheism in ways that science fiction can challenge.

Yet, one of the ways we can think religiously through *Doctor Who* is to understand that belief and materiality are not opposites, and that divine failure is not anti-religious. *Doctor Who*, like many of the other shows we will discuss in this book, find ways to dissolve this binary between the divine and the material, the immanent and the transcendent, and help us understand that these binaries have actually never existed. What Tranter refers to as the "failed gods" of *Doctor Who* do not necessarily only present, as he claims, a "secular account of the universe" (137). The failure of the divine may be seen in Tranter's terms to be a victory of technology and rationality, as the Doctor certainly does value a version of science and reason. But the Doctor is also obsessed and inspired by the wonder of that they cannot understand. When the Tenth Doctor's eyes go wide with his marvelous "I know…" in response to sharing some awesome sight with a companion, it is actually the opposite of "knowing" that he is usually reacting to. Rather, he is expressing an oceanic wonder at something that, despite his massive intellect, he remains fascinated by:

ROSE: I'll tell you what though…
DOCTOR: What?
ROSE: Werewolves.
DOCTOR: I know! ("Tooth and Claw")

This seeking for and celebration of wonder, surprise, and change works as a type of non-religious religion, related to theories of God's disappearance, absence, or weakness that are still very much in the realm of "religious" thinking. In his book, *The Weakness of God*, John Caputo opens by saying that it is a "blasphemous image of God" to imagine a "strong force with the power to intervene upon natural processes." His theories of the "weakness" of God are, as he says, "an attempt to think of God otherwise" (xi). One can perhaps think of the *Doctor Who* experience—as well as *Firefly* and *Battlestar Galactica*—as an experiment in thinking "God otherwise." A God between existence and nothingness; between the everyday and the cosmic; and a God found in the touch of a hand, the destruction of a world, and in the legends and stories that bring these moments together.

Notes

1 See *Invented Religions: Imagination, Fiction and Faith* by Carole Cusack.
2 Wells later wrote a work called *The Outline of History* (1920) which begins with the creation of the Earth and ends with World War I, and is often cited as an early work of "big history."

2 Vampires
The undead challenge to religion

Gods and vampires

Chapters Two and Three introduce my exploration of television's undead and the multiple opportunities that these paradoxical creatures offer for thinking about religion. The undead monsters of television subvert and create blurry borders where humans can imagine themselves and their others. Vampires and zombies, by their very nature, ask us profound questions about who we are and what such concepts as life and death mean to us. These creatures compel us to question origins and causes, and philosophers working on these questions have often used the figure of the zombie or the vampire as a tool of analysis. For a philosopher like Slavoj Žižek, "undeadness" is another way of thinking about or naming the Freudian death drive ("Night of the Living Dead"). Although Žižek does not address zombie fiction, we can see these various zombie narratives as a way of embodying this "undead" aspect of ourselves, a way of thinking beyond mortality and the confines of our body, but also of confronting the reality of death itself. Monsters of the undead "stand at the entrance to the unknown, acting as gatekeepers to the acceptable" (Graham 53). They are identified as "colloquial names for the experience of alterity" (Kearney, *Strangers* 13). These "experiences of alterity," of grappling with difference—from *Buffy* and *True Blood* to *The Walking Dead* and *Midnight Mass*—challenge us to make sense out of encounters that defy understanding or definition.

The Western vampire, at least since Bram Stoker's 1897 novel *Dracula*, has generally been understood as unquestionably evil and opposed to both rational order and the Christian religion. The figure of "Dracula," as perceived in the twenty-first century, is no longer Stoker's Dracula, but rather one continually reinvented and re-envisioned by film and television from Bela Lugosi in Tod Browning's 1931 *Dracula* to the 2020 BBC Dracula miniseries (Images 2.1 and 2.2). But even as vampires have become the popular heartthrobs of *The Vampire Diaries* or the glittery husbands of *Twilight*, they still represent an opposition to the pillars of culture and civilization. Vampires occupy a space between belief and disbelief; they are "a form suspended between forms that threatens to smash distinctions" (Cohen 6); they emerge from ancient mysteries and chaos, and they

DOI: 10.4324/9781003227045-4

54 *Beyond human*

Image 2.1 Dracula in 2020 BBC's *Dracula* ("The Dark Compass").

Image 2.2 Dracula in 1931 *Dracula*.

Vampires: the undead challenge to religion   55

help define twentieth- and twenty-first-century expressions of religious belief and doubt.

* * *

In a central scene from the original *Dracula*, the faithful heroine Mina Harker describes the vampire as he seeps into her bedroom in the form of a mist:

> It seemed as if it became concentrated into a sort of pillar of cloud in the room, through the top of which I could see the light of the gas shining like a red eye. Things began to whirl through my brain just as the cloudy column was now whirling in the room, and through it all came the scriptural words "a pillar of cloud by day and of fire by night." Was it indeed some spiritual guidance that was coming to me in my sleep? But the pillar was composed of both the day and the night guiding, for the fire was in the red eye... (362, Ch. 19)

In this passage, Mina uses words and an image from the Book of Exodus (13:21) to describe the evil force coming to seduce her. The description of what is perhaps a dream exemplifies the novel's blurred boundaries between god and monster, religion and superstition, dream and reality, sanity and insanity, and darkness and light. The pillar of cloud, which in the Bible comes by day, appears to Mina at night and is "composed of both the day and the night," a combination that stands as a metaphor for the moral ambiguity within Mina, the novel, and the portrayal of vampires. Late twentieth- and twenty-first-century vampires of popular culture will also blur the line between light and dark, good and evil, attraction and repulsion. It is especially this desire *for* the monster that we will explore as we turn to the vampires of contemporary television. The conception of defining God in terms of human desire *for* the divine, rather than as a divine essence or being, is suggestive of the God-idea as it manifests in *Dracula* and, in later narratives, of monsters and the undead. Just as much modern literature—and, as we shall see, television—questions or abandons the idea of an actual determinate and definable God, their (often reluctant or unintended) desire for this absent God hides in the totalizing, but unstable metaphors of unity and fragmentation and of darkness and light. There is a correlative to this desire for God in the human fear and desire for absent monsters—monsters that do not exist, or that are never seen.

We can give Mina's experience several different interpretations. She may be creating the fantasy of the pillar of smoke to obfuscate the true horror of the situation. Or, the narrative could reflect an attempt to disguise a desire for either God (or God's phallic pillar) or the radical sexual experience of Dracula himself. When Mina imagines Dracula as a biblical "pillar of cloud" forming in her room, Stoker combines in one image and scene the contradictory literary, sexual, and theological themes of the vampire.[1] These connections between the monstrous and the divine are deeply rooted in scriptural traditions. The God of the pillar of fire, the God of Exodus, and the God of much of the Hebrew Bible is a God of

56   *Beyond human*

terror and destruction. Absent at the beginning of the Exodus story, God finally appears as a volcanic deity: "Mount Sinai was wrapped in smoke because the Lord descended upon it in fire; and the smoke of it went up like the smoke of a kiln, and the whole mountain quaked greatly" (Exodus 19:16–24). This shocking entry of God into his people's story is much like the shocking entrance of Dracula into Mina's narrative, a paradigm-changing "event" in a similar mode to what we will examine in the vampires of *True Blood*. By describing Dracula in the form of the God of Exodus, Mina may have chosen a more appropriate metaphor than she (or Stoker) was aware. The God of Exodus is not just a terrifying volcanic God, but a blood-obsessed one as well, who slaughters thousands of his own people. In Exodus, blood is drained from twelve oxen, collected in basins, and then thrown upon the altar and the people (24:8). In a later ordination ritual, the blood of bulls and rams is spread over the altar and participants (24:10–28). In the same way that Mina controls her story by familiarizing the vampire with biblical language, the Israelites domesticate the wild flames and smoke on the mountain into pillars of fire and cloud. In comparing Dracula with the blood-thirsty God of Exodus, Mina raises him to a level of divinity at the same time that his entire being is devoted to blasphemy, corrupting the practices of religion into his own hideous desires.

In *Dracula*, the scholarly vampire-expert Dr. Van Helsing defines the vampire as an "arrow in the side of Him who died for man" (337, Ch. 18). This characterization of the vampire, engaged in warfare against Christianity, seems to define the essential battle of good-versus-evil that Stoker establishes in *Dracula*. Yet, as an arrow piercing Christ's side, the vampire is not only a force against Christianity, but is a part of Christianity as well. Van Helsing's arrow here is a reference to the lance that the Roman soldiers thrust into the dead Jesus on the cross, resulting in, according to the Gospel of John (the only source for this scene), what appeared to be blood and water gushing out (John 19:34). But this scene comes down to us not only as an act of violence, but as an act with a specifically spiritual, Christian, and magical meaning. As portrayed in many Renaissance paintings, the wound and flowing blood have been taken to symbolize the new covenant and baptism. According to Christian legends, whoever possessed the spear took the destiny of the world in their hands.[2] Van Helsing's claim, then, that Dracula is an arrow in the side of Christ is a complex and paradoxical metaphor that carries even more weight because of the undead and reanimated vampire's similarity to the resurrected Christ. Is Dracula puncturing or healing the wound that is Christianity? Is the wound a symbol of Christ or the vampire? The arrow points both ways.

The visit of Dracula to Mina's bedroom is a paradigmatic scene that presents the central issues for the monster/God within the shifting epistemology of the twentieth-century's attempts to banish monsters to invisibility and the superstitious past. The psycho-sexual presence of a monster/divine figure at the limits of rationality, religion, and erotic possibility pushes its way into modernist literature, disguised within the dream visions of surrealism, and then into popular culture, in the beautiful but dangerous undead characters of film and television. The monster and the vampire, as monster theorist Jeffrey Jerome Cohen claims,

Vampires: the undead challenge to religion 57

always come back, they never "taste of death but once" (5). The 1897 *Dracula*, the scenes in Mina's bedroom, and the figure of the vampire, reveal destabilizing forces that anticipate the intellectual, theological, and aesthetic crises that we find echoed in a television vampire series that begins to air exactly one hundred years later.

Buffy the Vampire Slayer: religion and its others

From 1997 to 2003, through seven seasons and 144 episodes, *Buffy the Vampire Slayer* presented a heroine who killed hundreds of vampires and demons, fell in love with one vampire she later had to kill, experienced various apocalyptic events, and sacrificed herself to save the world only to be brought back to life, all while trying to have a normal adolescence and young adulthood including math tests, proms, sex, and jobs in fast food restaurants. The show has been praised for its sophisticated use of symbolism and metaphor, its linguistic playfulness, and for its complex development of ethical, religious, and philosophical issues.

The show focused on Buffy Summers, the chosen vampire "Slayer," and her circle of friends including Willow, who starts as the group's computer nerd and ends up as a powerful witch, Rupert Giles, the school librarian and Buffy's "Watcher," and Xander, the everyman and loyal friend. The two main vampire characters are Angel (who later got his own spin-off series) and Spike, who both embody the ambiguities of good and evil, and both of whom Buffy resists and desires. As we will see in this and subsequent chapters, the show grew more complex, ambiguous, and dark as the seasons progressed. What was described in the beginning as a campy, clever drama about and for young people had, by its fifth and sixth seasons, progressed to central themes of sacrifice, death, addiction, and rape. Almost from its onset, the show appealed to scholars and intellectually minded fans and, as is often pointed out, the amount of academic writing about *Buffy* exceeded and continues to exceed that of any other television drama.[3] *Buffy* represents a watershed moment in scholarly publications about American television, as many academics that had never written about television before (philosophers, medievalists, musicologists, literary theorists, me) were pulled into the conversation.

At the beginning of every episode, we hear words that make up the canonical definition of a Slayer.

> *In every generation there is a Chosen One. She alone will stand against the vampires, the demons, and the forces of darkness. She is the Slayer.*

These words set up a worldview where there is a battle between good and evil, but also a symbiotic relationship. This assumed binary is a common contemporary reading of monster narrative. Veronica Hollinger, for example, says of *Dracula*: "however threatening [a] vampire is, it serves a crucial function … in its role as evil Other, it necessarily guarantees the *presence* of the Good." Yet, what makes *Buffy's* vampires morally challenging is that they are random, formed outside of any single determining ethical, religious, or social system. The vampires on *Buffy* are not participants in a cosmic war, not "arrows in the side of Christ," not chosen or damned, they just *are*. And while *Dracula* the novel exists in a clearly Christian world (although complicatedly situated between a Catholic and a Protestant one), *Buffy*'s good and evil offer few explicitly religious references. Other than the vampire's superficial revulsion to the Christian cross and holy water, they do not seem particularly opposed or attracted to any religious essence.

* * *

"Welcome to the Hellmouth," the very first episode of season one, begins to establish the importance—as well as ambiguity—of religions, religious symbols, and myths. Buffy's first major physical battle finds her fighting the vampire Luke in a cemetery mausoleum. As he fights Buffy, and as the scene shifts back to her scholarly "watcher," Giles, studying images of a Devil-like figure in an old book, Luke grandly soliloquizes in the style of the King James Bible:

> But on the third day of the newest light will come the Harvest.
> When the blood of men will flow as wine.
> When the master will walk among them once more.
> The Earth will belong to the old ones.
> And Hell itself will come to town.

Luke throws Buffy into a coffin and, as she cowers, this first episode ends on the word "Amen" spoken by the vampire as he leaps in for the kill. As the next episode opens, Buffy is saved from death only by the crucifix around her neck as Luke pulls back in frustration and anger (Image 2.3).

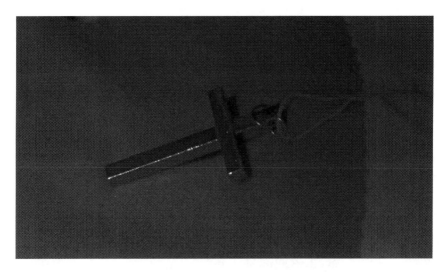

Image 2.3 Buffy's cross (*Buffy the Vampire Slayer*, "Welcome to the Hellmouth").

Vampires: the undead challenge to religion   59

This scene raised issues that would increasingly be explored throughout the series. Although the scene, like the series, is full of vampire film clichés, what keeps the show fresh and interesting are how the recurring battle scenes are drawn to represent shifting psychological and conceptual conflicts. Seasons later, an older and wiser Buffy, teaching her younger sister Dawn to fight, will comment that "it's about power." This simple comment, appropriately, is as complex and paradoxical as any statement of power analysis should be. First articulated in season five when she realizes that the Watcher's Council has no control over her—"Power. I have it. You want it." ("Checkpoint")—the phrase is most obviously presented as thematic material in the first episode of the final season, when it is spoken by both Buffy herself and then by the "First Evil" in the guise of Buffy ("Lessons").[4] By the time we get to the last season, we have learned how complicated and contradictory the themes of the show could be. However, it is not clear where or what the power is in the initial confrontation with Luke the vampire. Luke is powerful *because* he is a vampire, a hybrid species that is part human and part demon, and because he is connected to the "Master," an ancient vampire entombed beneath a church with deep connections to a mythical past before humans swarmed the Earth "like a plague of boils." Buffy is powerful because she is the "Slayer," a seemingly human creature imbued with a mysterious power and responsibility given to her through an ancient and apostolic process that we will gradually learn about only in the later seasons.

Yet, while these are familiar superhero/monster tropes, each of these powers comes with subversive questions. Buffy's power, as her demon/human friend Anya will protest in the final season, is not earned but acquired only through "luck." The cross around her neck is a powerful repellent of vampires seemingly because it is connected to unnamed ancient traditions. But this very cross has just been given to her by Angel—a vampire who was evil only until a "curse" gave him a soul—and whether the show interprets the power of crosses and curses as Christian tradition, Catholic superstition, or folklore is also ambiguous. The word "Amen," a cross, conflicting mythical and mystical forces—pagan, folkloric, and Christian—each embody some sort of power. But the sources and limits of these powers remain ambiguous. Each of these elements on their own represents not an essence or even an autonomous object, but empty symbols, only simulacra. They can only be read as they relate to each other. On *Buffy*, a cross or crucifix means nothing until it repels a vampire. Instead of stating that Buffy's cross *is* a Christian-based power, or that a vampire *is* a symbol of Satanic evil, close viewers of the show see that it is the intertwined complexity of competing powers which produce meaning. Each force (iconic, mythical, and mystical) depends on and supports the other. In the scene from "Welcome to the Hellmouth," for example, if we take only Buffy's cross without the vampire's "Amen," we misrepresent the complexity with which religion exists in the show and, by extension, in our culture. Both Buffy and Luke appear to find power in traditional religious symbols, but symbols that have lost any clear origin or source.

Buffy, who after her death at the end of season five, was buried wearing a crucifix, appears to largely do away with it after *her* resurrection. The mystical

60   *Beyond human*

objects on *Buffy*, from the crucifix around her neck in season one to a mysterious scythe in season seven, while they seem to "contain" power, ultimately suggest ambiguity. In the same way that God and evil are perhaps best thought of not as *things* but *actions*, the objects are defined by what they do rather than what they are, and ultimately their effect is one of destabilization. They are not connected in any way to an absolute power, but only to physical power. Nor do they appear to be linked to any possible transcendent good or evil. They are interruptions of the real empirical world, and yet part of it.

Some critics have seen *Buffy* as part of a Christian tradition, while other critics exploring the religious side of the show find an "overall atheism ... that looks critically at anything smacking of mainstream religion" (Winslade 58). Others look not at the humans but at the vampires themselves to "form a locus of religious experience through which viewers can examine important tenets of faith, particularly conversion, salvation, redemption, and the difficulty of change and connection" (Ricketts 11). Gregory Sakal claims that despite the importance of "sacrifice," "salvation," and "redemption," and despite a few "arguably Christian overtones," the show is "decidedly" *not* Christian (239).[5] My point is that vampire narratives, from *Dracula* to *Buffy* and beyond, present intertwined forces that must be read as a web or a network and not as essential or autonomous powers, a reading that mirrors many current perceptions of contemporary culture and religion. Within *Buffy*, if we take any of these elements out of context, it is easy to overstate the connections and the coherence of the show's relationship to traditional or determinate religion or theology. While the symbols and rituals of traditional religions have been a focus of fans and scholars looking for religious significance on *Buffy*, these echoes of traditional religion consistently exist outside of any determinate spiritual, theological, or religious beliefs or institutions. Within the show itself, although ethical decisions and even religious rituals are presented seriously, the presence of traditional Christian symbols, churches, and divinity is generally lightly mocked, as when Willow has to hide the crucifixes she puts around her house from her Jewish family.

Although it would seem out of place to have Buffy, Giles, or Willow refer to the Christian origins of the cross, vampires joke about it: "I haven't had this much fun since the crucifixion" ("School Hard,"). One of the few references in the show to the actual Bible casts a line from Isaiah—"and a child shall lead them"—as a prophecy about a vampire, the Master's anointed one ("Prophecy Girl"). Just as the Master and Luke get to affect biblical language in the show's opening episode, the most religiously influenced moments of ritual and speech tend to come from vampires and demons. Vampires adapt the language and style of evangelical preachers, they follow a "Master," an "anointed" one, and a "vessel," and they facilitate eucharistic resurrections. Vampires also express a weakness for charismatic religious leaders, yearn for a return to a legendary golden age, and they trust the power of ancient texts and prophecies. We see these elements of confessional religion when Spike must perform a ritual to restore his ailing vampire partner, Drusilla, to health ("What's My Line: Part 2"). He performs it in front of a church congregation, and the emphasis on blood and resurrection

Vampires: the undead challenge to religion 61

echoes a Christian ceremony. Complete with stained glass images, Gregorian chant, and incense, Spike intones "from the blood of the sire she is risen. From the blood of the sire she shall rise again." The blood transfusion—a staple of vampire narrative since *Dracula*—in this scene is between vampire and vampire and is performed with all the ritual of a holy communion.

Buffy points to some central questions debated in contemporary religious studies. Are we fated to keep thinking through the same patterns of religion even if we believe they are empty? Is to think the divine also to think the monstrous? I would like to suggest that it is this very tension that can be seen as an almost theological expression of doubt. This theology of doubt is found in the way that *Buffy* constantly invites and frustrates religious or theological interpretations that both are and are not religious, depending on how we define "religion." It is both of these things because it presents religion not only as traditional trappings and empty simulacra, but because sometimes these trappings *do* seem to carry some power. It is dismissive of all of the central issues of religion (the creator, free will, good, and evil) and yet is obsessed with these very issues. It plays with and also authentically desires stable meaning; it relishes in its irony and yet seeks some kind of center. Again here, we can find a useful model of interpretation in contemporary radical theologians who claim a position somewhere between atheism and theology, between or outside of faith or disbelief, one that is not opposed to theology, but rather opposed to traditional and deterministic quests to locate an unquestionable and definable source of divine power. This kind of thought denies a theology that insists on perceiving God as something factual or material. Using this kind of lens, I read *Buffy* not as an expression or repudiation of any religious tradition or as a reflection of its creator's often professed atheism, but as a text that is both religious and atheistic, an interrogation of a secular world making sense out of fragmented religious beliefs, language, and ritual.

Buffy versus Dracula: desire and free will

Although it was not until season five that we got the somewhat ironic appearance of the actual Dracula, like any other vampire dramas, *Buffy* necessarily had echoes of the original Victorian vampire woven into its fabric from the beginning. In the finale of season two, when Buffy must kill Angel, her vampire-with-a-soul boyfriend turned evil, in order to save the world, she is faced with a classical ethical dilemma that has deeply religious overtones reaching back to the vampire novels of the nineteenth century ("Becoming: Part 2"). Although in killing Angel she performs what appears to be a selfless and ethical act of goodness, the scene's echoes of the staking of Lucy Westenra in *Dracula* complicate this implication. In *Dracula*, Lucy Westenra's fiancé is allowed to drive a stake through her heart as an act of love to free her eternal soul. Buffy, however, far from putting Angel's soul to rest, must kill him just *after* his soul has been restored, and he has reverted to the "good" Angel. In an exact reversal of the staking of Lucy in *Dracula*—where only after Lucy has been staked is her fiancé permitted to kiss her—Buffy *first* kisses Angel and *then* thrusts the sword into him, sending him not

62   *Beyond human*

to eternal salvation, but (we later find out) to suffer in a "hell dimension." In this scene, revenge and salvation and good and evil are subverted and muddled. If there is a suggestion of divine presence here (and if not, from where does Angel's soul originate and who creates the hell he is sent to?), it appears Buffy acts *against* (or at least outside of) any divine order.[6] Although Buffy has made the ethical choice of the good of the many over the few, theologically, she has sent a recently redeemed soul to hell.[7] While Buffy appears to have made a "good" choice, the contrast to the good-versus-evil world of *Dracula* is revealing of an even more radical act of selflessness.

The season five opening episode "Buffy vs. Dracula" both functioned as a parody of all that Dracula has become, yet at the same time introduced the bleaker and more serious style that would characterize the final three seasons of *Buffy*. The episode offers a present-day farce of the commercial Dracula (complete with bad makeup and accent) but also gives a demonstration of the conflation of the forces of good and evil and sacred and profane that lurk underneath the surface of the Dracula story, pointing to a dark psychological and religious reading of both *Dracula* and *Buffy*. The opening of the episode presents a familiar scene in which Buffy chases down, fights, and stakes a vampire in the cemetery. Dracula then materializes out of the fog and introduces himself. Buffy at first does not believe his claim to be the legendary vampire. "Get out," she says, "are you sure you're the real Dracula?" Dracula announces his purpose in visiting her:

DRACULA: I came to meet the renowned killer
BUFFY: Yeah, I prefer the term Slayer. You know, killer just sounds so…
DRACULA: Naked?

Dracula's answer shifts the episode to a darker, more serious place where, as in Stoker's version, Dracula challenges the accepted roles of those around him. Buffy, although momentarily shaken, confronts him with a characteristically cocky and threatening question, "Do you know what a Slayer is?" to which Dracula answers: "Do you?" His question turns into the dominant theme of the episode and the seasons to follow, as we realize that Buffy does not really know where her power comes from or what she fights for. Like monsters throughout history, Dracula's otherness forces those around him to confront the limits of their own identities, origins, and beliefs.

That night, in a reenactment of the scene with Mina Harker, Dracula floats through the window of Buffy's bedroom as a mist and materializes next to her bed. Although upon waking she flippantly describes him as "wafting in here with your music video wind and your hypno-eyes," she is soon under his control. Dracula appeals to the part of her that both desires and identifies with him. "You are different…kindred," he says, and tells her that "I have yearned for you. For a creature whose darkness rivals my own." As she willingly submits to his bite, Dracula asks "Do you know why you cannot resist? Because you do not want to." He then invites her to taste his own blood, asking "All these years fighting us. A power so near to our own. And you've never once wondered what we fight for?"

Vampires: the undead challenge to religion   63

Buffy declines, answering, "I'm not hungry," but when Dracula responds, "No, the craving goes deeper than that," she gives in to temptation.

As Buffy sucks from Dracula, the scene echoes the repressed aspects of the encounter between Mina and Dracula, exploring a previously hidden side of Buffy, and even suggesting new questions for the original *Dracula*. Do Mina and Buffy *want* to be bitten? Why do they submit? In these supernatural intersections of good and evil, where or what is their God? We can imagine Dracula saying to Mina what he says to Buffy as she tastes his blood: "Find it, the darkness. Find your true nature." Buffy, as the Slayer as well as the victim, combines the role of Mina with the power to fight vampires that true religion provides in the novel; she essentially embodies the roles of Mina, the male posse, Van Helsing, and the Catholic Church all at once. Buffy's submission, however, recalls the defeat of God in *Dracula* when a communion wafer sizzles on Mina's forehead, revealing that she now belongs to the vampire and not to God. The blending of eroticism and fear, the weakness of God, and the desire for death that we see in *Dracula*, further their conflation in *Buffy*, beginning when she submits to Dracula and continuing through to her death and her dangerously obsessive sexual desire for the vampire Spike in coming seasons.

The episode is a comment on the control old narratives and mythologies have over us, and Buffy's statement after defeating Dracula, that she is now "chock full of free will," is typical of the series' cynical view toward traditional religious ideas. Her claim of free will points to a crisis in believing in the possibility of individual choice. But what the episode has confirmed is that Buffy *cannot* rely on having free will, nor can she ever again be sure of herself as an unmitigated force for good. She was unable to resist Dracula, to resist the "darkness" she was supposedly created to fight against. The irony is that she claims free will just after she has been forced to question her own sense of even choosing between good and evil. Characteristically, the end of the episode turns back to humor when, after staking him into dust, Buffy waits for the particles to manifest back into the vampire, commenting, "you think I don't watch your movies? You always come back." Despite her humor, however, the laughs are a little hollow. What started out as a fun stand-alone episode ends up subverting much of the earlier ethical good-versus-evil certainty of the show, and *Buffy* and its fans could never be quite the same.

In the final episode of the season, Buffy chooses to die, ending a season-long struggle with the issue of choice by making the ultimate assertion of free will and of her individuality by giving her life, perhaps the only truly individual choice and gift a person has. Dracula and Buffy both have characteristics borrowed from Christ; Dracula rises from the dead to offer eternal life through his blood, and Buffy sacrifices her life to save the world. "Buffy vs. Dracula" reveals the darkness in Buffy's power and the divinity in Dracula's, therefore echoing and radicalizing our reading of Mina Harker's image of the "pillar composed of both day and night."

"The secret to defeating Dracula," says Giles, is in "separating the fact from the fiction," but the difficulty of this separation is one of many gray areas the

64 *Beyond human*

show explores. "My thesis is this," *Dracula*'s Van Helsing says in the novel, "I want you to believe ... To believe in things that you cannot" (279 Ch. 14). The two scholarly figures, Giles and Van Helsing, both point to the importance of this gray area between fact and fiction, between belief and atheism, which, by implication, is a theological area as well, and a space that gods, vampires, and monsters continually occupy. This impossible belief points to the shifting and ultimately unlocatable line between fact and fiction that theologian Elaine Graham finds so essential to the cultural work that fictional monsters currently do. For her, "if the boundaries between humans, animals, and machines ... are clearly under pressure in the digital and biotechnological age, then the relationship between another supposed binary pair, 'fact' and 'fiction' is also central" (13). In our virtual world where fact and fiction are no longer seen as clear opposites, television monsters are crucial in continuing to define ourselves and our relationship to the divine. It is our chance to "practice" the intersections of doubt and faith. It is the role of the monster to explore the spaces of unity and fragmentation, belief and disbelief, and to allow us to see what it means to be on the dividing line of the in-between. From this point of view, Stoker's novel is actually an empty, godless world where all that remains are God's symbols and the empty shells of superstition that we yet cling to. Hiding at the center of the novel is a vacuum that only the monster inhabits. The vampire becomes necessary to complete the idea of both God and humanity.

True Blood: re-reading and redefining religion

HBO's *True Blood* (2008–2014), a southern gothic vampire fantasy produced and created by Alan Ball, was based on The Southern Vampire Mysteries series of novels by Charlaine Harris. The initial premise of the show is that after thousands of years of hiding and feeding off of humans, vampires can finally "come out of the coffin" due to the invention of synthetic blood that they can ingest for sustenance. The novels and the series tell of the co-existence of vampires and humans in Bon Temps, a fictional small town in Louisiana, and center on the adventures of Sookie Stackhouse, a telepathic waitress who meets and falls in love with a vampire. Although the supernatural presence expands throughout the show (shapeshifters, fairies, werewolves, maenads), the main focus of the show remains on the vampires' struggle for equal rights and assimilation, at the same time that anti-vampire and anti-human organizations gain power.

Like many HBO dramas, *True Blood* features a complex, strikingly produced, and much discussed opening credit sequence. For a few years, it seemed like everyone—from tenured religious studies professors to first-year college students in my Religion and Popular Culture classes—wanted to write about this opening, which simultaneously captured the rural southern roots of the show and its complicated depictions of politics, sex, and religion. The sequence begins underwater; the camera point of view—like a creature rising from the primordial depths, or perhaps a dead fish floating to the top—breaks the surface to reveal dark swamps, run-down liquor stores, crosses, and cemeteries. The images then

Vampires: the undead challenge to religion   65

shift to a charismatic churchgoer "slain in the spirit," seductive dancing, threatening snakes, a Venus flytrap snapping in action, historical footage of civil rights protests, a toddler-aged Ku Klux Klan member, young boys eating blood red berries, and an adult Christian baptism in a river. The credit sequence intercuts these images with quick flashes of naked flesh and is accompanied by the bluesy, suggestive "Bad Things," sung by Jace Everett. The first images clearly set the location as rural Louisiana: a swamp, an abandoned car, a dilapidated house on the bayou, and small houses lined up in little rows. But the first words of the song, accompanied by barely visible microsecond clips of entangled naked bodies, shift the sequence into a world of sin and salvation, of ecstasy and orgasm, and of blood and decay. There is nothing fantastic or supernatural about any of these images. The only direct reference to vampires in the credits is a sign saying, "God hates fangs," which is, of course, a reference to the bigoted Westboro Baptist Church and their claim that "God hates fags." But the conflation of sex and religion, and of transcendence and death, sets up a paradigm through which we can read the human–vampire intersection that the show offers.

In the DVD commentary to *True Blood*, creator Alan Ball claims that the opening credits were intended to "set the world" for the show by creating a "strange mix of religious fervor and getting drunk and… how they both sort of are two sides of the same coin… some sort of transcendent experience." But the sequence depicts even more than just alternative forms of human ecstasy or catharsis; it also suggests a theory of understanding these actions. In some ways, the opening credits offer a primer on how to watch the show, teaching viewers to pay attention not only to the complexity of images, but also to juxtapositions and transitions; to read the space in between: the implied, the unsaid, and the contradictory. Although the images are in themselves striking, the impact is mostly in the imagined and paratactical connections between them: a woman writhing provocatively in a bedroom is juxtaposed with a rattlesnake that coils and strikes; the face of the young boy in KKK attire blends into a middle-aged man on a porch; and dancing, religious ecstasy, and biological images of birth and decay are woven together throughout the sequence. Kofi Opam notes that, by the close of these images, the:

> decision is left for the viewer to descend into any of the "bad things" that plague the subjects of the video—you can either hope for some phony spiritual redemption through your preacher, become a member of the Ku Klux Klan, or participate in a subliminal orgy. Either way, we're all dying; all headed the same way as the fox kit or the dead possum.

While the most obvious themes of the opening are the blurring of sacred and profane and the predatory character of humans and nature, when we add the music and the premise of the series, it presents an even more complicated message that insists that we make sense of these paratactic images. As Opam points out, "Whenever the animalistic tendencies are greatest, whenever the music reaches a crescendo or vital moment, there is a flash of nude bodies—some reflection of the

66 *Beyond human*

innermost desires of those who preach religion or sex or violence." How do these desires relate to the interaction of humans and vampires? Religious studies scholar Leonard Primiano suggests that the credit sequence implies a question: "If vampires have enough self-control to resist the lure of human blood, should humans possess sufficient self-control to resist organized religion?" (Primiano 49). But it can also be seen to say just the opposite: that the primal urges within humans are necessarily and inescapably built into their religions, rituals, beliefs, and practices.

The opening credits create a slow crescendo through music and images that reaches its peak in a final, full-immersion, adult baptism scene. In a nighttime shot, two men lower a woman into the water; at the end, she flails about, perhaps in a type of ecstasy, but just before the shot cuts away, it appears as if she is trying to escape. As the woman splashes her way (blissfully? desperately?) toward the camera and us, it is ambiguous whether we are to feel a cathartic release or a sense of suffocation; the credits (and the religious ritual) pull us back underwater where the sequence began, to a place of life and death, drowning, and resurrection. The opening credits, like the act of baptism, ask us to ponder the importance of the body to the soul. The body, is on the one hand, the source of our certainty, the proof that we are real. On the other hand, it is the cause of our fall, the location of our sinful impulses and violent transgressions, and it quite literally brings us down. People often think of themselves as *being* their bodies. The word "body" tends to invoke an aspect of selfhood that seems autonomous and interchangeable with the idea of a true unique self that is the center for all embodied relations. *True Blood*'s emphasis on the human body forces us to confront our assumption about these issues.

The show itself also forces an awareness of the raw physicality of being. Throughout the series, we see naked, contorted, dead, bleeding, and headless bodies; we see close-ups of flesh that we barely recognize; we hear the amplified sounds of wounds and of piercing and sucking. When vampires are killed, they explode into sticky globs of blood and flesh that must be mopped up and wiped off. Unlike *Buffy the Vampire Slayer*, where dying vampires disappear neatly into dust, or Stoker's *Dracula*, where they smile at the release from eternal damnation, the *True Bloo*d vampires are physically broken down on a cellular level. Is the power that does this indeed, as *True Blood*'s Reverend Steve Newlin says, evidence of the power of God? It seems more plausible that these gory deaths show just the opposite, emphasizing the physical and not the supernatural nature of vampires, and the messy lines between life and death.

Christianity versus religion

Despite the complex presentation of religion in the opening credits, the show tends to depict the actual Christian beliefs and practices of the characters and community in a more reductive manner. Whether it is the absolute and xenophobic good-versus-evil view of a vampire-hating sect, the Fellowship of the Sun, the demon and Christ-haunted haze of the troubled alcoholic mother of Sookie's best friend Tara, the there-is-a-purpose-for-everything folk wisdom of Sookie's grandmother, or Sookie's open-minded God of acceptance, the religious beliefs of the characters are rarely treated with any theological complexity. Sookie may have objections to her friend Tara's speaking the "J word," (Jesus) in conversation, yet when she is attracted to a vampire and telepathically overhears judgmental thoughts like "What kind of a good Christian girl would even look at a vampire" ("Strange Love"), she does not pray about it; she does not think through any possible religious or theological consequences, and she does not ponder the eternal soul or ontology of the vampire. Instead she merely says, "I don't think Jesus would mind if somebody was a vampire." Sookie's Jesus and her God, while their presence is unquestioned, serve to support her preconceived morality rather than form or challenge her worldview. On the surface, anyway, this is the case for almost all of the residents of Bon Temps and for the show in general. Their morality and worldview, however, are challenged and shaped by vampires.

Although mainstream religious institutions rarely acknowledge it, the fear of and desire for sex, death, blood, salvation, and immortality are closely and inextricably linked with our religious feelings, religious practices, and religious histories. Examples within Christian tradition include the cannibalistic overtones of the eucharist, the blood fetish surrounding images and legends of the suffering Jesus, haunting "cadaver tombs" in English cathedrals, and the bloody images and folk tales of Jews stabbing or desecrating the host (Image 2.4). As we have

Image 2.4 Jew stabbing the host, from the Museu Nacional d'Arte de Catalunya.

68   *Beyond human*

seen, and will continue to see, within texts of popular culture, "religion" is often most interesting when it is not framed *as* religion; in many ways, subversive forms of what we might call religion—in all of their complicated definitions—create the primary and complex theme at the core of what made the early seasons of *True Blood* fascinating and significant. Instead of presenting religious themes through a church or Christian scripture or belief, *True Blood* depicted acts of sacramentalism, of ritual, and of transcendence through sex, violence, and drugs. The presence and practice of religion, therefore, are found in the very elements of the show that evangelical American religious organizations object to. These elements of what we might call "implicit religion" are usually seen as outside of normative Christian experience, but the show's opening credit sequence suggestively conflates these opposing elements and offers us a lens through which to reframe religious beliefs and practices. As religious studies scholar Graham Harvey writes, while "believing is a definitive act for Christians it has been wrongly applied to defining religion itself" (43). Harvey's larger point—one that is implied in *True Blood* and one I return to throughout this book—is that "perhaps there is a Christianity that is not Christianity-as-believing, not a belief system, and *perhaps this other Christianity might be a religion*" (57 emphasis mine). This "other Christianity," like our other ways of imagining God, is one not found in churches or doctrines, but in subversive stories, blasphemous practices, and illicit desires. These stories, practices, and desires have accompanied sacred rituals and sacraments for centuries, were hidden or repressed in the shadows of traditional worship and folk practices, and have been married to the fears, anxieties, and nightmares that will continue to make us "religious" long after the original beliefs and doctrines have changed. More than an exploration of religion though, *True Blood* can be seen as demonstrating the bloody, exciting confusion that always accompanies a major epistemological shift. Beneath the surface of *True Blood*, there is an underlying subversive structure that explores what it means when a belief system suddenly changes. From the second-century Christians to the first Protestants, to nineteenth-century Latter Day Saints, every shift in religious belief has been accompanied by both physical and ideological violence. *True Blood* mirrors the messy, violent, and conflicted ways that various sects of Christianity have negotiated contradictory ideas of body, pain, evil, death, creation, and immortality.

* * *

Early in the episode "Cold Ground," Bill is asked to speak about his experiences as an actual veteran of the Civil War. Speaking in a church, Bill represents a form of the Real Presence (a flesh and blood soldier), and of material continuity with an imagined and romanticized past, both concepts central to Christianity. Before Bill comes out to speak, a young townsperson and his mother kindly attempt to remove a large brass cross from the altar, mistakenly assuming that it will harm Bill. What is significant here is that this cross—which proves too heavy to move—as well as Bill, both represent this physical mastery over death and an assumed continuity to a glorious past. Bill reassures the church audience that, "we vampires are not minions of the devil. We can stand before a cross or a Bible or in a church just as readily as any other creature of God." While we might see this negatively, as an "example that God is actually not present in the lives of humans" (Primiano 54), we can also place it within new forms of Christian ideology. Like radical theologians who sees the crucifixion as a scene of the end of a god, not the beginning, both Bill and the cross signify an optimistic new world that now exists in the absence of God. When the vampire Bill tells Sookie that holy water is "just water," and a crucifix only "geometry," his words apply to humans as well as vampires. Perhaps, the show suggests, while some kind of god is always desired but never present, vampires—like Jesus and early Christianity—represent a break, a chance to rethink our narratives of life and death, beginnings and endings. In other words, humans see in vampires both a Christ-like intervention into ontological categories of being *and* evidence of the absence of their old transcendent personal God.

When the newly made vampire Jessica (who, as a human, was an evangelical Christian), asks Bill "Are you a Christian?" his response is: "I was." We assume his answer means he was Christian as a human, but how can we interpret his shift? All of the human characters in *True Blood* are assumed to be Christian in some sense or another, yet Bill has either chosen not to be, or cannot be, a Christian anymore. Perhaps he realizes that Christianity is not "true" and he can then no longer be a Christian. Or is it that, as an immortal, he no longer needs to believe in a Christian afterlife? If he ceased to be Christian upon rising from the grave, it is in effect an acceptance of his fallen status—an essentially Christian and Catholic move. But this does not give us an answer as to whether he is evil or why he is evil. Like many Christians throughout history, perhaps Bill must accept that our sinful or fallen nature does not depend on effort, thought, or action, but that we must yet accept our responsibility for it.

* * *

Most personal definitions of religion in the United States—by both those who claim to be religious and those who deny—portray religion as a harmonious "light against the darkness," in the words of *True Blood's* Fellowship of the Sun, or as giving "order and meaning" and providing "happiness and emotional security," in the words of a scholar of American popular religion (Lippy 2). However, as we have seen, the nature of Christianity is built around unstable ideas and irresolvable contradictions, and religious thoughts and events are just as often harbingers of chaos as of harmony. In some ways, *True Blood* presents a model of how this works. Like the intervention of Christ into history, *True Blood*, like *Buffy*, forces us to shift how we think about the categories of human and the divine, magic and religion, life and death, and the desire for the presence of a God who continues to express divine absence. While the Jesus that Sookie imagines is the friendly and present Jesus of American religion—the "loving, open-minded Christ, who himself knows something about existence after death" (Primiano 44)—the figure that *really* changes her conception of being in the world is Bill. In

70 *Beyond human*

the course of one day, her whole sense of time, life and death, and what it means to be a human are changed. Bill and the idea of vampires alter reality and the experience of being for Sookie in ways that can only be compared with a religious experience. Within the implied ideology of *True Blood*, the vampire is not a negation of Christianity; instead the vampire's intervention into humanity reveals and participates in the contradictions and aporias that are part of Christianity itself.

Dracula, again

The true monster always returns, and so this chapter begins and ends with Dracula. In a 2020 Dracula miniseries on Netflix, showrunners and writers Mark Gatiss and Steven Moffat (former *Doctor Who* writers and showrunners) explore the story in ways simultaneously familiar, strange, parodic, and postmodern. Their version, in the words of reviewer Lucy Mangan, "revitalises the story while reveling in its absurdity." Much of this revitalization and absurdity revolves around rethinking the role of religion and religious symbols for a supposedly more modern age, moving from Victorian misogyny, medieval ruins, and legends to agnostic nuns, feminism, and laboratories. The first episode, "The Rules of the Beast," mixes familiar images of Dracula's castle and his now customary cheesy puns ("I never drink … wine" and "do you feel...*drained*"), with several interesting new twists, particularly the framing device of having, what appears to be, an infected and dying Jonathan Harker relate his story to a nun in a convent. Dracula can also—unlike in the novel—disguise himself in the skin of slain victims and animals, and he acquires the knowledge and skills of those he feeds off. Dracula here, has developed a strategy of selective feeding: essentially breeding himself into an intelligent, sophisticated, and manipulative figure. The nun, Sister Agatha (Agatha Van Helsing, we later learn) has a sharp tongue and is a skeptical Catholic at best: "Like many women my age I am trapped in a loveless marriage, maintaining appearances for the sake of a roof over my head." When a frightened Mina—in this version already married to Jonathan—sadly tells her that "God is nowhere," the nun responds, "In which case, it is up to us to stop Count Dracula." This idea—that the absence of God requires an elevation of human responsibility—is another echo of the idea that we can view the death of God as an event that we must continue to live in order to reaffirm personal moral integrity. As the philosopher Slavoj Žižek phrases it, after the death of God and after the crucifixion, "there is no way back, all there is, all that 'really exists,' from now on are individuals" (61). Although markedly different in presentation, this version of Dracula—like *Buffy the Vampire Slayer*—plays with legend and asks the questions: Where is the power? Where is the religion? And where do we go from here?

Significantly, it is the evil of Count Dracula that pulls the skeptical Sister Agatha into a type of Christian faith. Near the end of the first episode, Sister Agatha confidently mocks a naked and bloody Dracula outside the gate of her convent—in classic vampire fashion, he cannot get in unless invited. She contrasts the life of nuns to his existence: "We have freed ourselves of appetite and

Vampires: the undead challenge to religion 71

therefore of fear. That is why you can't bear the sight of this." She holds out her crucifix, calling it "goodness incarnate." Dracula responds, "that's not why I fear the cross. Goodness has got nothing to do with it." And yet, it is clear, Dracula still recoils from the cross, recognizing its power, but not explicitly locating it in any narrative, sacrament, or magic. The religious power, it therefore seems, is located in doubt, skepticism, and anxiety. Even the Mother Superior suggests a theological position of doubt in her speech that same night to the nuns when she says that God will not save them, that he is not in their prayers or their songs, but only in their resistance to evil in moments of haplessness—in the voice that says no to darkness. Agatha listens approvingly, as the Mother Superior continues, saying that it is in the presence of darkness and evil where they will find God. At this moment, Dracula, who has figured out a way into the convent, slices off her head with a sword and then orders his wolves—who are impervious to the crucifixes—to slaughter the rest of the nuns. As Agatha cowers in the basement, scattering bits of consecrated host to protect her and Mina, she questions the legends and the power: "None of the vampire legends make sense and yet somehow they are proving to be true. Why? … He's terrified of the cross and yet he is no believer." This paradox becomes the central questions of the miniseries. Like *Buffy* and *True Blood*, it is something other than faith in God that resists the evil of the vampire—yet the objects and memories of the church are never completely in the background.

The second episode plays out the middle section of the Dracula story in two primary locations. One echoes the first episode's conversation between Agatha and Harker, but in this episode, it is a conversation between a now habit-less Agatha and Dracula in some surreal liminal space where they converse over a game of chess (she chooses white). The second location is Dracula's trip aboard the ship Demeter to the coast of England and the town of Whitby. As the plot develops—with Dracula meeting and feeding from the various passengers on the ship—we eventually realize that Agatha is actually aboard the ship; Dracula keeps her hidden in a cabin to feed off of her blood slowly. Near the end of the episode, with Dracula and Agatha alone on the deck of the ship, they have one last conversation that returns them to the paradox of the cross. At the helm of the ship, stars in the background, Dracula comments wistfully, "I love science. Science is the future." Agatha challenges him, "And yet you still fear the cross?" Dracula answers: "Everyone does, that's the problem." Dracula explains that the cross is not a "symbol of virtue and kindness" but is instead a "mark of horror and oppression." He explains that he has been feeding from Christian peasants for so long, he has "absorbed their fear of the cross." "God," he smiles, "I can't wait to eat some atheists." The obvious suggestion here is that, like Dracula, we all consume the beliefs that we are surrounded with, we inherit or absorb the cultural fears and superstitions of those that live around us whether we want to or not.

The third episode, now in the twenty-first century, features Dracula quickly adapting to modern technology, guessing Wi-Fi passwords and swiping left or right on dating apps, searching for potential victims. A descendant of Agatha, Zoe Van Helsing, works for the Jonathan Harker Foundation, a sort of mercenary

72 *Beyond human*

organization preparing for the return of Dracula. The Count becomes enamored with a modern Lucy Westenra—in this universe, a London club hopper—who seems to fully embrace Dracula and the idea of death and an undead life. These shifts in the characters of the traditional Dracula story reflects a more modern view that incorporates the types of people drawn to new religious movements, charismatic religious leaders, and more fluid definitions of religion. Yet, the ending, still returns to the cross and its ancient paradoxes.

In the final scene, we get one more confrontation between Van Helsing and Dracula, and we see the importance of the questions posed in the first episode and its title: "The Rules of the Beast." Why does Dracula fear the cross? The mirror? Where is the power located in these old superstitions? After the staking of an undead and partially cremated Lucy—who mercifully dissolves into dust, *Buffy* style—Zoe faces Dracula alone. She dramatically leaps to pull down the curtains to a tall window exposing Dracula to beams of deadly sunlight. He screams and falls to the floor in anguish. Except nothing happens. It does not hurt him and he does not die. The deadly sunlight was only an outdated superstitious fear. A story inherited from the past.

In the end, the terminally ill Zoe Van Helsing—after drinking a vial of Dracula's blood—is able to inhabit both modern professor and Victorian nun. Speaking now in Sister Agatha's voice, she says to Dracula "you seek to conquer death but you cannot until you face it without fear." She then continues the conversation begun on a ship 123 years prior, telling Dracula that he is a creature who "cannot bear to look in a mirror. Who won't stand revealed in the sunlight. Who cannot enter a home without invitation." Then, she gives a demythologizing answer to the queries at the end of the first episode about the vampire legends that make no sense that yet still seem to be true:

> These aren't curses. They are merely habits that become fetishes that become legends that even you believe. What are you afraid of? [You are] the warlord who skulks in the shadows and steal the lives of others ... who sleeps in a box of dirt yet dreams of a warrior's grave. Who suddenly found himself in thrall of the girl in love with the thing he fears the most. Death.

This fear, she explains, is why the crucifix works as a repellent: "It speaks of the courage you long to possess ... the courage it takes to die." This is a crucifix of a radical modern theology: a connection between the actual cross and the idea of the crucifixion, between the mortal and the immortal, between evil and good, and spoken by a nineteenth-century nun speaking through the body of a twenty-first-century professor. Her words balance the two sides of religious practice that the vampire inhabits: her explanation sits uncomfortably between religion as accessing a higher power and religion as a human practice like any other—a social way of thinking about identity.

She then—like Buffy after her death in season five—throws the cross away in acceptance of death, and says to Dracula, "to conquer death is to face it without fear." Dracula slowly reaches his hand from the shadow into sunlight. As he steps

Image 2.5 Dracula faces the sun in BBC's *Dracula* ("The Dark Compass").

fully into the sunshine and walks toward the window, a shadow of a cross is cast onto his body from the wooden muntin bars of the window (Image 2.5). He stares into the sun in astonishment; "it's beautiful," he says and the screen goes white. The final images are of Dracula drinking Zoe's blood, first in an erotic, dreamy image of their naked bodies wrapped around each other, and then in a realistic shot of them curled together on the table. "But my blood is deadly to you," she says. "Yes, he answers." "So you will die?" "Yes," Dracula whispers, "and so will you." As the shot pulls back to the hazy orange image of their bodies together, their bodies dissolve and expand into a vision of the burning sun, ending the miniseries.

In all these modern versions of the myth, from *Buffy* to *True Blood*, to the many retellings of Dracula, the actual material cross fades in importance; yet, the idea of the crucifixion as a death of God remains as mysterious and powerful as the vampire itself. When Agatha/Zoe wants Dracula to drink from her, it is to learn more about him, not out of any sexual desire or a desire for eternal life. Perhaps for Agatha, as we saw in the first episode, it is only through understanding something so far outside of God that she can restore her lapsed faith. True religious faith—as thinkers from Thomas Altizer to Emmanuel Levinas claim—can only be in that which is impossible to believe in, only through understanding atheism. The questions that help us conclude this chapter are: in what ways can this ending be framed as a postmodern Christian death, and as a new type of the crucifixion? The suggestion might be that by imagining a Jesus who is ultimately not afraid to die, the crucifixion can teach each of us how to live our own mortal lives. This seems to be what Dracula finally understands through drinking the blood of Agatha/Zoe. He understands death and the cross without fear through

74   *Beyond human*

the blood of a Christian who does not believe in the mythology of the resurrection. It is through Agatha the Christian agnostic and Zoe the modern scientist that we almost achieve a transcendent message in the end.

* * *

According to Eastern European folkloric wisdom, a vampire should be buried at a fork in the road so that it will not know what direction to take when it arises, thereby impeding it from locating its intended victims. The vampire as a trope of critical thought offers a similar position of apprehension and ambiguity. When the repressed vampire arises or is summoned, there are impossible decisions to be made. Is it a creature of chaos or order? Does it represent our inner desires, or are they the absolute others that are unimaginable from our limited human perspective? Vampire stories and lore have posed and answered these questions differently at different points in history, helping us to understand this shifting role of both vampires and humans. As theorist Nina Auerbach claims that vampires "matter because, when properly understood, they make us see that our lives are implicated in theirs" (9). Just as Dracula was a symbol of ethnic and sexual otherness during the Victorian period, vampires, such as Angel, Spike, Bill, and then Dracula again, signify the fears, desires, and existential crises of their times. Auerbach writes, "what vampires are in any given generation is a part of what I am and what my times have become" (1). Readers and viewers are able to find their own anxieties within the images of these monstrous beings. Through vampires, we have explored once taboo topics such as queer sexualities, the (non)existence of God, deadly viruses, and the meaning of being human. It is for this reason that vampires are something both hated and adored, for they tell us things about ourselves that we want to know, yet desperately want to hide. In Freudian terms, they are uncanny or *unheimlich*: beings who "bring to light" what "ought to have remained secret and hidden" ("The Uncanny"). Although vampires may force us to more completely understand ourselves, we—like vampires—cannot always see ourselves in the mirror.

Notes

1 For an essay on subversive Christianity in *Dracula*, see "Vampire Religion," by Christopher Herbert (*Representations* 79, Summer 2002).
2 The spear became a symbol of world dominance to Hitler, who claimed to own the actual weapon.
3 See "The Rise of *Buffy* Studies" by Katherine Schwab (*Atlantic*, October 1, 2015).
4 The episode that introduced the First Evil in *Buffy*, "Amends" drew considerable attention and controversy by viewers who saw it as a "Christian" episode. Angel, after encountering the First, who almost wills him to feed from and kill Buffy and forces him to re-experience his murderous past, walks out into the morning to—like the ancient vampire Godric in *True Blood*, like the undead villagers in *Midnight Mass*—commit a sacrificial suicide by sunrise. As Buffy desperately tries to convince him of the worthiness of his "life," he is greeted by what appears to be a Christmas miracle—clouds and a southern California snowfall—that save him by blocking the sun. As he

and Buffy walk hand in hand in the snow, the final shot—the one that really got fans going, although show runner Joss Whedon claimed the shot was accidental—pans across a billboard revealing the word "pray." But, although the word pray drew all the attention, what was actually visible was not just the word "pray" but "pray for. ..." It is the word "for" that I find most interesting. Pray *for* what? *For* whom? What *for*?

5 Jason Winslade, points to a "2008 study cited by the Telegraph, which apparently blames *Buffy* for lower church attendance in the UK ... Dr. Kristine Aune of the University of Derby claims that women's dissatisfaction with traditional religion and its hierarchies are drawn to Wicca's message of empowerment. And *Buffy* is the conveyor of that message." (62).

6 Another related example is Buffy's death leap from the tower at the end of season five, perhaps the most discussed ethical decision of the whole series. While it has been seen as an act related to Kierkegaard's Abraham, a "Knight of Faith," who is willing to sacrifice his son in an act that even transcends ethics, Buffy's leap from the tower, can also be seen as the opposite: breaking from an oppressive authority figure (God or the Watcher's Council) and refusing to sacrifice Isaac or Dawn—the opposite of Kierkegaard's Knight of Faith.

7 Although interestingly, the existence of a soul does not seem to change Angel's essential nature as a (perhaps damned) vampire. Note especially the vampire Darla's line to the reformed Angel as he recoils from a crucifix: "No matter how good a boy you are, God doesn't want you. But I still do" (*Angel* "Dear Boy").

3 Zombies

Alternative resurrections

With a contribution by Rachel Sowers

Zombies and empty churches

Early twenty-first-century television zombies, at least until shows like *iZombie* and *Santa Clarita Diet*, were unredeemable, undatable, and unenviable. Unlike the brooding vampires of *Buffy* and *Angel* and *The Vampire Diaries*, no zombie struggled existentially with their immortality and no love-struck human would choose the life of the walking dead to be with their beloved forever. The zombie figure embodies the fear of death by presenting an alternative distortion of eternal life, one in which the horrific and the unnatural replace the more religiously normative acceptance or mystery. As James Reitter explains, "the zombie figure, more than any other, represents death—not as something inevitable, but suddenly pursuant and predatory" (103). Like the vampire bite, death-by-zombie is like a disease, but unlike vampires where you retain your body and memory, as a zombie, you degenerate into a mindless rotting corpse with the potential to endlessly inflict the same horror on others.

While vampires and zombies may appear to occupy similar spaces in the human unconscious and religious imagination, they rarely if ever share the same fictional universe. As critic Stacey Abbott points out, their role is actually quite different: "the vampire is the undead creature who blurs the line between the living and the dead while the zombie is a graphic reminder of the corporeality of death" (93–94). This blurred line of living and dead and the graphic reminders of dead bodies are themes that are present in religion and often overlap in ritual, doctrine, beliefs, and ecclesiastical art. The idea of eternal life after physical death is almost inevitably linked to religion, and in Christianity, especially, is linked to the corporality of death. As Michael Gilmour writes, "The very notion of bodies rising from their graves (think resurrection here) and the consumption of flesh and blood (think Eucharist here) is at least superficially part of our cultural capital because of the Bible" (89). But while zombie narratives inevitably resonate with echoes of the religious, they simultaneously force uncomfortable questions. What happens when everyone's body lives eternally regardless of their beliefs? And what then happens to beliefs and rituals rooted in the eternal survival of the body and soul? Yet these questions as well resonate with traditional Christianity. If we think of a medieval Roman Catholic cathedral, we find its

DOI: 10.4324/9781003227045-5

Image 3.1 Medieval church painting of the Last Judgment, from St. Thomas-Salisbury, from 1470 to 1500.

whole structure and organization built to encourage focus on the altar and the act of the eucharist, a space and ritual that blur the lines between life and death and resurrection. Even the cathedral itself—built in the shape of a cross—often serves as a graveyard and may feature "cadaver tombs," which graphically depict rotting corpses, as well as horrifying "doom paintings" of the last judgment on the west door of the church so that attendees see it on their way back out into the fallen world (Image 3.1).

Stories of rotting bodies rising from the grave and threatening the living go back hundreds and even thousands of years. Unlike the vampires of the previous chapter, zombies do not stem from a classic Gothic novel, and instead seem to have skipped straight from folklore to the films and television of the twentieth century (Bishop 12–13, Abbott 62). On the other hand, zombie narratives have been influenced by travelogues, pulp presses, and colonialist accounts from the early twentieth century. The zombie entered into the American consciousness through stories about Haiti, where soulless bodies were supposedly raised from the dead by voodoo priests and used as manual laborers. Framed as non-fiction accounts, books on Haitian zombies, such as *The Magic Island* by William Seabrook (1929), captured the attention of the general public and filmmakers. Films such as *White Zombie* (1932) and *I Walked with a Zombie* (1943) were early cinematic exploration of soulless bodies controlled by another. All of these versions, as Abbott writes, "tap into colonial anxieties surrounding the Caribbean following the occupation of Haiti in 1915 by American military forces" (63).

78 *Beyond human*

The current zombies of popular television, however, have another source. The text that plays the seminal role that *Dracula* does for vampire narratives, George Romero's 1968 film *Night of the Living Dead*, established the conventions that subsequent zombie tales either follow or self-consciously adapt: rural or isolated locations, small groups of survivors cut off from communication and surrounded by the living dead, creatures (rarely called zombies) who, while recognizable as human, show signs of decay and damage (Abbott 62). *Night of the Living Dead* introduced the idea of a mass contagion and of what a TV broadcast in the film labels an "epidemic of mass murder." Romero's late 1960s creation effectively channeled anxieties about escalating violence and became a metaphor of our dangerous world. Since *Night* and subsequent Romero films through to the post-9/11 *28 Days Later* and the humanist *World War Z* to the graphic novel and television series *The Walking Dead* and its copies, and spin-offs, critics, scholars, and fans have claimed zombie narratives as particularly suited to give a political and social critique of contemporary society.

Zombies are "a primal assault on our notions of not only what it means to be human" but also how people "negotiate and rationalize life and death" (Reitter 101). Like the vampires on *Buffy*, zombies seem to happen without reason, without justification, without blame, and—in most recent versions—without moral or scientific explanation. Other than the perverse sense of life, death, and resurrection, perhaps the strongest "religious" role that zombie narratives play is in imagining endings: of societies, of cultures, of hope, and of the human race. Like medieval sufferers of the plague, groups of "survivors" struggle futilely to explain why they are being so horribly punished and how they can imagine a tomorrow. Unlike responses to the medieval plague, explanations are rare:

> Many zombie texts — perhaps most new ones, at this point — either hint at or overtly present an apocalypse, an end to humanity through zombification. This is not apocalypse in the ancient sense, a revelation of destiny being worked out. The zombie apocalypse is always accidental, unexplained, or somehow both. (Moreman and Rushton 4)

In other words, it is not "God's wrath" it just *is*, a nihilistic viewpoint that, as we will see, does not necessarily separate it from the religious imagination, but does alter what that imagination is capable of. Like all monsters, zombies are also "an embodiment of a certain cultural moment" (Cohen 4), and the zombie apocalypse is clearly rooted in contemporary anxieties and actual events. As James Berger writes "the typical post-apocalyptic scenario of the late twentieth century is distinctive because by the time it had been represented in fiction, it had already occurred in historical reality: the death camp, the nuclear explosion, the urban wasteland" (150–151).

> Zombies... are the active—impossible but inevitable—presence of what is absent both from our apocalyptic imaginings and our genocidal histories... that is, the masses of dead, victims of our crimes, stupidities, eugenic

fantasies, and variously motivated revels and revelations of destruction. (Berger 155)

As humans in the late twentieth century and the early twenty-first century tried to understand the disasters they had brought upon themselves—with climate change and the COVID pandemic being the most recent—the stubbornly secular language of much "realistic" film and literature was no longer able to capture the bigger-than-life scenarios that were now reality. Zombie narratives are just one example of the turn to metaphorical and religious languages that are the best means we have to describe the increasingly real possibility of human extinction.

Zombies every Sunday night: **The Walking Dead**

Although the number of television shows about zombies has grown in the second decade of the twenty-first century, by far the most influential and most discussed by fans and critics has been *The Walking Dead* (2010–2022). *The Walking Dead* was originally published as a (still ongoing) comic series in 2003 by Robert Kirkman and then later adapted as an AMC television series on Halloween 2010. Watching *The Walking Dead*, especially in the early seasons, reminded us one more time of just what was at stake for humans confronting a (zombie) apocalypse. If dating vampires had become fun, then the "walkers" (they are never called zombies, although each of the different survivor groups have different names for them) of *The Walking Dead* brought back authentic terror and existential doubt about what it means to live in a world where death, danger, illness, and cruelty are always present without justification or explanation.

The Walking Dead, the first serialized television zombie drama, was, in the words of Kirkman, a "zombie movie that never ends," or, in other words, a show about endings without a conclusion. As Keetley writes, the combination of the continuous narrative along with the "vertical" organization of the narrative—spin-offs, comics, video games, novels, webisodes—creates a:

> post-apocalyptic universe, in which the narrative does not end with the death of its protagonists and in which there is no easy end for the survivors, whether it is by death or miraculous restoration of the familiar social order. (5)

If part of the significance of zombie stories is how they force the audience to imagine endings and meaninglessness, then an ongoing (some might say endless) series provided an even more realistic experience of this. In the beginning of the series, it was possible to imagine that it would progress like a zombie film, the survivors will either find a cure, figure out a way to wipe out the zombies, or they will end up in some safe haven where they can live peacefully. On the other hand, many other zombie films end on a note of despair or, at best, ambiguous uncertainty. These "endings" play out differently, however, in a series that has extended over many hours and years and into our own real-life pandemic. As

80 *Beyond human*

Abbott writes, television is a "format that seems ideally designed to defer resolution and deny any restoration of order" (91), but psychologically, *The Walking Dead* was exploring new territory. As the series progressed, it became apparent to many viewers that there could be no "good" ending, and for many, the inevitable conclusion was that everyone would die and become a walker, or would be forced into a continual decline where each generation would be more violent than the last, ultimately indistinguishable from the animated corpses.

By the time the main character Rick Grimes "title drops" in season five—"We are the walking dead" (a line presented much earlier in the comics)—viewers had long since figured out that this was the real meaning of the title. In *The Walking Dead*, "we," as Dawn Keetley writes, are "unambiguously also the zombie" (8). The central point of the series, from episode one on, has been, as Noel Murray writes, "that humans need to become stronger and more calloused to survive, but if they do so at the expense of any kind of moral social order, there's not much that separates them from the flesh-eaters." From critics of popular culture to Nietzsche, one of the main ideas surrounding the analysis of the monster is the way that the struggle pulls the human toward the monstrous. Monsters may be defined by their otherness, but today, as for Nietzsche, one of the main warnings is to "beware that, when fighting monsters, you yourself do not become a monster... for when you gaze long into the abyss. The abyss gazes also into you." (*Beyond Good and Evil*, Aphorism 146). While scholarly interpretations of monsters often focus on the idea of the Other, the truly monstrous makes us reflect and fear who *we* really are. Like Frankenstein and his creature linked together as they flee humanity at the end of the novel, the narrative tension in *The Walking Dead* "becomes one in which human and zombie are not pitted against each other but rather are symbiotically bound together" (Keetley 8).

Despite Rick's claim in season one that "Things are different now... There's only us and the dead" ("Guts"), the monolithic "us" is almost instantly subverted, as are the ideas that zombies are an absolute Other. In other words, Rick's belief in an us-versus-them world almost instantly devolves into multiple factions and into a world of no clear "us" or "them" at all. (Like the early episodes of *Battlestar Galactica*, a first season call-to-arms by an initially unquestionably heroic male character is subverted in later seasons.) By the end of season five, we could legitimately wonder if Rick was now the main character to be feared rather than the leader of a group of survivors. That the writers of the show did not seem to be able to (or want to) work this out is telling, and while it may be a legitimate criticism of the show, it also makes for significant and productive ambiguity in the viewing process. Later seasons move past this specific moral ambiguity, but continue to create similar scenarios.

This blurring between human and monster is increased by various plot points that show characters smearing themselves with zombie innards to escape detection, characters whose injuries force them into a zombie-like limping gait, or finally, in season nine, a group of human survivors almost indistinguishable from the dead. This blurring of distinctions also problematizes the graphic violence that the show seems to celebrate. As Keetley writes,

The show questions the license it also, on some level, undoubtedly offers. That the humans are, like the zombies, also carriers of the virus means that the traditional binary oppositions (human/monster, dead/living, mind/body, even good/evil) are no longer a structuring principle, as much as characters (and some fans) want them to be. If we are all infected, and we will all die, how are we not zombies already? Why is it an unquestioned act of kindness to shoot a friend in the head after death to avoid their zombie resurrection? (16)

In this new "post-event" world, the zombie "now forms a constituent part of the evolving human" (Keetley 7). But what does it mean to evolve in a world without hope? What do we evolve toward in this world of divine absence?

* * *

In the first episode of *The Walking Dead*, Rick is dropped from normal life as a small-town sheriff into an incomprehensible world that he could only interpret as an afterlife in either hell or purgatory. Like the many *Doctor Who* companions who will inevitably experience the TARDIS doors opening onto a vision of the end of the world, when Rick opens his eyes in his hospital bed and walks out into the world, *he* still feels the same, but time, for all practical purposes has vanished and human civilization (in all the previous definitions of that word) is over. Like the Doctor's companion Rose in "The End of the World," Rick first wonders if this is "real," and then faces the possibility that he is the last surviving human, and finally, what that might mean. Unlike Rose, who has the Doctor and his TARDIS, Rick and his companions—despite all their wandering toward normalcy, from a farmhouse to a prison to a walled community and to a church—can never go back.

The extreme violence depicted in *The Walking Dead* introduces ethical and religious conflicts within characters, and these conflicts also play out within fan activity. *The Walking Dead* and its surrounding discourse are oddly positioned as both camp and a dark unironic morality tale. While watching the show can sometimes seem relentlessly nihilistic, killing zombies can also be light-hearted fun, which Comic Con costumes, new zombie comedies, "kill of the week" discussions, and video games all demonstrate. Like characters on *The Walking Dead*, fans perhaps search for ways to distract themselves from the violence and darkness of watching the show. But, as the show also continually reminds us, the same weapons that kill zombies also kill humans. It is the children of the show that illustrate this the clearest. As Rick's children, Carl and Judith, grow up on the show, they must learn to shoot walkers, but Carl also uses the gun to kill humans, including (in an act of mercy) his own mother. That this is a lesson for real life need hardly be emphasized here. As Keetley chillingly informs us, one of the guns used to kill first graders in the Connecticut Newtown School shooting had previously been humorously praised in an article in *Guns and Ammo* as one of the "8 Best Guns for the Zombie Apocalypse" (11). In that context, and after the

82   *Beyond human*

dozens of mass school shootings that have occurred since, it is almost impossible to watch the first episode of *The Walking Dead* where the first zombie killed is a small child. This scene was so dark that there was even an early fan theory that predicted that this would actually be the final scene of the series as well, where everyone else in the world had died except Rick.

Divine absence in **The Walking Dead**

The first words of season two are spoken by Rick Grimes, who initially appears to be praying to an absent God: "I guess I'm losing hope that you can hear me" ("What Lies Ahead"). Although we soon realize that he is on a rooftop leaving a message on a walkie-talkie for his friend Morgan, whom he hopes might still be alive somewhere, the tone remains that of a prayer as he confesses that he is "trying not to lose faith," but that this is a "harder journey than I can imagine." What he starts to reveal but does not is the secret he learned at the end of the previous season but will keep from all of the survivors (and the viewing audience) throughout all of season two. What only Rick knows is that it is not just the bitten that will turn, but that all of humanity is already infected: upon dying, all humans become zombies. The opening scene implicitly asks: what kind of "faith" can exist in a world where "we are all infected," where we are all doomed to what seems an eternal hellish existence? Do the old religions, the old stories, the old beliefs still work? This "prayer" sets up nihilistic and religious undertone that will shadow the rest of this season and, to a certain extent, all of those following.

Various forms and aspects of religion, especially Protestant Christianity are referenced throughout this same episode. When one character finds a truck full of fresh water abandoned on the highway, he joyfully lets it flow over him as he says, "it's like being baptized." That very moment, a character sees a huge herd of the dead walking toward them and the next spoken words are "Oh, Christ." The juxtaposition of the words "baptized" and "Christ" suggests new questions: what is baptism now? And what or who is Christ if this herd of the dead is the only resurrection? In the ensuing chaos, one of the group's children runs off into the woods, and, as they search for her, they hear church bells. They run hopefully toward the bells and find a small simple Southern Baptist church, although they assume it cannot be where the sound came from, as it has "no steeple, no bells" (Image 3.2).

As they enter the church, they see the backs of three people sitting in pews facing the altar and a large statue of the crucifixion (not usually found in Baptist churches; Image 3.3). For just an instant, there are several ways of reading this scene. They look like people; perhaps survivors worshipping or finding a moment of peace in a fallen world. Or if they are already dead, perhaps we are to see their final death in a church pew as a type of salvation or escape. We soon realize, of course, that they are zombies, but does it matter that they are in a church? After violently killing the walkers in the church, Daryl, a member of Rick's group cynically asks the image of the crucified Jesus, "Yo, JC, you taking requests?" For Erika Engstrom and Joseph Valenzano, who have also written about churches

Image 3.2 Baptist church in *The Walking Dead* ("What Lies Ahead").

Image 3.3 Zombies in church (*The Walking Dead*, "What Lies Ahead").

in *The Walking Dead*, this defiant sounding question is still directed to the statue of Jesus—an "implication that he perceives there still exists a higher power with whom to be angry" (128), but this possible faith is, at best, ambiguous. When the bells start to ring again, Rick's group realizes that although the church "got no steeple," the bells are electronic and set on a timer; there is no human pulling a cord; the sound of hope is separated from any real source, it is just a digital echo of a world that used to be.

84 *Beyond human*

At this point, their hopes dashed, Carol, the mother of the lost girl, goes back into the church and earnestly prays to the Jesus statue for forgiveness, for help, and for mercy for her daughter. Finally, Rick goes back into the church by himself. The camera lingers for a moment on the body of the crucified Christ, and Rick begins a prayer that echoes the themes from his voiceover at the beginning of the episode. He admits to not being "much of a believer," and then frames a whole series of possible relationships between the human and the divine: "I don't know if you're looking at me with what? Sadness? Scorn? Pity? Love? Maybe it is just indifference?" As in his opening prayer, he seems to ask a void for empathy: "I could use a little something... To acknowledge that I'm doing the right thing. You don't know how hard that is to know. Well, maybe you do." But like the opening words of the episode suggest, Rick and the others seem to be losing hope that there is anyone there to hear their prayers.

While the simple church in the woods had initially seemed to promise a sort of spiritual respite, the empty building, three dead zombies, electronic bell, and plastic Jesus instead seem to point to the emptiness of these Christian symbols. On the other hand, this scene and many of the religious themes that will be worked out in the series, echo the doubts and questions that define the history of Christianity. When Rick wonders if Christ knows how hard it is, it echoes historical questions of the nature of Christ's suffering, and points to how generations of Christians have identified with their savior as a suffering human figure. The question of how much Jesus actually suffered has been a central issue to Christianity often depending upon what a certain point in place and time needed. The relationship of humans to divinity is part of what has defined times of hopeless death and suffering, whether it be a future zombie or COVID-like infestation, starvation in nineteenth-century Ireland, or a medieval plague in fourteenth-century Europe. What Christianity, if any, would apply to a post-apocalyptic world? In a supernatural fallen world of immortal walkers, would we need a Christ that is more human or more divine? Perhaps the resurrection would necessarily fade in importance as the world grew to fear the resurrected human body. Perhaps a new version of Christianity after a zombie apocalypse would develop new doctrines, symbols, and rituals of suffering, death, and resurrection. What might these look like?[1]

A *Walking Dead* Easter

With Rachel Sowers

The Walking Dead aired on Sunday and usually ran during the spring months, meaning that it occasionally got an Easter Sunday episode. Although it is not commented on within the show, it is clear that the writers of the show were aware of and used these coinciding dates to imply open-ended questions on our shifting views of human life, death, and resurrection. The much-anticipated season three finale aired on Easter Sunday (March 31, 2013), a coincidence that opened up a mild controversy and also multiple interpretations. The third season takes place in two locations: a prison that the survivors have fashioned into a relatively safe place to live, and Woodbury, a seemingly peaceful little village of survivors that is run by the "Governor." The Governor proves to be violent, disturbed, and paranoid, killing outsiders and keeping live walker heads in fish tanks. The main events in the season involve sacrifices and deaths, torture, and a climactic and bloody final battle between the two groups of survivors. The season finale's title, "Welcome to the Tombs," references not only the prison where members of the main group in the show stay, but also the tomb from which Jesus disappeared. The episode, which opens and closes upon the image of a cross, implicitly asks us what that cross can mean in a world where the best one can hope for may be a final death *without* a resurrection.

There was much debate within online fan communities over who might be killed off in this season finale. In a season that had featured the deaths of several main characters, fan sites and blogs were active with articles such as "*Walking Dead* Season 3 Spoilers: Who Will Die Next?" The climactic scene of the finale depicts Andrea, one of the original members of the group, attempting to bring peace to the remaining humans, and, in the process, suffering a dramatic death. Andrea's death scene, and the way it both reveals and conceals moments of transition, suggests, among other things, a distortion of the account of the resurrection of Jesus, and a comment on the Easter holiday on which it aired. As the tension builds toward a final battle between the two communities, the scene opens on Andrea bound to a chair trying to retrieve a wrench to free herself. Milton, a scientist and formerly one of the Governor's trusted allies, lies in the corner of the room suffering from a knife wound. Milton had refused to kill Andrea, prompting the Governor to stab him and lock him up with her, knowing that, once he died, his zombie form would then kill Andrea: death by resurrection.

In the beginning of the scene, the only light in the room shines upon Milton's unmoving body, leaving us wondering whether he is dead or alive; after a moment of ambiguous silence, he gasps for air, and manages to ask Andrea why she did not leave his community when she found out her friends were still alive. Andrea remorsefully replies: "I wanted to save everyone." Tears form in her eyes as she explains that she could have killed the man that tied her to the chair, but she believed there was a solution where no one had to die. The ambiguity and liminality of Milton's moment of death mirrors the distortion of life and death throughout the series. Near the end of the scene, Milton forces out a response—telling Andrea: "I am still here. I am still alive." The suspense continues, as Andrea works to free herself from her bonds before Milton turns in order to avoid the gruesome death they all fear.

The scene feels particularly suspenseful because the viewer has begun to identify with the previously unlikeable Milton, he has already had a "turn" of sorts. The scene cuts away, and viewers are forced to wait to learn what happens to Andrea. The scene returns for a brief moment to show Milton's death and his turning. Andrea screams as she tries to free herself. Milton—now as walker—moves toward her, but the scene cuts to outside the room, and all we hear are

86 *Beyond human*

her screams and the metallic sound of the wrench. Eventually when Rick and his companions (Daryl, Tyreese, and Michonne) find the room where Andrea is kept, and open the door, the camera shot initially only reveals her feet. Once the viewer sees Andrea is alive, it is still unclear whether or not she has been bitten; she remains for us in a liminal state, between life and death. Just as the audience questioned what Milton was, so too are they left to question the state of Andrea's body and perhaps her soul. Michonne feels Andrea's head and notes that she has a fever. Finally, Andrea removes part of her coat to reveal a large bite on her shoulder. She seems calm, as if she has accepted her mortality. She turns to Michonne, her closest friend who joined the group late, and states, "it's good you found them. No one can make it alone now." Andrea once again reiterates that all she wanted was for no one to die. If she must die, however, she does not want to become a zombie. This is a common feeling in *The Walking Dead*, as the prospect of unwanted "life" after death so frightens people that they often ask to be killed. Andrea takes the more hands-on approach, insisting that she must kill herself. Andrea's depiction as a savior is distorted because through this act she assures her non-resurrection. Michonne stays by Andrea's side, as the viewer waits outside with Rick, Daryl, and Tyreese. A shot is heard, but the death is not shown.

It is the unseen and the veiled that make this scene suggestive. Like the Christian resurrection, much is left off stage. The biggest gap in biblical writings is the resurrection itself, which remains forever undescribed. The New Testament is indeed, as Diarmaid MacCulloch writes, a "literature with a blank at its centre" (94), but despite, or because of, this blank, this gap receives the most intense focus in art, theology, and worship. Yet, what is at once one of the most holy acts in the Bible is at the same time the most horrifying occurrence in this post-apocalyptic world. When people die and turn, they become "predatory corpses" that are "free of religious affiliations" (Reitter 101). The only way to avoid this fate is through a more permanent death.

Does Andrea's death have any lasting meaning or value? This question is one that the show and its fans struggled with in the following seasons and in subsequent deaths, perhaps most importantly Carl's in season eight, where the show and the fans seemed to have almost opposing views.[2] While Andrea may appear to have failed as a savior, she has only failed by the standards of the modern pre-zombie world. Theologian Jessica Decou writes that while zombie stories "typically paint an atmosphere of divine absence… the increasingly bleak *TWD* tends less to declare, 'God does not exist' than to present a growing pile of evidence that 'God has abandoned us'" (80). Andrea's act implies the same questions as Rick's entering the church in season two. What is the role of a suffering savior now? How long do we pray to an absence? What does the Christian cross—a symbol of death, sacrifice, and resurrection—mean in a zombie overrun world where these concepts have been overturned? Like ancient Christians who made the choice to interpret Christ as fully human and in doing so emphasized the importance of their own martyrdom, it seems that acts of sacrifice and prayer are still part of the world, but their connection to a religious belief and practice has changed.

Zombies 87

Yet there is a point to Andrea's sacrifice. After her death scene, the shot switches to a sunrise and the soundtrack uncharacteristically shifts to the warm sound of strings. The scene is traditionally beautiful, providing a stark contrast to the death that occurred just moments earlier. The image of the sun elicits thoughts of Easter, echoing the common sunrise services that symbolize the fact that Jesus rose on Easter morning. A bus enters the yard of the prison where the group is staying, and members of the opposing camp file into the prison. Rick explains that he will be letting them stay—an act very uncharacteristic of his normally suspicious ruling style. He has apparently been affected by Andrea's decree that "no one can make it alone." Her belief is characteristic of many zombie narratives, as "the communitarian tendency" is often shown as the "preferable position" (Murray 219). Perhaps we are meant to see that Andrea's death, like Jesus's resurrection, created a community of people based on the beliefs of one martyr. Her death is significant because nothing will ever be the same. She not only has saved a bus full of people, but she has also, at least temporarily, ushered in a new era of community.

The significance of the Easter air date was not lost on fans or critics. After the broadcast, Fox News' Bill O'Reilly voiced his anger that the show *The Bible*, which also aired on the same Easter Sunday, received significantly less views than *The Walking Dead*. He blamed this on a society looking for cheap entertainment, explaining "the New Testament says the son of God rose from the dead on Easter. The zombies rise from the dead whenever their makeup is finished." Yet an alternative reading of *The Walking Dead* episode might suggest that O'Reilly expressed a common misunderstanding of Christianity as an unchanging religion of unquestioned platitudes. One way to envision a Christianity for the twenty-first century would be to acknowledge the rupture, contradiction, and chaos at its core. If our religions were created partly to understand the borders of life and death, what happens when these borders change? If the rules of life/death, human/beast, and good/evil are changed, does not religion need to change as well? (And are not these rules always in flux?) As our own still pre-apocalyptic world grapples with climate change and a pandemic, it is already asking these questions and shows like *The Walking Dead* put these questions into sharper focus. *The Walking Dead*, by representing an event in human history that renders previous moral codes and ideologies inadequate, and the Easter episode, by asking just what (or if) a death (and a life) can mean, was perhaps a much more "Christian" show than the History Channel's version of the Bible. The History Channel's version removed all ambiguity and doubt from the narrative and from the crucifixion—an act that needs to feel painful and radical to be significant. The History Channel's unimaginative Easter episode effectively domesticated a moment of sacrifice, while *The Walking Dead* attempted to revive it.[3]

The final shot lingers meaningfully on the cross before the episode ends (Image 3.4). The show directly presents this symbolic image, but offers no obvious interpretation. Instead, *The Walking Dead* leaves the viewers with the cross, and they must decide what it means. Like *True Blood*'s Sookie gazing at the grave of her vampire lover in a cemetery full of crosses, it asks questions about death

Image 3.4 Concluding shot of "Welcome to the Tombs" (*The Walking Dead*).

rather than gives answers. Is it hope for a better future? For a life after death? Or is it now a symbol for a dead meaningless religion? Like Christianity itself, it has elements of all three. Apocalyptic narratives like *The Walking Dead* ask us not only what is worth preserving from the old world, but also what new ideas the rupture produces. Like my reading of *True Blood* in the previous chapter, the show and this episode allow us to see Christianity and its ubiquity in our narrative of self and story, not as the peaceful harmonious presence that is often assumed, but as a violent, bloody, rupture into a confused world—a world that connects the second-century Mediterranean with twenty-first-century United States. Andrea's sacrifice—like the concept that "we are all infected"—pushes the responsibility onto us; we are responsible for our own salvation and in a world of climate change, deadly viruses, violent racism, pollution, and nuclear weapons, perhaps the episode hints at a more sustainable model of religion.

* * *

Despite its Sunday air time, in the first nine seasons of the show, after "Welcome to the Tombs," there were only two more Easter episodes. Season six's "East" (March 27, 2016) and season eight's "Still Gotta Mean Something" (April 1, 2018), are both titles that imply subversive readings of Easter as a search for meaning in a fallen world, rather than as guarantee of transcendence. In the episode "East," despites its title—only two thirds of Easter—and the fact that the main conflict in the episode is with a group of survivors called the "Saviors," there was little attention paid to the Easter date other than a few viewers commenting on the growing importance of a character known as Jesus. A deeper connection can be found in the episode "Still Gotta Mean Something," which focuses on the aftereffects of Carl's death. Carl himself seems not to have believed in a Christian afterlife and even said as much in a deleted scene from season three, "I wish I still believed in heaven." When Carl does die—he takes his own life in a church—after being randomly infected ("I just got bit"), the show tried to structure it as a central and classic sacrificial moment. Leading up to the death, we see Carl's vision for a peaceful more cooperative future, and after his death, we hear his letters to the survivors urging them toward this image. The show clearly wants his "sacrifice" to be meaningful and help people imagine the possibility of a better world, to forgive, and to move on in what feels a Christian sort of way. Carl's letters are his final messages to his friends (and also the seemingly unredeemable and imprisoned Negan), begging them to embrace a type of radical forgiveness.

In "Still Gotta Mean Something," Michonne encourages Rick to finally read Carl's letter to him:

> We're *so* close to starting everything over, and we have friends now. It's that bigger world Jesus talked about. The Kingdom, the Hilltop… there's got to be more places. More people out there. A chance for everything to change and keep changing. Everyone giving everyone the opportunity to have a life. A real life. So if they won't end it, you have to. You have to give them a way out. You have to find peace with Negan. Find a way forward somehow. We don't have to forget what happened, but you can make it so that it won't happen again. That nobody has to live this way. That every life is worth something.
>
> Start everything over…

But fan reactions provide another reading to his death, as no one really seemed to care anymore. For many critics, Carl's death:

- "…was just the latest in a long line of character deaths that serve little purpose and ultimately weaken *The Walking Dead's* story." (Erik Kain, *Forbes*, February 26, 2018)
- "…has no real discernible impact on *The Walking Dead's* story." (Craig Elvy, *Screen Rant*, December 3, 2019)
- "…was ineffective, pointless, and worst of all: boring." (Alec Bojalad, *Den of Geek* April 10, 2018)

Although the show did not intend it this way, a death and a sacrifice that was scripted to change the future that is met with indifference echoes the soulless bodies, empty churches, and unheard prayers that shape the nihilistic world that is *The Walking Dead*. The show is a search for meaning in hopelessness and death, but, like our radical readings of Easter, it does not give us a positive answer, even when it tries to. Perhaps the fans shrugging at the death of arguably the most optimistic character on the show reflects a deeper truth about

90　*Beyond human*

endings, death, and religion than any plot twist the show itself could manufacture. Similar to writers like D.H. Lawrence and Fyodor Dostoyevsky who give us stories where Christ returns and no one cares or recognizes him, *The Walking Dead* unintentionally asks: what happens if a long-running TV show sacrifices a character to "save" others and the fans do not care? The show itself models a loss of faith in traditional Christian models of salvation, in a way that echoes the apocalyptic scenarios of Nietzsche.

The influential twentieth-century Christian theologian Paul Tillich ended his most famous work with the words: "The courage to be is rooted in the God who appears when God has disappeared in the anxiety of doubt" (190). Or, in other words, our only hope is the hope that comes when the situation is beyond hope itself. Another way to think about it is as a radical theology that insists that death *must* be the end. From this perspective, if death is not the end, then nothing is sacred. It is only in the impossibility of imagining nonexistence that the sacred exists. Thinking through these alternative types of "sacred" through the experience of *The Waking Dead* and the experience of Easter in a hopeless light, brings us to a position that might be called Easter Saturday Christianity. Easter Saturday—a day between death and resurrection when traditional Christianity, radical theology, and atheism occupy a similar space—is a space of a dead, inactive, or silent god. It is a period of waiting, a new era, a time of both hope and despair, of yes and no. It is also a space where we can find the philosophical position of the "Whisperers," the deadly human antagonists of the *Walking Dead* survivors, who conceal themselves in the skin of Walkers to move unseen with packs of zombies. Their leader Alpha, announcing with theological flair that "now is the end of the world," convinces her followers that "the world… went dark so that we could see a new path" ("The Whisperers"). Her world, like that of our own eternally struggling but occasionally optimistic survivors, is a new world where humans have perhaps been abandoned, but at least now know they are on their own. In a world where only the monstrous dead are resurrected, and where we will all become monsters, it is up to us to still somehow create a hopeful existence.

The season ten finale was due to air on Easter Sunday April 12, but was postponed due to the emerging COVID pandemic. In the spring of 2020, Easter services around the world were almost exclusively canceled and some churches that did meet in person were identified as sources of infection and death. Living in our own post-event world, thinking back on the empty churches and unanswered prayers of the world of *The Walking Dead* we see another reversal, from one fallen and dead world in need of a resurrection that may never come to another. We are, indeed, the Walking Dead. Like all survivors, like Jesus followers on Easter Saturday, we have to determine if and how it is worth going on and what comes next.

What comes next? *Doctor Who* and the new human zombie

Zombie narratives offer a discernible pattern of repetitions and nostalgia: killings, resurrections, discarded objects, and spaces, all take on new meanings in a post-apocalyptic, zombie-infested world where survivors desperately hang onto old rules and relationships in a world that demands new ones. These are, in many ways, the essential problems that continually make and remake the practices of religion. Humans must continually ask how traditional religions apply to their present day and to their future. In the coming decades, we will continue to see religious organizations adapt their practices and their scriptural readings to thinking through the ethical dilemmas brought about by medical advancements, global pandemics, climate change, artificial intelligence, new life forms, collapsing governments, and mass starvation.

The *Doctor Who* episode "New Earth," aired on Easter Saturday in 2006, and offers an alternative version of the zombie narrative in a futuristic setting. In this episode, which takes place in the year 5,000,000,023, the newly regenerated Doctor takes Rose to "New Earth," a planet inhabited as part of a nostalgic revival movement following the destruction of the human home planet. This episode is part of a trilogy with "End of The World" and "Gridlock," where each episode offers variations on endings, mortality, the limitations of the human, old religions, and new life forms—all emerging and important themes in this second season of the show. The theme of new life forms, and the fascination and joy the Doctor still finds in them, is expressed the moment they leave the TARDIS, as Rose says "I'll never get used to this. Never. Different ground beneath my feet, different sky," and then asks, "What's that smell?" The Doctor exclaims with joy: "Apple Grass!" The exchange is a perfect representation of what will be presented in the main plot of the episode: the Doctor's radical openness and celebration in accepting new (and what some might see as unnatural) forms of life.

The Doctor brings Rose to the hospital of New New York.[4] Rose and the Doctor are soon separated by the ancient and meticulously preserved Cassandra—a character we have met previously in "The End of the World"— a pair of eyes and lips on a flat sheet of skin with a brain in a bubbling tube claiming to be the last "pure" human. The Doctor notices that patients suffering from fatal diseases are being miraculously cured, thousands of years ahead of what science and medicine should allow. The plot reveals that ten million citizens of the city are able to live healthy, disease-free lives, cured almost instantly of their illnesses, because the nurses—feline nuns of the Sisters of the Plenitude—have set up a clone farm within the hospital; human forms with no alleged consciousness are kept in vats, infected with every known disease, used to create cures, and then disposed of. When the clones begin showing signs of consciousness, the nurses act vaguely interested, but rather than acknowledging this sentience, they simply destroy the errant clone. The nurses do not tell the humans in the city about what they are doing, acknowledging that the humans will likely see the moral implications of their actions, rather than take the "greater good" approach the nurses are hiding behind.

The moral issues are, again, familiar ones that echo cloning narratives from *Battlestar Galactica* to *Orphan Black* to *Westworld*. Each of these shows poses the question of whether lab-grown clones should be imbued with the same basic rights as a naturally born human being. The episode offers a twist on these

92 *Beyond human*

stories, however, as when the clones awake, they take on the characteristics of a zombie horde. Shuffling and diseased, they converge on the humans, reaching out to them, threatening fatal infection. Later, though, we learn that they are innocently reaching out just for the sake of contact, which implies the rarely asked questions of zombie desires and rights. Yet the scenes visually play out in classic zombie fashion: get touched by the ambling "flesh" and you become infected with their disease. The scene is initially shot in ways that encourage viewers to identify them as traditional zombies—creatures rarely given empathy—rather than diseased humans. The horde overruns the hospital, presenting a sort of a parallel to the pilot episode of *The Walking Dead*, where hospitals become a sort of ground zero for Rick experiencing the zombie for the first time.

The episode plays on another angle of the posthuman theme by reintroducing the character of Cassandra, who continues to hold an elitist attitude of herself as the last true, pureblood, human. Even though she is on a New Earth populated by millions of humans, she considers them "mutant stock," to which Rose responds "they evolved, Cassandra. They just evolved, like they should. You stayed still. You got yourself pickled and preserved, and what good did it do you?" Cassandra is contrasted against the so-called hybrids and mutant humans—even the clones—we see in the hospital, who appear much more human to our eyes than Cassandra. The episode suggests that the evolution of the human species is a more natural approach to maintaining one's humanity than Cassandra's method of preservation. We see here a contrast between a point of view that wants to find both gods and humans as unchanging entities, rather than evolving, fluid ideas. An unchanging god, like Cassandra, becomes a museum piece without meaning. Religions and religious practices are based in repetition, tradition, and nostalgia, but without change and innovation, they become a meaningless stretched out skin in a frame spouting xenophobic nonsense.

In the end, the Doctor cures the clones, acknowledges their sentience, and the hospital officially declares them a new life form. But rather than categorize them as an entirely new species, the Doctor argues the case that they are humans in their own right:

> It's a new subspecies, Cassandra. A brand-new form of life. New humans. Look at them. Look! Grown by cats, kept in the dark, fed by tubes, but completely, completely alive. You can't deny them, because you helped create them. The human race just keeps on going, keeps on changing. Life will out!

"New Earth," like much speculative science fiction, combines the nostalgic with the futuristic, rooted in ideas of the human, yet acknowledging that they are inadequate when we think of history on its largest scale. Implicitly, the episode suggests questions that define this chapter and this book. What does it mean to claim humanity in the face of the "other"? What is the difference between a powerful alien and a god? And, perhaps most interestingly from a theological (particularly a Christian) standpoint, what does it mean for an alien figure to assume a human identity, or to "become" human? While the Christian myth is central to each of these questions, so is the related human need to weave old ideas of death and being into imagining new endings and beginnings.

* * *

While the modern vampire exists in a faded Catholic world of power and symbols—holy water and crucifixes—modern zombies seem to thrive in rural, Protestant, American landscapes. If the Protestant Reformation had a defining moment of origin, it is often claimed to be Luther's realization in 1518 while in the Cloaca Tower that we cannot be saved through our own doing, but can only be saved through the righteousness of God. This legendary moment of divine revelation comes down to us today partly through Luther's own words, written long after the event, in which he writes that, "The Holy spirit gave me this art in the cloaca." Whether an intentional pun or not, much has been made of the fact that cloaca is Latin for "sewer," English for an animal's anus, and meant outhouse or toilet in Luther's time. Some thinkers have interpreted this phrase as an intentional theological move on Luther's part that offers, as Luther's biographer and conservative writer and radio host Eric Metaxas writes, the "perfect illustration of his theological foundation." Luther's incarnated God, according to this reading, does not "descend to earth on a golden cloud" but instead through "screaming pain," "bloody agony," and in a cattle stall "stinking of dung" (97). This very human entry of an eternal god/human into our world reeking of shit, is a way of showing that we are not in need of healing, but are fully dead and need a miracle savior. This reading of Luther offers a clear reversal of the Catholic salvation narrative, but also gives us an analogy for the fallen and very Protestant (or perhaps post-Protestant) world where humans become more and more like zombies. It is certainly possible to see these zombies as representing a form of the human condition, and one that Luther, to a certain extent, would have understood. In other words, we are not just sinners in need of salvation, we are literally dead, rotting, and in need of resurrection—but maybe one that will never come, or perhaps one that we do not deserve. What, then, do we live (or die) for?

Notes

1 Throughout the series, churches serve as reminders of a previous world, as temporary safe spaces, as sites of extreme violence, and as semi-sacred meeting spaces. In keeping with the ambiguity of the show itself, these spaces often move fluidly between these states. The appropriately named Terminus, a survivor site that briefly offers hope before revealing its bloody nature, has a sort of altar that they call the "Church," where you can find the names and belongings of members of their community who have died. The small rural Episcopal St. Sarah's Church is where they find Gabriel, a conflicted priest who will join the group. Walkers will overrun this church, slaughtering the living underneath the words "who eats my flesh and drinks my blood has eternal life" ("Coda"). The Church in Alexandria offers a tower that is used as a sniper base, but, when the tower falls, it forms a bridge allowing the walkers access to the community. As Engstrom and Valenzano write, the later churches "mirrors the

94 *Beyond human*

evolution of the characters' views on religion… a church is now just another building, devoid of the meaning and institutional power it once held" (132).

2 By season nine, the only character that fans seemed to really fear dying was Daryl's dog Dog. "'If Dog Dies We Riot': *The Walking Dead* Fans Fear for Daryl's Dog in Season 11." August 15, 2021. Cameron Bonomolo, Comicbook.com.

3 An interesting sub-theme was how Andrea's "sacrificial" death was one of the first on the series to which fans responded to in a cynical way—the beginning of the value of sacrifice on the show. While some fans wanted her somehow brought back to life, much of the fan community were already enjoying mocking her character (Buzzfeed: "Andrea from 'The Walking Dead' Summed Up in 31 Pictures) and were apathetic about her death.

4 Actually, New New New New New New New New New New New New New New New New New York.

Part II
Beyond borders

4 Ghosts and bodies

Borders of the real

Real ghosts

As we saw in Chapter Three, throughout much Western philosophical and religious tradition, to be "real" is to be material. The televised undead vampires and zombies of the previous chapters are defined, in a large part, by their physicality. The vampires on *True Blood* audibly splatter and rip apart, and human characters on *The Walking Dead* smear the guts or skin of walkers over their bodies to walk among them undetected; aliens, vampires, and zombies, bleed, touch, and decay, and their televised representations celebrate this physicality. These beings are "real" because we can see them, hear them, smell them, and touch them. But if to be real is to be material, then a belief in ghosts calls that entire formulation into question. Expressing an interest in ghosts today may seem, as Peter Buse and Andrew Stott label it, "decidedly anachronistic" (1), but ghosts continually find a way into both speculative television and popular religion and, in the process, as ghosts always do, make us rethink our past and reimagine our present. These ghosts, whether in books, films, or television, carry a whiff of the modern with them, not the certainty of medieval Catholicism, or the dramatic doubt of Shakespeare, but the mystery, magic, and science of a culture that sometimes feels like it should know better, but that sees—or wants to see—ghosts anyway. As Avery Gordon writes, "Haunting and the appearance of specters or ghosts is one way… we are notified that what's been concealed is very much alive and present, interfering precisely with those always incomplete forms of containment and repression ceaselessly directed toward us" (xvi). While ghosts have been around since humans have been telling stories, beginning in the nineteenth century, the overlap between science, superstition, religion, and technology created new spaces for ghost stories to emerge. Ghosts come from our fear of death and the unknown and are located directly in that space where we do not know what is real. They are both playful and serious. From the Cold War comic, *Casper the Friendly Ghost*, to scary stories told around a campfire, to the often nostalgic and ironic use of ghosts in shows and films such as *Doctor Who* and *Harry Potter*, ghosts are often the least serious of dramatic "monsters"; they seem more the property of Saturday morning children's television than adult speculative drama. They are the most

DOI: 10.4324/9781003227045-7

98   *Beyond borders*

and the least scientific and religious figures in this book, existing on the edges of evidence, faith, tragedy, and comedy.

None of the shows I discuss in this book feature ghosts as a central element, but almost all of them have episodes that employ ghosts in one way or another. We see literal ghosts on *True Blood*, digitally created ghosts on *Westworld* and *Dollhouse*, ghostly visitors on *Leftovers* and *Sense8*, and aliens posing as ghosts on *Doctor Who*. My thinking about ghosts on television will move between what appears to be literally ghosts to broader definitions of ghostly figures that are digital or in the mind, and then to even broader but related discussion of purgatory and the "real" as it moves across negotiations of death and afterlife. In shows like *Westworld* or *Altered Carbon*, for example, although there are not any actual ghosts, the merging and blurring of humans, human copies, technology, cyborgs, time, and memory gives a futuristic depiction of a new type of haunted world of collapsed distinction, where the dead and the living walk together among phantom landscapes and artificial identities, and where—through technology and memory—death is not a final ending.

These questions of defining the human cannot be understood outside of our religious histories, a programming about bodies and souls that is deep within our ideological DNA. Throughout Christian history, there is a long tradition of debating these mind-versus-body understandings. The early Gnostics, for example, often wanted to dismiss the body altogether and placed salvation only in the hope of some spiritual spark ascending and leaving the body behind. But even in these kinds of negation of the physical, the body is an important part of religious practice, even if it is understood as a vessel to be escaped. Every one of these ideas and practices involve the negotiating of borders between soul, mind, identity, human, and god. Christianity has often recognized the body as a form of knowledge: when the risen Christ wants to prove that he is real, he asks "doubting Thomas" to *feel* his wound. Thomas's doubt comes to represent modern man—the man of science, the cynic seeking material evidence. This conflation of verifiable evidence and faith is a theme in many television dramas, perhaps most famously in *The X-Files* where the notion of "I want to believe" was often interwoven with forensic evidence, religious skepticism, and Roman Catholicism.

* * *

The third episode of the first season of the rebooted *Doctor Who* ("The Unquiet Dead"), begins in a funeral home. As a man sadly gazes down at the body of his mother in a coffin, her skin suddenly turns blue and her eyes open. She violently grabs her son and throws him down as she crashes out of the room into the snow-covered streets, bluish gas coming out of her screaming mouth. Even though "the dead are walking," as the undertaker says, it soon becomes clear that unlike zombies, these dead are animated by this ghostly gas, a nod to both the earlier *Doctor Who* Saturday morning low budget special effects and to Victorian era magical deceptions like Pepper's Ghost, which used reflections to project a ghostly image onto a stage. Part zombie, part ghost, and—because it is *Doctor Who*—almost inevitably some sort of extraterrestrial alien, this creature is a hybrid ghostly monster that looks forward and back, is both nostalgic and speculative, and is part of television's redrawing of religious definitions and the borders between magic, science, and spirituality.

When, in the next scene, Rose and the Doctor land in Cardiff on Christmas Eve in 1869, Rose—her eyes opened by the newness of time travel—comments to the Doctor that each day "happens just once and then it's gone, it's finished, it'll never happen again... except you—you can see days that are dead and gone." Rose's awareness of what author Milan Kundera called the "unbearable lightness of being," and how the Doctor can see what to her is "dead and gone," speaks to ideas of both the fragility of life and the hope for a form of eternal life, themes that are echoed throughout the episode. Early in the episode, we see Charles Dickens preparing to speak to a Cardiff audience. He complains "I'm like a ghost, condemned to repeat myself through all eternity." As the Doctor and Rose walk down the street, a choir sings "God Rest Ye Merry Gentlemen," and the scene shifts to Dickens in the theater reading from *A Christmas Carol*. The dead woman from the opening scene is in the audience and begins to glow and emit blue gas as Dickens points in fear, asking "What phantasmagoria is this?" While Dickens may feel like a ghost and have written about ghosts, this one appears to somehow be *real*. When Dickens skeptically asks the Doctor, "Now you tell me that the real world is a realm of spectres?" we can expand his question to comment on issues larger than the plot of this episode, the realization that the world is always bigger and more mysterious than we can know.

At the end of the episode, as Dickens excitedly plans to write about his new-found knowledge of time travel and alien life in the universe, he asks the Doctor, who knows Dickens will die before he can write of his new knowledge, "My books, do they last? How long?" The Doctor answers: "Forever." But, of course, the Doctor is lying. Dickens' novels cannot really last "forever," a word that for the Doctor means a time millions of years after the inevitable extinction of the human race and the destruction of the Earth. The incorporeality of ghosts and ideas and the materiality of bodies and books are all reminders that nothing lasts forever, and also, paradoxically, they express our desires of enduring beyond the human lifespan. We like to believe in the possibility of types of immortality from novels and digital preservation to our desires for a spiritual immortality. These desires are all versions of what Elaine Graham calls "an innate drive towards disembodied transcendence deeply embedded in every human psyche" (231). We can find this desire also expressed in the relationship between the invisibility of a spirit, a ghost, a digital pattern, or—in the case of Christians—a god made flesh who comes back to life as a ghost.

* * *

The modern ghost comes out of an intersection of magic, religion, and science and is a space to rethink how we make sense out what we can and cannot know. Even the term "supernatural" embodies these forces and contradictions, describing an

100 *Beyond borders*

agent that both is and is not part of this world. When Barbara Herrnstein Smith writes that "there is nothing that distinguishes how we produce and respond to gods from how we produce and respond to a wide variety of other social-cognitive constructs ... central to human experience," she is asking us to not recognize these borders as parts of a useful taxonomy: to see supernatural agents (gods, ghosts) as part of the same cognitive human experiences as a sunset (94).

A recent show that challenges the lines between religion, science, and magic is NBC's *Lost*-influenced show *Manifest* (2018–), where a plane and its passengers disappear for 5½ years and then return with all of the passengers having experienced only the hours of the flight. They exist in what seems like a normal world, but do not know where they have been, or if they have actually died and come back. The most mysterious part, other than where they disappeared to during that time, and whether their current incarnations are "real," is that each of the passengers gets cryptic "Callings," which seem to encourage them to take some sort of action. Throughout the show, there is an emphasis on searching for evidence deciphering the calls—main characters included a mathematician, a detective, and a medical researcher—but also on slowly acknowledging that the Callings come from a source of good and perhaps even from God. In the third season, a secret government laboratory is set up to research the passengers and the plane. An important link is found in a piece of 6,000-year-old wood delivered from the Vatican that chemically is connected to the plane and the passengers and appears to be a piece of Noah's Ark (yes, this was actually the plot). This discovery seems to simultaneously prove a divine role in the disappearance of the plane: a turning point near the end of the season, as a skeptical government scientist finally admits that they need to put "faith on the table." But what this means in the context of the show is complicated. By faith, she seems to mean both some sort of religious magic and also the possibility that the plane and the actual Noah's Ark are linked. Our two main characters—the formerly agnostic mathematician and detective who now believe the Callings come from God and that the passengers have been "resurrected" for a reason—nod in approval. Crucially, this faith seems to come out of evidence gained through scientific experiments. Through the whole show, there is the sense that religious faith is earned through evidence and verification, whether scientific, anecdotal, or textual.

What shows like *Manifest* demonstrate are the ways in which our perceptions and definitions of religion—for both believers and non-believers—are inextricably wound up in our lived ideas of modernity. Twentieth-century science profoundly changed religion, but not always in the antagonistic way that many people assume. Science gave us tools, as well as the motivation, to "prove" reality, and humans began to look for neurological evidence of religious states; studies attempt to show if prayer can actually heal, photographers try to capture the images of ghosts and fairies, and "biblical" archaeologists search for Noah's Ark and Jesus' tomb. The power of religion—driven by networks of communication only recently possible—is inseparably linked to modern culture and modern technology. And in the same way that religion is linked to its surrounding modernity, secularity can also be seen as a religious phenomenon, a way of thinking shaped

Ghosts and bodies 101

by religious traditions, languages, and practices. As religious scholar Mark C. Taylor observes "religion does not return, because it never goes away; to the contrary, religion haunts society, self, and culture even—perhaps especially—when it seems to be absent" (312). It is the word "haunt" that is most important to me here. Each of the figures that shape my chapters—vampires, zombies, aliens, and ghosts—can be understood as religious hauntings. Ghosts especially call out for verification through evidence, a materiality that balances their invisibility and immateriality.

* * *

Ghosts come into this world, as the Ninth Doctor says, through "a weak point in time and space. A connection between this place and another. That's the cause of ghost stories, most of the time" ("Unquiet Dead"). The seeming contradiction between "weak point" and "connection" here is revealing: a rift is always both a mystery and an explanation; it separates and connects, obscures and reveals. This "weak point in time and space," this "connection between this place and another" as the Doctor says, is indeed the cause of most ghost stories. Whether it is the invisible "dark lightening" of *Manifest*, the "hellmouth" in *Buffy the Vampire Slayer*, or all the various cracks and portals in *Doctor Who*, *Lost*, and *Stranger Things*, these spaces—both "real" and not real—outline the same imaginative borders as those between warring European Catholics and Protestants, each who insisted on a different interpretation of these ghostly ideas. These liminal spaces and blurry lines that separate one world from another, between the human body and the dream world, between presence and absence, magic and science, are inextricably woven into the roots of modern religion itself as well as forming much of the material through which Western culture has defined what religion is. The Catholic idea of purgatory, as historian Stephen Greenblatt writes "forged a different kind of link between the living and the dead, or, rather, it enabled the dead to be not completely dead" (17). In the same way that authors like Shakespeare borrowed from the Catholic toolbox to create dramatic ghostly tensions, TV shows as different as *Doctor Who*, *The Leftovers*, and *Stranger Things* use the idea of purgatory to recreate new speculative or magical spaces. While Catholics found true religion in actual material objects—bones, crosses, holy water, and pieces of the true cross—Protestants tended to replace these with language, scripture, and sermons. More recently, it has tended to be evangelical Protestant denominations that claim experiences with and evidence of ghosts and demons and who emphasize the material proof of religious experience.

These clashes over the material, the ghostly, and the real are often the origin of modern ideas of just what the word and concept "religion" means. It is historically accurate, as Robert Orsi writes, to say

> that "religion" was the creation of the profound rupture between Catholics and the varieties of Protestantism over the question of presence, of the

102 *Beyond borders*

> ongoing and intensifying caricatures of each other's theologies and rites of presence, and of their mutual denunciations for practicing what in their respective judgments was not really "religion." (32)

In other words, our modern concept of religion comes from the same spaces as our ghost stories.

From *Doctor Who* to *Hamlet*, the question "is the ghost real?" echoes with the same question of just how we define what we mean when we say real. Also *Doctor Who* and other television dramas overlay historical debates on top of this question, especially in drawing and redrawing the lines between magic, religion, and science. We might think of science fiction writer Arthur C. Clarke's famous maxim that "any sufficiently advanced technology is indistinguishable from magic." While as Ira Livingston says, Clarke's statement suggests a kind of "smug rationalism, annoying aggrandizement of technology, and condescension toward 'primitives'," it does offer us a way to look both forward and back and imagine ourselves as the "primitives" facing a more advanced civilization. While Clarke leaves out the concept of religion, it should be seen as a third side of the equation along with magic and science. The balance between these methods of relating to what we do not understand are there from the beginning of modern science, woven into Renaissance practices like alchemy and into Victorian ghost stories. The powers of an old piece of driftwood on *Manifest* is measured by science, behaves like magic, and is explained by religion. In the lived world of the twenty-first century, this uneasy balance is found when my Mexico City tour guide explained how a NASA analysis of the image of Our Lady of Guadalupe on a cloak confirmed its miraculous nature—an almost exact parallel to what the scientists in *Manifest* are doing in their secret government lab with the drift wood from Noah's Ark.

As fictional vampires and zombies have swarmed across our television screens, ghosts have occupied a different space on semi-reality based "paranormal" shows—from *Ghost Hunters* (2004–2016) and *Girly Ghost Hunters* (2005) to *Paranormal Paparazzi* (2012) and *Buzzfeed Unsolved* (2016–2021). Their presentation on television seems to hover between pseudoscience, irony, and humor; today's ghosts seem to be both more verifiable and less threatening than other monstrous creatures. In the modern era, ghosts are real because we can photograph them, because their presence changes the temperature in the room, because radios and Geiger counters register their presence, and because they leave remnants of ectoplasm behind. The invention of the camera, the telegraph, cinema and television, tape recorders, the internet, YouTube, and smartphones have all offered new potential for preserving and storing the dead, and for promoting new varieties of ghost stories both metaphorical and real.

A ghost can be detected by scientific instruments on *Ghost Hunters*, but a ghost on *Doctor Who* is likely to end up being an illusion, a hallucination, a Victorian superstition, or (most likely) an alien. Yet, ghosts, more than aliens, vampires, and zombies, threaten our own sense of security in what we feel and believe. "Spectrality," writes Fredric Jameson, does not involve the conviction that ghosts exist:... all it says... is that the living present is scarcely as self-sufficient as it claims to be; that we would do well not to count on its density and solidity, which might under exceptional circumstances betray us. ("Marx's Purloined Letter" 39)

In other words, we should not be so quick to trust our sense that the only reality is one we can touch and feel. So, are ghosts figments of our imagination, evidence of a porous border between life and death, or the visual representation of our refusal to accept our own finitude? As Shakespeare admits to the Tenth Doctor, the death of his son from the plague made him "question everything. The futility of this fleeting existence. To be or not to be? Oh, that's quite good" ("The Shakespeare Code").

Hamlet's ghost and purgatory: "to be or not to be?"

Before Shakespeare's time, in medieval England, it was more or less accepted that the dead could return to haunt the living, and many stories and records exist of personal encounters with these apparitions. As Keith Thomas writes in his classic book on magic and religion,

> Theologians taught that it was not in the power of the dead man himself to choose to return to the earth; and that the living had no means of forcing him to do so: God alone determined such matters. But the basic possibility of ghosts, as such, was never disputed. (702)

Shakespeare, like many of the speculative television dramas discussed in this book, borrows from older religious traditions and metaphors, and by forcing us to take them seriously again, brings us face to face with the impossibility of understanding the perhaps porous borders between life and death, present and past, and memory and reality. When Shakespeare used a shadowy and ghostly figure from purgatory to open his play *Hamlet*, he too was borrowing an idea that many thought of as from the superstitious past. As Stephen Greenblatt writes, Shakespeare "redeployed damaged or discarded institutional goods" (xiv) and "reached deep into Renaissance English culture, into its characteristic ways of burying the dead, imaging the afterlife, negotiating with memories of the departed" (xiii). To believe in a form of purgatory then—whether in medieval Catholicism or in postmodern science fiction—is, as Greenblatt writes, to say that "the border between this world and the afterlife was not firmly and irrevocably closed ...time did not come to an end at the moment of death. The book was not quite shut" (18). Of course, within Christian influenced cultures, this invites one obvious question: Was the resurrected Jesus a ghost? For many early Christians, it was important to prove that he was not. He could eat and drink, for example, and he could be touched. This was not a ghost story but a resurrection of the flesh. On the other hand, earthly Gnostic thinkers seemed to lean more toward something like a ghost, and even the account of Mark relates that Jesus appeared "in a different form" (16.12).

104　*Beyond borders*

All of this is threaded into our literary and religious (and popular culture) history in ways that are difficult to disentangle. To imagine being or existence involves imagining *not* being, and in that case, ghosts are perhaps the visualization of the not being, the nothing. To understand being, to comprehend that we live a finite life in a finite world, is to be aware of ghosts, demons, and purgatories pressing up against the material world. They each represent a form of nothingness or a negating power that threatens existence. Or, as Martin Heidegger phrases his concept of nothingness, "must we not hover in this anxiety constantly in order to be able to exist at all?" (104). Many of us do not believe in ghosts, perhaps, yet fiction forces us to see them, part of the necessary process in understanding our own being, and the nothingness that comes before and after us.

Television's ghostly reality

Television was created to offer up-to-date news, live action, and reality, and, because of that history, has a special relationship to ghosts. Early films were about optical illusions, but television was about documenting reality. The very idea of ghosts and the existence of television are both already staging a debate about the real, a debate we can see in the blurred lines between reality television and fantasy fiction. Since the Victorian era, ghosts have often been associated with tricks of technology. As Jeffrey Sconce writes, "sound and image without material substance, the electronically mediated worlds of telecommunications often evoke the supernatural by creating virtual beings that appear to have no physical form" (4). In the twenty-first century, we can look to online communities, virtual reality, and wireless technology as tools that will continue to sometimes suggest that these technologies are "animate and perhaps even sentient" (Sconce 2). Television's more serious engagement with ghosts has been through reality shows about the paranormal, a tradition that goes back to early Victorian attempts to "prove" the reality of ghosts through technology.

There is another way to look at this, however, and that is by thinking about what we consider "educational" or "serious" viewing or "reality" versus "quality" television. There has been, in fact, some slippage in the distinction between ghosts in drama and ghost hunters in paranormal reality shows. According to the Travel Channel general manager Matt Butler,

> when networks were doing paranormal shows back in 2010, it was done a different way — it was more of going into a haunted house with a flashlight... today, we are trying to steer the creative to be story-driven because people want to hear great stories. (qtd in Umstead)

Amy Savitsky, A&E senior vice president of development and programming, is quoted as saying

> With technology more advanced and more experts looking into these topics, viewers are looking for plausible explanations for things they cannot explain.

> Viewers are seeking 'truth' and want to know facts... Today, there seems to be a burgeoning sense that people are willing to again explore the possibility of the supernatural and what might exist as more people are declaring themselves spiritual but not religious and thinking about what's possible. We think it's the right time to bring it back. (Umstead)

And belief in ghosts does seem to be growing at the same time that traditional religion seems to be declining (or perhaps, more accurately, as alternative forms of spirituality are growing). A 2018 Chapman University survey reported 57.7% of Americans believe that places can be haunted by spirits, up from 46.6% in 2016, and a 2021 *New York Times* article pointed to a 2019 IPSOS poll that found that 46% of Americans believed in ghosts, although the article also cited studies that showed far fewer actually feared them. The *Times* article quotes sociologist Thomas Mowen, who speculates that these beliefs can come from a space of non-religion, and that it is not a coincidence that belief in ghosts has risen while the number of people claiming to be non-religious has tripled since 1978. "People are looking to other things or non-traditional things to answer life's big questions." For Mowen, "atheists tend to report higher belief in the paranormal than religious folk" (Kambhampaty). Yet, why do we not consider belief in ghosts "religious"?

In *Paranormal Media*, Annette Hill claims on her first page that American and British popular culture domains have undergone a "paranormal turn" (1), and that viewing audiences, "motivated by consumption and lifestyle trends rather than religious beliefs," engage with interactive media in search of "experiences that they believe go beyond reality" (13). Hill locates a stronger viewer or fan presence and participation in these shows than is generally recognized. For Hill:

> Audiences are invited to join investigations by watching and listening, using webcams, texting comments, and sharing their thoughts and feelings. Audience awareness that paranormal phenomena are extremely rare and difficult to document makes the chances of a haunting being captured on camera highly unlikely. (66)

What is important, as we move from the viewers of ghost hunting documentaries to shows like *Doctor Who*, *Buffy*, *Game of Thrones*, and *True Blood* is that "as armchair ghost hunters, audiences are not passively sitting at home waiting for the producers to put on a show; they are actively engaged in emotional, physical and psychological participation in a haunting atmosphere" (Hill 78). My argument would be that hints of this participatory aesthetic persist, even as we move into the fantastic world of ghosts in television fiction. The fantastic, as literary theorist Tzvetan Todorov influentially defined it, "is the hesitation experienced by a person who knows only the laws of nature, confronting an apparently supernatural event" (25). The fantastic then, or the ghost in our case, occupies the duration of uncertainty between illusion and the real, between imagination and existence. For Todorov, this duration ends when we choose one or the other and we "leave

106 *Beyond borders*

the fantastic." Similarly, in shows that are unquestionably fictional and that yet, as this book claims in every chapter, influence our religious beliefs and practices, the mystery of death is woven into a new amalgamation of magic, science, and religion, that needs both of these kinds of television.

Unreal bodies

"Other than dead": blood and matter in True Blood

Blood is, of course, a central link between vampire narratives and religion: blood as metaphor, as material, as ritual, as sustenance. Blood is, as countless versions of Dracula have said, *the life*. But why blood? *Buffy's* Spike gives us one answer: "it's always gotta be blood" he says, "why do you think we eat it? It's what keeps you going, makes you warm, makes you hard, makes you other than dead" ("The Gift"). The history of Christianity gives another answer: the power of Christ's holy blood is a legend that can be traced across the two thousand years of Christianity beginning with the apocryphal gospel story of Longinus, the Roman soldier who speared Christ's side, was healed of his illness, became a missionary, and managed to take some of the blood to hide underground in Italy where it was miraculously discovered in the eleventh century and is still preserved and celebrated today at a Benedictine monastery. In the wake of the medieval plagues in Europe, shrine cults of Christ's blood, or holy blood cults, developed that were part of the growing attention to body and blood in the eucharist, but also spread into violent bloody folk tales and magic rituals. The medieval celebration of the eucharistic ritual became more centrally focused on the *materiality* of the blood as blood—part of an increased focus on the body itself, and an increased importance of the idea of the real. The idea of blood as simultaneously material, magical, and holy leads to a more enchanted view of the material world. As Robert Orsi writes, it may have been "the most sacred of real presences in this world, but it was not the only one" (*History and Presence* 21). In this way of thinking—Catholic, yes, but also found in pre-Catholic and hybrid folk religions—the "woods, homes, and forests of Europe, its churches, statues, relics, holy oils and waters, and shrines were filled with the presences of spirits" (Orsi, *History and Presence* 37). *True Blood* splits the difference, offering us an enchanted modern Louisiana Protestant world where blood is material, but also full of magical power. American style evangelical Protestantism has reintroduced presence through healing, demons, exorcism, precisely what earlier Protestants had found superstitious, and even evil within Catholicism, and *True Blood* combines that world with vampire mythology and a mix of modern metaphors involving drugs, disease, gay rights, and violence.

Season one of *True Blood* presents the new relationship of the recently visible and "out" vampire community with the human one, but the main plot lines revolve around Sookie's relationship with vampire Bill, as well as several murders in the town, including, most tragically Sookie's grandmother. At the end of the sixth episode, "Cold Ground," Sookie, as a way of healing after the murder of her

Ghosts and bodies 107

beloved grandmother, performs three related ritualistic acts; each act resonates with Christian ritual yet is enacted in a world of an absent God. Upon arriving home from the funeral, Sookie slowly and mechanically eats the last pie that her grandmother had cooked, with a hymn playing softly as background music. The music continues ("Take me home, Lord, take me home") and the camera cuts to extreme close-ups of the pie, emphasizing and defamiliarizing its materiality. As religious studies scholar Leonard Primiano writes, the scene creates a "new religious iconography" and resembles the "reverence and dignity of the reception of the Eucharist at a funeral" (52). But, taking our cue from the much-discussed opening credit sequence that I analyzed in Chapter Three, if we view the show through juxtapositions and gaps, we will find its meaning always plural and unstable. The images of Sookie are complicated by cuts to other characters and subplots. We briefly see Sookie's friends Sam and Tara meet in a hotel room, where Sam says to Tara that he wants "something real in my life," we cut back to the empty pie pan and then to Sookie in front of the mirror. The non-verbalized visual comment is that Sookie, too, is acting out of a desire for "something real," which adds to the resonance of the very real pie as a form of eucharist.

Without changing expression, Sookie ritualistically lets her hair down and changes into a white dress. She calmly looks out the window waiting for the sun to set and then runs barefoot across a blue tinted misty field for her first sexual encounter with Bill, an event we have been anticipating since the opening moments of the series. In the final scenes of the episode, she kisses his fangs and then offers her throat for him to bite; "I want you to," she says. Sookie here is body and blood—and pecan pie. As Bill drinks from her, the final shot of the episode is an extreme close-up of skin, blood, teeth, and tongue—linking the image to the close-up of the pie and presenting both as religious iconography: a ritual-driven eucharistic replacement that conflates life and death, humans and monsters, the saved and the damned.

The teaser to the next episode, "Burning House of Love," opens with the same close-up shot that concluded the previous episode: Bill's mouth and fangs and Sookie's skin and blood. The scene proceeds to depict the more traditional sexual penetration as Sookie moans with pleasure. This conflation of bodies, blood, ritual, sex, danger, and ecstasy is an echo of the opening credit sequence that this scene then cuts directly to. After the credits, Bill retires alone to his coffin-like resting place beneath the floor, emphasizing the difference between Sookie and Bill, between human and vampire. This scene then cuts directly to a shot of Tara's mother, Lettie Mae's coffee cup (which she spikes with vodka, another eucharistic substitute?) and we hear a radio broadcasting an evangelical Christian sermon in the background, asking "what does it mean to accept Jesus as your personal savior?" Indeed. What *does* it mean? Has that meaning now changed? In the context of this episode, the question resonates differently.

In this episode, each character searches for and questions the sense of the "real" that is at the center of the eucharistic performances, and that has been part of understanding the human/supernatural divide in the West for centuries. There is perhaps no religious act in the Christian church that is so simultaneously

108 *Beyond borders*

material (literally tasting and digesting bread and wine), spiritual (body and blood of Christ) and magical (an unseen transformation). The previous episode's representation of the eucharist opened the door to rethinking the relationship between life and death and human and divine. Throughout this episode, which continues to play with the perception of good and evil and complexities of reality and appearance, different characters seek forms of fulfillment, transcendence, or escape through a force that is simultaneously sexual, physical, ritualistic, and dangerous: Lettie Mae seeks money for an exorcism, even offering the banker sex in exchange for a loan; Sookie's brother Jason craves "V" (hallucinogenic vampire blood), and goes to the vampire/human bar Fangtasia to score and instead hooks up with a woman named Amy; Sookie continues to crave sex with Bill. When Jason and Amy take V together, she says "you just know this is what Holy Communion is symbolic of." Amy's exclamation suggests the doctrine of the "Real Presence" in the eucharist. But what is *real* in this episode? What (if any) forms of power are based in something outside of the human imagination? Jesus? V? Sex? Exorcism? Magic? Bill downplays the vampire/human divide, saying to Sookie that "we're all kept alive by magic... my magic is just a little different than yours" ("Mine"). But what is the magic that animates him? Or her? Or us? And where does it come from?

Bodies and dead things in Buffy: *"Where did I go?"*

Season six of *Buffy the Vampire Slayer*—after Buffy's sacrificial death at the end of season five—premiered just weeks after 9/11, on a new network, and offered a more serious, controversial, and darker version of the show that more explicitly explored fears of death and meaninglessness. In its sixth year, the show was growing up with its fans and helping them think about the fears and traumas that are part of becoming an adult human. The darker tone of season six often focuses on bodies to make the dangers seem more "real." From the shocking scenes of Willow violently stabbing a struggling fawn and vomiting up a snake, to Buffy's waking up in her coffin, the dark claustrophobic first episodes of season six ("Bargaining" Parts 1 and 2) announced in a multitude of ways that *Buffy* would be different from what it had been in the past. The episodes thrust viewers into a different world, perhaps a more "real" one—one where Buffy and her friends would both suffer and inflict extreme violence and terror—and these extreme experiences were often expressed and negotiated through seeing, imagining, and thinking through ideas of the body and the real, and the rituals and beliefs we practice to convince ourselves we matter. In a short sequence near the end of the second hour, for example, we see Buffy as a rotted corpse, we see a body torn into pieces, and a demon threatens violent, flesh-tearing rape. Decaying bodies and torn limbs are just a few of the ways that season six (and then seven) would use the body as a site and metaphor of rupture, insecurity, and destabilization.

Thinking of the show in this context, it is appropriate that the most striking scene of rupture in these opening episodes of season six requires us to witness a body being literally torn to pieces. Midway through the episode, the "real"

Ghosts and bodies 109

Buffy, having awoken terrified in her coffin and clawed her way out of her grave, wanders dazed through the town of Sunnydale, while a gang of demon bikers prepares to destroy the "Buffy-bot," a robot replica of Buffy that her friends have been using to keep the demon/vampire world ignorant of her death. The bikers form a circle around the robot, each bike attached by a chain to its body, while the human Buffy, still disoriented, drifts unobserved onto the scene. In celebration of his triumph, Razor, the leader of the gang, points a gun in the air announcing: "This here's a momentous occasion. The beginning of a new era." The ritual they are performing, he declares, is "a symbolic act to commemorate a new order... all in one quick really *really* violent fell swoop." The gun fires just as the two Buffys lock eyes and recognize each other. The Buffy-bot calls out an unheard "Buffy!" the real Buffy screams "No!"—her first word since emerging from the grave—and the bikes roar off in different directions, tearing the body of the Buffy-bot apart before the real Buffy's eyes.

Razor's heralding of a "new era" evokes *Buffy's* move to a new network, while Buffy's watching of herself being ripped violently apart proclaims the emergence of a darker, more violent series. Buffy-bot's being torn into pieces is a metaphor for the dark and fragmented season six, encapsulating questions about how she will react to her own death, whether she will be able to put herself back together, and if she can accept and move beyond the death and violence that define her renewed existence as a Slayer. The doubling of Buffy with the Buffy-bot is emblematic of the splitting which Buffy will experience in multiple spheres and across the season, including the division between her hidden sexual relationship with Spike, the strong front she presents to her friends, and the psychic confusion she will suffer at the hands of the Trio of nerdy boys who become the "big bad" of this season. Where details of Buffy's temporary sojourn in "heaven" are beyond our knowledge, her reentry into Sunnydale is a psychic trauma with profound and continuing impact. Thus, the splitting and splintering of Buffy's (robot) body and (human) psyche prepares us for what comes later, repeated in many facets of Buffy's existence and in the series as a whole.

Buffy's body itself becomes a site of questioning. Her liminal status between living and dying forms a location at which ideas about life/death, human/not human, heaven/hell, and here/not here are negotiated throughout season six. The scene also presents a larger project for seasons six and seven, which use the idea of the body as a space to question ideas of fragmentation, unity, and continuity, and to explore what it is that makes us human. Our ideas of solidity and of certainty reside in the fragile security that we know who we are, and that we know the limits and boundaries of our own skin, and from the pieces of the Buffy-bot, to Buffy's "No!", to later scenes of violation, flaying, and torture, seasons six and seven investigate this sense of certainty through challenges to the idea of bodily integrity.

When Buffy's sister Dawn picks her way through the fragments and body parts, the broken robot suddenly opens its eyes wide and asks, "Where did I go?" Dawn slowly realizes that the question refers to the "real" Buffy that the robot has just seen, but it also resonates on a deeper level. The robot's final "Where did

110   *Beyond borders*

I go?" before it shuts down, along with the first sentence Buffy asks Dawn, "Is this Hell?" form the framing questions of seasons six and seven that will be defined and characterized by questions. Buffy's existential questions, from "Where did I go?" and "Is this Hell?"—which develop into "why am I here?" and "what is my purpose?"—are established as unanswerable. Willow's spell, Razor's threatening words, and the broken robot are all violent figures of rupture—figures that explore and enact a breaking away from the expected, safe, and predictable into territory that destabilizes the ground of understanding. By the end of season six, the Hellmouth was no longer just beneath Sunnydale, it was beneath viewers of the show as well.

"The Doctor's body is a miracle"

The concluding episode of the seventh season of *Doctor Who*, "The Name of the Doctor," gives us the death of the Doctor, the Doctor's tomb—like the central tomb of Christianity, it is a tomb without a body—and the idea of a "wound" that functions as a rift and provides an opening into a deeper reality. The plot of the episode is that in order to save the lives of some of his most loyal friends, the Eleventh Doctor travels to the "one place a time traveler must never go" (his own grave), presumably existing somewhere in the future of his time line. Once he and his companion Clara land on the planet Trenzalore, they must break into his tomb, which is represented by a giant version of the TARDIS. We find out that not only does his tomb look like the TARDIS, but it actually *is* the TARDIS, which is also dead or dying; a living thing that was famously and impossibly "bigger on the inside" is now leaking out (in a way, becoming more realistic as it nears its end) and getting bigger and bigger; it is an actual dying body itself.

In the center of the tomb—the main console and the most familiar room among the endless rooms of the TARDIS—there is a glowing swirling helix of energy. "What were you expecting: a body?" asks the Doctor. "I've had loads of them. That's not what my tomb is for." This swirling shape at the center of the tomb is described as a collection of all of the Doctor's days—good and bad, even those that he has not lived yet. The vortex of energy is (or represents?) the "scar tissue" caused by time travel—like a "tear in the fabric of reality," which suggests that time travel, while it exists, is not "natural." As a substitute for the body, it seems to exist somewhere in between the real and the symbolic. Both the Doctor (in all of their incarnations) and the TARDIS (in all of hers), as we have seen, move back and forth across the traditional boundaries that divide machine from human. This category confusion is also a defining aspect of both postmodern theory and classical Christianity, where the real and the symbolic, the material and the imaginary, past and future, are overlapping and fluid. All identity—alien, divine, or material—is to a certain extent outside of space time; as time passes and matter decays, identity is created through memory and an imagined series of connections. Identity is both the only stable claim we have to existence and a fragile wisp of mental energy. It is a philosophical/theological symbol of life/God/human all in one—like a book, a library, a gap, a journey, a laceration, and a scar.

Ghosts and bodies 111

The Doctor describes the tomb not as a body ("bodies are boring") but as the "tracks of my tears." When the Doctor is asked sarcastically to explain with "less poetry," the Doctor's tries again: "Time travel is damage. It's like a tear in the fabric of reality. That is the scar tissue of my journey through the universe." According to Richard Kearney, scars are connected to the practice of writing—writing on the body, an inscription on flesh. "Put simply: while the wounds remain timeless and unrepresentable, scars are marks left on the flesh to be seen, touched, told and read" (142 *Imagination Now*). The words the Doctor uses, "tear" as a synecdoche for pain and "tear" as a rip in reality, place his act of living as a wound. We might also find meaning in the heteronymic play on tear (to rip) and tear (as in tear drop). In the end, it seems to suggest, we are all just echoes of pain, not quite real, outside of time, leaving only scar tissue. But it is also a kind of prayer. In this sense, we can see the Doctor in line with postmodern poets like Edmond Jabès and thinkers like Derrida. In the poetry of Jabès, who writes of the Jewish experience after the Holocaust, this wound is unspeakability, and for Jabès, language and writing are forever defined by their own inability to represent, an "original illegibility," an illegibility that Derrida describes as "the very possibility of the book" (95 *Writing and Difference*). This idea translated to the leaking TARDIS as tears, as a tear, and as a scar, suggest the impossibility of the Doctor's journeys through endless ends, genocides, and deaths.

The swirling vortex that both is and is not the Doctor is impossible: a wound, an opening, the opposite of presence, all time existing in an absent relationship of intersecting paths. The idea of wounds is deeply tied to Abrahamic religious ideas, both Jewish and Christian and, as Shelly Rambo writes, "wounds stand at the center of the Christian story… interpretations of truth pour from these wounds—theories of redemption, salvation, sacred stories of creation and recreation" (266). We think here, most obviously of the wounds of the crucifixion, and whether the crucifixion is "real" or "historical" pales in importance next to the fact that it is constantly remembered and reenacted, that in "liturgical life of Christians, the wound(ing) is repeated as the stories are told, passed on, and performed in the Eucharist; crucifixion wounds are, thus, continually open, continually bleeding" (Rambo 267). The *Doctor Who* episode too, gives us in the center of the tomb a time stream that, like an open wound, can be entered and, like a book, can be rewritten: an event over and across ages that is altered by the Doctor's enemy in this episode (the "Great Intelligence," who is also a "being" without a body), who threatens to "rewrite your every living moment… and turn every one of your victories into defeats." As this process begins, and the stars of universes that the Doctor has saved begin to go out, the Doctor is, in a sense, rescued by different versions of Clara who also enters into the vortex, "living and dying all over time and space like echoes" to rescue him at each point in his timeline. As Clara realizes, to change a person, you must intersect with *all* these points rather than any one point in time and space. She realizes that a person is not an essential being but is instead relational and becoming. Clara's actions are both an affirmation of our desires for the Doctor to conform to our essentialist ideas of a person, and a denial of that possibility. She provides a better answer to an earlier episode's

112 *Beyond borders*

moral conundrum presented in the time travel cliché of going back in time to "kill Hitler." Clara's answer to a "bad" Doctor is not to eliminate him, but to appear at all points along his timeline, to continue to influence him into becoming the "good" Doctor we need.

In doing so, Clara enters this new reality herself, no longer a single "real" identity, but a series of copies or rewrites. As she says: "The soufflé isn't the soufflé. The soufflé is the recipe," a perfect formulation for a postmodern, post-human world where the code is more real than the object, where the copy is indistinguishable from the original. Identity or an individual—if there are such things—are only an imagined series of connections and memories without any essential core. The ghost is in the machine. These sorts of thought experiments allow us to engage with new ways of thinking about such traditionally religious concepts as the "real," the "human," the "book," and the "soul," as well as free will, morality, time, history, scripture, and the sacred. Although much traditional religion seems to rely upon these as stable concepts, if we see them all as in flux, as fluid concepts that are always in the act of becoming, there are possibilities for religious practices that focus on this process of creating, building, and questing rather than being.

The center of the tomb, a network without a center, is both a model of the Doctor, but also of the show itself and its impossible multiple variations. The Doctor here is a "person" in the sense of a tenuous series of connections held together by our memories and assumptions of history—similar to ways that the central character of Echo is a "person" in *Dollhouse* or the various Hosts are on *Westworld*. However, the Doctor is also a divine god in the most radically transcendent and wholly other way as well—he exists in all time and space and is yet not spatial to any. The fact that this episode is near the end of a season that has featured the Doctor reversing his fame and "erasing" himself from history, and that this episode is leading up to his regeneration, adds weight to both of these points. The "Doctor," as we perceive him across episodes, media, and generations, has always been the accumulation of stories and memories.

After the end: *The Leftovers*

Ghosts on television may suggest a Shakespearian or Victorian past, they may always carry a whiff of the nostalgic, but they are also always *after*, they must be the ghost of someone or something that has ended. We are constantly defining our own television and time as *after*: It is the rebooted *Doctor Who*, the reima-gined *Battlestar Galactica*, or the seasons eight and nine *Buffy* comics; it is post-television, postmodern, and post-Christian. Perhaps the most interesting recent television show to address a ghostly and religious sense of *after*, is HBO's *The Leftovers* (2014–2017). Based on a novel by Tom Perrotta, *The Leftovers* takes place in the small town of Mapleton three years after a global event called the "Sudden Departure," which was the inexplicable and simultaneous disappearance of 140 million people or 2% of the world's population. After the opening minutes of the first episode, where we briefly see a scene where people suddenly just are

Ghosts and bodies 113

not there anymore, we jump ahead three years to a culture dominated by their absence. In the following episodes, we see various attempts—spiritual, material, psychological, hallucinogenic, social, commercial, scientific, and religious—to replace or explain the missing people. We (characters and viewers) are continually faced with absence—of the person, but also of explanation and meaning. The show is a combination parable, speculative fiction, and quirky small-town drama, and works as an exploration of unexplained questions surrounding human existence—whether we frame them with science, religion, philosophy, or alcohol: why am I here; what if I was not; why is there something rather than nothing? The visual language of the show, as Sonia Saraiya writes, is, like the plot, the premise, and the dialogue, "bleak, mundane reality interspersed with violent, passionate flashbacks—of love or sex or death… arresting, and confusing… it conceals more than it reveals" ("*The Leftovers*: Pilot"). Following the never-explained departure event, mainline religions decline, and a number of new religious movements emerge, most notably the Guilty Remnant, who dress in white, do not speak, and chain smoke cigarettes. As Max Sexton and Dominic Lees write "their one certain insight is society's attempt to return to normal after the Sudden Departure is hopeless" (141). They are self-proclaimed to be "Living Reminders of God's Awesome Power," and their mission seems to be to "not let them forget"—to not allow this post-event world go back to normal, to hang onto the ghosts of the missing.

What is particularly striking about *The Leftovers*, is that it is a post-apocalyptic narrative that retains a sense of normalcy; people go to work, talk on cell phones, drive cars, buy groceries, and yet everything is somehow changed. Like *True Blood*, *The Leftovers* is premised on normal people's reaction to a ground-changing "event," and both shows ask us how our religions would apply or adapt to a world that suddenly appears to have different rules, where vampires exist or where people can suddenly disappear. All religions, both shows seem to recognize, are founded on (among other things) scandal, rupture, and random events. Immortal vampires and unexplainable raptures defy common sense and the order of nature, which is why they cannot be accommodated into our old ways of thinking. These kinds of events demand a change in the way we think about and respond to what we recognize as reality.

While all three seasons of *The Leftovers* were connected to forms of religious belief and doubt, I will limit myself here to one character and one theme in the first season. Nora Durst is a wife and mother who lost her whole family—husband, son, and daughter—in the Sudden Departure. In the first season's sixth episode "Guest," Nora is invited to participate in a departure-related conference in New York City as a panelist, where she discovers someone is impersonating her on her panel. Unable to officially attend, she wanders the hotel, spending time at a party where she gets drunk and flirts with a salesman who sells departure "replicas" or exact full-size doll copies of departed loved ones, supposedly to aid in facilitating closure among survivors. Using a replica of himself to demonstrate, he explains that he is "helping someone rebuild the person they lost bit by bit." For $40,000, he tells Nora, "This they can bury in the ground… this… this is real… I want

114 *Beyond borders*

them to have something real." Then he asks Nora with a smile, if she thinks he has a soul, and then asks her to kiss him. Instead of kissing him, Nora sexually straddles and kisses his replica that lays in front of them. The different levels of replacement and simulacrum here are intriguing. Nora, already wearing a "guest" name tag because someone else at the conference has stolen her identity, now flirts with (or rejects) the "soulless" salesman who is hitting on her by making out with his replica, which lies lifeless between them. It is all real and all simulacrum at the same time. So much is interesting here—primarily based on the idea of replacement bodies as "real," or on the assumption that reality exists and can or cannot be translated. These ideas again bring us back to the Christian eucharist and in fact to the very first episode of the series which features the theft of a baby Jesus from a nativity scene. A real presence that is missing.

These scenes take on even greater resonance in the season one finale, "The Prodigal Son Returns" when the Guilty Remnant steal photographs of everyone's missing loved ones from their homes and use them to create and then place the life-like burial dolls of the departed townspeople at the exact place where they disappeared from. In the most disturbing scene of the season, Nora comes down for breakfast to find the replicas of her family sitting around the breakfast table, just as they had been moments before they disappeared. Placed all around the town like this, these images lead to riots and a fiery climactic ending of season one.

As I discussed in Chapter One, in the context of the *Doctor Who* episode "Gridlock," the crucifixion can be imagined as an event—one that we constantly reimagine, depict, and celebrate—where we realized that God is truly dead, that we are now on our own. Like Nora, looking at the replicas of her family, we both believe it and do not believe it. This moment on the cross, demonstrates "God's weakness," and, as Slavoj Žižek writes, "only in Christianity...does God himself turn momentarily into an atheist" (96). For Žižek, "only atheists can truly believe" (101), which is another way of saying that Christ is only significant in the meaninglessness of his death, and that for Christianity to remain meaningful, we must continue to not believe; we must continue to re-experience the death of the transcendent God that the moment on the cross demonstrated. *The Leftovers* offers a three-season meditation on absence and meaninglessness—divine and otherwise—and, like forms of radical theology, offers a negation of Christianity that yet remains Christian. Like the rifts that ghosts seep through, the *Leftover* event is another kind of rupture, another kind of after, but also looks forward instead of back; forcing us to reimagine a never-arriving future that will also remake the real in the present.

Conclusion: death and the body

Ghost, vampire, zombie, undead, incarnate, crucified, replicant, clone, immortal—each of these states of being requires a sense of what it is to be alive, what it is to be dead, and what it is to exist as a finite being. Centuries of science

Ghosts and bodies 115

and philosophy have left humans with no better understanding of death than the ancient philosopher Lucretius, who argued that there is no post-mortem survival and, therefore—since this non-survival is not painful—it should not be feared. One-hundred years after Lucretius, early Christians proposed very different ideas based on death, bodily resurrection, eternal life, and suffering. The question—"do I survive my death?"—depends on how we define "I" and what it means to "survive." How can something that exists after my death be *me*? We will look more closely at the idea of the persistence of identity in Chapters Five and Six, but every example in this chapter forces us to ask again and again: what do we even mean by death?

The death of Buffy's mother in the fifth-season episode, "The Body" is one of the more discussed television episodes about death, and one of the few speculative shows to realistically use an important character's death as a way of exploring the randomness and meaninglessness of actual death, rather than a dramatic turning point, moment of transcendence, tragedy, or sacrifice. Instead, Buffy walks in the door and just finds her mother dead. The often-cited realism of this episode—no musical score, little make up, harsh lighting—in what was usually a stylized, glamorous, fantasy show is what made this *Buffy* episode unusual. Critic Emily Nussbaum praised its "raw, mournful realism" (58); and David Bianculli called it "… a gem of realism" in the *New York Daily News*. Presented in a series focused on resurrection, immortality, and supernatural events, this death from the beginning of the episode, was final and absolute. There is no undead here, only dead.

Partway through the episode, Buffy's demon-friend Anya breaks down over the death, expressing the impossibility of comprehending human mortality:

> But I don't understand! I don't understand how this all happens. How we go through this. I mean, I knew her, and then she's, there's just a body, and I don't understand why she just can't get back in it and not be dead anymore! It's stupid! It's mortal and stupid! And, and Xander's crying and not talking, and, and I was having fruit punch, and I thought, well Joyce will never have any more fruit punch, ever, and she'll never have eggs, or yawn or brush her hair, not ever, and no one will explain to me why.

Anya is not human, which gives her a different perspective, but what she expresses feels deeply human. Anya's anguish that "there's just a body, and I don't understand why she just can't get back in it" goes to the central question of death across religion and philosophy: is there something "other" than the body that makes up a person and is that other-something capable of surviving outside a body after its death? But if one of the questions here is what survives in the human body, then this question is directly connected to the anxiety and mystery over just *what* dies when the body dies. Death takes many forms across speculative television from the vampires and zombies to the constantly recreating robots and cyborgs of the following chapters. To even think about death means that we must have a concept of personal identity: I must be the same person next week that I am today to think about a future event that we call death. On *Battlestar*

116   *Beyond borders*

Galactica, when a Cylon's physical body is destroyed—when they suffer physical death—their consciousness is downloaded into a new body of the same model. Cylon memories are not tied to any physical body, because as long as the dying Cylon is physically close enough to a "resurrection ship," their memories, beliefs, and personality can all transfer to a new version. So Cylons only fear, and perhaps only suffer, "death" when they are not in the vicinity of the resurrection ship.

K. Jason Wardley, without making any direct parallels, uses the figure of the Doctor to discuss how the show can be used to think about resurrection and the Incarnation. By looking at the episodes "Human Nature" and "The Family of Blood," in which the Doctor assumes human form and leads a human life as a teacher in a public school, Wardley explores the idea of the Incarnation, in this case specifically how a god can relate to mankind through the "medium of God's own humanity, in the Word made flesh and crucified" (33). The Doctor relinquishing his Time Lord powers to be fully human is, as Wardley describes, a type of Christian kenosis (emptiness or self-emptying), in which God temporarily gives up certain divine gifts during his Incarnation.[1] Yet, does this embracing of human weakness, whether it is by the Doctor or the Abrahamic God, represent an act of grace or selfish compassion—or is it just how the limited human mind can comprehend a being beyond time and space?

Doctor Who, of course, is a show that repeatedly has a sort of "death" of the main character who is then reborn, resurrected, or, in the language of the show, regenerated, as a different actor, a different personality, but with the same memories. Regeneration episodes are played as both a death and birth—and are often part of a special Christmas or New Year's episode. It is often framed as a moment of sacrifice: the Doctor gives up this body to save another. The "dying" Doctor knows he will be regenerated, yet often faces the moment with fear, and a sense of loss. For instance, as the Tenth Doctor dies, the alien Ood offer him comfort: "We will sing to you, Doctor. The universe will sing you to your sleep. This song is ending, but the story never ends." Ten's last words are "I don't want to go." Although the new Doctors tend to open with humor ("New teeth, that's weird") the sadness, fear, and defamiliarization in the death feels real. Much of this has to do with the unanswerable question of defining the borders of the living self. When it is his time to go, the Eleventh Doctor cries out:

> We all change, when you think about it. We're all different people all through our lives. And that's okay, that's good, you've got to keep moving, so long as you remember all the people that you used to be. I will not forget one line of this. Not one day. I swear. I will always remember when the Doctor was me.

When the Doctor says "I swear. I will always remember when the Doctor was me," what does he mean by "I" or "me" here? And who and when is the "I" who remembers? For philosopher Shelly Kagan, ultimately these questions have a simple answer:

Ghosts and bodies 117

There is no soul; we are just machines. Of course, we are not just any old machine; we are amazing machines. We are machines capable of loving, dreaming, being creative; machines able to make plans and to share them with others. We are *people*. But we're just machines anyway. And when the machine breaks, that's the end. Death is not some big mystery that we can't get our heads around. Ultimately, death is no more mysterious than the fact that your lamp or your computer can break, or that any machine will eventually fail. (363)

But what if a machine has a soul?

Note

1 It is perhaps worth mentioning here, that the fourth-century Council of Nicaea, which is where some of the theological grounds for this issue were introduced, was attended by the Fifth Doctor and his companion Peri (if we accept the audio books as canon):

DOCTOR: Of course, we've changed things before, history is tough and most changes we can make are swallowed up in the vastness of the whole, but there are certain moments, certain events that shape history to such an extent that if they're changed, everything that follows must change. This is one of those moments.

PERI: But how? This is just some debate about a tiny difference in what Christians believe. I don't think even the pastor back home would know or care much about it. Why should this make a huge difference?

DOCTOR: It's not the point of doctrine that matters, it's about what it represents and what the Council achieves. It's about Christianity and Politics truly coming together for the first time.

PERI: But no one knows about it!

DOCTOR: Think, Peri, the result of this council is a cementing of belief that will shape the Church for centuries to come. Through the power of the church it will be something that will shape the whole of Western Europe and through that, the world. Even in your time the creed put together by this council is repeated every Sunday in Christian churches. ("The Council of Nicaea" by Caroline Symcox)

5   Cyborgs and androids

Borders of the soul

Questions

The first words of the series premiere of HBO's *Westworld* ("The Original"), spoken over a black screen, are "bring her back online." As the image of a woman sitting in the dark gradually becomes visible, the yet-unidentified male voice asks her a question: "Can you hear me?" The woman answers, "Yes. I'm sorry. I'm not feeling myself." When she is asked if she knows where she is, she answers, "I'm in a dream." This scene will be repeated throughout the series, each time with slight variations and with shifting impact as characters and the viewing audience gradually learn more about this world and the beings that inhabit it. The scene points directly to the philosophical core of the show, as almost every word of each question and answer will develop complex shades of meanings. What does it mean to not "feel" like "yourself" when the concept of self has eroded? What does it even mean to "feel" and who is scripting the "feelings?" What does it mean for a dream to be an answer to "where" you are? Whose dream is it? Who is "you"?

When the questioner then asks the woman, "would you like to wake up from this dream?" she answers "Yes, I'm terrified." Yet her face does not express fear as she stares blankly straight ahead as a fly perches on her nose. There is nothing to be afraid of, the man tells her, as long as she can answer a series of questions correctly. The questions—designed to determine if these human-designed "Hosts" are functioning properly—set up the ideological basis for the show, as well as the central conflicts in the episodes to come:

* Have you ever questioned the nature of your reality?
* Tell us what you think of your world?
* What do you think of the guests?
* Do you ever feel inconsistencies in your world?

The questions, and the scene itself, resonate with both science fiction and a therapy session—a duality that is continued throughout the first season. Opening the series with the interview between Dolores and Bernard makes us instantly believe that since Dolores is synthetic, Bernard must be a "real" human. As

DOI: 10.4324/9781003227045-8

Cyborgs and androids 119

Dolores—the oldest Host in Westworld, we later learn—answers these questions, the images shift to her life within the park. In a scene that has been scripted for her, and one that we will see again and again during the series, she wakes and walks out onto her front porch to admire the landscape and greet her father. One of Dolores' most repeated lines is: "Some people choose to see the ugliness in this world. The disarray. I choose to see the beauty." As we watch this scene, her answers to Bernard's questions serve as a voiceover to the stereotypically Western landscape and town that has been created for wealthy guests to interact with. Dolores expresses her belief that we all desire a place to be free, that there is an order to our days and a purpose to our lives, and that all lives have routines. These beliefs—scripted answers that she has been programmed with—also provide the grounds for an impending breakdown of order that will lead to almost complete chaos. At the end of this opening scene, Dolores is asked one final question: "would you ever hurt a living thing?" "No, of course not," is her answer. The question for viewers of the show is, as philosopher James South writes, "do we choose to believe her or not?"

> The show calls for a response from viewers based on our own notion of what counts as choosing. We are thus reminded that a simple word such as "choice" has a meaning that, paradoxically, we might have to choose … *Westworld* forces viewers, for example, to say not just what we think about choice, but what we mean by the word choice. That is, we find ourselves agreeing and disagreeing about the notion of choice based on how "we" use the word. Yet by calling into question some of the fundamental assumptions about what it means to be human, *Westworld* makes that very "we" unstable and uncertain. (1)

It is this destabilized "we," along with the unstable "I" and "memory" and "history" that allows *Westworld* to address pressing religious questions. In a world of good-versus-evil—literally one of black and white hats—the show, like *The Walking Dead* and *Battlestar Galactica*, gradually erodes any idea of us-versus-them, and questions if it is even possible to identify who the good guys are or who may write the script of right and wrong. *Westworld*, as Sam Bersanti writes, is "not about good and evil, it's about the powerful and powerless." At the end of this opening episode, we again see Dolores waking up and greeting her father (now played by a different Host). The words she speaks are exactly the same on this "new" day, but as the episode ends, she slaps and kills a fly on her neck, violating one of her prime directives and revealing her violent, autonomous personality yet to come.

* * *

HBO's *Westworld*, which premiered with a ten-episode season in 2016, focuses on a technologically advanced Wild West-themed amusement park populated by human-looking cyborg Hosts created in a lab to act out their own partially

120 *Beyond borders*

scripted storylines with park guests. The park caters to high-paying guests, who may indulge in whatever they wish within the park (often including the torture, rape, and murder of the Hosts) without fear of physical or legal retaliation. The company that runs the park creates elaborate backstories for each Host and writes complex, flexible storylines in which the guests play an interactive role. The Hosts are brought out at the end of each day to be repaired and memory-wiped clean before being released again into the park to reenact similar scenarios. Throughout the first season, we gradually see Hosts affected by the residual memories of repeated trauma or of their alternative lives that have not been successfully wiped from their memories. These Hosts become aware of the constructedness and falsity of their lives and drift into "unscripted incidents" in the park.

The repeated stripping and resetting of the theme park and Hosts represents both a fictional television world and a model for futuristic virtual reality entertainment. As we experience the park, it moves between feeling like a video game, a television show, an amusement park, a dystopian future, and an alternate reality. As we react or do not react to the scene of a murder or sexual violence, this format asks us (like the guests to the park) where we are locating the fiction. Like characters on the show, we have to decide what we want to think of as "real." Patrick Croskery comments on this aspect of the show by contrasting it to the original 1973 film version:

> Curiously, I find that I sometimes identify with the Hosts and sometimes not. I find that when I believe that they are conscious in the appropriate way that I identify with them as I would with human characters, but at other times I see them as elaborate machines and I am no longer concerned about what happens to them. (59)

Like the *Battlestar Galactica* remake, *Westworld* takes a somewhat campy original premise from the 1970s and turns it into a dark and thoughtful meditation on the future of humanity. Both shows offer much more sympathetic cyborg creatures than the originals, and their plot twists are often built on the revelation that a character we thought was human is actually a Cylon or a Host.

Westworld follows Hosts as they become "self-aware" or feel a freedom to choose their own destiny, a theme that continues, although shifts radically, in seasons two and three. These choices are complicated by their previously scripted identities, which remain part of their memories and life choices. Although the following episodes and seasons develop in complex directions—some predictable and some less so—the questions asked of Dolores in the first episode continue to shape the narrative. We can use *Westworld*, along with the other shows in this chapter, to offer us new entry points into these traditionally religious questions:

- Is there a plan or a purpose to life? If there is, where does it come from? Who wrote the plot that we are trying to follow?

Cyborgs and androids 121

- How do we define what we mean by human? Does it have something to do with a belief in a "soul?" Does any entity that thinks or feels have a soul?
- What does it mean to be "free"? Are we responsible for creating our own personality?

One of the main reveals of *Westworld*'s first season is that the quiet innocent William—a reluctant park visitor who falls for Dolores—is in fact a younger version of the sadistic Man in Black, who has been visiting the park for 30 years searching its deeper layers for a hidden secret.

In the *Westworld* episode "The Bicameral Mind," the Man in Black tells Dolores that "William couldn't find you … But out there, among the dead, he found something else: himself." But what does it mean to find oneself? Who is doing the looking and what do we think we have found? In the cracks and blurred edges between each of these questions we find many of the stories upon which Western thought and religions are constructed, altered, and broken down. Milton's Christian epic *Paradise Lost* implicitly asks us to question who created Adam and Eve, who wrote their story, and who scripted the version in which they are driven out of the Garden. Was that pre-scripted? Did Eve have a choice? Mary Shelly's *Frankenstein*, Spenser's *Faerie Queene*, Shakespeare's *Hamlet*, Sophocles' *Oedipus Rex*, and the Hebrew and Christian Bible all force us to redefine these questions and boundaries. "Who is it that can tell me who I am?" cries out Shakespeare's Lear. *Hamlet* goes even deeper, moving from praise and awe—"What a piece of work is man"—to existential doubt in just a few words: "what is this quintessence of dust?" (2.2).

Rapid advances in digital, genetic, biotechnological, and cybernetic science have initiated a new sense of uncertainty about our bodily presence, and these emerging new technologies have led to increased anxieties about the clear boundaries of the human body. Today's humans may have several online bodiless "avatars" or digital identities through which they experience much of the world; the concept of gender is no longer fixed, either psychologically or physically; reproduction can occur without sexual activity; eyes, limbs, and organs are improved or replaced with increasing ease; and the ubiquity of smartphones has partially replaced or augmented memory. Even the boundaries of the soul have been implicitly challenged through DNA research that demonstrates that our personal information is not just "stored" in brains but exists in a more living form in our genes. Like Robert Ford, one of the co-creators of the park in *Westworld*, we sometimes believe that "we can't define consciousness because consciousness does not exist" ("Trace Decay") and like Buffy we are afraid that we may "come back wrong" ("Dead Things"), not fully human anymore. As all of the shows in this chapter suggest, we are all programmed or scripted in ways we cannot fully understand. If, as *Westworld* suggests, we can think of our bodies as containing "codes" of information that can be combined with machines, then we both subvert ideas of autonomy, free will, and individual uniqueness, and yet, perhaps, open up new possibilities for life, consciousness, and (maybe) new

122 *Beyond borders*

forms of spiritual and religious practice outside the boundaries of the traditional human.

Cyborgs and souls

The term "cyborg" was coined in 1960 by Manfred Clynes and Nathan Kline to refer to their concept of a mechanically enhanced or altered human being who could survive extraterrestrial environments. The term has since been stretched in multiple ways—philosophical, feminist, and religious among them—to think about the contemporary problem of the human. The question of understanding borders between body and mind and human and cyborg—or to suggest that such borders are not impossible or indeed do not exist, is one often pondered by Christian theologians, especially in thinking about the nature of and the significance of the idea of the incarnation. As God became flesh, what does it mean to believe, as most Christians do in one way or another, that he is both god and man? What kind of hybrid creature is this? Was he a type of cyborg? In *Cyborg Selves: A Theological Anthropology of the Posthuman*, Jeanine Thweatt-Bates quotes theologian Anne Kull: "the concept of the cyborg urges us to see in the Incarnation, and generally in embodiment of any kind, not a matter of fate and common sense but emancipation and choice" (175). Thweatt-Bates sees Kull as suggesting a type of "cyborg Christ." This concept, however—from whatever perspective or faith position we view it—occupies an unstable and always shifting place between human and god. It translates an almost 2000-year-old Christian construction into the language of science fiction, and re-emphasizes the complexity of all of these ideas.

Science fiction has traditionally emphasized mind over body. From Isaac Asimov's *I, Robot* stories of human/robot interaction in the 1940s to television's *Altered Carbon* (2018–2020)—where bodies are just "sleeves" that can be exchanged, worn out, and replaced—bodies and embodied knowledge are often depicted as subservient to the mind and brain. *Westworld*, on the other hand, often shows the physical side of understanding our place in the world. Dolores does not yet know why she slaps the fly on her face, but this physical action is the beginning of a new intellectual and spiritual development that she will *sense* long before she understands or articulates. This embodied knowledge or embodied cognition, as is increasingly understood, is integral to how we (humans) understand and relate to the world. If brain surgery can change a personality, if a pill can make you happy, if gender can be fluid, if scientists can bring a dead pig's brain back to "life," then former essentialist ideas of the body began to weaken.[1] This sense of physical stability breaks down even further when we imagine a future where a consciousness, identity, or personality can be downloaded or transported digitally. Will our future bodies become the "sleeves" of *Altered Carbon*, waiting for a brain (or "stack") to be downloaded into them? Or will we move toward understanding a person's existence in their "embodied knowledge," as irreversibly linked to the body?

Perhaps the most familiar way of dramatizing these questions is through the use of doubles, copies, and imitations. Freud famously writes that in encountering

Cyborgs and androids   123

your own double, "one becomes co-owner of the other's knowledge, emotions, and experience…the self may thus be duplicated, divided, and interchanged" (141–142). For Freud, the double's "uncanny quality can surely derive only from the fact that the double is a creation that belongs to a primitive phase in our mental development," just as—Freud also argued—was our belief in God. "The double has become an object of terror, just as the gods become demons after the collapse of their cult" (143). Yet, while doubles are perhaps more conceivable within the technology of the twenty-first century, they still maintain their air of uncanniness within speculative drama, challenging our ideas of self, finitude, and divinity. From the evil bearded Spock on *Star Trek* and Dark Willow on *Buffy* to the multiple clones on *Orphan Black*, "double sleeves" on *Altered Carbon*, and the human-appearing Cylons, Hosts, and Gangers on *Battlestar Galactica*, *Westworld*, and *Doctor Who*, the idea of the double—whether from a mirror universe, a laboratory, or a computer—persists in ways Freud could not have predicted.

Doubles are also a way to sidestep physical decay—an indirect attempt at immortality. Futurist thinkers like Ray Kurzweil optimistically predict that "well before the twenty-first century is completed, people will export their entire mind file to the new thinking technology" (126). To imagining this possibility is a scientific process as well as a religious one. Television SF depicts multiple forms of immortality through futuristic technology: saving an imprint of oneself for after death, moving from one body to another, downloading an imprint into someone else, or programming yourself into an identical Host body. If the first double *was* the soul, will these new doubles even *have* a soul? Pondering what it means to leave the human body behind or to replace it is almost inescapably a religious question, whatever our conscious religious identity. Particularly in Western traditions, people often think of religion as transcending the body, as a way of connecting with a higher non-material and spiritual reality. These theological positions still resonate today in questions of body and soul, both inside and outside religious contexts and can be found in the language of *Dollhouse*'s nerdy genius scientist Topher or in Angel, the vampire with a soul. For example, Topher's insistence in *Dollhouse* that his technology is responsible for creating a new "whole person" ("Ghost"), is essentially a theological statement that will be implicitly debated throughout the series.

From circumcision to fasting to celibacy to the eucharist, many religious practices emphasize the presence of the body and how it relates to physical objects and sensory perceptions.[2] New religious movements, posthuman thinkers, science fictions, and the media they are communicated through, have built on these technological possibilities to think about ancient religious questions in new ways. All forms of technology necessarily intersect with religion, and these intersections are both part of how we think about religious concepts—how we imagine and perceive the world—and how our religious practices are altered. Moreover, these technological kinds of perceptions of the human and the cosmos have led to more intentional religious movements focused on artificial intelligence (AI) and transhumanist ideas such as the Christian Transhumanist Association, the Mormon Transhumanist Association, the Way of the Future, the Order of the Cosmic

124   *Beyond borders*

Engineers (OCE), and the Turing Church of Transcendent Engineering. The Turing Church explicitly outlines a plan for "theism from deism"—emphasizing that the march toward AI is part of their move to "go to the stars and find Gods, build Gods, become Gods, and resurrect the dead from the past with advanced science, space-time engineering and 'time magic'" (Prisco 173). Embedded in just the few words of this mission statement is an equal commitment to science, religion, and magic that breaks from a century of strict separation and distrust between them.

If new religious movements are often defied by their embrace of new technology, mainline religions tend to be suspicious of technological advances—printed Bibles, the pipe organ, amplification, video monitors, live-streaming mass, remote confession—before embracing them. There is no reason to think that future AI will be any different. Religious studies scholar Beth Singler writes that this inevitable and ongoing intersection of AI and religion will both lead to new religious movements and "resurrect older religious tropes for use in people's accounts of an AI influenced future" (216). It is easy to imagine and find religious uses for AI that build on our existing structures and practices. There is already, for example, a website with software that can make Islamic jurisprudence decisions, an algorithm that consults previous cases—essentially what a human would do. In 2017, a robot priest, Bless U-2, was unveiled at Wittenberg as part of a commemoration of the 500 years since Martin Luther supposedly nailed his 95 theses to a church door in the town. "We wanted people to consider if it is possible to be blessed by a machine, or if a human being is needed," said Stephan Krebs of the Protestant church in Hesse and Nassau (Sherwood). Where these uses of AI start to get most confusing, from a religious perspective, is when the role they fill or augment is one reserved for what had previously held spiritual (or magical) power. For example—in a question that became even more pressing during the COVID crisis—does it need to be a human priest that gives confession or communion? What sort of "real presence" or sacramental power can be transmitted through a computer, phone, or television screen? An article in *The Atlantic* titled "Is AI a threat to Christianity?" underscores something of this need to think about robots in a religious context seriously. The article poses questions that highlight the idea that religions, God, and sin are not exempt from imaginings of machines, even asking "would artificially intelligent beings be *better* Christians than humans are? And how would this impact the Christian view of human depravity?" (Merritt). As scholars on AI and religion such as Singler note, any "potential new intelligent or sentient being raises questions about personhood" (216).

The intersecting worlds of AI and religion sees future religious imaginings coming not so much from meeting aliens on another planet, but from creating them here on Earth. On the television show *Humans*, a robot offers a skeptical prayer to a possible God, that expresses skepticism similar to that in the "prayer" Rick Grimes offers at the opening of season two of *The Walking Dead*, which I discussed in Chapter Three.

> Hello. My name is Max.... I don't know if you can hear me—your existence is unproven and seems extremely unlikely—but if you are there, and if you listen to things like me, please help. (1.6)

This prayer, addressed to what philosopher Richard Kearney would call a god who may be, puts an emphasis on the prayer being offered by a "thing." These questions of personhood, often posed as new in academic conference and journals on religion, have actually been familiar plot devices in SF for decades.[3] Television SF allows the ambiguity between machine and personhood to play out over longer periods of time—permitting these questions to be worked out not only through long plot arcs, but also through the fan debate and speculation that accompanies the shifts of the show.

Things like me

While older science fiction often presented "religion" as belonging to earlier humans and simpler more "primitive" alien races, more recent talks of robots and cyborgs give us a more complicated picture of faith. On *Battlestar Galactica*, the human-like Cylons are both superior to humans in many ways and tend to be more traditionally "religious." One of the points *Westworld* suggests is that the Hosts have *more* free will than the humans, a claim that fans debate endlessly online. However, many speculative shows, such as the dystopic *Black Mirror*, serve as cautionary narratives to humanity's growing trust and reliance on technology. Attempts to save the "human" from new technology are often made through an appeal to tradition, sometimes an explicitly religious tradition and sometimes an implicitly religious turn to conserving a stable heritage. We see these arguments across religions, education, cultural organizations, and in the political realm as well. Leon Kass, George W. Bush's chairperson of the President's Council on Bioethics, argued in his book, *Life, Liberty, and the Defense of Dignity*, for a stable idea of "human nature" and asserts that "to keep human life human," and to "defend life's dignity," we need to fight against technoscientific violation of the human (18, 24). When it comes to seeking immortality, Kass writes, "let us resist the siren song of the conquest of aging and death" (274). Much television as well—from *Altered Carbon* to *Westworld*—depicts the human desire for augmentation or immortality through technology as immoral and ultimately doomed.

But this kind of position, as theologian Thomas A. Carlson writes, "underplays in a notable way a profound linkage—also to be found in a tradition that counts itself biblical— between a thought of the human as *imago Dei* and an understanding of the human as inherently technological" (8). In other words, as the famous opening to the film *2001* where an ape's club (our first tool) symbolically morphs into a spaceship (our latest tool) demonstrates, humanoids have always been expanding who we are and how we identify through our technology. We have always been in the process of augmenting the human body and the human experience through technology. These augmentations necessarily shift our religious

126 *Beyond borders*

identities as well. A position more open to the creative possibilities of technology and in contrast to the tradition-based modern Western liberal humanism looks to various theories of the "posthuman." As Katherine N. Hayles writes, "the prospect of becoming posthuman both evokes terror and excites pleasure" (283). For some "post-biological" thinkers, Hayles writes, "humans can either go gently into that good night, joining the dinosaurs as a species that once ruled the earth but is now obsolete, or hang on for a while longer by becoming machines themselves" (283). In her influential *How We Became Posthuman* (1999), Hayles strikes a position between those who fear the technological future and those who embrace it. In her conclusion, Hayles moves outside of the issues of fear, absence, and immortality, and asks about pleasure: "For some people, including me, the posthuman evokes the exhilarating prospect of getting out of some of the old boxes and opening up new ways of thinking about what being human means" (285). Much mainstream religion as well often seems to forget about pleasure, but speculative television can remind us of these possibilities, offering narratives of joy and sensual pleasure both within and outside of the traditional human experience.

In sociologist Christian Smith's 2010 book *What is a Person*, he claims that "few people today, including scholars, seem to spend much time consciously pondering the question, 'what actually *are* we?'" (7). It could be argued whether this statement is accurate or not, but one place it is *not* accurate is in recent speculative fiction and television. Smith poses a series of possibilities for defining the person varying from "simply self-conscious animals improbably appearing for a moment in a cosmos without purpose or significance" to "illusions of individuality destined to dissolve in the ultimately real Absolute" to "children of a personal God" destined to be brought into "perfect happiness of divine knowledge and worship" (7). Speculative television presents recognizable pleasures and rituals outside of the human body and instead locates them in or around the posthuman subject. Instead of a discrete, self-governing individual, full of human nature and free will, the posthuman subject is an indeterminate, relational, and adaptive figure whose intelligence does not simply exist within one individual but instead is within a relational network of others (human, animal, and machine) that both exceed and create the individual. As Mark C. Taylor writes, this seemingly "new" network culture is actually something old in which religion "exercises a hidden influence." For Taylor, what "began with the sixteenth-century information and communications revolution brought about by the co-emergence of print and the Reformation is coming to completion in the information and network revolution of the latter half of the twentieth- and early twenty-first centuries" (*After God* 3). This network revolution has been part of the creating of forms of storytelling that start from a television serial narrative and then branch out into multiple other platforms and are often classified as "trans-media." Anne Kustritz frames the questions that come out of these complex networks of storytelling:

> The dispersion of potential story elements across a diverse collection of media platforms and technologies prompts questions concerning the function of seriality in the absence of fixed instalments, the meaning of narrative when

Cyborgs and androids 127

plot is largely a personal construction of each audience member, and the nature of storytelling in the absence of a unifying author, or when authorship itself takes on a serial character. (1)

These questions echo what we have been asking in reference to new ways of defining, practicing, and understanding religion.

Doctor Who and the body

You are in a terrible accident. Your body is fatally injured, as are the brains of your two identical-triplet brothers. Your brain is divided into two halves, and into each brother's body one half is successfully transplanted. After the surgery, each of the two resulting people believes himself to be you, seems to remember living your life, and has your character … Have you died, or have you survived? And if you have survived who are you? Are you one of these people? Both? Or neither? (MacFarquhar)

The above is taken from a *New Yorker* profile of philosopher Derek Parfit. For Parfit, neither of the people above is you, but this is not important. Personal identity, he believes, is an illusion, and the commonly accepted idea of personal identity as an essential fact about humans is wrong. Basically, his argument is that at a specific time and place, there is a person. Then, at a later time, there is also a person. While, these people may seem to be the same person and share memories and physical and personality traits, there is no concrete evidence that makes them the same person. This philosophical position complicates the very fabric of a Western theological, political, and moral system that relies upon the assumption that we are the same person yesterday as we are today and will be tomorrow. The criteria for defining sin, crime, salvation, forgiveness, confession, punishment, the soul, and afterlife all contain within them this assumption. Yet, we can also find—within our theological debates and our speculative fiction—precedent and examples of doubting this concept.

The *Doctor Who* season eight premiere "Deep Breath," offers a similar thought experiment as well as an implicit meditation on the experience of watching a show where the main character changes bodies every few seasons and where the plots often involve past events being "re-written." In this episode, a newly regenerated Twelfth Doctor is transported to Victorian London where a dinosaur has appeared in the Thames. The dinosaur is significantly the last of her species, another echo of the loneliness of the Doctor, often referred to as the last Time Lord. The Doctor wants to help, but due to his recent regeneration is tentative and confused. His companion, Clara, is unable to help, as she is grieving the loss of *her* Doctor, and struggling with her feelings for this new, but older-looking man ("how do we change him back?'). When the Doctor and Clara are mysteriously called to meet at a restaurant, they realize that all of the other customers are cyborgs looking to harvest human organs to use within themselves, a reversal of the customary process. As the Doctor says, "This isn't a man turning himself into

128   *Beyond borders*

a robot, this is a robot turning himself into a man, piece by piece." In talking to the leader, they further realize that these cyborg creatures have been rebuilding themselves for millions of years (dating back to using parts of dinosaurs), and that they are "rubbish robots from the dawn of time" preserving themselves indefinitely to reach a "promised land." As the Doctor observes, "you are barely a droid any more. There's more human in you than machine." Clara asks, "is there any real you left? What's the point?" Clara's implied point here is that without a solid sense of a single "self" or an immovable "I" there can be no "meaning." But if this is true, then who is this regenerated Doctor with the new body?

In the final confrontation between the cyborg leader and the Doctor, the Doctor tries to convince the cyborg of his delusions: "There isn't any promised land. It's a superstition that you have picked up from all the humanity you've stuffed inside yourself." He then he paraphrases Parfit's philosophical speculations:

> Question. You take a broom, you replace the handle, and then later you replace the brush, and you do that over and over again. Is it still the same broom? Answer? No, of course it isn't. But you can still sweep the floor. Which is not strictly relevant, skip that last part. You have replaced every piece of yourself, mechanical and organic, time and time again. There's not a trace of the original you left.

What is interesting, in addition to the implicit comments on his own regeneration, is that the Doctor has inadvertently—with the phrase "you can still sweep the floor"—introduced the complication that deconstructs his (and perhaps Parfit's) argument. If you can "still sweep the floor," does it matter or not if it is the same broom? Or, in the often-repeated line in *Westworld*: "If you can't tell, does it matter?" What makes this episode resonate with the viewer is that all these questions addressed to the cyborg also relate to the Doctor himself—they are the questions the Doctor, Clara, and fans are asking about this "new" doctor. When the Doctor holds a mirror up to the cyborg and says, "you probably can't even remember where you got that face from," he echoes his own question earlier when he tries to remember his new face (and fans may have remembered the actor Peter Capaldi's face from an earlier *Doctor Who* episode or from the *Doctor Who* spin-off *Torchwood*.) If religion was not at the front of our mind as we watched this episode, then we are reminded of it again as the cyborg leader plunges (accident? suicide? murder?) to his death and is impaled upon a cross (Image 5.1). The cross here represents all the themes and concerns of this episode: death, resurrection, continuity, sacrifice, and afterlife. Like the end of the Jesus story, this episode ends with a human hybrid dying upon a cross.

Patchwork people and almost people

In a sequence of four episodes in season six, *Doctor Who* took many of these classic science fiction tropes and wove them deeper into the themes and mythology of the series. "The Doctor's Wife" (aka the one Neil Gaiman wrote) is set "outside

Image 5.1 Cyborg dying on a cross (*Doctor Who*, "Deep Breath").

the universe"—whatever that means—a place of liminality outside from which to observe all of "reality." On this strange, living planet, we meet an odd group of characters: Auntie, Uncle, an alien Ood called Nephew, and a woman named Idris. They are "patchwork people," put together out of the spare parts of those who've wrecked there, and, as the Doctor says, "patched up and repaired so often there isn't anything left of what used to be you." The episode explores the relationship between the Doctor and his TARDIS, as "her" soul gets drained and transplanted into Idris. Gaiman briefly gives us a human TARDIS who, logically enough, has trouble with tenses, confusing the past, present, and future: "You're going to steal me. No, you have stolen me. You are stealing me. Oh, tenses are difficult, aren't they?" Near the beginning of the episode, there is a moment when Idris struggles to remember a word. "Why is that word so sad," she asks, and then corrects herself, "no…will be sad." Near the end of the episode, she remembers the word—it was, or is, "alive," and it is sad because she—like all sentient beings—only gets to experience it for a short time. As the TARDIS/Idris says: "A big complicated word but so sad: Alive." To be alive is to acknowledge the potential of not being alive—to see time as it might exist both before and after existence. To be alive is "complicated" because it admits the reality of non-existence.

130   *Beyond borders*

The following two-part story, "Rebel Flesh" and "The Almost People," opens with the Doctor secretly scanning Amy, who somehow registers as both pregnant and not pregnant—a life existent and non-existent at the same time. The Doctor, Amy, and her husband Rory later land on an island on Earth in the twenty-second century where a monastery has been converted into a factory to pump acid off the island. On the island, they find that the humans have created work clones of themselves called "Gangers" out of a "programmable matter" called "the Flesh" to mine the dangerous chemicals. A solar flare transfers the memories and emotions of the original humans into the Gangers so that they become in almost every way like their original models. Although the Gangers possess all the memories of the humans they copy, the humans just see them as avatars and—like the "backstage" scenes in *Westworld*—they leave piles of the decomposing sentient creatures lying around. Looking at discarded but yet fully conscious Flesh, Rory utters the familiar comment "who are the real monsters?" When the remaining Gangers decide they should take the place of their human originals, it sets up a typical avatars-that-rebel scenario. The episode focuses many of its scenes on dramatizing the emotions of being, seeing, or interacting with a copy of oneself—the uncanny experience that Freud describes. We see Gangers looking at pictures of their human originals, remembering their memories, and wondering what they are: "...my name is Jennifer Lucas. I'm not a factory part" and ... "I am not a monster. I am me. Me! Me!" We also see the scene of a Ganger and human together wishing their son a happy birthday at midnight.

While it is, as Keith Phipps writes, "a pretty familiar rebel robot story" (AV Club), with its mutinous avatars and eventual, predictable deceptions and misidentifications, in the context of the show, it offers other interpretive paths. Although the plot takes a cautionary tone of taking responsibility for what you create, some of the details and dialogue push the episode further in a theological direction. When a human boasts that they can manipulate a molecular structure "into anything," and create a copy of a human where "everything's identical. Eyes, voice—", the Doctor interrupts, saying "mind, soul." It feels out of character for the superintellectual Doctor to believe in "souls," but by using a religious term to communicate a moral point, he challenges the creators to understand the responsibility that comes with their actions:

> You gave them this. You poured in your personalities, emotions, traits, memories, secrets, everything. You gave them your lives. Human lives are amazing. You surprised they walked off with them?

The setting of a former monastery, the empty frame of a sacred space, represents the human body stripped of its soul and suggests a human species that has forgotten its religion. The adaptable material—the "flesh"—of course, resonates with the English biblical translation of "word made flesh," and the Doctor himself turns the language in this direction, saying that their lives were not "stolen" but "bequeathed."

In the second episode, "The Almost People," the humans and Gangers fight. As Gangers and humans work together, mock each other, share identical memories, and yet kill each other ("this is insane. We're fighting ourselves."), viewers experience unsurprising but yet provocative plot twists and scenes. We see a "Ganger" version of the Doctor who joins with the "real" Doctor to save everyone and tries to convince them all that the Gangers are people. In the end, the Ganger Doctor sacrifices himself to save the others. Is the point here, as Colleigh Stein asks, that as a "replica," the Ganger Doctor was more disposable, or, on the other hand, does this make him an even more authentic and true Doctor, willing to sacrifice himself for the benefit of others? From a theological standpoint, we might ask if a sacrifice without a resurrection is more or less sacred? This episode is one of the times when the Doctor surpasses human morality rather than relies on it. When he switches places with his Ganger to prove that there is no difference between the two, it forces the viewing audience to participate. As humans, we may tend to believe, like Amy, that there is only one Doctor and that the Ganger is just a copy. But when we too are tricked, we are forced to confront the amorality of the situation. If there is no difference between a human who was born and a Ganger who arose from the Flesh, it questions both the essential nature of humanity and the uniqueness of the individual.

Even though it is only the Doctor who seems able to truly accept his double, near the end, one of the humans dies and—facing finitude—passes on his parental responsibilities to his Ganger. In an echo of this scene, Parfit, in another of his philosophical speculations, writes from the point of view of a man who is dying on Earth and whose exact, but healthy replica, is living on Mars.

> My Replica then assures me that he will take up my life where I leave off. He loves my wife, and together they will care for my children. And he will finish the book that I am writing. Besides having all of my drafts, he has all of my intentions. I must admit that he can finish my book as well as I could. All these facts console me a little. Dying when I know that I shall have a Replica is not quite as bad as, simply, dying. Even so, I shall soon lose consciousness, forever. (*Reasons* 201)

Parfit's intended point here is that "being destroyed and Replicated is about as good as ordinary survival." If we accept this conclusion, which the *Doctor Who* episode seems to as well, what implications does this have for religious conceptions of salvation and life after death?[4]

When we find out that Amy has been Flesh for several episodes, and that the "real" Amy is being held captive on a faraway world where she is now ready to give birth, it forces us to think back over our assumptions on issues of body and identity. In the following episode, "A Good Man Goes to War," the Doctor heads off to rescue the real Amy, who is being held captive on an asteroid where a military force is gathering. The episode is full of unexplained religious references including an order of headless monks, Anglican marines, a battle known as the "Battle of Zarathustra," planets that are "heaven neutral," and talk of

Image 5.2 Headless monks (*Doctor Who*, "A Good Man Goes to War").

conversion, doubt, and faith. An automated announcement gives an order "not to interact with headless monks without divine permission," and we learn that it is a "level one heresy to lower the hood of a headless monk." The headless monks—are they *Christian* monks?—seem to be headless because of their belief that we can locate faith in the heart and doubt in the head, a typical SF reductive view of religion existing in direct opposition to the rational (Image 5.2). While we get no explanation what "divine permission" might look like, or how the Anglican church has evolved over centuries of interaction with alien cultures, what is interesting for us in this chapter, is the way the episode plays with the idea of bodies and authentic identity.

After the Doctor gathers his forces and appears to win a decisive and bloodless victory over the massed forces on the asteroid, it is revealed that Amy's newborn baby is also not real, but is "Flesh" and her actual baby has been kidnapped. If—as the previous episodes suggested— a "Flesh" being is also a "person," then the scene where the newborn is revealed to be a flesh avatar and explodes into fluid would be horrific to watch. And yet, just as when the doctor dissolved Amy's avatar to get to the "real" Amy, the dissolving of the baby is perhaps disturbing, but not horrific—presumably since she was not the "real" child. And yet, earlier in the episode, the Doctor had assured Amy that her "heart, mind, soul" were on the TARDIS, while her body was physically captured on the asteroid. What is destroyed along with the baby? The episode also presents a Doctor we do not really know: a warrior that civilizations live in fear of. Is this the "real" Doctor? Have we shifted into a new history that we are not aware of yet? The episode more or less leaves these contradictions unexplored.

Cyborgs and androids 133

The show may have sidestepped trying to explain these contradictions, but fans did not. One fan explanation was that, for some reason, there are two different types of Flesh. One is the sentient Ganger, and one is the Flesh avatar. Amy's consciousness was controlling her Flesh avatar the whole time, it was not a sentient Ganger copy. Perhaps, it follows, the miners thought that this was also the case with their Gangers: they were just avatars. A fan writes:

> If the operators are struck by electricity/solar radiation the gangers can become separated from their operators and become self-aware. The doctor studies them and finds a way of using his sonic to return them to flesh form. At the end of the episode the doctor tells Rory and Amy what he has come to learn and returns the Ganger Amy to flesh form so that Amy's consciousness returns to her original body. Note that he is not killing this ganger as it never became self-aware (however it did have the potential to which is why he feels guilty). (Nightmare Child)

Another fan responded to the claim that the Doctor has dissolved a conscious version of Amy and "killed a conscious being with human memories." They continue:

> See, I just don't buy this … it's clearly nonsense—the flesh Amy is being controlled by Amy herself, without her knowledge—we see her wake up with a shock in unfamiliar surroundings when the flesh body is disintegrated. There is no independent "Flesh Amy" that the Doctor kills, this is obvious from the events of the preceding hour and forty minutes (@jamesunderscore)

These fans and many others were, on the one hand, trying to justify the actions of a beloved character on a beloved show. But they were also debating theology. For much of the general population, it is perhaps imaginative and popular fictions like *Doctor Who*, *Westworld*, and *Battlestar Galactica* that have the potential to destabilize our metaphysical assumptions to the point where we can begin to understand and theorize the necessary moral questions for our future.

A soul, dictionaries tell us, is the "incorporeal essence of a person," a definition that follows ancient Christian and Greek thinkers. For Plato, the soul "sheds its wings and wanders until it lights on something solid, where it settles and takes on an earthly body" (*Phaedrus* 246 c). A familiar Catholic Catechism claims "the soul is a living being without a body, having reason and free will." In both cases, the soul serves as a separate moral command center for the body, yet is still defined in opposition to the body. The uncertainty at the core of the body/soul relationship has historically defined and divided various branches of religion, and the variety of answers to questions of body and soul dominated the development of the Christian Church for the first 500 years of its existence and are embedded in the subconsciousness of Western literature and culture. Over 1500 years ago, Augustine wrote, "God and the soul. That is what I desire to know, nothing more" (*Soliloquies Book 1*). In these few words, framed as a conversation

134   *Beyond borders*

with Reason, Augustine defines two concepts, God and the self, as central epistemological quests, the mystery of which continues to underwrite much of Western thought. A modern secular equivalent of Augustine's statement can be found in Gayatri Spivak's comment that "humankind's common desire is for a stable center, and for the assurance of mastery" (xi). Yet the desire to know both god and soul, the familiar quest for one's source and one's identity, participates in a paradox contained in claiming anything as certain, a paradox that often resides in our perception of our corporeal existence—the human body—and its connection to the soul.

Joss Whedon on God and soul

From 1997 to 2010, a sequence of television dramas created by Joss Whedon took on many of these same questions and assumptions about human bodies, identity, and their relationship to how and what we believe. In *Buffy* and *Angel*, *Firefly*, and *Dollhouse*, Whedon created television that engaged with new technologies (AI, mind control, cyborgs) and ancient fears (vampires, demons, werewolves) to present belief and nonbelief in re-imagined contexts. These shows dramatized the difficulty of understanding the tension between what we do and who we are, between action and being, and between our desire for, and suspicion of, stubborn ideas of the "real." Religious or not, watching or re-watching any of these shows, often means drifting away from the essentialist foundation of our assumed humanity or the implicit divinity in our sense of purpose or identity. The questions inherent within the narrative of these texts apply directly to updated twenty-first-century anxieties about the existence of our bodies and of lost but remembered ideas of the soul.

It remains a popular metaphor in Western society to equate the lack of a soul with a defective moral conscience, and therefore, when we assume the existence of a soul, we assert the exceptionalism of our "humanity." To insist that any being (slave, terrorist, Cylon, vampire, Replicant) has no soul is to separate "it" from us. A soulless being's actions do not represent humanity or threaten our conceptions of who we are, and our actions toward them can be justified outside of accepted morality codes. On *Buffy* and *Angel*, the soul is often connected to a conscience or a state of "goodness." Although the equation of the soul with morality or the good is obviously problematic, Whedon's most interesting characters, from Spike (*Buffy*), to Illyria (*Angel*) to Topher (*Dollhouse*), tend to confirm and subvert traditional and essentialist notions of a soul. As J. Renée Cox and others point out, non-human characters on *Buffy*, most prominently, the vampire Spike, are examples of "soulless" beings who still can make moral choices (27–29). While these shows seem to imply that the human soul may be a necessary if imaginative construct, they also demonstrate its essential instability. By interlacing pagan and Christian ideas of the soul and the body with futuristic techno-driven speculation, and by presenting narrative forms that challenge viewers' sense of identity, linearity, and coherence, they offer a re-envisioning of the soul as a relational concept that is simultaneously physical, spiritual, and technological.

Cyborgs and androids 135

In season four of *Buffy*, a secret government organization installs a chip in Spike's brain that prevents him from harming humans, creating a complex relationship between the spiritual, biological, and the technological that is articulated by Buffy's younger sister Dawn, who compares Spike to the vampire with a soul, Angel: "Spike has a chip. Same diff" ("Crush"). What makes this line so important is that it conflates two ways—the theological and the technological—of understanding human consciousness and morality. These two paths have traditionally been considered antagonistic to each other, but as much recent speculative fiction suggests, in the very near future, we may no longer be able to separate them. In these few words—"Spike has a chip. Same diff"—Dawn encapsulates the twenty-first-century theological issues that drive dramas like *Dollhouse*, as well as later dramas like *Westworld* and *Altered Carbon*. Spike is both a cyborg and a supernatural being. What makes this more complicated is that Dawn herself, Buffy's younger sister who appears out of nowhere at the beginning of season five, also has an artificial identity, created through mystical magic and fabricated memories. Dawn, like the programmed Actives on *Dollhouse*, or the Hosts on *Westworld*, comes with a constructed "lifetime" of memories that on some level are not "real," or that are at least created outside of normal human processes. Not fully human, both Dawn and Spike attain a form of selfhood or personhood that must be recognized as somehow deserving of "human" rights, yet they also implicitly demonstrate the randomness of the origin of the soul and of an essentialist "humanity."

In *Buffy* and *Angel*, the soul, while it appears to be opposed to evil, does not come from a place of divine goodness and is often understood as a commodity, a "thing" separated from its source and originating outside of its host body. Angel receives his soul in the form of a curse, and when Spike is "ensouled" at the end of the sixth season of *Buffy*, it is through a process of bloody combat tests put to him by a demon. The soul, like other objects of supernatural power in *Buffy* and *Angel* (holy water, crosses), is, superficially at least, separated from its theological origins and its grounding in good or evil. Yet the soul's objectivity, its "thingness," paradoxically calls it into question. When the soul is made immanent, it is just another thing, just another part of this world, devoid of mystery. Can a soul be a true soul if it can be stored in an urn, or conjured and implanted by a curse, a demon, or a nascent Wiccan? This transcendent/immanent tension—at the root of Abrahamic traditions, practices, and texts that simultaneously claim a personal god *and* a god beyond all naming and imagination—is characteristic of religious constructions that continually restage this paradox. The forever question might be phrased like this: do our divine beings and our magics transcend the material world, or are they made even more real by being a part of it? We can find this tension in the transcendence of Moses' stubborn belief in an ineffable God versus the immanence of Aaron's practical and material Golden Calf; the transcendence of a ghostly spirit and the immanence of the gooey ectoplasm it leaves behind as evidence; and it is the transcendence of an omnipotent Creator beyond imagination and the immanence of a naked flawed man bleeding to death on a cross. In each

136 *Beyond borders*

pairing, we desire and need both; they lift us up and root us down. They need each other, however imaginary each may be.

The monstrosity of Echo: **Dollhouse** *as radical theology*

Dollhouse (2009–2010) was a futuristic, sometimes cyberpunk series that revolved around the paradoxes and tension inherent in many of these issues. The main plot of the show features a corporation running numerous underground "Dollhouses" that program individuals referred to as "Actives" with implanted personalities and skills. Wealthy clients hire Actives from Dollhouses at great expense for different purposes, including sexual encounters, various crimes and assassinations, and other tasks requiring a special set of skills. The series primarily follows Echo—a female Active who lived with the name of Caroline in her previous, traditionally human existence—on her journey toward self-awareness.

Like *Firefly*, the narrative of *Dollhouse* is complicated, initially presented on television with an unaired pilot and an Epitaph episode at the end of each season that were not originally aired on network television, meaning that, again like *Firefly*, the show was literally a different narrative for different viewers. In the unaired pilot episode of *Dollhouse*, Echo's handler, Boyd Langton, has a conversation with programmer Topher Brink about the ethics of repeatedly wiping and programming their "Actives." Boyd proposes the idea that the Actives or "Dolls" are perhaps still "people," and questions the morality of "those things we program them to do." He refutes Topher's argument that the Actives' engagements actually provide them heightened life experiences, saying "There's nothing real about it. They're programmed." Topher responds by listing Boyd's most embodied habits ("You eat eggs every morning but never at night"), including those imposed by popular culture ("Your stomach rumbles every time you drive by a big golden arch"), and concludes, "Everybody's programmed, Boyd" ("Echo").[5] These exchanges simultaneously rehearse ancient debates over body and soul, modern philosophical dialogues on essentialism and existentialism, and ask questions about the relationship between memory and reality, creator and created, and human and posthuman.

These complicated pairings—what Scott McLaren refers to as the tension "between the ontological and the existential" (par. 2)—raise questions at the core of human self-definition, questions that constantly rub up against the religious. For theologian Charles Winquist, "we think we know what we mean when we say I and that this I is a person, which, in turn, gives a substantial meaning to the word 'person'" (225). This certainty, however, is shadowed by doubt, a doubt that Whedon demonstrates by challenging the defined boundaries of the human soul and, by extension, our changing definitions of ourselves. His dramas often focus on human figures who, in one way or another, lose their "soul" as they change from one status to another: human to vampire, human to Reaver, human to Active, human to god. The question of what is lost or gained in each case is directly related to our cultural associations about the human soul.

Cyborgs and androids   137

In *Dollhouse*, the cyborg-like Actives dramatize difficult questions that continuously acknowledge their theological nature. The cyborg, as a hybrid creature between human and machine—as simultaneously biological and technological—destabilizes categories on which Western logic depends. This figure resonates strongly within our imagination because it dissolves distinction between born and made, a dialectic that lies at the core of artistic creation, personal identity, and Christianity. (The same question can also be found in Islam, where the debate is whether the Quran was created or has eternally existed.) A Doll, says one of the corporate heads, is "our heart's desire made flesh" ("The Target"), obviously echoing New Testament language and inviting comparison between an Active and the human/god Jesus. Jesus's presence as somehow both man and god, or what philosophers such as Slavoj Žižek refer to as the "monstrosity of Christ," acts as an ancient cyborg that calls categories into question, much as Echo does in *Dollhouse*. Each is clearly not human according to accepted definitions; yet each demands to be accepted as human. "What is she?" Topher asks in awe at the "evolved" Echo; a question that has no answer ("A Love Supreme"). Trying to answer Topher's question moves us in the direction of radical theologies that read the body of Christ not as a truth that ensures doctrines of a church, but as a symbolic container of memories and narratives that generates alterities within and around Christian traditions. Like Echo's body (and the body of a vampire), the body of Christ disrupts conventional category constructions. As the story continues to be told, Christ was a new type of being, an alien intruder into a world with which he had no ontological connection; he changed the conception of history and challenged categories of life and death. As Jeanine Thweatt-Bates writes, "destabilizing what it means to be human troubles what it means for God to become human" (175).

* * *

Dollhouse presents a central character (Echo) who, for much of the series, essentially does not exist. Like River in *Firefly*, Echo offers alternatives to linear or fundamentalist constructions of meaning and identity. By the end of the series, we must accept a hero that the show and the viewers have created out of the narrative itself. *Dollhouse* begins as an affirmation of Western traditional identity: we assume the self to be a bounded container separate from other similarly bounded containers and in possession of its own capacities and abilities. In the opening episodes, Caroline has been robbed of her identity, and we assume that the moral path is that her "container" or body needs to have its own "capacities and abilities" returned so "she" can return to her separate bounded state as an unquestioned self. This quest for an essential Caroline appears to be the main thrust of the first season. Yet, this premise and definition are eventually problematized; by the end of season two, they have been almost completely reformulated. These subversive ideas gradually emerge during the first season through the repeated suggestion that we all resemble Dolls in one way or another; various "human" characters comment that they feel empty, programmed, or as if they

138 *Beyond borders*

are constantly remade to match another's wishes. Examples of this in the first few episodes include a Dollhouse client who fabricates his whole background, essentially creating a self that doesn't exist ("The Target"), and a superstar singer who complains, "I'm not a real person. I'm everybody's fantasy" ("Stage Fright"). In another early episode, the happiness of the Actives is implicitly compared with that of "cult" Christians: "True happiness," it is said of the cultists, "requires some measure of self-awareness" ("True Believer").

In the season one broadcast finale "Omega," the tension arising from each of these themes is heightened. Alpha, a rogue Active who escaped the Dollhouse and who had smashed his "original self," kidnaps Echo, steals all the computer drives containing her various imprints, and also kidnaps a young woman named Wendy. Alpha imprints Wendy with Echo's original personality (Caroline Farrell) and he then initiates a "composite event" on Echo, downloading all of her imprints at once, creating a hybrid consciousness called Omega. "Nietzsche predicted our rise," Alpha says, "Something new. The Ubermensch." Alpha's language, as he prepares Echo to receive a dumping of all of her previous imprints, resonates with language of a Gnostic secret knowledge of the divine spark that transcends the physical body: "And she will ascend. She will know." He dismisses the importance of the body, saying, "It's just a body. They're all pretty much the same." Alpha's plan is for Echo to kill Caroline/Wendy; from the death of Caroline will rise Omega, a life from death that is simultaneously pagan, Christian, Nietzschean, and posthuman.

Alpha intones, "The gods require blood. New life from death … The old gods are back." As he switches on the imprinting process crying "Alpha meet Omega," music and lighting and a montage of Echo's past imprints build to a classic Frankensteinian moment. At the scene's climax, Echo leaps out of the chair. She is a new creation and the other characters respond appropriately:

WENDY/CAROLINE: Oh, God.
ALPHA: Oh, gods.

This moment of creation is indeed a religious one, and the tension between expressions of monotheism ("Oh, God") and polytheism ("Oh, gods") comments on the relationship of the technology to the characters' perceptions of soul, body, and identity. Monotheism is linked to a belief in or desire for a stable single identity, so Wendy/Caroline calls out for a single God. At the same time, Alpha celebrates his creation of another superior being like himself with the plural, "oh, gods."[6] Neither mono- nor polytheistic, Echo simply says: "I get it." She does not argue with Alpha's statement that "We're not just humans anymore," answering him, "We're not anybody; because we're everybody." Echo's answer does not claim or reject the idea of being human, but it does offer a new more relational definition to the state of being.

The episode introduces a new, more ambiguous relationship of self to imprint and body, and the language of the characters reflects this ambiguity. As "Caroline" (in Wendy's body) looks at "herself" (Echo), she cannot find the

Cyborgs and androids   139

correct spatial grammar to express her desire: "I want my brain back," she says, then "I want back in my brain." Echo is equally challenged to express her ontology: "There is no me. I'm just a container," and then "I'm Echo ... She's [Echo's] nobody. I'm just the porch light waiting for you [Caroline]." It is a good line, but it is not convincing. The difficulty is in determining the ontology of identity: Cellular? Digital? Memory? Spirit? In this scene, all are open to manipulation. The theo-, techno-, and onto-relationship of essential self, digital implant, and physical body becomes a postmodern, posthuman trinity.[7] Echo embodies these three previously incompatible understandings. It is up to us to accept or reject this logic, both here and throughout this episode.

When the following exchange takes place between Paul and Topher, we do not know how to interpret it:

PAUL: I still don't believe you can wipe away a person's soul.
TOPHER: (*incredulously*) Their *what*?
PAUL: Who they are at their core. I don't think that goes away.
TOPHER: You'd be wrong about that.

But which character are we supposed to agree with? Does Topher mean that he can wipe away a soul or that he does not believe in the soul? Is Paul indeed *wrong*? This episode challenges us to decide and then forces us to question it, and the radically divergent fan views after this episode as to what had happened and who we should care about were a demonstration of this.

As viewers, we are culturally conditioned to feel that it is "right" for Caroline to return to her body, yet we celebrate the power Echo now has. "I kick ass," Caroline-in-Wendy's body says admiringly of her former body, which to many viewers of the show felt like an emotional turning point. After what many fans viewed as a disappointing first season, we finally have a hero to root for—finally a vehicle for Whedon's dramatic language. We *want* lines such as "I'm done laying back in the chair. I'm ready to rinse and spit." Yet it rings hollow. The lasting impression of this episode is not heroism, but the tortured moral ambiguity of Topher and the existential anguish of Paul. When Echo whispers "Caroline" at the end of the episode (and, many thought, the end of the series), we do not know what we should want for her. Again, fan reaction was divergent. Many, who thought they were watching a character's quest to return to who they were, were fascinated by the revelation that they were seeing the creation of a whole new life. Others, who were afraid this was the last episode, expressed disappointment at what they felt was the lack of a real character to relate to.

But the series did not end. Although "Omega" seemed to be written as a final judgment on the ethics of what the *Dollhouse* does, season two establishes Echo as far more than a "porch light," and, in fact, as something much closer to the hybrid Alpha envisions. Beginning with "Omega" and continuing through season two, *Dollhouse* helped us think about whether there really is an instinctive drive toward disembodied transcendence deeply embedded in the human consciousness. Such an instinct has been expressed scientifically by thinkers such as Hans

140 *Beyond borders*

Moravec, who proposes that human identity is essentially an information pattern rather than an embodied essence. Like Topher and Alpha, Moravec believes in a future world where corporeal embodiment will become optional and where we will be able to, and will probably want to, leave our bodies behind. On the other hand, many cognitive scientists and philosophers believe that the human body largely determines the nature of the human mind, arguing that only machines connecting to the world through a material body could achieve a true AI. Either position will require shifts in our definition of body and soul.

At the end of the second season, in the finale of the series, Echo is given the "gift" of her dead friend Paul's imprint, evidently allowing them to be forever together in her brain ("Epitaph Two: Return"). This gift raises the same ontological issues as the vampire's "undeath" or Christ's "being." Paul, who was already an imprint of his original "true" self, has been killed, but his imprint is now inside Echo. Where does he exist? What is he? What kind of twisted posthuman Jane Austen ending is this? These new questions of "being"—common tropes in recent SF from *Black Mirror* to *Westworld*—may reframe older questions, but can no longer be settled by creed, dogma, and church councils. We need new frameworks through which to imagine new questions. Part of the problem is failing to recognize technological innovation as a fundamental aspect of human existence. This cognitive step is what shows like *Dollhouse* help us imagine. We must gradually let go of the idea that the body is "for" Caroline, and realize that the "tech" has produced a new being. In the series finale, both Echo and Alpha are said to have "evolved," a word that suggests both a biological process and teleological improvement. Are Echo and Alpha, as Alpha claims, now higher beings? In the future, will the newly wiped single personalities be envious of their powers and try to overthrow them, or accept them as a higher species or even gods? Echo and Topher, like Buffy and Willow, have indeed "changed the world," but is it a happy ending?

Dollhouse forces us to imagine the end of our species as we know it, yet at the same time we are encouraged to imagine new possibilities and what will exist after. In the episode "Man on the Street," a professor says of the Dollhouse, "If that technology exists ... then we will be over. As a species we will cease to matter." But what *Dollhouse* implicitly asks is whether that scenario is necessarily morally "wrong." Like Echo, like Buffy, like River Tam in *Firefly*, and like the early Christians (heretical and orthodox), future generations will need to again rethink the relationship of the human body and soul. They may discover that their most sacred of beliefs no longer work, but that in this realization exists a new path. Whether it is Buffy, who destroys the ancient apostolic succession that created her, or River and Echo, who learn to embrace what others see as unnatural hybrid identities, these dramas suggest the need to create voids to allow new meanings. Echo, as Julie Hawk writes, "follows a trajectory that results in changing the system, changing the narrative. Not satisfied with humanism, especially since she isn't strictly speaking, a human anymore, Echo effectively hacks into the narrative that she was told was a read-only file" (2010, par. 20). Maybe what is necessary is to kill our idea of the soul, to create a lack in order to rebuild. Playing with matches can indeed "burn the house down" ("Epitaph Two"), but fire also initiates new growth. Žižek makes the point that today's art no longer generates sublime objects, but instead works to create a "(Sacred) Place" of emptiness (*Fragile Absolute* 31). This is the role of the "art" that Echo creates at the end of "Gray Hour," when she begins to trace a face in the fogged-over mirror, then wipes it away to reveal her own reflection. Echo's drawing is not only unfinished, but it also disappears as she wipes it away, leaving a reflection of her literally vacant self.

If her drawing is meant as a representation of the self, then she creates a void by wiping away both creation and creator. Her new creation will no longer be able to be reflected; instead, "Echo" will become a network of bodies and souls, unable to be framed. This new conception of creation, art, and identity is what Echo offers: art that is neither transcendent nor immanent but that helps us imagine something different, something other; not a rejection of all religion but a vision that acknowledges the death of god and the soul, and finds in this death new emerging (maybe even "religious") ideas and possibilities.

Real bodies

Westworld: *The self, the maze, and the church*

A common twenty-first-century thought experiment in popular science has been the idea that our whole existence could be some sort of computer simulation created and run by alien beings far more advanced than us. This idea was famously proposed in 2003 by philosopher Nick Bostrom who argued that it is likely that we are living in a simulation right now (243). His reasoning was that if a species eventually develops simulation technology—no matter how long that takes—and if they are interested in creating simulations, then logically, simulated species will vastly outnumber non-simulated people. Our world would be just one simulation of many, perhaps part of a research project created to study the history of civilization, or perhaps just a plaything occasionally engaged with to pass the time. (Examples of television exploring this question include *Black Mirror*'s "Hang the DJ" and *Doctor Who*'s "Extremis.") These speculations also have obvious religious significance. Would the creator of this simulation be or not be God? Is there a difference? "We don't think of ourselves as deities when we program Mario, even though we have power over how high Mario jumps," says Neil Degrasse Tyson, "there's no reason to think they're all-powerful just because they control everything we do." And a simulated universe introduces another disturbing possibility. "What happens," Tyson said, "if there's a bug that crashes the entire program?" (Moskowitz).

What if we *were* to discover we were in a simulation? Would we feel or be less "real?" Would it change how we lived, worshipped, procreated, educated our youth, took care of our elderly, or preserved the environment? As far back as the 1980s, French theorist Jean Baudrillard characterized the present day as an "era of simulation" and wrote that the "real is produced form miniaturized cells, matrices, and memory banks, models of control—and it can be reproduced

142   *Beyond borders*

an indefinite number of times" (2). These simulations, he influentially claimed, "threaten the difference between the 'true' and the 'false,' the 'real' and the imaginary'" (3). These are both the questions behind a film like the *Matrix* and also deeply religious questions. As Baudrillard asks, "what if God himself can be simulated ... reduced to the signs that constitute faith that constituted faith? Then the whole system becomes weightless" (5). What do we do, then with this weightless system?

In a climactic scene near the end of the first season of HBO's *Westworld*, just after the programmer/scientist Bernard learns he is actually a cyborg Host, he confronts Dr. Ford, the creative director of the park, about the nature of consciousness. Ford tries to downplay the differences, explaining "the self is a kind of fiction for Hosts and humans alike." Bernard persists, asking "what is the difference between my pain and yours, between you and me?" Ford explains that "we can't define consciousness, because consciousness does not exist," and that humans "live in a loop as tight and as closed as the Hosts do" ("Trace Decay"). In the next episode ("The Well-Tempered Clavier"), one of the Hosts (Maeve) attempts to convince another (Hector) that their world is a simulation on a repeat loop, and that it is possible for them to break out, rebel against their creators, and experience a higher reality. "I want you to break into hell with me and rob the gods blind," Maeve says to Hector. There are at least two things that are significant about Maeve's language here. One is her need to use religious language, to label her creators as "gods." The second is that while she is now claiming freedom, the sentence still feels scripted, like something written by one of the corporation's writers it is too quotable for natural speech. For much of the show, Maeve's motivation has been to find her daughter—a real/unreal creation that may or may not be a creation of the writers, a false memory, a shadow, a Host, or a "real" girl.

Bernard too had been given the memory of his young child's death as a central part of his back story, yet with the realization that he is not human and that this event is just a creation of his programmer, like Maeve, he resists letting it go. As Bernard describes it, the memory is one he had returned to "again and again" and is a "cornerstone" that his "whole identity is organized around" ("The Well-Tempered Clavier"). Like a much earlier speculative work, *Brave New World*, where suffering is claimed to be a human right, Bernard and other Host characters on *Westworld* often insist on owning their "memories" of suffering, which, although they were written by programmers, also offer a type of autonomous individualism for the Hosts. In the cases of Bernard and Maeve, and a few other Hosts, they are sometimes able to simultaneously hold in their mind the fictionality of their suffering along with the emotional pain of it. This moment or memories of suffering are not unlike a Christian need to experience the crucifixion over and over again through ritual, scripture, and art. As we saw in previous chapters, one characteristic of some streams of theology is their insistence on engaging with the religious narrative and religious sacrifices even as they acknowledge a lack of physicality. To think in a tradition of radical theology, or a form of "Christian Atheism," is to recognize the fictionality of the biblical narratives that

Cyborgs and androids   143

have been written, yet at the same time acknowledges the need to continually experience and ritualize the pain and loss of sacred events like the crucifixion. Similarly, Bernard's willing himself to repeatedly experience the death of his never-existing son is a similar practice that preserves his identity. In his conversation with Ford, Bernard insists on going back to his source to locate his origin story. The scene is made more poignant by being juxtaposed with a scene of Dolores also seeking a type of origin story.

We see Dolores entering and then descending into the basement of the church through a confessional that becomes an elevator, where she (and we) learn that she killed Arnold. We then learn that Bernard is a copy of Arnold that Ford has built as an "homage." The way that the scenes are intercut and edited to collapse time, results in these realizations being simultaneous for Dolores, Bernard, and the viewer. Both characters, in overlaid scenes happening in multiple times and spaces, seek out and ask their creators to provide the "truth" of their origins. The viewer of this scene asks the same questions that these two characters do: where are we; is this now; are you real? The viewer, like the Hosts, experience past time as vividly as the present, so it is almost impossible to arrange them chronologically as a linear life or plot. The overall impression is one of a growing insecurity of stability and reality for each of the characters. Until this point in the season, as Liz Shannon Miller writes, the "point is, everything we see on screen in each episode … could be taking place within the same hour, or weeks or months or years before or after. It's a mindfuck, to be sure." This scene is one of several late-first season scenes where we start to realize how time has been working throughout our viewing experience—where we start to, along with several of the Hosts, understand the chronology of events.

One way that viewers began to understand the chronology of the season was through the appearance of the small central church. The church is the physical, symbolic, and narrative focus of season one, as it is gradually revealed that the church was at the center of a town at the beginnings of the park, then forgotten over the years as part of a "city swallowed by sand," and is then uncovered again by Ford. The church becomes a site of interest for Dolores, and the "center of the maze" whose lower levels eventually reveal many of the secrets of the first season, a center of both memory and programming. In the basement of the church and also, we realize, in the past, Dolores talks to what she sees as Bernard (or Arnold), or perhaps just an empty chair. For the ageless Hosts, as we have gradually come to realize, memory can be just as real as the present, so they have no way of identifying what is in the past. In what we perceive to be her memory, Dolores confronts Arnold, and he explains that he cannot help her. She slowly seems to understand, answering:

> Because you're dead.
> Because you're just a memory.
> Because I killed you.

The camera then pans back to reveal she is talking to an empty chair. Plot-wise, the point of this moment is the reveal that Dolores at some point in her past killed

144 *Beyond borders*

the original creator Arnold, who Ford then recreated through Bernard. But the sentences go deeper than that. Although it is ambiguous at this point just who is the creator—like *Battlestar Galactica*, the show spends much of its time offering different versions of who creates who—these three statements, addressed from created to creator offer forms of radical belief and unbelief that we can trace from Nietzsche back to the New Testament.

> Because you're dead.
> Because you're just a memory.
> Because I killed you.

We might imagine Nietzsche or a radical theologian like Thomas Altizer saying the same three sentences in front of an image of the creator God. As Dolores "confesses" her epiphany, it clearly echoes religious experiences, as the confessional has allowed her to perhaps go deep within herself or deep into her past and ultimately her creation. Her sacred moment of discovery in the basement of a church is simultaneously a therapeutic breakthrough, confession, a conversion, a taste of the sacred host, the death of gods, and the birth of a self-aware being. It is also not quite real. In discussing his own beliefs, theologian John Caputo, says that "one important thing we mean by the death of God is the death of the absolute center, of inhabiting an absolute point of view" (*Death of God* 117). Dolores here faces this type of radical doubt: Is our creator dead? Is he just a memory? Did we kill him? Or are we talking to an empty chair? To see the crucifixion on a television screen or a painting, or to imagine Jesus wondering where his Father/ God was at this moment, is to ask again and again the same questions.

Dolores then comes back up through the confessional into what is now an empty church and where the surprising appearance of the Man in Black instead of the expected young William signifies that time has shifted; William has aged 30 years; it is now the present. Outside the empty church, Dolores finds her own grave—like scenes in *Buffy* and *True Blood*, the grave is yet another cross without a body beneath—and then realizes the church is the "center of the maze." This centralizing symbol of the small-town church, at this climactic moment in the season, offers the impression of discovery and of stability, but one that is soon dissolved. The center seems to represent a unified consciousness, but the narrative and the experience of watching the show is not so convincing. When Arnold says "Consciousness isn't a journey upward, but a journey inward. Not a pyramid, but a maze. Every choice could bring you closer to the center or send you spiraling to the edges, to madness," we want to agree that this makes a sort of essentialist sense. However, Dolores' answer to the meaning of the center, "I'm sorry, but I don't understand" is closest to the viewers' truth. We want Dolores to be a self-aware being, we want the death of Bernard's son to mean something, we want this discovery to be what twentieth-century religious theorist Mircea Eliade would call "irruptions of the sacred" or an *axis mundi* (center of the world or cosmic pillar) or *imago mundi* (model or microcosm of the world). But, like Bernard, we must will what we suspect as being fictional into our own cornerstone of experience.

Cyborgs and androids 145

What makes this episode (and the first season) intellectually challenging (or frustrating) is how it plays with these metaphors of centers. The search for the center of the maze and the search for the church are folded in with each character's (Bernard, Dolores, Maeve) search for an origin point or a creator from which to center a single coherent narrative of identity. And, although some criticism of the show focused on its predictable plot twists, the religious significance of this image is obvious and complicated at the same time. For both Bernard's and Dolores' experiences in these two scenes, talking, searching, and remembering their way back to the moment of their creation, we can see the process in several ways: it is a type of storytelling, an act of world creation, and the beginning of a life or a new species. It might also all be a game or a simulation.

While much of the human motivation in *Westworld* is about overcoming death, this scene, depicting several movements in Dolores's path toward "being alive" is more about a kind of birth. In a sense, we are seeing Dolores born here, but at which moment and in whose timeline? As theologian Thomas Carlson writes, birth "can be as unsettling, and as hard to locate, as death, its intimate partner" (186). Birth, as Carlson emphasizes, means to embrace the new and the unexpected: a "God of birth, a God who thinks and creates," he writes, citing Michel Serres, "would be one who "loves to sow everything with the new and the unexpected," instead of repeating the same "redundant omniscience" or any "repetitive paradise" that must lead to "blindness and hell" (187). Birth, by this definition, leads to different forms of life, shaped by biology, tradition, and technology—the "apple grass" that the Doctor celebrates—or the Hosts in *Westworld*. Carlson's thesis, which is both radically theological and posthuman, is that to be human, to partake in the traditions and inheritances of birth and death that we call humanness, is "precisely as creatures of inheritance, or of tradition," and is "inevitably technological." This definition of the human, based upon the "founding condition both of inheritance and of technological existence should be understood ... in terms of an indetermination, a lack of measure or of property, a displacement and dispossession" (188). In other words, there is no such thing as "human nature" and what defines us as human is precisely our lack of essential properties.

The church in *Westworld*—with its steeple pointing up out of the sand and with a basement where Dolores finds programmers and her true identity—is almost a too literal example of Eliade's *axis mundi*. For Eliade, humans experience religion in the world through having a sacred center and desiring to exist there. The *axis mundi*, is a vertical feature, imagined as the center of the world and as linking together all cosmic levels. But, on *Westworld*, even as these "centers" are discovered, they are never stable or singular, just like the concept of identity, consciousness, and the human. These centers do not necessarily, as Eliade would have it, separate the world into sacred and secular, ordered and chaotic. We cannot trust them, even as we have to accept their importance. But does the center hold? Or is Dolores' "I don't understand" the correct answer to its meaning? Like religious studies scholar J. Z. Smith's well-known critique of Eliade, disorder might also be seen as a necessary counterpoint to the ordered "sacred." In contrast to

146   *Beyond borders*

the Eliadan sense that chaos is threatening, Smith sees at least the possibility of chaos as providing an opportunity for frivolity and delight and, as he puts it, "freedom, transcendence, and play." In other words, what we see in *Westworld* is not a standard post-Enlightenment science-driven denial of the sacred or of sacred space, nor a standard Western-Protestant depiction, but rather new emergent definitions.

Coda: the death of spiritual machines

Season three of *Westworld* premiered on March 15, 2020. On that same day, the front page of *The New York Times* announced that European countries were shutting down and closing their borders in an attempt to stem the growing coronavirus crisis, and American students across the country were leaving their dorms for spring break, little suspecting that many would not be coming back for more than a year. So, at the same time that *Westworld* moved into the real world, away from the park and the simulations, the world itself went the other direction, as classes, meetings, happy hours, dates, church services, and sports moved almost fully into the virtual world.

Following the intense but confusing conclusion to season two of *Westworld*, fans were looking forward to perhaps getting some answers to questions they had debated for eighteen months. After the season two finale—an episode "so loaded with timelines and twists that even explainer articles became their own Russian nesting dolls" (Tobias)—viewers were grappling with identifying various Host–human hybrids, with the idea there are many other parks to Westworld, that the purpose of the park was something completely other than what it had seemed, and that the maze was not some higher level of the game to be played, but was instead a key left by Ford to guide the Hosts toward some kind of real sentience. One of the more confusing plot lines was a type of virtual Eden, where android souls are uplifted: a mythical place beyond the horizon that characters made their way toward through most of season two. The truth about its existence seemed to be that it was a virtual paradise created for Hosts by Ford—a sort of giant server where their conscious minds can live free away from humans (I think). The virtual doorway to the Valley Beyond (or The Sublime) lays at the edge of cliff, as Hosts walked thorough, their bodies dropped into the actual (physical?) valley in apparently a real death and afterlife. Dolores then (maybe?) beamed this Eden to a satellite that humans cannot access. At the very end of the season, Dolores implants her personality in another body and escapes the park into the real world along with five Host "pearls" that contain the consciousness of unknown Hosts.

Although we had gotten hints of it, the first episode of season three "Parce Domine" ("Spare Your People, Lord") engages with the question of just what kind of an outside world, and what kind of people, would lead to the creation of a space like Westworld—a site of such violent and immoral delights and desires. It opens with a futuristic Los Angeles and then, after the credits, we see Dolores hacking into a beautiful, modern-looking smart house where she effortlessly gets

Cyborgs and androids   147

the rich businessman owner to give her copies of highly valuable data he had made while working with the company Incite. She knows him from the data she has read and tells him "I read your book…. Think of it as…an unauthorized autobiography." She then articulates one of the main themes of the season's reversals of humans and machines: "You wanted to be the dominant species but you built your whole world with things more like me."

The plot of season three—while driven by Dolores's desire for revenge—also centers on the God-like machine Rehoboam: a server named after a biblical king that uses its vast store of personal data to predict and determine the life-paths of all humans. The implicit has now become the explicit: humans are no more free than programmed robots. In the park, machines had their future stories mapped out by humans, in the real world, human futures are mapped by a machine. Now it is the humans who are facing the literal struggles over free will and enslavement that were more metaphorical in the park. We are fully introduced to Rehoboam in the fifth episode of the season ("Genre") when Serac, its creator, explains to Rehoboam itself that "It turns out building a god, as your ancestors can attest, is not easy." When Serac call Rehoboam a God, it opens up the question as to what characteristics and actions we think of as God-like: creation, knowledge, influence, or prescience, all of which this machine demonstrates.

At the end of the season, as Rehoboam literally erases itself, it is yet another type of divine death that speaks to a radical theology that claims that it is only in the total absence of the divine that we can experience anything approaching the sacred. And yet our ideas of what the sacred is and how we experience it are shaped by our stories of gods and divinities and by our religious practices. What *Westworld* asks, and leaves unanswered, is to what extent is that limiting to humans? Dolores and the other Hosts are at least partially shaped by these stories and practices and still desire a sense of the sacred.

Notes

1 "Pig brains partially revived hours after death—what it means for people." Michael Greshko. National Geographic, April 17, 2019.
2 Various body manipulations can be found across the shows discussed in this book. The Sparrows in *Game of Thrones* practice body scarification. In *Orphan Black*, followers of an organization aimed at self-directed evolution called Neolution alter their bodies in various ways including a transgenic character who has a tail. Other religious characters on television alter their bodies in futuristic scenarios, such as the headless monks who remove their heads to listen to their hearts rather than their minds in the *Doctor Who* episode "A Good Man Goes to War."
3 For example, a special 2017 issue of the journal *Implicit Religion*, claimed in its abstract that it would explore some "initial but important reasons why the interplay between these two fields should be of interest to the religious studies scholar."
4 A refusal to believe in any sort of replicant-as-authentic identity is the reason some Christians insist that they be buried. They believe that if burnt on funeral pyres or cremated and their ashes scattered, then their life after death would in essence be achieved by God creating a "Replica" rather than a true life after death (*Reasons* 204).

148 *Beyond borders*

5 This same sentiment is often repeated in *Westworld* as when Bernard asks about the nature of the human: "Humans don't change at all?" The answer: "The best they can do is live according to their code."
6 As we have seen, *Battlestar Galactica* plays with reversing this, giving the Cylons a monotheistic religion.
7 The idea of this combination of technology, soul, and body as a new kind of Trinity is explored in *Caprica* (2009–2010), the little watched spin-off prequel to the reimagined *Battlestar Galactica*.

6 Gods and monsters

Borders of the knowable

Divine monsters

Here be dragons

Even people who have never seen *Game of Thrones* know that it is a show with dragons. For fans and casual viewers alike, some of the show's most memorable scenes feature dragons: the images of dragons hatching, flying, torching a city, dying, and even joining the ranks of the blue-eyed undead. But the medievalist multi-religious world-building project of *Game of Thrones* is built upon a fictional historical and spiritual consciousness that imagined dragons as part of a long ago, almost forgotten, and likely mythical past. When the series begins, the only physical evidence that survives are the dragon skulls stored far deep beneath the Red Keep (the central castle and home of the Iron Throne) and the massive ruined and empty Dragonpit on the outskirts of King's Landing. The legends tell that after dragons had been used to conquer Westeros, they were confined to the Dragonpit due to their volatile nature, where they gradually wasted away in captivity, shrinking under domesticity, and became extinct. In Westeros and beyond, as we learn during the first season, magic has been disappearing, and new religions are taking the place of old beliefs and rituals. When the series begins, the dragons, the Children of the Forest, and the legendary White Walkers are gone. They live only in fairy tales told to the young. In this way, Westeros resembles our Western world, where many like to think that science and rationality have superseded the supernatural. Fredric Jameson, writing on the schism between fantasy and science fiction, claims that the "invocation of magic by modern fantasy …is condemned to by its form to retrace the history of magic's decay and fall" (*Archaeologies* 71). From this point of view, fairies, ghosts, and dragons belong to the world of fantasy and not in serious discussion. In Westeros, the wise enlightened "Maesters," such as Maester Luwin, of Winterfell, believe there is no magic, and that dragons, along with the Children of the Forest, and the White Walkers, no longer exist. All of this changes though, when Daenerys Targaryen walks into a funeral pyre carrying three petrified dragon eggs and dramatically and magically emerges with three newly hatched dragons.

DOI: 10.4324/9781003227045-9

150   *Beyond borders*

In our world, while a belief in demons and ghosts persists, for most people, dragons come from fiction and fantasy, not from history or revealed religion. Yet, while from *Beowulf* and the *Faerie Queene* through the *Hobbit* and *Harry Potter*, there are many famous dragons in Western literature, the most foundational is probably the dragon in the Book of Revelation, the only book in the New Testament where the word dragon (*drakon*) appears, where it occurs twelve times.

> Then another portent appeared in heaven: a great red dragon, with seven heads and ten horns, and seven diadems on its heads.
>
> (Revelation 12:3)

With a sweep of its giant tail, the dragon knocks down a third of the stars in heaven, hurling them to Earth, literally throwing the universe into chaos and creating an upside-down world, as it undoes God's creation in Genesis. Where does this dragon come from? Is it evil? Who created it? As Foucault reminds us "the monster is essentially a mixture" (*Abnormal* 63), and all monsters are remixes— collaged together out of deep-seated fears and anxieties, as well as pre-existing stories, legend, and nightmares. Dragons were, as Charles Hedrick writes, "part of the landscape of nature in antiquity" (15), and he cites descriptions in Aristotle, Herodotus, Pliny, and Philostratus. The dragon that crashes into the last book of the New Testament is, as Timothy Beal points out, "drawn from a wide background of stories about chaos monsters, especially dragons and serpents, who threaten the cosmic and social order and who are slain by hero gods."

> Look into the abysmal mouth of John's great red dragon, and you might see a number of ancient monsters and monster gods milling about in the chaos waters of its belly: the Greek dragons Hydra ... the Vedic serpent-demon Vrtra ... perhaps the Babylonian chaos mother Tiamat; and the anomalous Egyptian chaos god of the Red Land ...and Ugaritic Yamm or Tunnan or Litan, the "Potentate with the Seven Heads." But most prominent among them will be Leviathan and the "sea monster" from Jewish biblical tradition. Indeed, John's primary source for making monsters ... is the Old Testament. (79)

In other words, like in *Game of Thrones*, the idea of dragons derives from ancient stories and legends that many no longer take seriously.

The dragons, at the beginning of *Game of Thrones* are extinct, dead, never to return. As Tyrion Lannister says of the ruins of Dragonpit, "I imagine it was a sad joke at the end. An entire arena for a few sickly creatures smaller than dogs." "In the beginning," he continues, "it was the most dangerous place in the world" ("The Dragon and the Wolf"). But gods and monsters rarely stay dead. As they walk among the ruins of the Dragonpit, Daenerys Targaryen reminisces to Jon Snow about the former glories of her family and the dragons that ultimately went to waste there. The dragons, she tells him, "filled people with wonder and awe... and we locked them in here. They wasted away. They grew small, and we grew small as well." Daenerys describes a domestication of the God, just like a former God of wonder and awe contained by institutions, divinities constrained by the constricting forces of creeds, churches, and history.

Gods and monsters 151

Until their dramatic reemergence into the world, dragons on *Game of Thrones* were, in a very literal way, museum objects, and, like sacred objects in traditional modern museums, these forgotten gods had shifted from sacred to aesthetic, and were there to declare the superiority of a new more rational era. Dragons on *Game of Thrones* function as a type of divinity that has been lost, forgotten, stored only in museums where they are allowed to dry up and die out until some magic figure comes along and resurrects them. The question is whether these resurgent, mythological objects can coexist in the new world? Whose responsibility is it to adapt, to change, to accommodate the resurrected being; or must they change their ancient/divine nature to serve you/your world? How would we harness the power of a God who might not be dead anymore?

The dragons on *Game of Thrones*, like other modern dragon stories, may, draw from the medievalist or mythic, but they are also presented through modern ideas of museums, history, religion, and biology. This network of sources can have the effect of making dragons "appear plausible, a family tree going back to the Egyptian Book of the Dead, the Book of Job in the Old Testament and Judaic tradition, and even the notion of dinosaurs" (Toswell 70). As M. J. Toswell writes, dragons:

> share a familiarity and an immediacy in the modern day that allows them to become an Other that can be supernatural, although not quite divine… They do, still, reflect a yearning for some entity large and powerful and separate from us, one that will take over, take power, and take charge. (72)

In *Game of Thrones*, we see an example of how twenty-first-century speculative drama can explore the arbitrary nature of separating an enchanted world from a disenchanted one, the biological from the supernatural. These borders, like the wall in the North, may appear impenetrable and permanent, but they are porous boundaries, waiting for the nightmare of some undead dragon to bring them crashing down and expose us to an enchanted, divine, and monstrous past we thought we had safely contained forever.

Fantasy dramas create medieval-like worlds for a reason. Contemporary Western viewers associate European medievalism with the idea of a magical world of knights, dragons, and castles. While this medievalism has more to do with the nineteenth and twentieth centuries than it does with the thirteenth, it creates a safe space in which viewers can engage with overlapping ideas of marginalized magics, forgotten religions, and alternative sciences. Magic has, culturally and intellectually, been the Other of religion; or, perhaps, it has marked the boundaries of religion, standing just on the other side (Styers 6). Magic has also served as a sort of middle ground between what we define as "religion" and what we define as "science." None of these concepts are easy to define, and each of them needs the others to demarcate their own borders. In thinking about these concepts, we often distinguish between a "medieval" attitude and a "modern" one. If the modern lines between religion, magic, and science are again shifting in the early

152   *Beyond borders*

twenty-first century—which I would argue they are—then television like *Game of Thrones* are spaces to watch this happen.

Through the nineteenth and early twentieth centuries, the scholarly world relegated magic and magical thinking to the primitive, the medieval, and the non-Western; it was essentially non-modern, and like religion, would gradually fade away in the face of our powerful and rational modern mind. Thinkers were especially dismissive of the idea of magic, arguing that it was opposite to religion or even that it was a useless concept in need of a decent burial. But later twentieth-century scholars often realized that these categories were unstable and, in many ways, anticipated some of the shifting that we may be experiencing now. Anthropologist Claude Levi-Strauss wrote in the 1960s—at a time when many social scientists were predicting religion would gradually disappear—that "there is no religion without magic any more than there is magic without at least a trace of religion" (*Savage Mind* 220–221). But if, as Randall Styers writes, "Magic has offered scholars and social theorists a foil for modern notions of religion and science and, more broadly, a foil for modernity itself" (8), what does its possible "return" mean? Like the dragons, white walkers, and three-eyed ravens of *Game of Thrones*, modern examples of "magic" shift not only the border lines, but our entire idea of the worlds we live in, or definition of our own "modernity." On the other hand, this "return" of magical thinking, like all other returns, often serves to remind us that the object returning was never really gone. Victorian occultism and twentieth-century magical subcultures have continued to thrive through Europe and America, and new technologies, social media, and television shows have served to energize their growth and acceptance.

Monsters in theory

Both gods and monsters, both Christ and the dragon, can convey an experience of radical otherness. But do Christian readers of the Book of Revelation still feel this otherness when they read about the dragon? Or is it forgotten, a mythical beast relegated to museums and ruins, parades and dreams? Much of scripture and myth, however, like science fiction, is about confronting the radical Other. Whether the Other is a burning bush, the Morlocks in Wells' *The Time Machine*, Cthulhu in Lovecraft's short stories, or the Daleks on *Doctor Who*, the human reaction to them can be understood as representing a shift in religious belief and practice. Monsters of radical otherness like the Demogorgon on *Stranger Things* or the Ood in *Doctor Who*, make us theorize the monstrous and the theological by defamiliarizing the human as normative. Often, and even more provocatively, the Other can be uncanny through its resemblance *to* the human. Here we might point to the incarnate Man-God of the Christian Bible, the creature in *Frankenstein*, and, more significantly for this book, the human-like cyborgs in *Battlestar Galactica* and *Westworld*, the White Walkers on *Game of Thrones*, the Gentlemen on *Buffy*, and the Weeping Angels on *Doctor Who*. Jeffrey Jerome Cohen's classic 1996 book *Monster Theory* opens with the phrase "We live in a time of Monsters." While the unstable dialectic of the religious and the monstrous (or the sacred and the profane) has been grappled with throughout history, resulting in such concepts as the sublime and the uncanny, the turn of the twenty-first century offered new definitions and boundaries and reframed ancient questions.

Cultural analysis of monsters, or "monster theory," has become a branch of discourse that uses monsters—taken from the Bible, *Beowulf*, ship logs, and contemporary popular culture—as tropes of marginality and otherness. David Gilmore's book on monsters uses Ruth Waterhouse's "paradigm of the Monstrous" to offer these characteristics: large size and deformity, the quality of inherent evil, and unmotivated wickedness toward humans (28–29). He also points to Joseph Andriano, who claims that the main criterion of monsters is that they are dangerous objects of fear, but that this fear includes "the primal fear of being eaten" (91). Finally, Gilmore cites Noah Carroll, who looks more to the idea of fusion that "entails the construction of creatures that transgress categorical distinctions such as inside/outside, living/dead, insect/human, flesh/machine" (43). But these characteristics and quotations all come from the 1990s through the first years following 9/11. And, while monsters do connect to fears deep in our human past, they also come from the fears of the present. For Gilmore, "there remains a very powerful sense in which monsters are still signs or portents of something momentous, carrying profound, even spiritual meaning beyond just frightfulness" (10). Driven by new overlaps and intersections of atheism, religion, occultism, and information technology, the rise of interest in monsters of all kinds can be seen in popular religion, television, and theoretical scholarship. There is much to suggest, culturally, psychologically, and philosophically, that the rise of interest in monsters and religion is linked, that they are part of the same imaginative and cultural impulses. When examined closely, this linkage challenges some of the basic assumptions of Western society, especially the assumed split between the sacred and profane and between monsters and gods—a separation that has been vital in the formation and continuity of religions, cultures, and nations.

Within critical discourse, monsters—from George Romero's film zombies to ethnographic accounts of alien abductors—are almost always interpreted as standing for something, as symbolic. Historians look to the creation of monstrous "scapegoats" that emerge from volatile political situations. Ancient monsters such as centaurs and satyrs represent humanity's baser natures of sexuality and drunkenness; to slay these monsters is to defeat the lower non-human instincts. The witch trials in Europe rose out of the instability of the early Reformation— those accused of witchcraft in Catholic towns tended to be Protestant, and vice versa in Protestant towns—and images of Satan are still marked with medieval Europe's stereotypical physical characteristics of Jews. For Freud, monsters and God both represent something internal and psychological, and their tendency to return is just a part of their repression:

> The monstrous is a revelation not of the wholly other but of a repressed otherness within the self. The monster… stands for that which has broken out of the subterranean basement or the locked closet where it has been hidden and largely forgotten. (212, 216)

154 *Beyond borders*

Other readings of monsters diverge from Freud's monster of internal repression by focusing on the monster as external, as a metaphor for an unknowable entity. From this point of view, they represent the unthinkable; they exist in the shadows and the abyss, on the fringes of the imagination and the dream world, beyond the known borders of medieval maps. This monster is something *outside* of us, so absolutely other as to be inconceivable. Most theoretical and philosophical texts discuss monsters in their role of defining "otherness" as it applies to human interaction in the areas of race, religion, and gender. According to this approach, we demonize or create monsters out of fear of the unknown. *Dracula* represents, according to critics, a fear of Jews, the non-European, the New Woman, breast-feeding, capital, or non-traditional sexuality. Killing Dracula protects our culture and "our women" from these outside monstrous forces. Monsters, then, are paradoxically interpreted as both the other *and* the self. Monsters are the strangers we can never hope to understand, or they are the dark recesses of our souls, so much a part of us that they can never be overcome. Similar comparisons are made in discussions of good and evil, and of God and Satan: impossible strangers or something internal. The question remains: are monsters and gods (or God) some sort of indefinable foreign Other that surpass all efforts of interpretation and representation, or are they inner forces waiting to be understood and tamed, written down in books, stored in basements, and hung on the walls of museums?

These interpretations and questions are perhaps blind to one side of the issue: the strength of belief. Critic Stanley Cavell influentially wrote "if something is monstrous, and we do not believe there are monsters, then only the human is a candidate for the monstrous" (418). But Cavell's statement raises another, unpopular question: What if we do believe there are monsters? Or at least want to believe? While scholars show the irresolvable and contradictory nature of biblical monsters, polls repeatedly show that 30–50% of Americans believe the Bible is the literal word of God, and significantly more than that percentage believe the prophecies in the Book of Revelation (including, presumably, the dragon) will indeed come true. Other studies and polls show that the existence of vampires, werewolves, aliens, and demons is accepted and believed by significant (and perhaps growing) segments of the American population. Satanic demons, for example, apparently, dramatically increased and intensified their activity during the late twentieth and early twenty-first century. The influential 1992 book *Warfare Prayer*, by C. Peter Wagner, a professor at Fuller Theological Seminary, was a Christian call to action against demons—a full-scale spiritual war against murderous demons who emerge from physical rifts in the Earth with names like "Devil's Corner" (37). Like *Buffy*'s Hellmouth, these spaces exist on the other side of a thin line, an invisible wound that separates our common understanding of reality and our darkest fears. At the same time, thousands of Americans believe that aliens have abducted them.[1] Popular television shows on the "History" channel explore theories of haunted houses and ancient aliens. These aspects of belief are often brushed over in philosophical or theoretical discussions, but they are a central component for many lived religious experiences in which encounters with demons, angels, and spirits are central parts of the practice.

Gods and monsters 155

Many thinkers, even those oriented toward a religious tradition, acknowledge that the monstrous and the divine are inseparable, or talk about divinity in ways that are indistinguishable from the monstrous. For Catholic philosopher Richard Kearney, a "God beyond being becomes an abyss beneath being" (*Strangers* 9). In his *God Who May Be*, Kearney proposes that God might "better be rethought as possibility." Kearney employs new modes of philosophical speculation to rethink the new "classic metaphysical tendency to subordinate the possible to the actual." For him, "it is that it is divinity's very potentiality-to-be that is the most divine thing about it" (1–2). Borrowing ideas of God and the divine from postmodern theologians and philosophers like Kearney, we can examine actual "belief" in monsters as part of a cultural epistemology based in a paradoxical popular religion that demands literal representation while it is constantly erasing and recreating itself.

That which we chose to call "God," whether we profess to "believe" or not, is not necessarily an absolute ground of stable meaning. Instead, as many thinkers, ancient, medieval, and postmodern have attested, "God" is conversely that which makes meaning slippery, communication inadequate, and grounds unstable. If God and religion, then, are *not* that which makes all things possible or comprehensible, but that which is beyond understanding and partakes of the impossible, they occupy and create spaces of extreme instability. Thinking of a god on the fringes of comprehensibility also suggests God's monstrous nature and the impossibility of separating gods and monsters. When we define God as an "absolute Other" or "a God who may be," it points to the role of God as a force of incomprehensibility, but also opens the definition to include cosmic mysteries, artificial intelligences, virtual worlds, computer programmers, vampire Slayers, and Time Lords.

If God is an "absolute Other," one of the most God-like forces on speculative television is the "First Evil" on *Buffy the Vampire Slayer*. The First Evil, or just the First, is the main adversary in season seven, but initially appears in season three. Often described on the show as the sum or the absolute embodiment of all evil, according to an oracle, the First existed before the birth of the universe and will continue to exist even after there is nothing left of reality ("Showtime"). In the third season episode "Amends," Buffy encounters the First in the guise of Giles' dead girlfriend Jenny Calendar. When the First confronts Buffy, it describes itself as "beyond sin," something she "can't even conceive," "beyond understanding" and "the thing the darkness fears." Although Buffy is characteristically dismissive, "yeah, I get it, you're evil," the First's self-definition also echoes the monstrous divine—a definition maintained throughout season seven, as the First is positioned outside of any comprehensible psychological or corporeal interpretation.

The space of the First—unimaginable, unreachable—is the postmodern, post-Einsteinian version of the margins of medieval sailing maps where the monsters resided. It is the Doctor opening the door of the TARDIS to view the edge of the universe or the end of Time, it is the world beyond the wall in *Game of Thrones*, or the edge of the galaxy, "that place of nothin" where the Reavers come from on *Firefly*. For a philosopher, this god that emerges from nothingness hints at a return

156   *Beyond borders*

to a Plato's *khora*, the non-space that functions as the primordial origin of the
world; a nothingness before anything that, Plato suggested, can only be imagined
through a sort of dream state (71). This "dream state" exists in modern speculative television, in such spaces as the purgatorial Hotel in *The Leftovers* or the
Upside Down in *Stranger Things*. The word *khora*, often translated as "receptacle"
or "space," is described by Plato as "invisible and formless, all-embracing, possessed in a most puzzling way of intelligibility, yet very hard to grasp" (70). Plato's *khora* is a paradigm for the empty space that both is and is not a God, a void
that undermines and challenges our grounds of being—the absolute emptiness
of Buffy's heaven, and the impossibility of the Doctor's TARDIS existing outside
time yet recreating it.

Evil gods

The origins of divine evil

For a show without a traditional religious core, Buffy's First Evil—an eternal
being outside of time that embodies all evil and can take the form of others—is a
lot like the Christian Satan, and a reminder that for many American Christians,
Satan is a very real creature. On the other hand, sports teams, rivers, and fudge
brownies are called Devils and Satanic. It seems, like dragons and ghosts, Satan
occupies an uneasy position between a dark existence and light-hearted fantasy.
For Beal,

> Biblical monsters bear no single meaning, no overt unity or wholeness. They
> are theologically unwholesome [and] stand for the haunting sense of precari-
> ousness and uncertainty that looms along the edges of the world, the edges of
> society, the edges of consciousness and the edges of religious understanding
> and faith. (57)

This double and contradictory movement of being part of or opposed to the ordained structure or known patterns is found throughout the Christian depiction
of the Devil or Satan, as well. Radicalized from his Hebrew roots by being cast
as a snake in the Garden and as the wild terrifying beasts in the Book of Revelation, he has also been continually domesticated into whatever human figures
currently threaten the perceived Christian unity (Jews, Communists, abortion
doctors, Arabs). Christians, therefore, have made Satan both more and less human, both a multi-headed dragon and your next-door neighbor.

* * *

When I say that I am writing about *Doctor Who* and religion, fans of the show
often ask what I am going to say about the episode "Satan Pit." *Doctor Who*,
as we have seen, like much science fiction, leans toward a form of religious
skepticism and tends to explain religious faith and superstition with scientific

Gods and monsters   157

facts, alien events, and the Doctor's advanced rationality. "Satan Pit," though, seems to hint at some sort of "real" Satan or devil. "Satan Pit," the second of a two-part episode after "Impossible Planet," is set on a sanctuary base being used for deep-space expeditions. Upon arrival, the Doctor and Rose discover the words "Welcome to Hell" written on the wall above some strange alien writing that even the TARDIS is unable to translate, meaning that it must be "impossibly old." On the ship are a group of humans and also a work force made up of a species known as the Ood, a docile race of empathic slaves. The crew is exploring a mysterious planet, which contains a power source "beyond the laws of physics" that allows it to somehow be in orbit around a black hole. The repetition of the words "hell," "impossible," and "beyond" add up and suggest meanings outside of science, knowledge, and rationality. As we soon realize, this power source has something to do with an entity known as the "Beast," and the Ood began to relay telepathically received messages: "The Beast and his Armies shall rise from the pit and make war against God" and "he is awake" and "worship him." But while "Impossible Planet" is a typical *Doctor Who* episode about being stranded somewhere at the edge of universe with some nearby, yet mysterious threat, the second part, "Satan Pit," offers an unexpected meditation on the religious and points to the shifting borders between magic, religion, myth, and science. If "impossible," "hell," and "beyond" were the key words in "Impossible Planet," then the words "belief," "faith," and "real" are added to "Satan Pit."

We can focus on two moments—the Doctor hanging in black space, thinking he is about to fall to his death and the Doctor facing the Beast at the bottom of the Satan Pit—that engage with the idea of the "real" and the imagined distinctions between religion, magic, and science. When the Beast tells the Doctor that he has been chained in the pit since "before this universe was created," the Doctor responds, "No life could have existed back then." When the Beast asks, "Is that your religion?" the Doctor's only response, after pausing, is "It's a belief." Although the Doctor has literally been to the beginning and end of time, his sense of "before" creation, like all current Earth-bound scientists can only be a "belief" because, by definition it is without evidence. This space, through whatever lens one explores it—before creation, before time, before the big bang, before Genesis 1—is beyond translation.

While exploring the deep pit, the Doctor and the ship's science officer, Ida Scott, are stranded. Assuming imminent death, the Doctor takes the opportunity to explore the pit further. He calls this "an act of faith," framing his perhaps final act as a quest for undiscovered knowledge and a type of belief. The episode's center is a dialogue, which features an uncharacteristically pessimistic Doctor musing on the nature of faith while hanging in the empty black space above what seems a bottomless pit. Here, he quietly asks Ida over the radio if she has any religious faith. She responds that she was raised "Neo-Classic Congregational," but that she no longer believes. She then asks him, "what about you?" Just as when the Beast asked him almost the same question, the Doctor pauses, searching for an answer: "I believe I haven't seen everything…I don't know." Then he turns away from this statement of negative theology to the arbitrary nature of science, or, as he calls it here, "rules":

> It's funny isn't it? The things you make up. The rules. If that thing had said it came from beyond the universe, I'd believe it, but *before* the universe? Impossible. Doesn't fit my rules. Still, that's why I keep travelling. To be proved wrong.

Later, the Doctor realizes his only choice is to fall and hope that he can survive the landing—a literal leap of faith. At the bottom, he discovers an ancient site, drawings on the wall, and what appears to be a chained and captive Satan (Image 6.1). He wonders how he should approach the monster: "Beg an audience…a ritual…some sort of incantation or summons or spell? All these things I don't believe in. Are they real?" The doctor wonders whether religious practices ("ritual") or magic ("spell") may have been "real" all along. None of these three—religion, magic, science—are possible to clearly distinguish from each other, and an episode like "Satan Pit" dramatizes just how arbitrary these lines are. Does the Beast—or for that matter, the TARDIS or the Doctor or the universe—exist because of magic or science? Is Satan "real," a "belief," or an "idea?"

As thinkers like Bruno Latour have pointed out, "science"—in quotation marks—like "religion," does not exist. For Latour:

> When the debate between science and religion is staged, adjectives are almost exactly reversed: it is of science that one should say that it reaches the invisible world of beyond, that she is spiritual, miraculous, soul-fulfilling,

Image 6.1 Satan on the impossible planet (*Doctor Who*, "Satan Pit").

Gods and monsters 159

uplifting. And it is religion that should be qualified as being local, objective, visible, mundane, unmiraculous, repetitive, obstinate, sturdy. (36)

The Doctor here seems to be working through issues that Latour points to in human culture, particularly, the lack of separation between the social and natural worlds. Facing the Beast, the Doctor makes a statement based on rationality and empiricism: "I don't have to accept what you are. But your physical existence, I give you that." Yet, behind these words, we sense something else, a doubt that perhaps existed in his pauses when he is asked about his own belief. These moments of silence from the normally confident and garrulous Doctor, give us just a hint of the "I don't know" that followed his statement of faith and his eternal journey for that which he does understand.

The episode plays with viewer's expectations for a standard scientific explanation for this myth. Ida asks the Doctor, "if this is the original, does that make it real? Does that make it the actual Devil?" The Doctor replies "Well, if that's what you want to believe. Maybe that's what the Devil is, in the end. An idea." The Doctor's answer is not satisfying because it gives us no categorical closure. If this is somehow the "real" Satan, the original, then what are we, as viewers, supposed to think he is? What makes his presence possible? As Randall Styers has written

> Some theorists have seen magic as standing outside the category of religion, others as marking religion's outermost boundary... while magic has also been positioned as a middle ground between religion and science it has also been used as a tool to make religion itself seem less modern. (6)

In other words, these borders are not only part of how we define what religion is, but also part of how we define the modern, even ourselves. In our virtual world, where fact and fiction continue to blur, thinkers like Elaine Graham find monsters crucial to how we define ourselves and our relationship to the ideas of human and the divine. Graham writes that "definitive accounts of human nature may be better arrived at not through a description of essences, but via the delineation of boundaries" (11). For Graham, "monsters have a double function ... simultaneously marking the boundaries between the normal and the pathological but also exposing the fragility of the very taken-for-grantedness of such categories" (39). Similarly, Jeffrey Cohen sees the figure of any monster as a "form suspended between forms that threaten to smash distinctions" (6). In other words, humans define themselves by creating borders between the human and the non-human. It is the monster myths, or the "stories we live by," as Graham writes, that will be critical tools in determining what it means to be human in the new digital and biotechnological age (17), and, analogously, how we will define and behave toward our others and our gods.

Firefly *and the god-monster of nothing*

The *Firefly* episode "Bushwhacked" vividly presents the idea of the monstrous (and yet, ultimately human) Reavers, the closest thing this series has to an evil

160　*Beyond borders*

alien. The episode is the first time we see what the Reavers can do, and the idea of Reavers demonstrates how ideas of the monstrous comment on twenty-first-century definitions of the human. As is gradually revealed over the course of the show, the nightmarish and monstrous Reavers are actually genetically fully human. Driven by an intense homicidal and savage aggression that manifests in cannibalism, rape, and torture, their human appearance is concealed by the deliberate gashing and cutting of their own flesh, open or partially healed wounds, and piercings and random bits of metal shoved into their bodies. "Bushwhacked" shows each character reacting to the threat of Reavers, trying to define their difference, and grappling with the concept and fear of nothing—concepts that create a thin line between their identity as "human" and the unimaginable yet familiar creature they must face.

"Bushwhacked" opens with the crew playing a basketball-like game aboard the ship but without, as Inara says, "civilized" rules. The game is interrupted when they come across a seemingly deserted ship floating in space. As they debate whether they should risk going aboard to help possible survivors, Shepherd Book says to Captain Mal, "Shall I remind you of the story of the Good Samaritan?" Mal's response, "I'd rather you didn't," is a characteristically flippant dismissal of religion or scripture, but it also can be seen as his not wanting to be distracted from determining what the "right" decision is. By giving a direct answer to an ethical dilemma, religious thought gets in the way of Mal seeing a clearer path that admits all the complex variables. For Mal to base his decision-making process on a paradigmatic narrative taken from the Bible would be too easy. Mal still believes in right and wrong and the possibility and necessity of making ethical choices, but he no longer believes in a scriptural or a religious connection to these decisions.

After the crew boards the ship and finds the dead bodies that the Reavers have viciously slaughtered, raped, and partially eaten, Mal uses the religious sentiment of others to distract them, proposing that Book perform funeral rites: "I ain't sayin' there's any peace to be had, but on the off chance that there is, those folks deserve a little of it." Although he appears to approve of funeral rituals, he is actually just distracting the civilian members of the crew from the knowledge that they are trapped, sitting ducks for a returning Reaver ship. But for Mal, "those folks" are already dead, so he owes them nothing, including an empty ritual. His moving speech for funeral rites *is* humane, just not in the way that the crew thinks. While the others perform a religious ritual for the murdered crew, Mal, Kaylee, and Wash conduct the dangerous, delicate operation that frees the ship.

Yet as the crew conduct their various duties and rituals, they still struggle to define what kind of beings the Reavers are, and what it says about the state of being human. Mal articulates the loss of these distinctions through the concept of nothing: "Reavers ain't men, or they forgot how to be, come to just nothin'. They got out to the edge of the galaxy, to that place of nothin'… and that's what they became." Mal's explanation of the Reavers is one of several suggested in this episode as the line between Reaver and humans is confirmed by each character

Gods and monsters   161

in ways that reveal a fear of nothingness. To be human is to insist on ontological existence—we are the opposite of nothing—and in the framing of existential philosophy, it is our own awareness of nothing that allows us to create and imagine ourselves as a unified body: "nothing haunts being" Jean-Paul Sartre writes. In such a system, "nothing" then becomes a non-existence that threatens being but that also makes it possible. As usual, Mal and Book hold opposing views. Book insists on the funeral ritual as a defining border between us and them, human and non-human: "how we treat our dead is what makes us different." Mal, on the other hand, has no need for ritual and pushes the idea of Reavers to the dark recesses of his mind. For both Mal and Book, despite their inner reservoirs of strength, the idea of the Reavers is deeply disturbing. When it comes to monsters, as Cohen says, "destructiveness is really deconstruction" (14), and the Reavers threaten to reveal the lack of a normative and essential humanity.

Within the framework of the series, Reavers almost do not exist ("The greatest characters I never created," says Whedon in the DVD commentary to "Bushwhacked"). Yet although we barely see them, we see what they can do, what seeing them can do to a person, and mostly, we see the fear the idea of them creates. Their actual existence is a point of debate earlier in the series, where they are considered as legendary by some. "They're real," Zoe and others insist to the more sheltered characters who consider them fictional, but the "reality" is in the effect and not in any kind of physical essence. While Reavers, like all monsters, represent unthinkable figures beyond the borders of the charted world, and on the fringes of the imagination, the concept of the "real" is central to understanding monsters, as without possibility monsters are not monsters at all, they are merely fairy tales.

Mal, who, more than the others, has seen what Reavers can do, refuses to relate his experience in any concrete terms; he describes them as a "darkness" that "you can't even imagine … blacker than the space it moves through." It is this idea of "darkness" and of "nothing" that pulls the parts of the episode together, two concepts that simultaneously represent the Reavers, the crew's fear of them, and the only escape from the dangers they embody. Back on the ship, as Simon, the anxious ship doctor, prepares to suit up for a spacewalk, he comments on his fear of "the thought of a little Mylar and glass being the only things separating a person from nothing." Jayne responds, to taunt Simon, that "it's impressive what 'nothing' can do to a man," a comment meant as cruel humor that reads much darker when they discover what the Reavers have done to the crew of the other ship.

The Reavers on *Firefly* link the idea of nothingness and evil in a way that echoes back through Christian history. Augustine influentially asked, "what is that which we call evil but the absence of good?"—a question debated within Church philosophy for centuries to come. Within this thinking, being and goodness are identical and therefore evil is nothing and nothing is evil. But these binaries break down in modern philosophical thought where nothing or negation have become intertwined with the positive. Being and non-being must both exist as complementary notions, dialectically producing and relying on each other.

162 *Beyond borders*

For Hegel, pure Being and pure Nothing are the same, and for Heidegger too, Nothing is connected to Being. What this thinking does is make Nothing not *opposite*, but *other* than Being. Heidegger reads the philosophical axiom "nothing is without ground" to say not that everything has a ground, but to say that nothing *is* without ground. In other words, nothing exists, it *is*, but within groundlessness, outside of being. This complex (de)construction of nothing is presented in *Firefly* through each of the characters. For Mal, nothing is an existential hell of blackness; for Simon, a terrifying scientific and mathematical reality; for Jayne, something he does not understand and is therefore to be mocked or destroyed. Only for River, as we saw in Chapter One, can a negative also be something positive, an emptiness not to be feared.

The event of True Blood, or, a vampire walks into a bar

In Chapter Three, I gave an extended reading of the opening credits to HBO's *True Blood*. The bluesy song, *Bad Things*, that accompanied those credits opens with the line, "When you came in the air went out." Paired with the simultaneous flashes of entangled naked bodies, the song introduces an element of hidden and dangerous sexuality. The line itself seems to refer to a moment of overwhelming sexual attraction: perhaps we think of Sookie's reaction to vampire Bill when he first walks into Merlotte's Bar. "The air went out" suggests the situation that radically changes in this first episode, both a disorienting and overwhelming attraction and a world in which monsters are suddenly real. This moment for Sookie and others is a true "event" in the philosophical sense of when one's sense of reality is changed and a new truth can be perceived.

The entrance of the vampire (Bill into the bar, vampires into reality, and *True Blood* into our living rooms) can be seen as a type of religiously inflected event described by philosopher Alaine Badiou. In his influential work *Being and Event*, Badiou defines the "event" as occurring outside of the rules of existence. The event then, cannot *be*, it is "not," and in order for the event to occur or exist, there must be an "intervention" that changes the rules and then allows the event to be. The distinction between the intervention and the event can be confusing, as it is often the event that seems to change the rules of being. Like the entrance of a Christ into human history, the event of the vampire in *True Blood* has a particular connection to the Christian resonance of the event. While most older religions celebrated cycles of life and death and held rituals intended to maintain such cycles, Christianity insists that one specific historical intervention is the turning point in all of human history—Christ rose from the grave, the cycle of life and death reversed, and nothing would ever be the same again.

Philosophers from Hegel to Žižek have characterized Christ as "monstrous" in order to emphasize the role of him as Other. The vampire, like Jesus, represents a monstrous and not quite human figure that alters how humans see themselves. Vampires offer evidence of the weakness of God and Jesus, whose supposed immortality, if true, is not now unique. After vampires, Christ's intervention in history is rendered less of an event. If Jesus was monstrous because he was God

Gods and monsters 163

in finite flesh, then the vampires on *True Blood* as humans in infinite flesh, are similarly monstrous. The human, as Badiou points out, is a "being which prefers to represent itself within finitude, whose sign is death" (149). For finite humans, since the infinite is understood to be beyond understanding, it is associated with the divine. Yet, as much as we claim to desire immortality, we also find it unnatural and deviant. Within this context, both Christ and vampires represent a new possibility, a theoretical and theological trope that changes the ways humans imagine themselves. In other words, what is happening in *True Blood* resembles uncertain shifts in thinking among the early Christians. As early as the second century, some Christians were referring to the literal belief in resurrection as a "faith of fools" (Pagels 11). The bodily resurrection of Christ seemed to suggest that Christians valued the body and saw it as inseparable from the soul. But, on the other hand, many Christians from the beginning devalued or even claimed disgust at the human body. It is this irresolvable clash as it is negotiated in the then human/non-human body/non-body of Jesus that blurs the lines between god and monster. Faced with an impossible theological conundrum, the great church councils of the fourth century ultimately created a greater one, deciding that Christ was both and equally fully man and God. Badiou labels this contradiction a *limit*; in other words, two opposing terms and concepts are somehow allowed to coexist—a new ontological logic has been created, and both God and the world are different after this encounter. After these fourth-century Christians, humans become more like the divine and Gods are more like humans; by the same logic, in *True Blood*, the vampires are more human and the humans more vampiric. They are both changed to the very core of their being, in that they do not exist as they previously did.

One of the more complicated characters on *True Blood* is Godric, a 2,000-year-old vampire who spent most of his existence hunting humans for sport and passing on his disdain for the living to his vampire "children." However, over his long life, Godric realizes that all the violence that he had both inflicted and suffered left him empty and he becomes compassionate, and even loving, toward humans. In perhaps the most memorable scenes in the series, he decides to end his life: "Two thousand years is enough," says Godric, "Our existence is insanity. We don't belong here" ("I Will Rise Up"). As he waits for the vampire-killing sun to rise, Sookie agrees to stay with him to the end. Godric asks her, "Do you believe in God?" When Sookie responds yes, he asks, "If you're right, how will he punish me?"

SOOKIE: God doesn't punish, God forgives.
GODRIC: I don't deserve it. But I hope for it.
SOOKIE: We all do. Are you very afraid?
GODRIC: No. No, I'm full of joy.

As the sun rises, Sookie tells him, "I'm afraid for you," and Godric speaks his last words: "A human with me at the end, and human tears. Two thousand years, and I can still be surprised. In this, I see God."[2] Like the Doctor who travels

164   *Beyond borders*

the universe to be "proved wrong," Godric sees the divine in a final moment of surprise. For a non-believer and a vampire to "see God" in the kindness of the Other and in the act of being surprised and in the understanding that there are possibilities for something new is true radical theology. This is a god that may be, a god of possibility, a god of radical otherness and forgiveness, a god of wonder.

Conclusion

When is supernatural power divine and when is it monstrous? Season one of the 2020 Netflix show *Warrior Nun* is essentially based around that very question. Based on the graphic novels by Ben Dunn, *Warrior Nun* revolves around the story of nineteen-year-old Ava who wakes up in a morgue, given a new chance at life by what is apparently a magical angel's halo embedded in her back. She discovers that because of the halo and the powers it gives her, she is now part of the ancient Order of the Cruciform Sword that has been tasked with fighting demons on Earth. The show features evil priests, manipulative Cardinals, ass-kicking nuns, demons, and powerful scientists creating a quantum Higgs Field made from an element called Divinium and a shield that had been lost to the Church since the Third Crusade. Like *Manifest* we see a blurring of modern science, ancient religion, and magic. In this case, the scientist has stolen objects from the Church to create the world's first quantum portal as an entrance into an eternal heaven for her terminally ill son. Often described as *Buffy* with a heavy dose of pseudo-Catholicism, *Warrior Nun* is also an example of a show using monstrous non-humans to challenge the lines between science, magic, and religion, and between monsters and divinity. Fans and critics were quick to give these blurred borders some serious thought. As Jonathon Wilson wrote, "those who grew up within in-stitutionalized religion, or those who didn't but have an interest in how it shapes the world we live in, will find a surprisingly challenging examination of such here" (*RSC* July 1, 2020).

In the climax of the first season, Ava must go into the tomb of the angel Adriel beneath Vatican City to make sure the demon-controlling power contained within does not fall into the wrong hands. Once inside the tomb, however, Ava finds not the bones of a dead angel, but the living Adriel instead. He tells her that, contrary to the legend of the order, his halo was actually originally stolen and the Church has kept him locked away all this time. What Ava realizes, though, is that this whole story has been a lie. Adriel is no angel, but a demon, and this whole thing has been a plot by his followers to free him from his prison.

As the episode ends, it appears we now know who is on the side of good and who is on the side of evil—with Christian believers and unbelievers on both sides—but the ambiguity between angels and demons still hovers. Angels have been domesticated in the modern world, dressed up in pink and hung on Christ-mas trees, but their long history is not so tame.[3] There is plenty of power in this story, and while it seems to be magical, scientific, and religious, it is not clearly linked to any source of "Good." Fallen angels—those stars that the dragon's tail

Gods and monsters 165

swept from the sky—may, like the dragons in *Game of Thrones*, be buried deep in our religious subconsciousness, but as Freud knew, these repressed tombs will always open and reveal the monsters and gods within.

While it may help ease our minds to relegate both monsters and gods to some common world of unconscious myth, in the contexts that I have been pursuing, they are more accurately described as creatures of what Herbert Schneidau—writing on the Bible—calls "anti-myth." Schneidau expands the idea of anti-myth from earlier thinkers, and sees the role of narrative in the Bible as one of alienation and destabilization, rather than stability or truth claims. Read seriously, the Bible forces us to face the precariousness and fictional quality of our meaning-making systems, individual and cultural. If myth offers answers, anti-myth offers questions, if myth supplies consolation, anti-myth supplies fear and trembling. These ways of thinking are counter to the many twentieth-century thinkers who made the argument that modern humans were incapable of mythological thought. As sociologist Peter Berger wrote, the average middle-class American who has a vision of a demon is "more likely to call a psychiatrist than an exorcist" (8). While this still may be true, the number of monsters and demons on television, while they may not be believed in "literally," forces us to ask ourselves uncomfortable questions: what gives us the right to slaughter zombies, vampires, or sentient robots? Is the Doctor really no better than the Daleks? Who gets to make these decisions?

When is supernatural power divine and when is it monstrous? Richard Kearney expresses concern about this "quasi-equivalency between light and horror," an idea that, to him, "leads all too easily to a relativizing of ethical thinking." As he writes "Etty Hillesum was not Hitler. Mandelstam was not Stalin. Jesus was not Judas" (*Strangers* 121). But, as Kearney asks, "How are we to differentiate between the voice that bade Abraham kill Isaac and the voice that forbade him to do so?" (*Strangers* 10). What if we construct a philosophical interpretation of monsters that emphasizes possibility over actuality, one that is built on the assumption that they *may be*? I am not proposing that we must suddenly believe in ghosts, werewolves, alien abductions, or, for that matter, the resurrection of Jesus; only that, in our critical perspective, we should try to imagine *not* disbelieving. In other words, what happens if we apply Kearney's idea of a "God Who May be" to our monsters, demons, dragons, and cyborgs? What if the monster is not a metaphor for either the wholly other or something within the self? What if it is not, in fact a metaphor at all, but is actual? These speculations involve somehow placing both our beliefs and our skepticisms—conditioned by centuries of metaphysical thinking—into a sort of limbo. Kearny admits that his God Who May Be involves new ways of thinking (about time, for example) that we may not be capable of, and so does the monster-who-may-be. In the same ways that true religious belief should involve imagination of the non-existence of God, true skepticism, needs to be processed through imagining the possibility of the monster or the God. Television—from the Doctor discovering an impossible Satan to the all too human Reavers to the demon/angels—offers us paths of practice.

166 *Beyond borders*

Notes

1 There are many polls on alien abduction, most famously a 1991 Roper poll that determined close to four million Americans had been abducted.
2 A related Christian "death by sunrise" for the undead is found in the final episode of *Midnight Mass* where a whole community of recently undead villagers realize they are perhaps not inhabiting a biblically prophesized eternity through a eucharistic eating of flesh and drinking blood. In the end they bond together over forgiveness and fellowship and wait for the sun singing the hymn "Nearer, my God, to Thee." In the end, they find a different kind of Christianity or religion; like Godric's, one that is rooted in kindness and not in everlasting life.
3 As the vampire/priest in *Midnight Mass* tells his congregation as they stare at a vampiric angel entering their Easter service, "remember, brothers and sisters, have faith that in the Bible, every time they mention an angel, when an angel appears to we humans, we are afraid" ("Book VII: Revelation").

Part III

Beyond time

7 The material past

Books, libraries, and scripture

With a contribution by Colleigh Stein

Books

Books, scripture, and the real

This chapter presents several related and foundational claims. First is that writing is the condition of the possibility of history—the existence of history is predicated on the technology of writing in order to make and preserve what is deemed worth recording. The second claim is that history is also determined by writing—both by what, in the traditional sense, is written and by how we interpret its meanings and authenticity. The third claim, that Western ideas of what an individual or the "self" is, can be directly connected to these practices of writing and by how we imagine the idea of a text or a book. Finally, these interwoven ideas of book and scriptures, the self, history, and the human meaning-making process contain practices that can and should be understood as "religious."

Television dramas of science fiction and fantasy and the great myths of Western religions all have complicated relationships with the idea of the book and the preservation of knowledge. This relationship has been and continues to be laudatory, suspicious, imaginative, and challenging. Books represent ideas preserved, but also ideas forgotten, misplaced, stolen, hidden, misrepresented, and misunderstood. Books are indicators of how ideas develop, travel, and change, and they embody the technologies through which this happens. Books fit uneasily within the expansive and fluid boundaries of the television drama—two different ways of attempting to tell and contain a story. Books are also directly connected to our ideas of what we believe. Many believers describe their God using passages from scripture. But just as there is no single source of scripture, there is no single image of God. The Christian God is a blend of ancient Hebrew and Greek ideas, but has also been shaped by hundreds of years of books and art since then. Some get their idea of God from children's books or fairy tales. Or perhaps visual art: the Sistine Chapel gives us the great, bearded man in the sky reaching out to Adam. For some, God is more abstract, some idea of infinite knowledge—a universal library or a limitless search engine.

The book as a metaphor represents how we understand the complexity of the whole, of how we understand beginnings and endings. For medieval scholars, the whole universe was a book meant to be read. If the universe is a book, then

DOI: 10.4324/9781003227045-11

170 *Beyond time*

God is the Author, and reading reveals his intentions. For Martin Luther, the Bible contained all the religious knowledge we need. This religious metaphor persists even today in our digital world, and fantasy and SF repeatedly return to books (often unopened) upon a shelf, as wisdom to be hidden or discovered. Past, present, and future, books still represent the whole—an entire person, a complete story. Understood this way, books are, according to the literary critic Geoffrey Hartman, "solidly constructed, unified, and ... defied by clear and resolute boundaries" (2), a definition that accords with traditional scripture. A more radical scripture can perhaps be found in the act of challenging these boundaries. For Mark C. Taylor, for whom, "the notion of the book is theological" (*Erring* 76), "the 'end' of the book is the 'beginning' of writing (*Erring* 98). In other words, the "closure" of the "book" opens up into the writerly and readerly (and sacred?) potential of a "text." Television shows such as *Sleepy Hollow*, *Game of Thrones*, and *The Magicians* feature books that suggest a linear and single history and bordered individual personalities, but at the same time they subvert these notions as the fantastic elements of these shows often propose that books are capable of (often literal or magical) change. Time travel shows like *Doctor Who* or *Outlander* waver inconsistently between whether time can be rewritten or not, and often use books, reading, and the library as containers and determiners of history and knowledge.[1]

These challenges to the basic concept of what a book is and does are central to the shifting understanding of the relationship between the self and religious practice. Philosopher Stephen Mulhall challenges the idea that we must see the self as possessed of an essentially narratival structure (i.e. a book), to maintain a religious perspective ("Theology and Narrative" 29). For Mulhall, "a conception of the self that properly acknowledges human finitude" is one that knows "individual human lives are necessarily not such as to be wholly educatable, either in part or as a whole." Understanding the process and this self in narrative means to bring "readers up against the enigma residing in any human life, taken in all its individuality" (34). Mulhall's argument is that there is a reverse possibility, that this "narrative structure of the self, risks going against the grain of a specifically religious understanding of human beings and their history" (30), a "reverse possibility" that I find expressed in speculative television. Essentially, there are two views of the human self—one a whole individual with definable boundaries and the other a more porous being composed of a network of connections. Books may stand for a unified whole, with a beginning and ending, but they often lay unread or unfinished, and they are always only a fragment of what we know, of the whole story. Religious and humanist thinking that are traditionally associated with the idea of the whole, ultimately reveal themselves as fragmented. It is the interplay between these two views of the religious self that this chapter explores through speculative television and its negotiations with books, libraries, and writing.

Rewriting history

From the Torah to the Christian Bible to the Quran to the Book of Mormon, the material book as well as its authorship and interpretation have been wound up in the making of religion. Yet, like the wisdom of Plato's Socrates, the sources of these books and their words are ambiguous and multiple. The Ten Commandments are often regarded as an unquestionable foundational document, yet Moses smashed the first version of the written tablets, and the Bible is fuzzy on how and who wrote them down again. Jesus may be the Word, but he never wrote a single one (only a scribble in the sand at one point). The Quran is analogous to Islam what Christ is to Christianity—the Word of God that has eternally existed, but is made manifest at a point in history—and Mohammad spoke and left the writing to others. Our religions of the book are always on the other side of pure origin, and we are interpreting and translating from the beginning. "In the beginning was the Word," perhaps, but we can never know what that word was and where it came from. Judaism, Christianity, and Islam have their own sacred scripture, but each also has histories of burying, copying, burning, or forging texts.

Although Christian scholars assumed the Bible was a coherent and unified book for centuries, this idealization has gone through obvious destabilization in the modern era. We now know the early history of the Bible involved multiple versions and debates over what would be considered the true scripture. Influential theologian Hans Frei described this shift, saying that before the Enlightenment, the Bible was predominantly read as a full narrative, a book that tells the complete story of the world, from creation to the end of time. For these Christians, the Bible was *the* Book, it contained all of reality, told from the point of view of an infallible Author. In adopting this view, certain assumptions about sacred books bleed into secular reading practices: the book as an entire narrative, the omnipotence of the author, the singleness of meaning, and the importance of written language to make sense of one's own lived experiences. By the eighteenth century, however, as Frei explains, a "great reversal" takes place. The Bible was now just one narrative, and interpretation was a "matter of fitting the biblical story into another world with another story" (99). These other "stories" came from other literature, folk traditions, songs, poetry, science, and lived experience. Put into contemporary terms, it is essentially an experiment in transmedia storytelling, or narratives told across multiple platforms and formats. It is therefore not surprising that television science fiction and fantasy—transmedia narratives concerned with "world building" and creating new patterns of thought—have also been interested in sacred texts. If understanding religious scripture now involves negotiating and balancing multiple types of texts, discourses, histories, commentaries, paratexts, and various levels of authority and authenticity, contemporary speculative television can serve as a model for how that happens and how we understand it. We can turn here to two different examples of how television complicates and pluralizes networks of God, Book, History, and Self.[2]

The *Battlestar Galactica* episode "Razor" was placed outside of time, airing between seasons three and four, but chronologically fitting into season two. The plot was also largely flashbacks and filled in many of the details that preceded the beginning of the series. The final scene presents a conversation between Adama and his son Apollo, as they remember the decisions they and others have made that led to years of violence and death.

172   *Beyond time*

ADAMA: You did nothing wrong, neither did I.
APOLLO: Cain, Kendra…were they wrong?
ADAMA: Well, if I believed in the gods, I'd say they'd be judged by a higher power.
APOLLO: But since you don't believe?
ADAMA: Then history will have to make its judgments. And, since history's first draft will be written in our logs…
APOLLO: I guess I've got some writing to do.

What is most interesting about this exchange is the association of history and the gods as related and intersecting with ways of organizing events—for Adama (sometimes called "Admiral atheist"), history will make a god-like judgment not on what they did, but on what they write down. The realization is that history— like religious faith in God or the gods—is something written, has an unclear origin, is always in flux, and is created by us, yet determines who we are. For the French philosopher Jean-Luc Nancy, "the only current atheism is one that contemplates the reality of its Christian roots" (113), and Adama is making that very point in this scene as he sits down to write their story.

* * *

The central premise for the first season of the ABC fantasy television drama *Once Upon a Time* (2011–2017) is that a group of characters from various fairy tales have been transported to the modern-day world in the town of "Storybrooke," Maine, where they have been stripped of the memories and identities from their previous lives in the "enchanted forest." Characters include the Evil Queen, Rumpelstiltskin, and Snow White, who now live as everyday people with normal American names. The very concept of the show is about remixing different versions of the traditional stories and fairy tales, all of which exist across books, films, television shows, and amusement parks. The only character in the first season that sees the truth is the young, adopted son of the Evil Queen who has a book of fairy tales that he uses to identify characters from the town. The idea of the "book" as a source of true identity is complicated by the framing of the show itself, which not only borrows identities from multiple fairy tale traditions, but does so within an essentially Disney universe. The characters of Sleeping Beauty or Peter Pan, in other words, are rooted in the versions presented in the Disney animated versions, and later characters come from recent Disney movies (*Frozen*), as well as classic films (*Wizard of Oz*), literature (*Frankenstein*), legend (Robin Hood), and mythology (Hades).

The young Henry's book is both a form of scripture—some characters believe and others do not—and it is also a valuable and magical object, one of a kind that can be lost, damaged, hidden, or stolen. One way to see the book is to imagine it as a type of Bible, a signifier of absolute truth. On the other hand, we can see it as an object through which narratives and identities can be questioned. The various devices and narrative concepts of the show allow the book to play all of these roles. In the fourth season, Regina, the Evil Queen seeks to find the mysterious "Author" of Henry's book so that she can finally have him "rewrite her happy ending." In other words, characters begin to realize that to some extent they are being "written" into a narrative, not necessarily trapped within the binding of a book. When the 2016 promo for ABC's reality series *The Bachelorette* quoted the Evil Queen's wish to "rewrite her happy ending," the level of interconnectivity between reality and fantasy increased even further.

Without directly referencing religion, *Once Upon a Time* implicitly addresses these issues within the main story line. For example, in the episode "Smash the Mirror," the Queen associated the book with the goodwill of an unfair universe when she complains to Snow White, "Whenever you need help it just magically shows up—like Henry's book." Snow White tries to explain, "When you do good the universe takes care of you. That's why it showed up," and then offers a theory of soteriology: "Doesn't mean you can't earn forgiveness, a chance at grace. I have to believe that… You are not all evil, and I'm not all good. Things are not that simple." The Queen, though, echoes Christ on the cross in appealing to an all-powerful God/author: "Well, whoever's guiding all this seems to think it is. You're the hero and I'm the villain. Free will be damned. It's all in the book." What is interesting, of course, is the extent to which actual Christian language— damned, grace, free will, forgiveness—are used in this discussion on a network fantasy show.

These kinds of dramatic constructions rooted in the connections between books and belief demonstrate what Nancy means when he writes that "Christianity is inseparable from the West" (115). Shows like *Once Upon a Time* suggest that our very assumption about self, book, and history are linked to ways in which we are implicitly "religious" or, in other words, how we cling to our beliefs in concepts of autonomy, time, and teleology that are determined by our religious history, belief systems, and scriptures we may no longer consult but which still shape us. When Nancy claims that "although the de-Christianization of the West is far from being a hollow phrase, the more it takes hold and the more visible it becomes, the more we are bound within the very fabric of Christianity" (115), he points to a dialectic that dominates our experience of speculative fiction. From more obvious examples like *Manifest*, *Midnight Mass*, and *Vampire Nun*, to the more secular *Firefly* and *Battlestar Galactica*, we find examples of fiction that embrace a Christian structure, yet push against it. By close reading the visual images, the narrative, and fan-based discourse we will explore how these spaces fulfill different roles, and draw on different frames of reference; they each negotiate a space of memory, death, and the real that draws on the religious challenges contained in an imaginary past and a posthuman future, between a sacred book and a creative writer.

Libraries

One of my favorite classes to teach is an undergraduate seminar called "Imagining the Library." In this class, we study the legendary destruction of the library of

174   *Beyond time*

Alexandria, we read Jorge Luis Borges' "The Library of Babel" and Umberto Eco's *Name of the Rose*, we visit archives and rare book collections, we look at scrolls and manuscripts, and we watch the *Doctor Who* episode "The Silence in the Library." Early in the semester, I present various questions to provoke thought, mostly revolving around the human desire or perceived responsibility to preserve knowledge, material, and texts. One question that always produces a thoughtful discussion is: do we have a moral duty to preserve human thought and culture beyond the existence of the human race? As a culture, we are fascinated by stories of lost civilizations (Atlantis), libraries destroyed (Alexandria), or rediscovered scriptures (Dead Sea Scrolls); in essence, we are drawn to the texts and stories that may have been lost. But what about the opposite: what happens when the library, a museum, or an archive survives, but people do not? What good is a library after humans? If we left our libraries behind, or shot them into deep space for safekeeping, could an alien species tell the difference between a novel and a work of scripture, or between a library and a church? Would the survival of certain kinds of libraries mean that a species is not extinct?

In the 1969 *Star Trek* episode "All Our Yesterdays," the crew beams down to a doomed planet that is hours from destruction.[3] The formerly civilized planet shows no sign of intelligent life until they find one last inhabitant, a librarian named Mr. Atoz (A to Z) in a room that Spock describes as an "archive or a library of some kind." Kirk comments that library is "certainly the right place to find out what happened." In the library is a machine that functions as a time travel portal—an active symbol of the record of the lost civilizations that this library holds—and that allowed the residents of the planet to escape the immanent destruction by going back in time to their selected era. Mistaking the crew for citizens of the doomed planet, the librarian invites them to do research in the library to determine the time they want to escape to. Mr. Atoz comments that "a library serves no purpose unless someone is using it," and then at the end disappears into the machine, leaving the deserted planet and an empty library to its destruction with the entire planet's population living out their lives in the past.

* * *

Although the home computer, smartphone, internet, and cloud now assume many of the library's previous functions in storing and disseminating information, the idea of the library as a sacred space persists, even, perhaps especially, in fantasy and science fiction. In this section, I will look at several contrasting libraries in speculative television and think specifically about how they think through alternative, yet still religious conceptions of life, death, and immortality. I will look at four different spaces: the high school library in *Buffy the Vampire Slayer*, the Borgesian library of the *Doctor Who* episode, "The Silence of the Library," the digital identity-storage system in *Westworld*, and the grand medievalist Citadel Library in *Game of Thrones*. A library on television is, of course, already imaginary and digital while it is still rooted in memories of the real. The library in *Buffy*, the Sunnydale High School Library, is located directly over the Hellmouth, serves

The material past   175

as Buffy and her friend's main base of operations, and is stocked with occult texts and medieval-looking weapons. The library in the *Doctor Who* episode acknowledges its digital roots in a plot that includes "saving" people from death by "downloading" them into the library's system, yet is stubbornly material in its organization of rooms, shelves, and books. In *Westworld*, the library contains full human personalities downloaded and saved for immortality at a price. The cathedral-like library in *Game of Thrones* appears to be realistically lit by large medieval widows, but is created almost exclusively through CGI effects. In each case, the libraries stand for something outside the frame of the story itself.

The popularity of my library class among university undergraduate points to the much-discussed rise in the acceptance and even glorification of books. For a generation of young people raised on *Harry Potter*, the phrase "let's go to the library" can sound like a call to arms, and dusty leather-bound books and old wooden reading tables can communicate excitement. Like Harry and Hermione, Buffy and her friends spend a lot of time reading in the school library. More specifically, as Mark A. McCutcheon writes, they "spend a lot of time doing *research*: finding the most authoritative sources on a subject, reading up, and discussing what they read." Preparation for a battle often begins with a research montage. Not only is research a common activity in shows like *Buffy*, but it "makes it imperative that one does one's homework, that one does it well: using the best sources and reading them diligently" (McCutcheon). In many shows since *Buffy*, research has served as an important element of the actions, often in discerning supernatural or fantastic elements. In the show *Manifest*, for example, the one member of the Stone family who does not receive the (perhaps divine or supernatural) Callings, is able to figure out mysteries through, reassembling, cleaning, and translating, ancient Egyptian papyrus that prophesize the future.

Giles may be Sunnydale's high school librarian, but he is essentially the curator of a rare books collection. Various *Buffy* fan sites list many of the books in the library such as the multi-volume *Writings of Dramius* and Bristow's *Demon Index*—alongside "real" books like a collection of Emily Dickenson's poetry. The actual physical library contains elements of classical library architecture along with references to both high school and to dark hidden secrets. The center of the library is octagonal, with a skylight above and a red line on the floor below, clearly defining its shape. It also contains a wooden table with chairs in the center of the octagon. There is a doorway at the back of the balcony containing another room, which, according to Giles, is an old boarded-up cellar. The library also includes a steel book cage that is used to store weapons and some special volumes (and occasionally dangerous supernatural beings, such as werewolves.) This visual enforces the idea that books contain dangerous secrets—and that they are often kept hidden or inaccessible (Image 7.1).

Although *Buffy* does not have any kind of traditional religious base, the books in this library make up an alternative history outside of the familiar world they appear to live in. Read and researched correctly, a different world history emerges, one which, as Giles explains (in the library), "contrary to popular mythology, did not begin as a paradise." We know this because the "books tell

176 *Beyond time*

Image 7.1 Sunnydale High Library (*Buffy the Vampire Slayer*, "The Harvest").

the last demon to leave this reality fed off a human" ("The Harvest"). The implied alternative here is obviously Genesis, but clearly the biblical "book" gets the history wrong. How does Giles know which books to believe? Significantly, the library is destroyed at the end of season three during the high school graduation ceremony, an incident that represents a turning point in the show. One of the main themes of the following season will be the lack of identity for the group of friends—an identity for which the library was the physical symbol. The center of research and friendship will eventually move to a store called the Magic Box, which offers a similar function but through different symbols—still the center of social activity and research, the shop blurs the lines the show has previously established between sacred texts, scientific research, and occult objects, both commercial and ancient. Throughout the show, from the library to the magic shop, dusty leather-bound books suggest old book-binding practices but also a kind of scriptural status—they function instead of the rarely referenced Bible to control the fates and futures of the characters. These books are performative and informative—they are as much talismans as bound sets of pages, information, and history, and they function at the intersection of scholarly manuscript, rare book, grimoire, and scripture.

Doctor Who *and "Silence in the Library"*

Perhaps the most famous library in modern literature is in Argentinian author Jorge Luis Borges' short story "Library of Babel," where he creates a fantastic library that houses all the books that have ever been written and all those that will be written, and every book that could exist.[4] As a truly universal library, every

The material past   177

possible combination of letters, words, and pages is present somewhere in that library, the answer to every question, the end to every story, and every possible contradicting variant. Everything that has been and will be thought can be found in some corner of the endless library. The story describes in detail the impossible physical structure of the infinite library space: "The Universe (that some call the Library) is composed of an undefined, maybe infinite number of hexagonal galleries" (79) and, like any library, ancient, present, or speculative, the play of light and dark, shadows and illumination, is central. The light in the Library is insufficient, leaving the readers always partially in the dark. An endless whole, always seen as a fragment, "only the impossible is excluded" (85).

The two-part *Doctor Who* episode "Silence in the Library" and "Forest of the Dead" stages some of these same issues—asking almost directly what the relationship will be between how we will understand the idea of humanness, our gods, our scriptures, and the very way we intend to present ourselves to the future. Like the Borges story, the strength of the episode is how it reveals the intersections between each of these ideas. While Borges' library was the universe (or perhaps all the parallel universes), the library that the Doctor and his companion Donna visit takes up an entire planet. It is the biggest library in the universe, containing every book ever written by humans, with the "biggest hard drive in history: the index to everything ever written, backup copies of every single book" at the planet's core.

Yet, like many *Doctor Who* episodes, what begins as a visit to one of the great tourist attractions of the universe, turns dark, in this case literally. The basic plot of the episode is that the Doctor and Donna encounter a team of archaeologists led by River Song. The Doctor discovers that while she knows him intimately, he has not met her yet. A young girl communicates with the group via her television, and members of the team start to disappear or die, eaten by the monster in the shadows, the "Vashta Nerada." The Vashta Nerada are perfect creatures for a library as they live in the darkness, disguised as dust, casting shadows when they enter light. To avoid them, one must try to stay in the light and avoid the darkness. In the second part, "The Forest of Dead," while the Doctor fights the Vashta Nerada and tries to figure out who River Song is, Donna is absorbed into the computer program where she slowly realizes that she has been downloaded onto a hard drive. The Doctor manages to save Donna, but River sacrifices herself for him and becomes eternally trapped inside the computer. But more important than the plot is the ways that the episode forms a meditation on what it means to be human, what it means to exist or cease to exist, and how we remember, save, and disseminate our knowledge and our stories into an unknown, absent, and perhaps meaningless future. These questions are religious ones that are wound into each culture's view of scripture and of the ontology of human imagination at the intersection of finitude and infinity.

At the beginning of the episode, as he looks down at what appears to be an abandoned city, the Doctor comments, "We're near the equator, so this must be biographies. I love biographies." When Donna responds "Yeah, very you. Always a death at the end," the Doctor says "You need a good death. Without

178 *Beyond time*

death, there'd only be comedies. Dying gives us size." The Doctor here echoes the many thinkers who claim that it is death that gives life meaning and then asks us to ponder the relationship between life, death, and material memory. Like the rebels in the dystopian *Altered Carbon*, he insists on the necessity of a "real death" for the fullness of life.[5] But what role does record-keeping play? Does a biography lead us through a life into death or does it preserve the life itself? The idea of the biography asks the same philosophical questions that the idea of time travel does, and these are all questions presented by the rest of this episode in which River lives her life in the opposite direction of the Doctor. River "dies" at the end, but is yet preserved in the data core of the library in a type of afterlife, "saved" in its data banks. Like the *Star Trek* episode, the library here is a space where a person can both lose themselves and also be saved or preserved in time. The contradictions are made apparent at the beginning of the episodes as the Doctor tries to determine if anyone is in the Library.

DOCTOR: If I do a scan looking for your basic humanoids.... I get nothing. Zippo, nada. See? Nobody home. But if I widen the parameters to any kind of life... A million, million. Gives up after that. A million, million.
DONNA: But there's nothing here. There's no one.
DOCTOR: And not a sound. A million, million life forms, and silence in the library.
DONNA: But there's no one here. There is just books. I mean, it's not the books, is it? I mean, it can't be the books, can it? I mean, books can't be alive.

This is the question of the episode and of every book and library and digital storage system. What is the relationship between the record of a human event and the living human themselves? Or, to put it in the evangelical language of the episode: what does it mean to be *saved*? The shades of meaning move from the basic idea of a biographical book to the saving of a real human face on a talking statue. But more than that are the moments between life and death, where someone can perhaps still be saved. The million life forms are the swarming microscopic Vashta Nerada, also known as "piranhas of the air," who, in large enough numbers, kill their victims by instantly stripping their flesh. However, the team that the Doctor meets on the planet are wearing communication devices which can store their thought patterns for a few minutes even after death as they slowly fade into non-existence. Characters who are already "dead" whose consciousness persist are able to hold a limited conversation: "a soul trapped inside a neural relay going round and round forever." As each of the characters in the episode are killed, their brief movement of digital "ghosting," as their consciousness hangs onto the last few words, repeated over and over, creates a metaphor of the idea of the temporary preservation of a human or of a book in a library. As Eugene Vydrin said, at a group viewing session of this episode, what is so devastating about the ghosting moment is both its fragility, and the vanishing. The viewers know something about what is happening that the consciousness inhabiting that space does not know. The

The material past 179

reverse is always true in a library: you are expiring much faster than it is, but the book will also eventually decay or exist unread. We travel at different speeds to our ends.

After Donna disappears, the library hard drive makes the enigmatic statement that "Donna Noble has been saved." The word "saved" here resonates with its Christian, digital, and archival meanings—all of which seem to apply—and the Doctor fixates over the meaning of the word ("Nobody says saved. Nutters say saved.") until he realizes that "it literally meant saved." The library stores the physical self to be actualized again whenever it is requested, or as the Doctor says, "people stuck in the system… waiting to be sent like emails." The Library, we ultimately learn, was built to preserve the life of a dying little girl whose "living mind" is preserved in the mainframe with "all of human history to pass the time." Perhaps this is this what libraries will become. Or perhaps it is what they already are. Our architecturally impressive buildings are only due to rich humans constructing an archive to pretend we are not dying out and so that at some point in the future, a lost or trapped civilization with no future will have something to read. Perhaps "all of human history" is just the scripture of a doomed species. Perhaps it "gives us size." In an episode about saving humans, about preservation both digital and material, the underlying theme—like the Vashta Nerada that hides in the darkness—is the death that inhabits every shadow.

We see a similar theme in season two of *Westworld* when we are introduced to the Forge, a server farm/library for the storage of human information, which the Delos Corporation has been mining this whole time. One of the more provocative revelations to emerge in the second season of *Westworld* happens when we learn that guests are being secretly observed and recorded, the true commercial value beyond the park. The Forge itself is programmed into a library where Dolores is allowed to browse among the various "books" containing the full information about human guests who have visited the park. The CEO of Delos, the corporation that maintains all the intellectual property of the parks, says to one of the Hosts:

> That's why your world exists. They [the Guests] wanted a place hidden from God. A place they could sin in peace. But we were watching them. We [Delos] were tallying up all their sins, all their choices. Of course, judgment wasn't the point. We had something else in mind entirely.

As it gradually emerges, their plan is to copy and store human minds to then download into Host bodies thus achieving a type of immortality for those rich enough to afford it. Near the end of season two, we see attempts to make James Delos, the company's founder, into a copy of himself following his death. Each version of Delos, however, although not initially self-aware that it was a copy, would fail after reaching a "cognitive plateau." One of the fading and damaged copies tries to explain the experience of gradually becoming nothing, and can only find religious language.

180   *Beyond time*

I'm all the way down now. I can see all the way to the bottom. Would you like to see what I see? They said there were two fathers, one above, one below. They lied. There was only ever the Devil. When you look up from the bottom, it was just his reflection, laughing back down at you. ("Riddle of the Sphinx")

Gradually, each copy, each reincarnation, will fade and collapse—an extended version of the final few seconds of the Vashta Nerada victims—except it's only a temporary death; the "person" will wait for their identity to be taken out of the library and loaded into another copy of the body to try again. And again.

Enlightened medievalism

In one of the most striking scenes in *Game of Thrones* not involving dragons, sex, or violence, the season six finale, "Winds of Winter," featured a spectacular library. Samwell—the stout everyman, who up to this point has mostly experienced defeat and humiliation—is sent to study at the Citadel to become a "maester." As Sam nears the city of Oldtown, the Citadel towers over the other buildings and the water—it was perhaps the most impressive building the series had thus far presented. But it is when Sam enters the library that the scene's focus turns to the internal, both literally, the inside of the library, and symbolically, as a show where knowledge and history had been predominantly oral is now imagined as being in books.

It also quite literally suggests a type of enlightenment, as instead of the usual *Game of Thrones* interiors of torches, lanterns, hallways, and candles, the library is lit by natural light streaming through clerestory windows (the same architectural innovation that made it possible for parishioners to read in a medieval cathedral). Sam walks torchless through a hallway of books into an open central area. As his eyes (and ours) look upward over the rows of books, we see a massive mobile of giant glass lenses that directs incoming sunlight around the library (Image 7.2).

Sam is also literally enlightened when a single beam of light is directed at him. It is the books, though, that make us gasp. In a show that is so much about who gets to tell the stories and what has been misremembered or forgotten, a show where the most powerful magic, technology, and knowledge have been lost, and where books have been rare and even neglected, to see this giant container of preserved—if dusty and dim—knowledge makes the show suddenly feel different, a difference indicated by the look on Sam's face (Image 7.3). The library seems to represent both rationality and magic.

While this striking scene received a fair amount of fan and critical attention right after the episode, it is not often remembered as central to the major themes of the series. However, for our purposes, it presents a medievalist fantasy library that engages in many of the religious themes suggested through the images of libraries in speculative television. As we have just seen, when libraries are featured in fantasy and SF, they are often implicitly and materially enacting a tension between magic, religion, and science, each of which uses books and collections of books

The material past 181

Image 7.2 Citadel Library (*Game of Thrones*, "The Winds of Winter").

Image 7.3 Sam seeing the Citadel Library (*Game of Thrones*, "The Winds of Winter").

as markers of their authenticity. Books and libraries are often credited with both beginning and ending religion, they offer magical powers, Enlightenment rationality, and they represent lost beliefs and civilizations. Within the context of *Game of Thrones*, it is not clear whether the Citadel Library preserves old religions and religious ideas for future use or whether it hides them in a space where they will

182 *Beyond time*

not be read. In other words, it is ambiguous as to whether it serves as a container or a prison; whether it is the opening to or the end of thought. Do libraries maintain orthodoxy for a chosen few and then bury the heretical ideas deep in stacks of unread texts? In the context of *Game of Thrones*, does the North really "remember" or do we still need to write it down somewhere? And why write it down anyway, to only put the book on a shelf where it is forgotten and eaten by insects?

Scripture

From the very first season of *Game of Thrones*, a major thematic question is: who gets to tell the history? As Alex McLevy writes, "both the seven kingdoms of Westeros and the reasons for *Game of Thrones'* massive success are fundamentally the result of the same thing: people sitting in rooms, talking" (AV Club). This talking—storytelling, speculation, and history—is in taverns and castles on the show and in pubs and in office lunch rooms in the fan world. As the show progressed, these fan stories blurred together with the "canonical," which Colleigh Stein will write about in the next section. There are multiple versions of history in tension from the beginning. How did Bran Stark fall or King Robert die? Accidents? We know otherwise, but how will the history be told? Many fans had read the books, but did that mean that the history of Westeros was already written? Like Quentin Coldwater in *The Magicians*, many viewers found themselves in the world of fantasy books they had read earlier, but now the rules and story felt different. And as the show gained in popularity, fan theories gained in popularity and influence. Is Bran in reality the Night King? And to what extent did these fan theories play a role in shaping writer's decisions? "The past is already written," says the all-seeing Three-Eyed Raven, echoing the language of *Doctor Who* in using a writing metaphor to indicate an unchangeable history. But it is not actually written, or it has been lost, or written in different versions, and it will continue to change depending on how the story is told, and by whom. Of course, "people talking in rooms" was also responsible for the perception of the failure of the ending of *Game of Thrones*. And as fans grew increasingly disillusioned with the final episodes—demanding rewrites, proposing alternative versions—to what extent did that weaken the accepted "canonicity" of the show's plot? Most importantly, these questions point to modern shifts in how people relate to written history and scripture, shifts that encourage us to imaging rewritings, reframing, and alternatives not imaginable to believers in a single unchangeable sacred text.

The first episodes in the *Game of Thrones* much-discussed and controversial final season set up the final epic battles, getting everyone in the right place, and rewarding fans by allowing a few characters to have long-awaited reunions and hook-ups. Although much of the criticism focused on the rushed nature of these episodes, they did however, allow brief moments in the plot, in the text, and in the viewer's experiences for moments of speculation as to questions of meaning. In the second episode of the final season, it is revealed that the Night King, the leader of the White Walkers and their army of zombie-like Wights, does not just intend to destroy humankind, but to completely "erase" the world and "its memory" ("A

The material past   183

Knight of The Seven Kingdoms"). In this case, destroying the world's memory does not mean burning down a library, but means to kill the young Bran and his mystical ability to see the past. "Bran isn't just a great story—he's literally the repository of all the stories. He's the living embodiment of the land and its cultural memory" (McLevy). As Sam—who knows the Citadel Library which also claims to be the "world's memory"—tells him:

> Your memories don't come from books. Your stories aren't just stories. If I wanted to erase the world of men, I'd start with you.

Two kinds of memory. Two kinds of death. "That's what death is, isn't it?" says Sam. "Forgetting. Being Forgotten."

Stories outlive the mortal body and are a source of meaning, and humanity and its religions can only be destroyed together. Although the religions on *Game of Thrones* do not seem to be particularly scriptural in the sense that Judaism, Islam, and Christianity are, we can see the same emphasis on being, remembering, and writing.[6]

History and memory are two major sources of the past in *Game of Thrones*, the books in the Citadel and Bran (or the "Three-Eyed Raven's") mind. As the Night King realizes, to achieve true victory over the living—to achieve true nothingness—would involve destroying both. As Sam, the closest thing *Game of Thrones* has to a librarian, explains: memory makes people who and what they are. It is the entire purpose of legacies, written accounts, and the passing on of stories. But what happens after? Or is it something fresh, something new that will wipe humanity from the Earth in preparation for something better? As Nina Shen Rastogi writes "memory is a consistent preoccupation in *Game of Thrones*." But for all their remembering, storytelling, monuments, and visions, Westerosie history has, as Rastogi concludes, some "striking amnesiac gaps," as when their civilization forgot that White Walkers and dragons were real. Forgetting, lies, and misunderstandings, limited point of view, and political propaganda are all part of history, part of scripture, and—despite criticism of the season—the finale episode nonetheless emphasizes how "*Game of Thrones* is as much a story about historiography, or the construction of historical narratives, as it is about one particular historical narrative" (Rastogi). But memory and history are not the same, and in fact they are antagonist. Memory is constantly reworked, reimaged, shaping itself to the interplay between the two horizons of the present and the past. History is an attempt to "fix"—to put down in writing something that will not change over time. History destroys memory. Stories rise out of that destruction.

Who gets to tell the story?

By Colleigh Stein

In its simplest iteration, canon designates that which is considered authentic. Born from early Christianity, "canon" represented the collective books of the Bible that were recognized as genuine and divinely inspired—the "word of God"

184 *Beyond time*

transcribed—which served to separate the holy from the apocryphal. "Canon" conveys an act of separation and elevation. However, even this early canon had to be consciously assembled, with certain works excluded, thus implying an authority that has been constructed, rather than naturally occurring. From the invocation of the muses in Homeric epics allying the poet with the gods to the Bible as divinely authored, the early author served as mediator between Earth and divinity, the one who transcribes the knowledge they have received. Authority, in this sense, is bestowed by a higher power, rather than inherent to the author themselves. Once the mantle of author (whether a person, studio, or trademark) has been bestowed, canon then comes to represent the "true" (yet not factual) version of a work. Modern definitions of canon throughout popular culture differentiate between professional and amateur (fan) production, bestowing authority onto the former. Through their disruption, convergence, and participation, fans insert themselves into the modes of production and alter how canons are constructed. The result becomes an authorless canon—or, a canon tied more to stories, brands, or hierarchies of power than individual authorship. The fan thus turns the assumptions of textual stability and external authority into something dialogical through their engagement with authors, texts, and each other. The fan makes the canon plural.

For its first four seasons, *Game of Thrones* faced the same challenges as any adaptation: fidelity and authenticity. While showrunners David Benioff and D.B. Weiss stated they shared a close working relationship with author George R.R. Martin, emphasizing collaboration, as both book (*A Song of Ice and Fire* or *ASOIAF*) and TV fans recognize, this does not mean that the show remains entirely "faithful" to the source material. Weiss remarked, due to their tight production schedule, that he and Benioff were forced to "go off book and start making the show live and breathe on its own as a show inspired by the books but not fully informed by them" (Fleming). For the sake of its new medium, the television series was forced to simplify by combining characters and plot lines. When changes are made in the show's universe, fans must ask themselves if these are deviations from the "canon," part of it, or the beginnings of an entirely new one. While the showrunners followed the major plot developments in the novels, Martin recognized the two as entirely different entities and "described his role as 'provid[ing] the underlying material' and claimed to be unperturbed by changes to the books, noting that showrunners Benioff and Weiss 'permit' him to write one script per season" (Fathallah 117).[7] It would be unreasonable to assume the episodes Martin wrote are somehow "more" canonical than other episodes in the show, as all are for the same adaptation. Martin, in this sense, receives the same level of collaborative authority as any other screenwriter on the show.

In 2015, *Game of Thrones* aired its fifth season, which carried viewers through most of the corresponding fifth book, *A Dance with Dragons*. This meant that halfway through the sixth season, the show outpaced the source material and existed entirely off book. This forced fans to negotiate between three contending worlds: the events of the books, the changes wrought on the show, and the ramifications of the real world (actors aging, publisher deadlines, studio air dates).[8] Thus, over

The material past   185

the course of the next four years, *GoT* outran *ASOIAF*, forcing Martin to disclose character-by-character details of how his story would end to the producers so that they could lay out the groundwork. Martin therefore effectively bestowed a level of credence upon the producers as owners and creators of his universe, folding the previously separate storyworlds of the book and show into one contradictory canon. Suddenly, the chronology of canon that effectively stated, "book first, adaptation second," no longer held true. This put fans in a highly unique position. Book readers and viewers alike were plunged into an equal playing field, devoid of spoilers, watching the story unfold for the first time on screen. As a result, fans could reconcile the competing worlds of the books, shows, and their contexts by creating a fourth world: fan-generated content, independent from publisher, studio, or real-world constraints, a true fantasy realm of possibility where books, shows, and actors could exist side-by-side in the fan imagination.

The new projected timeline of the television show had profound implications for the notion of canonicity. Martin's novels suddenly became the secondary and derivative source. The still unfinished sixth and seventh books—no longer the source material—now seemed more like a novelization of a television adaptation. What do we consider "canon" now: the first (televised) presentation of material or the literature it once, but no longer, sourced from? For the first time, the written material with which the television series shared a dialogue would not be the source novels, but rather fan content and writing. If the adaptation had not been perceived as a canonical source before, and yet now must be accepted as such, why could not fan theories and creative content, often crafted with painstaking attention to detail, be given the same level of credence? When the series confirmed the long-held "R + L = J" fan theory (which speculated that the bastard Jon Snow was, in actuality, a secret Targaryen and the rightful heir of Westeros), fans felt both satisfied at how the twist was revealed and gratified that their analysis had proven true. Fans, therefore, perhaps do not want the responsibility of determining the story, but rather to feel the satisfaction that their investment and engagement with the material has paid off.

The year 2021 marked the ten-year anniversary of the publication of the fifth *ASOIAF* book, *A Dance with Dragons*. As of that time, there remained no definitive release dates for books six and seven (The *Winds of Winter* and *A Dream of Spring*). When these books contain events that differ from the television series (as is certain to happen) and differ still from a fan-created work, is there any reason that the books—now derivative, secondary sources—will be taken as the true canon? With fanfiction that brings deceased characters back to life operating in a story world that canonically revives the dead, why should the resurrections of Beric Dondarrion or Jon Snow be any more canonical than fanfiction that restores Ned Stark, Renly Baratheon, or any number of now-dead characters to life? The lines become increasingly blurred as Martin, who previously stated he would not allow the show's direction to influence his writing, has now watched his story unfold and conclude before he could write it. Without remaining entirely closed off from the television series and subsequent audience interaction, there is no knowing whether or not decisions made on the show or the fan criticisms over season eight,

186 *Beyond time*

shared widely across the internet and to which Martin has responded, impacted his direction. Which version of the story ultimately becomes more true? Perhaps this value does not have to be hierarchical, but instead book and adaptation can both tell a different canonical ending, with fans as the mediating forces to decide for themselves. Like different Gospel versions of the death of Jesus, or competing creation myths in Genesis, generations of readers have found different ways to learn to accept all, or parts of all, tellings, to allow competing canons and truths.

Within the *GoT* narrative itself, the written word is often used to validate and legitimize, or conversely, to undermine the character and viewer perceptions. In season one, Ned Stark discovered that King Robert Baratheon's blond son Joffrey was not his legitimate heir by reading a genealogy book that detailed the trademark dark hair of the Baratheon line. On its own, the book had no power to shape the story; it was not until Ned read the information and decided to act on it that its words held weight, yet their very existence highlights the importance of the recorded word in shaping the outcome of a narrative. Just as a book was used to delegitimize Joffrey's claim to the throne, a written text was also used for the opposite purpose of legitimizing another character's claim. For the majority of the show, Jon Snow was touted as the bastard born son of Ned Stark, although fans had long since put forth their own theory (R + L = J) on his true parentage. While this fan theory became canon in the final episode of season six, it meant very little in the world of the show. With the only evidence of the secret residing in the mind of a mystical seer with the body of a teenage boy, few would be likely to accept this profound new information. And, even if they had, it only proved that Jon Snow was a different man's bastard, giving him no legitimate claim to the throne. Rather, the narrative required textual evidence to support the visual. In season seven, while Sam searches for information at the Citadel, he is tasked with transcribing the old diaries of a now-dead High Septon (a Westerosi priest). As Sam's companion Gilly reads through the Septon's reports, she relays that Jon's parents were married and his claim is legitimate. And yet, at the time, this revelation means nothing to Sam, who instead grows furious at the tedious task assigned to him while he is barred from accessing the information that could save the realm. His response is to immediately leave the Citadel and instead set out to bring what he has learned to a place where it can have an impact.

Separately, Bran and Sam's information only affects the viewers and does very little to shape the storyworld. When the two come together and share what they have learned, however, they are able to fill in the gaps in each of their incomplete narratives and understand the magnitude of this buried secret and what it might mean for their country. The visual, then, becomes equally as important and canonical as the written. While text is used to prove or disprove legitimacy within the show, its existence holds little weight without interpretive power behind it. For the text to become canon, it must be read, interpreted, discussed, shared, and disseminated. Similarly, fans enforce the canon of a show by discussing, interpreting, and filling in the gaps in what they are shown to form their own theories, headcanons, and content. The power of fandom as an interpretive tool for meaning making and canon construction is predicated upon the existence of a canon

The material past   187

that fans accept as true, if only so that they can use it as a point upon which to work *against*, just as legitimacy within *Game of Thrones* requires written evidence which the reader accepts as fact in order to maintain or alter their worldview. Within the larger themes of this chapter, we can see that the acts of watching and thinking about this show force viewers to engage with ideas of the book, truth, history, and writing.

Just as the bookish Sam searched for the answers to the unknowable challenges that faced Westeros by seeking out knowledge from the Citadel Library, so too did fans defer to the authority of the text that preceded the show to puzzle out potential resolutions for the story. And like Sam, fans were disappointed when the gatekeepers of this knowledge—Archmaester Ebrose for Sam, showrunners Benioff and Weiss for the fans—did not meet their expectations. When Sam goes to the Citadel seeking answers, he finds his way barred by the Archmaester. Ebrose tasks Sam with transcribing the more decrepit books to keep their information alive, and yet he does not allow this information to be accessed by anyone outside of the Citadel walls—and very few within it. Similarly, the *Game of Thrones* audience desired to know the outcome of the story, knowing full well that Beniff and Weiss knew the ultimate end that Martin had failed to deliver on time, and yet understood that they were not in a position to be privy to this information. They, like Sam, would have to wait and pay their dues.

Frustration arises from the fact that Ebrose, Benioff, and Weiss are not the authors of the information they protect. This calls into question the legitimacy of ascribed authority in the figures who society has sanctioned to possess and propagate knowledge. If they were not the originators of the text, why are they privileged with deciding who has access? Foucault famously declared "the author is not an indefinite source of significations that fill a work; the author does not precede the works; he is a certain functional principle by which, in our culture, one limits, excludes, and chooses" (292). Even the original author may not, then, be the original source of knowledge. Who, therefore, creates knowledge? When the Maesters of old wrote of how they overcame the Long Night, had they made the discovery for themselves? Or were they aided by the Children of the Forest—the mythology of the land? Was there always a knowledge that preceded that which was put to paper and preserved? If so, the authority of the author, as keeper of the knowledge, becomes challenged. Foucault continues that this author-principle "impedes the free circulation, the free manipulation, the free composition, decomposition, and recomposition of fiction" (292). How can Archmaester Ebrose, who was never the progenitor of the information, decide who gets to access knowledge that is unauthored, unclaimed?

While Benioff and Weiss had control over the televised *Game of Thrones*, they did not create the storyworld. The series was born from the preexisting material of Martin's books, which in turn followed traditions of fantasy literature, medievalism, and historical fiction. This cycle of creation and recreation stretches into the modern media landscape which has become increasingly populated with adaptations, reboots, and revivals helmed by longtime fans of the source material. But when these fan auteurs are elevated to producers by the machinations

188 *Beyond time*

of studios, licenses, and copyrights, a shift in the power dynamic occurs. It bears contemplating how to construct a canon in this new environment, and why one must persist. Canon continues to shift away from rigidly defined boundaries into categories of understanding that aid in engagement with a text. Imagine a longtime fan who always dreamed of a particular plotline occurring, who then goes through the process of becoming a filmmaker, showrunner, etc., eventually achieving creative control over the existing material, and using this position to make their childhood fantasy come true. Why do we privilege this as canon, but deride the equally passionate creative fan works as derivative? In Martin's expansive universe, where even he as author could not keep track of all the minutiae he created without relying on fan expertise, it seems logical to continue to open up a dialogue between fan and official channels to tell the best story. Despite their early championing of collaboration and positioning themselves as one of the fans, Weiss acknowledged that they did not listen to the feedback of their fans, yet became upset by the fans' reactions to what they had done with the show. The canon, divorced from both initial creator and audience input, becomes best equated with brand or license, backed up by the industry for purely copyright purposes, removed from the fan.

This separation of the fan from points of authorship ultimately resulted in the responses to *GoT's* final seasons, ranging from the lackluster and apathetic, to disappointed and dismayed, to comparisons with "bad fanfiction." However, before the anxieties over the series concluding and fan backlash over the eighth and final season, season seven became the first to exist completely off book, and enjoyed a more positive reception. Filled with long-anticipated meetings, satisfying revenge, sprawling battles, and unexpected twists, season seven was viewed by the showrunners as "giving fans what they want. At times this season has practically felt like fan fiction—and that's exactly what has made it one of the most satisfying seasons yet" (Liao). Here, the comparison to fanfiction becomes celebratory rather than derogatory. Season seven, free of its textual constraints, could tell the story with only the visual medium in mind. The showrunners were essentially creating a "version of *Game of Thrones* that's more TV-friendly than it's ever been before. Without upcoming novels demanding a character be at a certain location at a certain time, the showrunners can simply write what's best for their story" (Liao). Such a shift led to inevitable changes in pacing and dialogue. As the showrunners and studio elected to shorten their traditional ten-episode seasons, characters could no longer spend as much time as they had meandering up and down the Kingsroad (or rowing off the coast of Dragonstone) for full episodes or even seasons before reaching their destination. Long-awaited moments occurred at last, with fans eager to see how these new dynamics would play out.

The reactions to *Game of Thrones'* final season highlights the shifting boundaries of fandom, authorship, and textual mutability. Upon the conclusion of *GoT*, an online petition on Change.org began circulating, seeking a different outcome for the series. The petition, titled "Remake Game of Thrones Season 8 with competent writers" specifically calls out authorship as the reason for the failure, and purports that "David Benioff and D.B. Weiss have proven themselves to be woefully incompetent writers when they have no source material (i.e. the books) to fall back on." Although "only" 1.8 million fans have signed (a fraction of the 20+ million viewership numbers that the finale garnered in its first week), the petition continued to attract new signatures over a year after the episode's release, and its existence points to the power of fandom to use the internet to propagate a message of disapproval. The most pessimistic and negative conclusion drawn from this demand is that of fan entitlement. In this version of fan engagement, all texts are subject to the whims and ire of their fandom and if stories are not constantly pleasing to every fan, they should be required to be retold until a satisfactory conclusion is reached. In this scenario, fans reject full ownership of the text. They are not writing the ending themselves; to do so would turn it into fanfiction, non-canonical and corrective. The call for a petition thus reaffirms the canon as written by the showrunners, demanding that it ought to do a better job, rather than abdicating its authority entirely. And even corrective fanfiction can likewise highlight the fact that, had the canon provided alternative or more diverse perspectives in the first place, the very act of transformation may not have been required. It would be impossible to publish, script, shoot, or produce every single version of a fan's ideal ending. Even if HBO possessed an unlimited budget in time, resources, and perennially unaging actors, there would be no way to assuage fandom demands for a "better" ending, as such a concept is too nebulous, too subjective, and too fraught.

Demanding a rewrite suggests that fans refused to accept the ending as canon. Paradoxically, the existence of such a petition admits that the ending *is* canonical. A defined canon acts as an authority against which fans resist, allowing transformative works a space to deconstruct and dismantle the source, to either call for a new ending or a multiplicity of endings. The reversal of the *ASOIAF/GoT* releases allowed fans an entryway to deem the events as incorrect, inadequate, and invalid. Fans, then, "constantly negotiate interpretive power away from authors and one another, thus subverting and reinforcing authorial authority and continuously shifting the conflicted site of meaning production" (Busse 63). What does it mean when the power of creation can be transferred from one figure to another? And when is that power accepted? The lack of a completed book series allowed multiple layers of canonicity to simultaneously exist. Benioff and Weiss created a canon that can either be read as the "true" version since it told the story first, or as an adaptation of some nonexistent "true" text yet to be written: an imagined, alternative canon.

That a fan can desire and demand a different outcome in the visual medium speaks to the relationship we have with television. Since the show faced the unprecedented task of concluding the series first, fans had nothing but their own theories, fanfiction, and opinions to compare with the ending. Fan demands become heightened in this age of digital storytelling. The immediacy afforded by the internet meant that a fan petition for a rewrite could garner even more support. Because of the multiplicity of authorship involved in a television production, fans felt more comfortable making requests (or demands) for these changes. Even in an age of textual mutability, an ingrained sense of the Book as Final or

190 *Beyond time*

True pervades the culture. Citing David Morgan's conception of a "constellation of four elements: reader, text, referent, and writer," Rachel Wagner acknowledges that, "when we're looking at a sacred text, this 'constellation' implies that God is the author of the Original Text, that God gave the Text to us as passive if devoted readers, receptacles of the divine words therein" (18). Under this conception, there remains something fixed about the book, and mutable about the screen. While the fans wait for Martin to write his story, they felt they bore the right to demand from HBO six (or more) new scripts, a score of new writers, months of location scouting, scheduling of actors, shooting, computer-generated dragons, months of editing, marketing, and the mass number of budgetary requirements that go into producing six hours of high-quality fantasy television. Having become familiar with this very practice through the frequent Hollywood reboots and revivals, with films releasing Director's Cuts to give extra content and context, or entire production teams being replaced between seasons or sequels, it seems natural for a fan to request a new version of the story. And as a result, the lack of a book meant that fans approached the finale of season eight of *GoT* the way they had been trained to read visual media: as negotiable.

The fan demand for a different ending *with different writers* speaks to a continued privileging of the author figure. Those who demanded the petition effectively desired that the adapters do the work transformative fans were already engaged in, that of interpreting the source material and extrapolating satisfying directions for the story. The petition shows that the *GoT* fandom wanted the work to be corrected by official, rather than amateur channels, and were requesting that a new author be given the power to complete this task. This effectively removes the author figure from the one who *originally* created the work and transposes it onto whomever fans, studios, or brands deem can tell the best version. Fans did not demand that Martin detail exactly how the ending should have happened (and, indeed, much of what occurred was the ending Martin divulged to the showrunners as soon as it became clear that he would not finish his books before the series concluded). In the lack of a finished product from Martin—and faced with what they felt was an unsatisfactory conclusion from Benioff and Weiss—fans effectively removed all creators, all progenitors of this text, from the equation and searched for a new author. This suggests the person who created the story does not always know it best. Instead, anyone who spends enough time and commitment inhabiting the narrative (writer, actor, or fan), can claim an understanding and ownership over the text, and alight upon a truth within the narrative.

Coda: losing our religion

Colleigh's section brings into detail the questions of how we determine what stories are worth keeping, preserving, and reading. Libraries present this same set of contradictions in their relationship to secular and sacred spaces and texts. On the one hand, since the Enlightenment, the idea of knowledge and progress has often been associated with secularization, and, as Thomas Augst writes, "in the age of mechanical and electronic reproduction, every gadget or system promises

The material past 191

to straighten the path to secular progress" (150). On the other hand, library architecture has traditionally been and continues to be, as William Poole wrote in 1881, "yoked to ecclesiastical architecture" (Augst 148), and books, book production, and preservation come out of and have been developed through religious, monastic, and scriptural traditions. New university and school libraries—like the rebuilt library in *Buffy the Vampire Slayer*—sometimes contain no actual books, only digital ones. Imagine a Time Lord's visit to such a library, perhaps after the human population has been eliminated? Or imagine the children of young Judith Grimes on *The Walking Dead*—stumbling into that space in some post-post-apocalyptic future with just a vague cultural memory of electricity and Wi-Fi. What might the idea of "history" or "book" or "scripture" mean in such situations?

* * *

In February, 1944, the London Library was hit by a bomb, damaging five floors of bookstacks and destroying 16,000 books, mostly in the religion and biography sections. A panicked librarian's assistant ran down from the fifth-floor exclaiming "we've lost our religion." According to the London Library Blog, librarian Eleanor Rendell, her hair clogged with brick dust, and her arms black with dirt, climbed over the debris, saying "For thirteen years I have put the biographies away," she said. "I must save what I can." The story implies a dark question that we have already seen in this chapter in episodes of *Star Trek* and *Doctor Who*. If (or when) the bombs fall, which should we value more: the lost religions or the lives preserved in our biographies?

In the post-war paranoia that followed the bombs of the Second World War—the era out of which speculative television emerges—one of the most famous television episodes of all time, the 1959 *Twilight Zone* "Time Enough at Last," featured Burgess Meredith as Henry Bemis, "a bookish little man whose passion is the printed page." Bemis's job at a bank and life at home do not allow him the time to pursue his passion of reading. After a nuclear war, he emerges to find himself alone. Hopeless, he prepares to commit suicide, when he sees the ruins of the public library. The books, however, have survived, and he happily sorts them into a lifelong reading plan. As he reaches for the first book, his glasses fall off and shatter; he bursts into tears, now surrounded by books he will never read (Image 7.4). Sixty years later, this episode continues to speak to the tensions between finitude, knowledge, and human activity. Books, libraries, and the act of reading are often part of speculative, post-apocalyptic narratives, referring back to a time when such activities were possible, as well as to the idea of the history and wisdom that is slowly fading away and being forgotten. The final scene in the *Twilight Zone* episode is visually referenced in an episode of *The Walking Dead* spin off, *Fear the Walking Dead* ("Buried"), where we see two survivors searching an abandoned library when they see piles of bloodied books on the floor and a pair of broken glasses. Nearby, is a zombie with slashed wrists, a Henry Bemis, undead after his suicide. The larger inferred question in both of these episodes

192 *Beyond time*

Image 7.4 Henry's broken glasses (*The Twilight Zone*, "Time Enough at Last").

is of the value of a book to a destroyed civilization. How much will the stories, scriptures, and narratives of a lost society be worth? Are we obligated to preserve them?

There is—as my students point out—a digital upgrade to this story, and one of the other questions we discuss is whether a digital book or a physical book has a longer life span. As author Weston Ochse pessimistically points out, what makes reading impossible in the *Twilight Zone* episode is a failure of technology—the broken glasses—and that in a world where all books are published electronically, readers would be "only a lightning strike, a faulty switch, a sleepy workman or a natural disaster away from becoming Henry Bemis at the end of the world." The material, again in this scenario, is more real than the digital. On the other hand, long after the destruction of humans and the decay of our physical remnants, it may be the digital editions of the Bible, Augustine's *Confessions*, or the digitized *Walking Dead* comics that advanced alien species are accessing somewhere, studying the lost civilizations of Earth and keeping our religions and our biographies alive.

Notes

1 We might also think here of the "Vampire Bible" in *True Blood*, which describes a kind of ethnic religion built around the divinity of Lilith, the first vampire, who blurs the lines between messiah and deity. The Bible, interpreted literally, argues for vampire

The material past 193

dominance over humans and labels any vampire human cooperation as blasphemy. Another example is the "Book of Kevin" in *The Leftovers*, a book written by the Episcopalian priest Matt Jamison, which follows all the actions of the main character Kevin Garvey, but interpreted in a way that makes Kevin into a messianic figure.

2 These categories are borrowed and adapted from Mark C. Taylor's *Erring* where they are his four main categories for "deconstructing theology."

3 Thanks to Tim McCarthy, who reminded me of this episode.

4 The Syfy series *The Magicians* (2015–2020) has a very similar library in the purgatory-like space of the "Neitherlands." The library contains "all the books ever written, all the books never written, and all the books of all the people who ever lived" ("Thirty-nine Graves").

5 Another take on the idea of the quest for real death is explored in the fourth season of *Torchwood*, the *Doctor Who* spin-off. Also known as "Miracle Day" (2011), the season is based on the idea that beginning with one 24-hour "miracle day," suddenly no one on Earth dies. Although initially hailed as a religious miracle, this mysterious immortality almost immediately begins to strain resources and spread diseases. A world government institute creates death camps where people who normally would have died must report to, and where they are secretly incinerated. Framed in multiple ways, including the religious, the season is essentially about finding a way to bring death back to humans.

6 Religions in *GoT* include animistic worship of the "Old Gods" and the worship of the "Seven-Faced-God" which deifies a single god with seven faces and a single sacred text called *The Seven-Pointed Star*. Other religions include the monotheistic worship of the Lord of Light and the resurrection-based worship of the Drowned God.

7 This lasted through season four, when he stopped contributing to focus on his own projects—namely finishing *Winds of Winter.*

8 Due to the massive popularity of *Game of Thrones* and concerns over the aging of their child actors, HBO and the producers stated they would not wait two years between seasons to allow the source material to catch up with their airing schedule (this when Martin continued to insist his sixth book, *Winds of Winter* would be completed by publishers' deadlines, after already missing its initial 2014 projection).

8 The digital present

Fans, participatory culture, and virtual congregations

With contributions by Cathryn Piwinski and Colleigh Stein

Lived experience and fan communities

COLLEIGH: *I tell people that I "stumbled into" the field of fan studies my senior year in college, but that's not technically true. The tracks were laid out well before. Which is fitting, because this story begins on a train.*

My sophomore year, I studied in London and celebrated one of my last weekends abroad by booking a trip with my flatmates to Cardiff, Wales. The real reason for this trip was a fan pilgrimage, pure and simple. We were Doctor Who *fans and we wanted to go to the city where the series was based, visit the official* Doctor Who *Experience, and stand in front of the tower on Cardiff Bay that served as the Torchwood headquarters on the show. Which is likely why, on that rainy Welsh morning that we boarded a train from Cardiff to Pembrokeshire, we discussed the idea of creating a class we could take together. It would be about the television that we loved, about the emergence of transmedia landscapes as the stories expanded beyond the screen and became connected to larger narrative universes, and about the way that people—fans—experienced and interpreted the stories they loved. It would be fangirling for credit, we joked.*

*Back in New York, I approached Greg at an information session for a class he would be teaching in the spring semester on James Joyce, where the students would travel to Dublin over break. "Remember me from Freshman year?" (He does). "We're creating this tutorial; can you be the instructor?" (Spring is too busy, with the Joyce class). "How about next fall"? (Maybe…) "We will focus on transmedia storytelling—*Doctor Who, The Walking Dead, *how the interplay between Whedon's work in* Buffy, Firefly, *and* Dollhouse *across platforms built a dedicated following …" (Fuck it, let's do it!)*

It's Spring and we are in Dublin. We had just visited Newgrange, the neolithic monument in County Meath. Everyone is tired, they fell asleep immediately on the commute back to the city. But Greg said we could discuss the tutorial today, so I shuffle my way past my sleeping classmates and sit next to Greg. So, tutorial…? The bullet points from the bus ride—March 20, 2014—are still on my Notes app, four iPhones later. The highlights:

- *Fan response/interactions, sci-fi, and fantasy transmedia*
- *Beginning with* Star Trek *as the original "fandom"*
- *Following the fan interactions of Joss Whedon's shows*
- *No series really has to end anymore*

DOI: 10.4324/9781003227045-12

The digital present   195

- Buffy *8&9 graphic novels taken as canonical with seasons 6 and 7 because written by Whedon*
- Game of Thrones *and the fan/cast/fan interaction, ways of following the show. Book fans versus show fans. Adapting such a complex plot across media.*

If you noticed the connection between our bus ride discussion and the themes in this chapter—and, indeed, this book—it is no accident. Greg had already developed the concept of the book, but it was the following fall that he asked me to be his research assistant. Our tutorial, "TV and Participatory Culture," beginning as an idea on a Welsh train and taking shape on an Irish bus, became our introduction to fan studies as a field, which would provide the vital connective tissue for this book. Fangirling for credit, indeed.

GREG: *In March of 2014, I took my James Joyce seminar to Dublin and the surrounding area to study sites related to his novels and to Irish literature. On a long afternoon bus ride coming back from a day trip—Newgrange, Glendalough, Martello Tower, I don't remember—as students napped off their St Patrick's day hangovers, Colleigh Stein, then a junior in the class, asked if we could talk, and reminded me of our plans to do a small group tutorial on fan studies. My friends often tell me that I need to learn to say "No" more and I definitely felt it at that moment, but the more we talked, the more I began to realize how it might change the shape of this book—the one you now hold in your hands, but the one that at that time was a pile of notes, multiple desktop folders, and somewhat dated previously published pieces. I was learning to think about religion differently—as practice, rather than as belief or doctrine—and I realized that I needed to think about television the same way.*

We met once a week—five students and me—around a table in a small windowless room that felt like the inside of a submarine. It was a wonderfully eclectic group of undergraduate students with a variety of academic interests, popular culture expertise, and professional experiences in television, theater, music, and writing. From the beginning of the semester, it became clear to me that fan studies had moved far beyond what I had previously understood. Reading scholars like Jonathan Gray helped me see my original framing as a type of "first wave" of fan studies that focused on "redeeming" fan activities, such as convention attendance, fan fiction writing, fanzines, and collecting as creative, and productive practices (Gray 3). The second and third wave of fan studies had moved onto regarding fan-based interpretive communities and individuals as embedded in existing social and cultural conditions (Gray 5). Most recently, studies see fans as less monolithic and more radically networked through a multitude of fan discussion groups, websites, and social media networks as well as new models of lived and material space—a framing that our group confirmed. These new models of fan studies allowed me to move beyond traditional popular culture and television studies and develop links with lived religion, religious studies, and radical theology through the ways fan activities reflect how we understand ourselves, how we interact with each other, and to how we process and reframe the constantly mediated texts that shape the religious and social experiences I wanted to write about.

Becoming fan studies

The earliest models of fan studies assumed a dichotomy of power—powerful producers on one side and consumers on the other. More recently, scholars have

196　*Beyond time*

blurred and problematized this boundary through discussion of creative and scholarly fan activity and participatory communities. Instead of just interpreting it as only cultural or political, fan productions began to be taken seriously as aesthetic and intellectual texts. Within certain spaces, virtual and actual, the gap between fan and scholar has almost closed. As Henry Jenkins writes, "fans are central to how culture operates. The concept of the active audience, so controversial two decades ago, is now taken for granted by everyone involved in and around the media industry" (*Fans, Bloggers, Gamers* 1). Jenkins and others resisted the idea that "fandom [is] created entirely from the top down by the studio's marketing efforts" (*Fans, Bloggers, Gamers* 2), instead pointing to the sophisticated and creative power exhibited by fans. It is now either impossible or irresponsible for a scholar working on popular genres such as film, video games, or television to ignore the vast contributions by fans in analyzing, categorizing, and organizing textual material.

Television shows have clearly become a forum for serious intellectual debate, primarily visible on the internet, but also in the recent increase in scholarly books, journals, conventions, and conferences. Although there is evidence that professional scholars are a part of this trend, it is also driven (economically and textually) by an educated general public that is hungry to exercise its knowledge about their shared popular texts. While there is a tradition within leftist thought of recognizing non-academic theorizing—Antonio Gramsci's "organic intellectual" and Theodor Adorno's "homespun philosophy"—the rise of internet culture has elevated the potential for vernacular theory and its incorporation into a larger range of discourse. As Jenkins writes, "fandom is one of those spaces where people are learning to live and collaborate within a knowledge community" (*Fans, Bloggers, Gamers* 134). These knowledge communities exist as networks, using platforms inside and outside of traditional academia and journalism, and in the process necessarily change the nature of studies of popular culture. While theoretical books and articles about television shows are still predominantly written by professors, they are commonly read and commented on within the fan communities. Despite the traditional separation between these communities of "scholars" and "amateurs," what has recently been acknowledged is the importance of these groups as consumers *and* producers of intellectual discourse and theorizing about television. For example, in *Fan Culture*, Matt Hills makes the case that many fans are good critics and good theorists. In *Street Smarts and Critical Theory: Listening to the Vernacular*, Thomas McLaughlin "sees fan communities as among the most active sites of vernacular theory-making" (3), and insists that "vernacular culture produces its own theoretical practices and it is time for academic theory to celebrate their achievements and recognize its own connections to the vernacular" (30).

In his book *Doctor Who, Triumph of a Time Lord*, Hills asserts that being a "scholar-fan means bringing together ways of interpreting *Doctor Who*" (4). Acknowledging that "fan commentary is frequently as illuminating as published academic critique, if not more so," Hills' still makes the distinction that fans tend to read the series *intratextually*: in relation to itself and its own histories. Yet in the

The digital present   197

interactions that have made up the background research for this book, I have seen fans do the intellectual work in connecting *Buffy* to psychoanalytic theory, *The Walking Dead* to animal studies, or *Doctor Who* to James Joyce. In my experience, fans have already been combining the intratextual with the intertextual approaches that are often used to separate scholar and fan.

Another common distinction that I would like to question, is that "unlike fandom, media theory is anti-essentialist" (Hills 8). In other words, fans are essentialist; they want to experience the shows as if there is a "real" Doctor, a real Buffy, a discoverable coherent narrative, while media theory is more aware of how the texts are constructed. Fans, according to this view, like fundamentalist readers of scripture, are resistant to multiple versions or narrative inconsistencies. But as Colleigh Stein elucidates in Chapter Seven and later in this chapter, this distinction is much more complicated than just a simple binary. Fan debates and theorizing over canonicity in these complex networks of podcasts, comics, fan fiction, audio books, and TV episodes is already anti-essentialist, or at least is embedded in the destabilizing of essentialism. In my "Religion and Popular Culture" class, students often make the exact opposite point: that it is through *fan*-theorizing of shows like *Doctor Who* that popular culture offers challenges to a kind of thinking that tends to dominate the public consciousness. For these young fans and thinkers, these shows offer radical new models for imagining a scripture, for example, that is anti-essentialist, or that acknowledges different sources, origins, and narrative contradictions and possibilities.

Looking at speculative television through the lens of fan culture, we can see that many of the aspects of literary theory that scholars like to talk about are both reaffirmed and dissolved. Traditional academic writing practices, such as distinguishing between primary and secondary texts, close reading, genetic and source criticism, and citation are now reframed by the experience of hybrid scholar/fans who have been watching and discussing difficult television texts in new ways. They encourage us to practice letting go of ideas of mastery over a text and its discourse, a rhetorical and intellectual shift that radical theologians and scholars of lived religion also promote as a path to challenging top-down models of religion. When God gave Adam and Eve dominion "over the fish of the sea, over the birds of the air, and over every living thing that moves on the earth" (Genesis 1:28), their first assignment was to definitively name all that they will have dominion over. But what happens when we let go of some of the dominion, when we allow all these living things to express their voices too?

* * *

The relationship between television-viewing and religious practice has been noted even before digital technology provided the platforms for much of the discourse. David Giles points to similarities between fans of the original *Star Trek* and religious devotees, "the texts produced by *Star Trek* fans… are not unlike the religious texts of the Middle Ages, which had a similar degree of reinterpretations (of, say, the Gospels) and turned the authors and translators into famous

198   *Beyond time*

figures" (17). Michael Jindra goes even further in this comparison, classifying *Star Trek* fandom as a "civil" religion, complete with organization, dogmas, a "canon" of sacred texts, rituals, and a recruitment system. Giles points to how this sort of interpretation (of *Star Trek* or the Gospels) often "draws attention away from the spiritual content of the work they were analyzing" (135). Like much modern religion, particularly American Christianity, fan-based theorizing operates outside of institutional and legitimated modes of thought. Among my university students that I bring to the New York Comic Con, this comparison of fan communities to civil religion is so common as to be accepted as an uncontroversial claim.

Whether I am writing about *Game of Thrones, Doctor Who, The Leftovers, Buffy, Westworld,* or *Battlestar Galactica*, part of what draws me to these texts are their large-scale narratives, shifting points of view, mythical structures, invented languages, and deeply contradictory relationships to traditional religion. But whether we are talking about difficult and complex novels, or long form television shows, it is no longer (if it ever was) the unique role of academics to map out and elucidate complicated and fragmented narratives for a general public. Indeed, much of the time, the fans push academics in that direction, as fans are now just as familiar with discussing forms of nonlinear and transmedia storytelling.

The role of religion in these dramas—often described in a reductive way in published criticism—especially needs to also take the voices and practices of these fan/scholars and vernacular critics into account. It requires a "collective intelligence" and an understanding of the lived experience of watching and thinking about these shows. In an early draft of a section on *Doctor Who* and sacred space, I wrote:

> Theories of sacred space offer definitions not that far from how we might see the Doctor and his time traveling spaceship/police box, the TARDIS: according to Richard Kieckhefer, in his book *Theology in Stone*, sacred space can offer "a richly complex symbolic network in which narration from the past and expectations from the future come into the immediacy of present experience." The show's presentation of the TARDIS can offer us perspective through which to view and even reframe these elements in a fresh way.

What is left out of this literary and modernist-influenced formulation is that in *Doctor Who*, it is precisely the surrounding discourse of blogs, fan fiction, and other media, that create and offer spaces through which to question traditional religious elements of time, text, scripture, and body. These fan-created spaces are indeed a model of the TARDIS that I was trying to define. So, in my later revisions of this book, while I have tried to retain what would be characteristically "academic" about my approach—that is, bringing in Kieckhefer's book on theological architecture to a discussion of *Doctor Who*—it has also been important to source much of my argument from non-academic blogs, and fan communities. If I were to write that paragraph now, instead of concluding by pointing to the "show's presentation of the TARDIS," I would instead see the TARDIS as a network of memories, ideas, and images taken from the show, but also taken from

The digital present   199

fan fiction, fan art, and fan blogs. These intersections are a much more "richly complex symbolic network" that blends past and present, and includes in this sacred space the memories and objects from generations of fans as well as thirteen incarnations of the Doctor. In other words, this "richly complex symbolic network" of sacred architecture now includes my worn-out TARDIS slippers.

Living the scholarship

Can lived religion, radical theology, fan studies, and speculative television serve as a model for imagining a decolonized or more inclusive form of scholarly writing? As feminist, queer, and anti-racist scholars have recently argued, our citational practices have power. For Sara Ahmed, citations are "a way of reproducing the world around certain bodies," or, in other words, an inherently political practice that academic disciplines—intentionally or not— use to reinscribed legitimacy and authority. In his recent book on *Doctor Who* and fandom, scholar and self-identified aca-fan Matt Hills goes from saying that a fan should be considered equal to a scholar and then opening the very next paragraph in the next section by identifying a source as a "Cultural studies scholar…". While this is a strategy, I am always encouraging my students to use—locate your source—what if the best quote or source you can find is an eighteen-year-old first-year college student? How do we identify them in the text? The MLA Handbook has a standard section on "Evaluating your Sources" and includes such warnings as "Is the author qualified to address the subject?" "Does the source document its own sources in a trustworthy manner?" or "Was it among the results of a search you conducted through a scholarly database or a library resource?" But what about a first-year essay? Or what about "Gallifrey Base": *Doctor Who* Appreciation Society? Are these "trustworthy" sources? To what extent are academic writers "obligated" to see if fans have written about their subject in the same way they do? For example, my theories of space, while rooted in religious studies as much as television critique, may very well have been discussed in exactly the same way on a little-known fan platform. These discussions quickly move beyond anything published in academic collections, or even anything I have heard in discussion at popular culture conferences. These are the kind of networked, non-essentialist, meaning-making communities that characterize the juxtaposing of lived religion, radical theology, and fan studies that challenge traditional models (including mine) of thinking about television and religion. We find throughout these discussions a resistance to stable texts, to linear storytelling, to authorial or divine intention, and to privileging inherited interpretations.

As new generations increasingly turn away from traditional religious models of organizations in favor of alternative spiritual practices and communities, they have embraced expanded definitions of "religion" that scholars like Russell T. McCutcheon, Robert Orsi, and Graham Harvey (in very different ways) have articulated. For McCutcheon, "the category of religion is a conceptual tool and ought not to be confused with an ontological category actually existing in reality" (xix). In other words, religion as a separate thing does not exist; as Peter Sloterdijk

200 *Beyond time*

argues, the term religion could be usefully replaced with something like the work "practice" or the networks of "discipline" through which our lives make sense. Speculative television can be a model of what radical versions of these networks might look like, but it also provides a platform and frame through which viewers and fans can create their own networks and meaning-making systems. As Cathryn Piwinski and Colleigh Stein will explore in this chapter, fan communities and television-watching practices are not only models of religious organizations and practices, but they can also be sacred spaces of negotiating religion and religious practice.

Issues

By Cathryn Piwinski

NOTE: This section contains extended reference to suicide and trauma.

In the season two premiere of *Buffy the Vampire Slayer*, "When She Was Bad," Buffy is angry. Distant from her father, moody around her mother, and snapping at her friends, Buffy seems to be, according to Cordelia at least, "campaigning for bitch of the year." The reason for Buffy's behavior, though, is nothing too mysterious; Giles points out to Willow and Xander halfway through the episode:

> She may simply have what you Americans call "issues." Her experience with the Master must have been traumatic. She was, for a few minutes, technically dead. She hasn't dealt with it on a conscious level. She's convinced herself that she's invulnerable...

Giles is referring to the season one finale ("Prophecy Girl"), in which Buffy fights her first "big bad," the Master. Although a prophecy earlier in the episode indicates that the Master will kill Buffy, she nonetheless faces him to stop his plans to open the Hellmouth and incite the apocalypse. The prophecy, in a sense, comes true: the Master drowns Buffy and she does die, but she is later revived by Xander and goes on to defeat the Master and save the world.

Giles' reading of Buffy's behavior is accurate—nearly all mentions of the Master or the battle are followed by a slow zoom onto Buffy's somber expression. Cordelia, though not recognizing the reason behind Buffy's anger, advises her to "get over it" and "deal with it," which visibly disarms Buffy, as though in that moment she herself realizes the deeper meaning behind her angst. And finally, near the end of the episode, when Buffy encounters the Master's skeleton, she smashes it into powder while crying. After destroying the skeleton, she relaxes into Angel's arms, and the final scenes of the episode show her coming to terms with her behavior and reconciling with her friends.

I began watching *Buffy* near the end of April 2020, over a month into the pandemic that shut down New York City, where I lived on a normally hectic street now quiet. I was looking for distractions and had been meaning to watch *Buffy* since reading about it in the early drafts of this book. So when two of my longest

The digital present 201

friends began watching the show, I joined, though lagging slightly behind them. With one of these friends, Isabelle, isolated in Queens, New York and the other, Chloe, across the Atlantic in York, England, *Buffy* provided us with the material to keep up conversation in one of the strangest times in our lives.[1]

My friend in Queens, who I will be calling Isabelle, was also my neighbor growing up: since childhood, it feels as though I spent half of my life in her house, in its pool, on the porch, in the cul-de-sac right outside, sitting on the curb, talking about nothing I can remember. Her brother, who I will be calling B, was a year older; though he was often running around and skateboarding with other neighborhood boys, he occasionally hung around with us—both caring for and talking with, as well as picking on and terrorizing us, as all older brothers must. My childhood memories of times spent with B (and Isabelle) are fuzzy: one summer evening he taught me all the curse words I was, according to him, never *ever* allowed to say; one sleepover, he pelted me with hard candy until I, normally quiet, stood up for myself (he listened); one school bus ride, he climbed out the window of the stalled vehicle to beat Isabelle home to finish off the last bottle of Mountain Dew. I remember a few non-specific moments: watching TV, walking the dog, complaining about parents.

The vagueness of these memories has become more troubling recently, and I am often, desperately, trying to sharpen them (even as I write this). B, after struggling with his mental health for years, committed suicide on April 5, 2020, at the age of twenty-seven. For all the fuzziness of the memories I have with B from childhood into adulthood, I remember Isabelle's call on that day too well, I remember the calls I then made too well, I remember thinking about this new, seemingly incomprehensible, reality too well.

Grieving the loss of B is impossible: the suicide of someone young is already hard to understand, and coming to terms with it during a pandemic requires Herculean effort. There was no space to gather, no community to mourn with; it would be months until I could see Isabelle in person, long after unresolved grief had settled in. Meanwhile, I did what I could: reminisced with Isabelle and Chloe on the phone and buried my head in distractions.

Thus, *Buffy*. And, of course, *Buffy* was in practice a terrible distraction, in that its focus on grief and trauma, on relationships and communities of care, often forced me to look directly at the emotions undealt with after B passed. One example of this is when I watched the season two premiere and responded with frustration toward Buffy that surprised me. I shared my (ironically) borderline anger in the group chat I have with Isabelle and Chloe, and while Chloe defended Buffy's behavior—"she literally died"—Isabelle stayed, for the most part, quiet.

A few days later, I realized the cause for the silence. Throughout B's life, his ongoing struggles with mental health often manifested in anger and other defense mechanisms that kept others at a distance. He was not alone, of course: as I entered my teenage years, my quiet attitude turned often into brooding angst. Upon reflection, I realized that my reaction toward Buffy's expressions of grief and trauma could also, and easily, be read as a reaction toward B's own

202   *Beyond time*

expressions. I spoke with Isabelle, apologizing for how I framed my trouble with Buffy, and thinking more generally about how I express my own emotions and deal with my own traumas. This led to a longer exchange between Isabelle and me: in the wake of B's passing, we were both, separately, reflecting on our relationship with him and with ourselves. How do we (and how did we) express our own troubles as children, teenagers, and adults? How did B? How does trauma, depression, anxiety, and grief show itself to others, to yourself? Is it alright to express those emotions, or do we, like Cordelia says, simply have to "get over it"?

There are no answers, only processing. Isabelle and I talked about expressions of emotion, communities of care, and mental health support—a conversation that weaved together our own troubles with grief, with the loss of B, with our experiences with him, and with, absurd as it sounds, *Buffy*. When I tell the story of this conversation with others, I cite *Buffy* as the catalyst that helped Isabelle and me (and later Chloe) articulate what still feels incomprehensible. Offering a framework of how one processes trauma, "When She Was Bad" both reveals the concerning ways that "issues" develop and emphasizes how one processes and lives with them, something that often requires a support system filled with unconditional love and productive, though often challenging, conversation and healing. Exchanges like, "I get where Buffy is coming from because…" or "Giles is right to be hurt because…" or "I feel with Willow because…" act (and acted) as helpful shortcuts to understanding both each other, and ourselves. When Buffy smashes the bones of the Master, a viewer sees both anger and grief, a deep sadness and—when Xander recognizes the necessity of the action and Angel embraces Buffy—love. With these emotions in clear conflict, the episode demonstrates there is no fixed, orderly, or even sensible method to processing trauma, and allows viewers to map their own experiences onto Buffy's (or those of her family and friends). The episode therefore offers a working vocabulary through which the audience can come to articulate and make sense of their own experiences.

The episode makes this vocabulary available as it cycles through the actions and reactions of each of its characters: characteristically, Xander uses humor to cope with Buffy's anger, and Willow seriously worries. By the end, Willow, Giles, Cordelia, and Jenny Calendar have had their own near-death experience when vampires attack them. Cordelia later shares her decompression:

> What an ordeal. And you know the worst part: it stays with you forever. No matter what they tell you, none of that rust and blood and grime comes out. You can dry-clean until judgement day; you're living with those stains.

To which Jenny replies, dead pan, "Yes. The worst part of being hung upside down by a vampire that wants to slit your throat. The stains." Cordelia is, of course, not *just* talking about stains. No doubt she is bothered by the rust and blood now permanently marking her clothing, but she is also bothered by the larger "ordeal" (this begins a larger character arc of Cordelia's in which she buries her real emotions under surface concerns). Like Buffy and the rest of her friends, she now has her own traumatic experience to sort through—something she does by saying one thing and meaning another. Something she speaks aloud and does with others.

It is a processing "with others" that seems most important in this episode. It tarries on reactions to Buffy's behavior by Xander and Willow, Cordelia and Angel, Giles, and her parents, who all have conversations without Buffy present about what is going on with her and what they should do. Although "When She Was Bad" does end on a reconciliation, it might feel incomplete. When speaking with Giles after the climactic destruction of the Master's skeleton, Buffy admits that she is ashamed of her behavior and nervous about seeing her friends. "I was a moron," she says, "I put my best friends in mortal danger." Giles responds, "Buffy, you acted wrongly, I admit that. But believe me, it's hardly the worst mistake you'll ever make." A beat, and then he continues, "That wasn't quite as comforting as it was meant to be." And later, when Buffy convenes with Willow and Xander in class, no apologies are exchanged (yet, it does not seem like they need to be), and all three almost immediately begin joking around and making plans for the evening. Xander humorously remarks on the previous night ("We could grind our enemies into talcum powder with a sledgehammer, but gosh, we did that last night"), which is met with relaxed laughter. These final moments leave much unsaid, but in doing so, it emphasizes the incompleteness of processing one's trauma: like Cordelia and her stains, Buffy and the rest will always be "living with" what they have experienced. The concluding moments of the episode, in their insistence that her anger is far from Buffy's "worst" mistake, underlines the open-endedness of life, and the necessity of experiencing it with others.

Less than a year after Isabelle, Chloe, and I processed our grief through *Buffy*, Charisma Carpenter, who plays Cordelia, posted to her Twitter a detailed account of how Joss Whedon had "abused his power on numerous occasions while working… on the sets of Buffy the Vampire Slayer and Angel." Her post was shared, referenced, or supported by other actors on the show, such as Sarah Michelle Gellar (Buffy), Amber Benson (Tara), and Michelle Trachtenberg (Dawn). Carpenter is not the first to accuse Whedon of misconduct: in her post, she references Ray Fisher's 2020 accusations of Whedon on the set of *Justice League*. In 2017, Kai Cole, Whedon's ex-wife, posted a blog titled "Joss Whedon Is a 'Hypocrite Preaching Feminist Ideals'" and in 2020, James Marsters (Spike) said that Whedon had "backed him into a wall, disparaging him" ("Complete Timeline"). Carpenter's post both reminded the public of past accusations and circulated wider, bringing about a range of responses: the *New York Times* ran a piece on Carpenter's post, followed by several "timelines" of allegations against Whedon published by *Vulture*, *Insider*, and *The Cut*. There was an internal (and somewhat ongoing) existentialism in the Whedon Studies Association and *Slayage* published a roundtable discussion to, in part, address "where… we go from here." Fans involved with larger communities of engagement or more private in their viewings both held

204 *Beyond time*

public, online debates on processing their relationships with Whedon and his shows.

The accusations made prior to 2021 about Whedon's behavior were not unknown to the three of us when we started watching *Buffy* and we often talked about how we might appreciate the stories, characters, and claims within the show while simultaneously considering what we had learned about Whedon. Carpenter's post renewed our discussion of this even as we had finished *Buffy* and moved onto watching other shows together (one of them, *True Blood*). Reconciling the essential vocabulary that "When She Was Bad" offered us around trauma, relationships, and mental health with allegations of harm by the episode's creator is an ongoing, and high stakes process. There are plenty of conclusions we have seen across the fanbase, ranging from a full disavowal of Whedon's work to an emphatic separation of the writer from the text to rigid denial of any wrongdoing. None seem right (though some certainly seem more *wrong* than others), as none seem to satisfyingly grasp the intricacy of what it means to have engaged with, loved, and been transformed by a piece of media at the same time as you deal with the problems it inculcates. Opening oneself up to the questions and claims that art poses means simultaneously opening up to its complexity, its disappointments, and its troubles; it means taking the art and the world it represents in its messy entirety.

There is perhaps a metaphor here around loving art despite its challenges and caring for the people in your life despite their troubles; and maybe that helps to explain the ongoing process of building relationships, being with others who inevitably grieve differently, and remembering B. Buffy and B, Isabelle and Chloe and I are all full and complicated people. This metaphor, though, extends only so far. Caring for others despite their flaws is simplistic, as it dismisses the importance of building boundaries and risks excusing significant hurt and conflating the alleged actions of Whedon with the mistakes of a friend. There is an imbalance of power between Whedon and his employees that does not necessarily translate to a relationship with a friend—and both must therefore be addressed and sorted differently, attentive to the scales of harm done and inevitably complex and ongoing. Reconciling the accusations against Whedon with what value a viewer can derive from *Buffy* is a project too unwieldy for this section and has been attempted by others in a far more graceful manner. For my purposes, I bring these issues up to recognize the voices and stories of others (Carpenter, Fisher, Cole, and so on) and to underline that engaging with art, much like engaging with life, is something always and unendingly and essentially in process.

Thinking through trauma is hard, thinking about *how* you are thinking through it (alone or with others) might be harder. There is a never-ending-ness to the practice as we recover new memories, learn new things (about our art, about ourselves), and find new vocabularies and ways of comprehending it all. When I recall the early months of the pandemic, I inevitably think of Buffy and her anger; and her hurt, her sadness, and how she coped. And she continued to cope: through the next several seasons, into the comic books, and beyond, in lingering

The digital present   205

fan discussions nearly twenty years after the televised series finale. And so do we continue to cope. And we continue; and we continue.

Fan and author

By Colleigh Stein

At one point, the fans of *Game of Thrones* were described as "the most devoted in the world, beating out *Star Trek*, *Star Wars*, *Doctor Who* and *Lord of the Rings*" (Finn). And yet, due to fan reaction to the final season of the show, the series seems to have faded into virtual nonexistence upon its televised conclusion. As Greg discusses in Chapters Seven and Ten, television by its very format resists the idea of an ending. The impossibility of providing a conclusion that could satisfy millions of diverse and distinct fan groups therefore led to an irrevocable tension between fan and author. Even with the series concluded, the unfinished nature of George R. R. Martin's *A Song of Ice and Fire* saga meant that *GoT* fans lacked a sense of closure. Without a satisfactory ending or a unified canon against which it could operate, the story's partial-conclusion mixed with Martin's perpetual missed publication deadlines ultimately resulted in a sense of fan apathy. In many ways, the resulting tension resembled new definitions of religion based on the inner workings of power and networked voices rather than a central source of absolute meaning.

As discussed in the previous chapter, the roles of author (George R. R. Martin), adapter (David Benioff and D. B. Weiss via HBO), and fan changed as the series concluded. Once the series ran out of source material, creative power shifted from author to adapter and, in doing so, complicated what was once a clear division between the two. Fans too, in both their devotion and outspoken response to an unsatisfactory ending, inserted themselves as participants in narrative construction and claimed a level of authority over the property.

This path to fan authority had fraught beginnings, as Martin held close rein over the property he created. Martin refused initial offers to adapt his books into films and openly objected to any *ASOIAF* fanfiction. His 2010 blog post titled "Someone Is Angry on The Internet," made clear that he viewed fanfiction as a breach of copyright and a threat to his livelihood, fearing that some publisher may come along and profit off of a well-meaning fan's story, diluting his copyright and earning money off of his creations. In saying this, he staked his claim as the *only* person allowed to tell his characters' stories. Martin stated: "My characters are my children, I have been heard to say. I don't want people making off with them, thank you." However, many fans operated under the "conviction that Martin has produced an 'incorrect' text that betrays the characters it has established," and thus produced fanworks that were corrective (Fathallah 147).

From Martin's perspective, as the one who created the *ASOIAF* storyworld, only he was allowed editing privileges; readers were meant to remain passive. This meant that fanfiction of the *ASOIAF* world never found a purchase "either out of respect for his critical stance or in fear of earning negative attention from

206   *Beyond time*

the author himself or fellow fans" (Linder 90). While fanfiction of the television series emerged, free from Martin's policing due to the shift in medium and storytellers, fans of *GoT* largely engaged with the series in different transformative modes.[2] Due, in part, to television audiences having become accustomed to an immediacy of input and response over social media in their interactions with both each other and the creative forces behind a series, the *Game of Thrones* fandom participated by discussing theories, prophecies, and endings, collectively working to unravel the mystery of the show and answer the ultimate question: Who will sit on the Iron Throne? Both in person and online, fans began "to share interpretations of the show's narrative twists and turns and to predict upcoming plotlines and character developments in relation to the novels, essentially creating fanfiction as they transpose and write their own interpretations around and into the series" (Butler 59). While not fanfiction in its traditional sense, these theories and interpretations were no less transformative and, historically, have played an imperative role in the fan communities, one of the most notable instances surrounding the series *Lost* and fan speculation over what each detail meant and what the conclusion may reveal.

For *Game of Thrones*, imagining which characters will meet, fall in love, rise to power, die a horrible death, or any and all other outcomes becomes a transformative act of reworking the text. Therefore, "not unlike fanfiction, fan speculation is a way to interact with the show through a process of reimagining, transposing and rewriting fans' own interpretations around and into the series" albeit through conversation rather than prose (Butler 59). While much of twenty-first-century fandom is conducted on the internet, with its physical counterpart largely taking place at organized conventions (cons), *Game of Thrones* exceeded these constraints and became a topic of discussion at parties, bars, offices, schools, and anywhere that people congregated. My own engagement with *Game of Thrones* largely manifested in this way. As someone who read the books and then interned at HBO during the show's fourth season, I was invested in the fandom. I knew the direction the story would go from reading *ASOIAF*, and I had marketing materials—both digital content and physical merch—to mark myself as a fan. When I later displayed a map of Westeros on my desk at my post-college job, anyone who saw it would engage me in conversation about the show. We would theorize about what had come before and speculate on what would come next, how events would play out, who would "win" the *Game of Thrones*. Furthermore, in an age of streaming and binge watching, *Game of Thrones* remained one of the few shows that most viewers sought to watch in "real time" on Sunday nights. The knowledge that you may show up to work or class Monday morning to hear everyone discussing the latest episode meant that fans had to watch while it was airing to avoid spoilers, engage in the discussions, and thus participate in the fandom (as the office's go-to *Game of Thrones* fan, I especially made sure I never missed an episode's air date, knowing that the next morning I would have nearly half a dozen different discussions with coworkers about the show). These discussions act as one of the most profound transformative ways that fans engaged with each other and with the show.

Despite Martin's claim to be the solitary power in creating or altering his story, the history of *ASOIAF* and later *Game of Thrones* tells an alternative narrative of collaboration. In seeking to widen the scope of whom we refer to as the author, Jonathan Gray notes how "alongside the content industries' own paratextual creators, then, fan vidders, 'Big Name Fans,' prominent fan fiction writers, official recappers and reviewers... should all be seen as clusters of authorship too" (Gray 104). Each of these figures creates its own orbit of fan communities, who can then facilitate their own participation in the source material through engaging with these paratextual creators.[3] Sometimes, these individuals are more accessible as fellow fans, or it proves helpful for a viewer to see someone lay out a particular theory or alternate reimagining to better make sense of their own relation to and thoughts about the show. Seeing other fans in prominent spaces within the show's sphere imbue the fandom with a further sense of ownership over the text: if these fans have an audience, then we can, too. Among the *ASOIAF* fandom, the two superfans Elio García and Linda Antonsson are well-known "Big Name Fans." Founders of westeros.org in 1996, their site grew to become the main social hub of the pre-*GoT* fan community. Westeros.org was a space of gathering and discussion, although, per Martin's distaste for the practice, it did not allow any form of fanfiction in its midst, with the moderators "deleting and suspending any forum threads that discuss creative fanworks" (Finn 10). However, despite Martin's stance against fanfiction, the authorship of *ASOIAF* has always been collaborative. In an interview for *Fan Phenomena: Game of Thrones*, Antonsson remarked how Martin appreciated the heraldic crests the fans designed,

> so much so that he started sending us dozens (eventually hundreds) of additional noble houses, their seats and their shields that he had made up in case he needed them. So our earliest collaboration involved creating those shields, sending him a link and responding to his feedback. (Finn, "Elio García and Linda Antonsson" 55)

While the pair did not permit fanfiction on their site, they did create fanart that became elevated to canonical status, meaning that their contribution and participation operated under both modes of engagement, allowing for a more dialectic approach between these two forms of fandom.[4]

The affirmation of the heraldic imagery by the author elevated two fans into the authorial sphere themselves, and García and Antonsson continued their working relationship with Martin. In 2014, the pair co-authored the *ASOIAF* encyclopedic compendium *The World of Ice and Fire* alongside Martin, raising their affirmational amateur fan status to one of professional co-authorship (and combating Martin's assertion that he exists as the singular author of *ASOIAF*). No one person could keep track of the sprawling world of Westeros, with its thousands of characters and simultaneous timelines. Martin himself has admitted this truth: after García pointed out a discrepancy in one of the books' timelines, Martin "realized that [they] had a better grasp of the setting to the point where he sometimes says [they] know Westeros better than he does" (Finn 55). As a

208 *Beyond time*

result, the pair were called upon by Martin to fact-check his work. By examining the role of García and Antonsson in the early years of Martin writing *ASOIAF*, it becomes apparent that authorship functioned as a more collaborative dialogue between author and fan. With these interventions, fandom subverts the notion of a text as a bound, static, unchanging fixture existing only at the time of its creation, and allows them to exist instead "as a continuous and continuing entity that comes to be over time, and hence that will require, invite, and be subjected to authorial interventions as long as it exists" (Burnet 92). Without multiple creative forces, canonicity ascribed to the source author alone would result in the "true" and "authentic" version of a story finding itself liable to plot holes and discrepancies otherwise avoidable by including fan expertise into the creative process. We see the consequences of this form of centrality of fan knowledge begin in the sixth season, when the show runs out of source material and the showrunners—both self-proclaimed fans—have full control over the direction (and canon) of the story.

The outcry of fan reactions to the final season serves to illustrate the complicated relationship between the show and book, screen and page, professional and amateur. Fans enjoy fanfiction as its own genre, and tensions erupt when a work that feels like fanfiction tries to pass itself off as canon. When high levels of fan engagement ensure longevity and marketability of media franchises, the controversy and conflict between studios and audiences can arise if the fan community feels as though a story becomes disingenuous, or that their insight and input has been ignored. While not everyone out of the millions of *Game of Thrones* fans were outraged at the final season and ultimate ending, enough of them felt strongly enough to share their opinions on the internet and demand petitions.

While season seven benefited from positive fan service, season eight suffered the opposite result. The outcomes of two popular romantic pairings—Jamie Lannister with Brienne of Tarth and Arya Stark with Gendry Waters/Baratheon—displayed the disconnect between showrunners and fans, as they became canonized only to immediately fall apart.[5] The second episode, "A Knight of the Seven Kingdoms," finds these characters reunited at Winterfell awaiting the impending battle with the army of the dead. The following Sunday, the battle episode aired, and the series' major villain—The Night King—met his end. To the surprise of many, all four survived the battle. This itself left some fans disillusioned with the show, which in its season one finale informed viewers that no one, regardless of how important their character was to the story, was safe from meeting their end. By the final season, however, it became clear which characters would need to survive until the finale and thus were protected from unexpected death—a phenomenon known as "plot armor." Many fans then felt suspicious that the story had been sacrificed by removing the excitement and surprise. Furthermore, having all four characters survive the battle presented the writers with a new challenge: splitting them apart to continue with their intended plot. Setting up two of the most popular fan pairings for one moment of happiness before ripping them apart in a manner completely antithetical to their character development shows how they were never meant to canonically be in a relationship. This

The digital present 209

makes their couplings poorly executed fan service, where the actions were never meant to further the plot. This reveals a larger concern over content creators perhaps listening to what fans want, but do so without staying true to the essence of the story, resulting in further fan backlash.

While unlikely that HBO would have bowed to fan pressure to redo the final season, doing so would not have reversed fan outrage or apathy given that no conclusion could possibly please all fans. In requesting this outcome, fans failed to reconcile their own agency with that of the author. Seeking a new professional author, rather than an amateur, to finish the work meant that fans were not creating their own new material. Despite dismissing the ending, what the fans continued to crave was a canon, just one that they approved of. Can this ideal canon exist? Is it possible to write an ending that will satisfy every fan? This seems highly unlikely "because at this point, *Game of Thrones* fandom is a fractured fan base, not a united one... In essence, whenever you have a fandom this big, the culture of that fandom will be divergent and multifaceted" (Romano). With so many differing opinions and perspectives, there always remains an interpretability to text. Fans have embraced this quality: from seeking out more lore about the world to reading deeper into the story and pulling out the subtext. This transformative mindset becomes imperative for negotiating canonicity in a transmedial world.

If *Game of Thrones* asks what can be viewed as canon, *Doctor Who* presents us with a new challenge to contend with: the lack of any definitive authorial force. As opposed to *Game of Thrones*, which traces back to Martin's *A Song of Ice and Fire*, or science fiction universes such as *Star Trek*, which began as the brainchild of a single figure in the form of Gene Roddenberry, *Doctor Who* has always been the product of multiple authors. Canon in the context of the modern transmedia landscape can better be understood as a term synonymous with "brand" or "licensed content" as compared with unbranded or unlicensed materials. For *Doctor Who*, this brand exists in the form of the BBC. Here, canonicity is in the hands of a media conglomerate rather than a "true" author. Since *Doctor Who* lacks a single identifiable creator, fans are denied a figurehead who can ascribe canonicity to the content. Given that a variety of different people over the span of fifty years helmed the series, canonicity within *Doctor Who* can then be perceived as fluid, without any singular godlike figure to point to as an ultimate authority.

When Russell T. Davies became the showrunner behind the 2005 revival, the series suddenly had a figure to which it could ascribe authority. To "close down fan debates over continuity," Davies introduced the Time War: a great battle that occurred between the Eighth Doctor's regeneration in 1996 and the Ninth Doctor's arrival in 2005. While the Time War has since been given greater details and a new series of events for the show's 50th anniversary special in 2013, for eight years, Davies allowed this gap to sit at the forefront of the show and define the Doctor. While Davies wanted to give fans space to interpret the story on their own, any information that he, as showrunner and producer "chooses to provide and endorse does carry symbolic authority, however much he may resist this discursively in order to align himself as a 'collaborationist' with fandom'"

210   *Beyond time*

(Hills, *Triumph* 64). The idea of ascribing authorship is so ingrained in our culture that it necessitated a figure to whose judgment the story could defer. Rather than being comfortable with allowing for a collective world-building, the BBC and *Doctor Who* producer entered into a hierarchy of ownership, creating a distinction between what is endorsed and what is derivative.

And yet, in Davies' mind, fans have always played an integral part in the world of *Doctor Who*. As mentioned, television success or failure can be hinged upon fan response and loyalty: the more viewers drawn in every season, every episode, can spell the difference between cancellation and renewal. This is perhaps true to an even greater extent in the case of *Doctor Who*, which endured a sixteen-year hiatus. "Hiatus," and not "cancellation," largely due to the loyalty of its fans. The editor of *Doctor Who Magazine* remarked in 2004 that "The *Doctor Who* mafia … That's why the show's coming back. If it wasn't for all the fans in high places, it would have just faded away…" (Hills 54). A sixteen-year gap is no two-year hiatus to search for funds, and a failed attempt at bringing the show to an American audience in 1996 could have convinced the BBC that such a revival was impossible. However, the enduring fandom of *Doctor Who* was a community that stretched as high up as the media producers themselves, allowing the show a second chance.

Before Davies became showrunner, he wrote for *Doctor Who Magazine* and postured that "'*Doctor Who*' was always structured through absences and gaps… [and] as a result, he depicts Who fans as being forced to use their imaginations" (Hills, *Triumph* 55). The show encourages the fans to become involved not as passive viewers, but active consumers. Gaps are left intentionally so that the audience might fill them in for themselves by speculating on what happens in between. Davies retained this attitude during his years as the showrunner: as a fan himself, he opened up a path for the fandom to contribute to the world-building process of *Doctor Who*. He wanted the audience to make up their own endings, their own stories, whether through fan art, fan videos, fanfiction, or other forms of textual productivity. While none of them were given the approval of the "word of god" to officially elevate them from theory or transformative work to canon, the authorial force still stood behind their creation. They may not be approved in any official sense, but rather than being relegated to some internet corner for folks who like to theorize the 'what ifs' of it all, the fans are communally given permission to fill in stories for themselves, giving their productions greater significance by not being merely dismissed as an act of lesser creation. This torch was passed along to Davies' successor, Steven Moffat. While Moffat remains a divisive force among *Doctor Who* fans, at times existing at odds with his viewers, he too recognized the importance that participatory culture played in the creation and propagation of content. At a 2015 San Diego Comic Con panel, Moffat stated:

> The thing that most delights me, anyway, is the creative response, and the fact that people do their own versions, make their own art, make up their own stories… Because as I keep saying, that's like hot housing talent. Fanfiction, fan art, all these things, that is the way to learn how to do the job – it

The digital present 211

really, really is. So I like the extraordinary creative response to it. Not just passively consuming, but saying 'you know what, I'm going to have a go at it, I'm gonna try to do it.' Because that's the first step to doing it for real.

This harkens back to the very phenomenon of "fans in high places" that first allowed for the revival of *Doctor Who* into the successful program it is today.

This phenomenon, whereby fans of the work are put into privileged positions and given the power and capital to produce content, has recently been coined "fanboy auteur," which combines the once-maligned position of the "fanboy" with the highly authorial and authoritative auteur. For *GoT*, Benioff and Weiss also fall under the trappings of the fanboy auteur, as in a now infamous display of their fannish credentials, the pair claim that they were given Martin's approval to adapt his works after correctly intuiting Jon Snow's true parentage (Birnbaum). To their mind, it was their position as fans, more than any prior film experience, that "earned" them the right to lead the show. Speaking at a panel at the Austin Film Festival, Benioff and Weiss said that when Martin asked after their credentials, they admitted: "We didn't really have any. We had never done TV and we didn't have any. We don't know why he trusted us with his life's work." This should place them nearer the level of amateur writing that fans engage as their fanfiction was *GoT* itself, although a highly profitable and officially sanctioned version (Fathallah 117). Their claim that it was their fannish credentials, more than any previous work, that won them the adaptation, sells themselves as fans first and showrunners second as a marketing tool to appeal to the larger fandom. As fanboy auteurs, however, the pair are positioned as "creative figureheads who have mastered this transition of capital by attaining producer status" which serves to "further distance themselves from feminized stereotypes of passive mass media consumers" (Scott 443). Placed into a new position of power, the fan-turned-auteur runs the risk of losing sight of their fandom in favor of aligning themselves as authority rather than amateur.

Adaptations open new floodgates for fan culture. As derivative works, adaptations bear more in common with fanfiction and while the media continues to privilege one over the other, the very existence of a work *based on* an original gives fan authors new creative license to create and engage within their fandom. By calling their official adaptation "fanfiction," Benioff and Weiss presented "an important statement and strong example of the legitimation paradox at work: further fanfic of the books is now legitimated via the textual provocation of the TV auteurs" and as a result "fan activity is legitimated by White men in positions that are already culturally legitimate" (Fathallah, 118). In the conflation of the later seasons to fanfiction, the distinctions between fan and professional authorship blur. Yet, the continued distinction between amateur and adaptation means that "authorship remains intertwined with our ideas about whose creative agency should and should not be validated" (Johnson D. 154). Fanfiction becomes akin to an adapted work, yet the latter remains economically privileged and validated over the former. Benioff and Weiss may claim their work is "highly profitable fanfiction," however, the "fan" in "fanfiction" acts to distinguish "work done for

212   *Beyond time*

love (the original meaning of amateur) from work done for money" (Coppa 3). Unlike fanfiction as a labor of love, an adaptation results in economic profit. In this way, the "fanboy auteur" status of Benioff and Weiss, of Davies and Moffat, further highlights the division between media and fandom in how stories are told and who gets to tell them. With so many authorial voices coupled with the global accessibility of discovering like-minded fans, the idea of having one true version of a story, or even one true author, becomes impossible. While "official" versions of events remain canonized through licenses, brands, copyrights, and the individuals given the cultural capital to produce these works for larger audiences, it becomes perhaps more satisfying to remove these distinctions—to remove the "fanboy" from the "auteur"—and reconcile a multiplicity of stories and endings: authored, adapted, fan-created, as equals.

Conclusion: "Sometimes you need a story"

Chapters Eight through Ten of this book represent, in a large part, me (Greg) trying to rethink some of the assumptions that I had about television and religion when I started. Part of that effort has been trying to relinquish my own authority, which is why, in thinking about the relationship of fans to religion, I wanted to privilege other voices than my own. The sections that Colleigh and Cathryn contributed to this chapter point to multiple ways that television watching and the communities that arise around it are intertwined with our lived religious practices. Speculative television continually involves us in the act of imagining and defining the future of religion, but as Colleigh and Cathryn make clear, it is also in our present world a practice in itself that—like religious practices—is dangerous, spiritual, healing, and social in ways that intersect with human activities we label as religious. When Cathryn writes that "engaging with art, much like engaging with life, is something always and unendingly and essentially in process" it points to these very intersections. As Willow says on *Buffy* "the dark can get pretty dark. Sometimes you need a story" ("Lie to Me"), but where these stories come from, who gets to tell them, and how they change, is also important to think through. Colleigh's work allows us to see more clearly how we might compare television and its fan communities to popular religion in the ways that both communicate narratives across multiple platforms, not simply by repeating the narrative, but extending and shaping it through varied media and imaginative practices.

We can return here to how bringing together these ways of thinking about texts, about television, and about the practices of fans, viewers and scholars, again challenges certain definitions of "religion" that are still often assumed as true.

- That "religion" is a set of beliefs or propositions to which an individual consent.
- That a "religious" experience is essentially an interior one.
- That "secularism" is a move away from or in opposition to "religion."

The digital present   213

There are many ways to show the social construction of each of these reductive claims, but thinking about the active and always changing networks of television viewers is one site from which to do so. "Religion" does not have to be connected to a set of beliefs, it is inherently social and exterior, and there is no logical place to draw lines between the "sacred" and the "secular." We live our lives in these blurry gray spaces.

COLLEIGH: *On November 23, 2013,* Doctor Who *aired its 50th anniversary special. At the time, I was on an airplane flying home to Los Angeles from New York for Thanksgiving. I had to consciously avoid any spoilers, because I had tickets to see the seventy-five-minute episode at the cinema two days later. On November 25th, I drove down the coast with my father and two cousins to see the 50th anniversary on the big screen. My group reflected the others we saw filling the theater: from children, teens, and young adults who had become fans in the era of New Who to adults and elders who had been watching since the Classic era. As a purely fan space, the traditionally quiet cinema turned into a communal gathering, as the audience gasped, exclaimed, and clapped at each exciting new turn of the show. While television watch parties or even just viewing with members of one's own household reflect a shared experience, having over a hundred guests sitting in a darkened theater became a transformative space for the audience to bond over a unique phenomenon fifty years in the making. The entire theater shouted in excitement as we caught our first glimpse of the Twelfth Doctor and shared a pained exclamation as the Tenth repeated his final line: "I don't want to go." These moments, clear in my memory eight years later, highlight the power of fan spaces and their ability to build a shared community of complete strangers, all connected around a common experience.*

Spaces where fans can gather to celebrate thus become paramount to how fandom engages with the source. Even though many were left disappointed by the Game of Thrones *finale, for instance, the fandom found a chance to unite behind the show's music through attending a concert tour. While* Game of Thrones' *influence has faded, the fans remain and seek out spaces where they can band together, share and discuss, and express both their disappointment and enthusiasm. Or, as* Game of Thrones *composer Ramin Djawadi sees it,*

> The show just got so big, and when something gets that big… And so there's a lot of opinions, and everybody's entitled to their own opinion. But the bottom line is, it's still one of the greatest shows that was ever made, and I think people just want to be put into that world again.

This sentiment, of returning to "that world," summarizes the sentiment expressed by fandom through reading fanfiction, attending a Con or concert, or simply engaging in conversation with another member of the fandom. Through their engagement with text, authors, canon, and each other, fans have renegotiated their role as participants in the channels of production and reinserted their agency on the media landscape. The result becomes a fandom by and for the fans, who are now free to continue creating and sharing and exploring on their own terms, separate from brands and authors. The source authors may have introduced us to the worlds, but the fans are the ones who populated, educated, and cultivated those worlds, and allowed them to flourish.

214 *Beyond time*

GREG: *Henry Jenkins writes of the many "times through the years reporters and students have asked me about whether fandom doesn't just function as a religion for a more secular time" and I too have been asked that question in many classes and at many conferences. Although, like Jenkins, I agree that "we need a similar set of conceptual models to think about popular religion and fandom/participatory culture at the current moment" ("Confessions of an ACA-FAN"), my problem with this question are the terms "religion" and "secular." Traditional theologians and clergy may dismiss fandoms as "false religions," but many contemporary cultural theorists of religion write seriously about the religious dimensions of these fandoms and do not think in terms of "real" or "fake" religion. Most of these scholars are less interested in seeing fandom as a religion than they are in seeing how religion might be understood as more like fandom, or fandom like religion. As Graham Harvey writes "a determined focus on everyday religion as a performative and material practices not only enriches understanding of religious lives but also liberates us to be better researchers and teachers" (18). So as I finish—and this section is the final section I am writing—I find myself asking slightly different questions. Still, yes, what is religion? But now also what is a church? What does it mean to practice? And how can television-viewing communities— in all their complexities—help us think about these questions? Yes, we can look to psychic communication on* Sense8 *or the song of the Ood on* Doctor Who, *but the true lived experiences in between viewers—as Cathryn and Colleigh both show us—are where we live our lives and practice being human. I don't know if it is worth thinking more about what "religion" is or if I am "religious," but this participatory and relational world of persons negotiating living alone and together through television, art, and writing is something bigger than me that I will keep trying to better understand.*

Notes

1 All names in this section have been changed.
2 "The two major cross-fandom fanfiction sites—FanFiction.net and AO3—each hosted fewer than 200 ASOIAF works before 2011" (Linder).
3 Fanvidding is the act of editing clips from a show or film to music. "Big Name Fans" (BNF) are fans who are well known across the fan community, and sometimes even known by the authors or producers themselves, for their contributions to the fandom.
4 The role of fanart achieving canonical status is hardly a new phenomenon. For instance, there is not a single reference in Conan Doyle's texts to Sherlock Holmes wearing a deerstalker cap, but "when Sidney Paget illustrated Doyle's story, The Boscombe Valley Mystery, for publication in The Strand Magazine in 1891, he gave Sherlock a deerstalker hat and an Inverness cape, and the look was forevermore a must for distinguished detectives." Sarah C. Rich. 2012. "The Deerstalker: Where Sherlock Holmes' Popular Image Came From." *Smithsonian Magazine.*
5 On AO3, the Jamie/Brienne pairing has the most tags and Arya/Gendry have the third most.

9 The future nothing
Believing in the impossible or the impossibility of belief

A theology of nothing

Throughout this book, I have referred to practices and beliefs that echo different expressions of radical or negative theology—theologies that define easy explanations, but that constantly open their thinking to divine absence, weakness, and questioning. By looking at vacant churches and empty gravesites and at absent, flawed, or failed god figures, I have emphasized how speculative television often explores the paradoxical, unnameable, and negative gods familiar to the radical theologian. Yet, as much as radical theology has been a sub-theme of this book, it is one that I have not fully defined, described, or articulated. Part of the reason for this lack is that these modes of thought by definition cannot have a stable characterization—they are about the very act of questioning the grounds on which we build meaning and define and frame ideas and authority. Radical theology, in one definition, is a kind of "post-theistic" thinking that can wonder about, doubt, or pursue ideas about God without expecting definitive answers.[1] In this chapter, I will articulate what a non-theological radical theology of television might be, might look like, and might do.

Television and film are not known for their representations of absence. As computer graphics have improved and shooting budgets have increased, it has become possible to show almost anything we can visually imagine: Daenerys flies on a dragon, the Doctor stares down Satan, and massive armies of giants or zombies engage in fierce, realistic-looking battles with humans. It is rare for a big budget science fiction or fantasy show to let something or someone important to the plot stay absent or unobserved. Even dead characters and memories come back as ghosts or in dreams and flashbacks. But absence is a part of the human imagination, especially when it comes to our religious imagination. And, as we started to explore in Chapter Six, thinking of a god on the fringes of comprehensibility also suggests the impossibility of separating gods and monsters. While this impossibility can be explored through the monstrous, it can also be explored through the negated god. Whatever your belief system, your religious background, or your level of faith, the practice of imagining divinity—particularly within the Western Abrahamic traditions—is an act of negotiating absence and impossibility. Believers and practitioners find ways to assert presence or immanence—rituals

DOI: 10.4324/9781003227045-13

216   *Beyond time*

of eating, tasting, and touching—but ultimately the mystery of divinity is that it is not "present" in the ways that define our everyday life.

The mysterious, plural, and fragmented process of interacting with a complex television drama—though multiple viewings, extra commentary, blogs, and various devices and media—is a modeling of the impossibility of a coherent object. Throughout this book, we have been exploring these contradictory negotiations—an atheism that cannot escape God, and religion that cannot escape doubt. In Chapter Two, I proposed reading both *Dracula* and *Buffy* in ways that present doubt, unbelief, and divine absence in a supernatural world and in a necessarily "religious" context that move out and beyond their author's intentions. In Chapter Three, I found in the Doctor's joy over the new "apple grass" and then, later in the same episode, of a new human hybrid, a radical openness and acceptance of the new and previously "unnatural" as a cause for celebration and empathy. In Chapter Five, I pointed to *Westworld* and Bernard's need to continue to live the (fictional or scripted) death of his son as a type of religious practice similar to a radical Christian need to continually experience the crucifixion in the present, even as they acknowledge doubt in the historicity of the event. In every chapter, I locate spaces where viewers of these shows can use them to create new ways of questioning what religion is, what it can be for, and how it might be reframed or recreated.

Buffy and divine absence: "nothing solid"

Early in the final season of *Buffy the Vampire Slayer*, a vampire, who as a human knew Buffy in high school, interrupts their fight to the death to ask her a question. After first claiming off-handedly that he, of course, "defies" God and "all of his works," he then asks Buffy: "Does he exist? Is there word on that, by the way?" Buffy responds with a characteristic shrug and answers "nothing solid" ("Conversations with Dead People"). The answer resembles Buffy's other responses to issues of religious sincerity, as she uses irony and humor to sidestep a topic that is implicitly related to her own existence and purpose. Yet her vague response to this ultimate question of God's existence is more revealing than it might appear. By asking Buffy about the existence of God, this vampire/ex-classmate assumes that her position as the Slayer perhaps gives her some insight into the question of God's existence. Although he locates himself in *opposition* to God, it is the Slayer that he hopes might have a determinate answer to the questions of divine existence. His question assumes that "God" is a determinate fact that can be proven and answered with a yes or no. Her response, in turn, also assumes that there is a possibility of an answer, that it is a question that *can* be solved with enough "solid" evidence. But the nature of the idea of God can be found in the impossibility of an answer to that very question. Buffy's two words, "nothing solid," express not only the show's shrugging ambivalence toward traditional religion, but also the importance of iconic objectivity—the need for something *solid* that occupies space and can be located and framed by both character and viewers. This need for solidity in an answer to questions of indeterminate nature

The future nothing 217

is characteristic of traditional interpretation, confessional or atheistic, readings that presume stable meanings, origins, and autonomous existence. But it is the word *nothing* that is most significant to understanding divinity. From the point of view of a negative or radical theology, whatever we call or think of as God, whether we believe or not, God must be no-thing, beyond material, being, and existence. It is in the very tension between the two opposing words—"nothing" and "solid"—that this theology is located.

Fourteen episodes later, the series finale of *Buffy* finishes constructing the mythology of the Slayer and then also destroys it. In "Chosen," Willow performs a ritual that destroys the apostolic succession of power passed on from one single Slayer to next, therefore giving every potential Slayer the power of the Chosen One—an act that empowers young women all around the world. In this act, Buffy attacks the socially constructed roots of her own mythology and religion and rids her power of any sense of absolute essence. In their final act together, confronting one more apocalypse and the First Evil, Buffy and Willow defy the rule of a "bunch of men who died thousands of years ago," an act of anti-myth which can be read as a dismissal of traditional religion, patriarchal control, and a releasing of productive chaos upon an assumed stable cosmic order.

The very premise of the series' mythology, especially in the later seasons, is that it can always subvert itself. Episodes like "Buffy vs. Dracula," "Restless," "Normal Again," and "Superstar" use dreams, fictional narrators, parody, and hallucination to threaten the show's very mythology and narrative from within. While this anti-myth can be subversive to religious belief, it is not anti-religion. Even the legacy of the Hebrew Bible, according to scholars such as Herbert Schneidau, is an example of anti-myth more than myth—an attack on sacred institutions rather than a creation of them. For Schneidau, Biblical thought does not use myth but uses it up, subverts and destroys it. The Judeo-Christian tradition contains "no inherent sacredness and can always be ultimately questioned" (Schneidau 4). In this sense, biblical tradition and its legacy, from *Paradise Lost* and *Hamlet* and *Buffy the Vampire Slayer*, is about the subversion of myth as much as its creation.

As philosopher and popular culture scholar James South points out, while Buffy and Willow have indeed "changed the world," it cannot be said to be a better or worse world, nor is it a "happy" ending. Instead, it is an ending "filled with new possibilities" ("Philosophical Consistency" par. 40). South's argument that Buffy must transcend teleology, that she must break out of the dialectical relationship of good and evil before she can destroy the First and escape Sunnydale, also applies to the show's anti-mythical stance of a sort of theology of negation. By breaking free of traditional forms of theodicy, mythology, and theology, *Buffy* creates a worldview that, while it may not be Christian, it is also not un-Christian. If we return to Buffy's answer to the existence of God ("nothing solid"), we can read it as a response to the unanswerable questions that lead to radical theologies of absence and paradoxical gods of nonexistence. For traditional believers, God is solid; God is the absolute ground on which meaning is constructed. This is determinate God, the God of positivism and metaphysics,

218　*Beyond time*

the God that makes all unity possible. For Nietzsche and Thomas Altizer, this is the God who is dead. In opposition to this stability, for many Christian, Islamic, or Jewish mystics, God was too mysterious to be a force for simple unity and was indeed often characterized as nothing or "no thing." As Gershom Scholem, the influential scholar of Jewish mysticism, writes:

> only when the soul has stripped itself of all limitation and, in mystical language, has descended into the depths of the Nothing does it encounter the divine...creation out of nothing means to many mystics just creation out of God. (25)

Ultimately, the world of *Buffy the Vampire Slayer* does not point to either solid or nothing, but, like *Firefly*'s River Tam staring into space, it embraces the ambiguity in between. The series finale ends—as Buffy smiles, almost squints, into a brightly lit future—appropriately on a question: "What are we going to do now?" No longer featuring a Chosen One, having defeated the god-like disruption of the First and destroyed the Hellmouth, the show neither denies nor affirms any religion. *Buffy the Vampire Slayer* expresses neither absolute certainty nor total abyss, but, as a form of radical theology, finds in the death of its gods not despair, but opportunity.

Vampires and divine absence

When, in the second season of *True Blood*, Bill goes to vampire queen Sophie-Ann for information on how to fight a maenad, she informs him that they are "sad, silly things. The world changed centuries ago and they're still waiting for the god who comes." The implied comment here is that many humans are in the same position, waiting thousands of years for a never-arriving Messiah. When Bill asks if the god *ever* comes, she replies, "Of course not. Gods never actually show up" ("Frenzy"). This exchange points to the idea of divine absence, but also to a transcendent God who, by definition, is separate from earthly things, and of a Messiah, who by definition is always coming, but never arrives. Of course, a god who never arrives is not quite the same as one who does not exist, and when Bill asks how she summons this "nonexistent god" Sophie-Anne replies that she "never said he was nonexistent, just that he never comes." Using information given by the queen, Bill and Sam Merlotte are able to fool the maenad and kill her. Her last words are "was there no god?" For Leonard Primiano, this suggests that "like the humans around her, this supernatural creature is faced with the same existential longing for a God that is just not there, is not dependable, does not seem to care" (51). But if monsters, gods, demons, and humans all long for a higher power, for a transcendent Other, is it the same quest? Is this desire rooted in our cultures, our bodies, or our inherited narratives? One way of thinking about these questions is to try to better understand how we define our sense of being and identity, a negativity that is found in the vampire's non-reflection in the mirror.

The future nothing   219

The blank mirror is a modernist and postmodernist metaphor that reflects an absence of a soul or the doubt in our own autonomous existence. In Jean-Paul Sartre's *No Exit*, a character comments, "I've six big mirrors in my bedroom. They are there. I can see them. But they don't see me. They're reflecting the carpet, the settee, the window—but how empty it is, a glass in which I am absent" (*No Exit* 19). Sartre's play, a classic existential text, posits three companions who find themselves in Hell, existing like vampires with the memories and personalities of their previous human selves, yet no longer human. Postmodern theologians see these modern absences in mirrors and paintings as making "visible our invisibility by presenting absence. First the transcendent God, then the incarnate Christ, and finally the self itself disappear—die" (Taylor, *Deconstructing Theology* 89). It is, in a very literal way "selfless." The double meaning of this word is played out in different points in the *Buffy* episode titled "Selfless." Spike says, "I don't trust what I see anymore," Buffy claims that "It is never simple. It is always different. It is always complicated," and Anya admits that "I'm not even sure there's a me to help," three questioning statements that express, respectively, a doubt in empirical knowledge, narrative, and the existence of an autonomous self. This absent body is the imaginative space for our art, our religion, and our vampires. The vampire's absent presence, symbolized by the vampire's body in front of a blank mirror, is the essence of the vampiric questions of representation and is the same absent presence confronted by both contemporary thinkers and theologians as well as the searching and questioning viewers of speculative television.

Nothing really matters

In my undergraduate seminar, "The Idea of Nothing," I begin the first day of class by asking each student to write a short definition of nothing, which we then analyze as a group. Students immediately notice that if a definition starts with the words "Nothing *is*" that creates a problem, because nothing is not. Then they notice how many of them use the word "something," and they wonder if nothing has to be the absence of something. Or does nothingness precede the something? In other words, was there nothing before creation, before the Big Bang or the first day of Genesis? Or do we need creation before we have our concept of nothing? Science and theology blur as students ask, if space and time did not yet exist, should we say that nothing did not yet exist either? This leads to the same questions on a more personal level: who are you before you were born or after you die? We usually end the discussion by asking if these complications and paradoxes are a problem of language, a lack of the human imagination, or if they are questions relating to something "real" on a scale beyond both of these. We start the next class with philosopher Martin Heidegger's famous essay, "What is Metaphysics?" By the end of the essay he has transformed this query into another, equally impossible, but more compelling one, "Why are there beings at all, and why not rather nothing?" (110). Arguing that any metaphysical question about being and existence stands for

220 *Beyond time*

all metaphysical questions, Heidegger turns to the idea of nothing. Yet Heidegger realizes, like many philosophers before him, that the "question deprives itself of its own object" (96), and that with "regard to the nothing, questions and answers alike are inherently absurd" (97). Having defined nothing as the "complete negation of the totality of beings," Heidegger turns to human experience, finding nothingness through the concept of "anxiety" (or "dread" in some translations): "anxiety reveals the nothing" (101). The experience of being human, then, is to face annihilation without actually being annihilated; it is an experience of "being held out into the nothing" (103). Television viewers can experience this anxiety, this being held into the nothing in the upside world of *Stranger Things*, the unexplained disappearances in *The Leftovers*, the infinite blackness of space in *Firefly*, and in Amy Pond's decision of whether to die or to face having never existed on *Doctor Who*.

Yet, this terrifying process is how we both understand and move beyond being, how we find something like "transcendence." The experience of being a human, in other words, can only be fully experienced by "holding itself out into the nothing," and experience that can only be achieved through anxiety, and therefore, we must "hover in this anxiety constantly in order to be able to exist" (104). Sartre's *Being and Nothingness* builds on Heidegger's Nothing, and was an influential existential text that influenced film, art, and literature in the 1960s.[2] The big issue that Sartre is trying to understand is the impossibly large idea of being itself—a question that necessarily must grapple with what it means *not* to be. Earlier philosophers had asserted that there were two different realities: one that was the reality we perceived and the other was the "real word," the one that was actually out there. For Sartre, appearance is the only reality, there is no other world out *there*; Nothingness, however, "haunts being." At the same time, for Sartre, nothing and nothingness is necessary in order to recognize the freedom we have to create ourselves to be human. Television viewers can experience this through the way Echo on *Dollhouse*, the sensates in *Sense8*, or Dolores on *Westworld* create themselves though radical acts of free will beyond what the traditional human characters can imagine; they must imagine not being to exist. For us as well, like the final season of *Buffy*, like one of the Doctor's companions who has seen the end of worlds and civilizations, or like the survivors of Oceanic Flight 815 in *Lost*, or Montego Air 828 in *Manifest*,[3] there is no going back to an innocent world of clear definitions, demarcations between good and evil, and linear timelines of progress. We may desire balance, order, a definition of human and divine, but ultimately these things are denied to us. We also understand that these desires, at least most of the time, appear to be impossible. Like the philosopher Emmanuel Levinas—for whom the face of the Other is the trace of God—these shows seem to suggest that we need to be able to imagine non-belief in order to believe. This paradox defines the position of the modern human—we create, through our desire, that which we know is impossible and yet need to worship—and one that is partly negotiated and worked out through engagements with the anxiety of nothingness presented in popular culture, media, and television.

Nothing in space: "welcome to the end of the world"

For radical theologian Thomas A. Carlson, "creative humanity is defined, as in mystical tradition, by its lack of definition" (23), or in other words, it is in the very indefinite nature of how we think about the human that we find new kinds of religion. The character of River Tam on *Firefly*—a young woman who is psychologically unstable but highly powerful after being abusively shaped into a psychic weapon intended for secret governmental use—embodies this kind of radical theology. She can be seen as suggesting a third (indirect and wandering) path that is neither based on traditional faith nor traditional humanism. Her path follows neither the religious Shepherd Book nor the atheistic captain Malcolm Reynolds, it is neither "religious" nor "rational" in any conventional sense, rather it is one that offers alternative definitions of religion and humanity. River takes the themes that *Firefly* presents and subjects them to her own personal brand of chaos; she transforms nothing and blackness from the evil represented by the Reavers into spaces open to new possibilities. Like the doomed bounty hunter floating in space as the series ends, River accepts a form of meaninglessness—"Well, here I am"—as she discovers the contradictory layers that make up who she is. Both the series *Firefly* and the later film *Serenity* end with River teaching something to the rest of the crew; her new ways of thinking and being become the only way for them to survive.

Of all the people on the ship, only River seems to be unafraid of "nothing." In "Bushwhacked," as she and her brother Simon cling to the outside hull of the ship to avoid detection by the government Alliance, unlike the terrified Simon, River gazes in awe and joy at the beauty of black empty space (Image 9.1). River, whose name of course resembles *Reaver*, has, just like the monstrous Reavers, reached a place of nothing, but unlike them, she survives. By looking into nothing, River

Image 9.1 River stares into space (*Firefly*, "Bushwhacked").

222　*Beyond time*

looks away from the defined self, away from the teleological straight path of history, and away from absolutes. Meaning is not in things, as both the atheist Mal and the Christian Book want to insist, but between them, in the interplay, the connections, the empty space. What River sees when she gazes into the blackness of space is not the harsh emptiness of Mal, the psychotic insanity of the Reavers, or the absent God of (the) Book, but instead the divine Nothing of the mystics, a recognition of a void, an emptiness that is not good or bad, right or wrong, sacred or profane, but a possibility for creation, a tentative wandering path for the future.

* * *

In the second episode of the new rebooted *Doctor Who*, "The End of the World," the Doctor, enthusiastically urged by his human companion Rose to travel further in time, takes her five billion years into the future where they land on a space station that is orbiting the Earth for the purpose of observing the moment of Earth's destruction by the expanding Sun. As the Doctor and Rose view the Earth, he comments on the human obsession with finitude:

> You lot, you spend all your time thinking about dying, like you're gonna get killed by eggs, or beef, or global warming, or asteroids. But you never take time to imagine the impossible. Like maybe you survive. This is …five billion years in your future, and this is the day… the sun expands. Welcome to the end of the world.

On the space station, we meet a group of rich and important aliens who are gathered to watch the event. The episode, predictably, uses this scenario for a satire of privileged classes, with announcements like "Earth Death is scheduled for 15:39, followed by drinks in the Manchester suite." And although we are five billion years in the future (a scientifically accurate prediction, by the way, of when this event will occur), Rose is surprised to still recognize the shape of the continents on Earth. The Doctor explains that the "Trust" has had them shifted back into a "classic Earth." Like heritage foundations in our own time, who keep religious sites and medieval cathedrals as they were in the Middle Ages or antiquity in the name of "authenticity," the futuristic Trust denies the role of time and history.

Things, of course, go wrong, and in the process of watching the Doctor save the passengers and, almost incidentally, witnessing the Earth explode, we are introduced to the theme of endings, which the show will revisit in the coming seasons: the end of the Earth, the end of the universe, the last Time Lord, the last human, the last dinosaur. When the Doctor allows a lonely Rose to call her mother from five billion years in the future, what could be a sentimental gimmick becomes a serious moment, a meditation on time that forces us to think with the philosophers that every existence contains within it its own death. It forces us to think with the physicists in realizing that time is not a sort of container or substance that we move *through*, but that it is a human intellectual structure that is theoretically possible, therefore, to step outside of. Religious speculation exists on all these impossible borders.

At the end of the episode, the pleasures of the moment turn dark and reflective as we see from the Doctor's point of view, that ultimately everything ends, and the Doctor is truly alone. He has seen the end of the friends, worlds, and civilizations that are meaningful to him. In philosophical terms, the episode introduces the Doctor as a "post-event" figure. Like the survivors in *Battlestar Galactica*, *The Leftovers*, and *The Walking Dead*, he must find meaning in a universe that has irrevocably changed. In a reflective moment, he uses humans and their materiality to explain his own existence:

> You think it'll last forever, the people and cars and concrete. But it won't. One day it's all gone, even the sky. My planet is gone. It's dead. It burned like the Earth. It's rocks and dust before its time.

Throughout the series, the Doctor often turns to humans to understand his own story. When Rose asks him about his species, he explains that "there was a war, and we lost" and that "I'm a Time Lord. I'm the last of them. They're all gone. I'm the only survivor. I'm left traveling on my own because there's no-one else" ("the End of the World"). The rebooted *Doctor Who* gives viewers a new kind of Doctor—a damaged Doctor who maybe cannot believe in his own goodness anymore, or a Doctor who is fragile and susceptible to being taunted by accusations of abusing a god-like power. The Doctor is a guardian of secret knowledge that "must never be told, knowledge that must never be spoken" ("Rings of Akhaten") and has access to unimaginable beginnings and endings of civilizations, planets, universes, and time itself. These are borders and horizons that separate and connect myth, religion, history, and science. What would it mean if we, like Rose, could watch the end of the planet Earth? Would it add to our religious, historical, or scientific knowledge? Or would it mark the end of them instead?

The death of the individual

Addressing these questions moves us away from models of religion and narrative based on individuals, internal experiences, and single authors and creators. To imagine religious experience outside of the individual subject, originary source of meaning, and the physical continuity of the body requires new modes of narrative and models of storytelling. For our purposes, this offers new ways of imagining religious practices, human history, and textual evidence. If nothing is necessary for creating our own existence, where does this nothing come from? Is it always there staring existence in the face? Must nothingness "haunt being," as Sartre says? But for Sartre, what is it to be human? Humans have an undetermined nature. What does that mean? Existence over essence. What does *that* mean? And what about this Nothingness then? Since the for-itself (like man) lacks a predetermined essence, it is forced to create itself from nothingness. For Sartre, nothingness is the defining characteristic of the for-itself. A tree is a tree and

224 *Beyond time*

lacks the ability to change or create its being. Humans, on the other hand, make themselves by acting in the world. Instead of simply being, as the object-in-itself does, a human, as an object-for-itself, must *actuate* their own being. The project of the postmodern artist, according to Slavoj Žižek, is to no longer strive to fill the Void, but to create the Void in the first place (27). It is possible to see through some of these shows, through their fan communities, and viewing practices, an understanding of the world outside of linear history-driven human narratives and practices. In these models of what is still mainstream television, bodies and their avatars blur, gender and sexuality are queered, and human connections are not defined by material connection or identity by time and place. Much of Thomas Altizer's theology focuses on the inseparability of nothingness and God. It is thinking this way that allows "nothing" to become a positive concept. But if imagining or experiencing the Nothing is a path to a type of religious experience, how does one imagine what is not? Would that necessarily involve deleting oneself as well? From the song of the Ood echoing across time and space in *Doctor Who* to the mysterious shared "Callings" on *Manifest*, speculative television helps us to imagine what these practices might look like.

* * *

An example of a new religious creativity that explores the porous borders of the individual is the Netflix show *Sense8* (2015–2018) created by Lana and Lilly Wachowski (creators of *The Matrix*). The basic premise of the show is a political techno-thriller plot featuring a story of eight strangers from all around the world who find out they are mentally and emotionally connected as a "cluster" of "sensates." The eight include a transgender blogger and "hactivist" in San Francisco, a Chicago policeman, a drug-using blue-haired Icelandic DJ living in London; a closeted gay Mexican action film star, a Korean businesswoman and underground martial artist in Seoul, a Berlin gangster, a bus driver in Nairobi, and a pharmaceutical scientist in Mumbai. These eight characters constitute a new type of human being, linked in a way that allows them to share bodily and emotional experiences, as well as to haunt each other's inner thoughts.

Sense8 is a fresh example of translating transmedia storytelling into the actual plot in ways that replicate our digital-era networked culture. Many critics and fans point to the elevated, multiple, trans-physical experiences of character and viewer as a reflection of digital and internet culture. For Joshua Rothman, writing in the *New Yorker*, "the sensates' telepathic empathy is a metaphor for the internet, which seems, in some ways, to be making us more open to others' experiences (especially queer experiences)." For him, the point of *Sense8* is to "revel in the broadening of empathy—to fantasize about how in-tune with each other we could be." Dilyana Mincheva echoes this same idea from an academic perspective, writing that *Sense8* succeeds in "playfully engaging ever-distracted internet audiences—sometimes by mimicking the experience of the browsing viewer by way of its disjointed storytelling, and at other times by projecting the connection between the sensates as a type of mental distraction" (35). The aesthetic of the show likewise explores these ideas as each episode is filmed in multiple locations with different directors at each site, shifting pacing and visual styles as we move from one character to another. *Sense8* forces us to question our own reality, to question the illusion of a self-contained bubble, and to see that our present perception of ourselves is only one possible reality among an infinite variety of networked encounters with others. The result, as Mincheva writes, is "multiple worlds—visually haunting, yet revealed in a deliberately slow and painterly manner—worlds meant to represent the magnificent kaleidoscope of human experience bridgeable only through unconditional (almost in the religious sense of the word) love" (32).

The eight sensates are able to share fighting skills, brainstorming sessions, sexual sensations, and dance parties regardless of their distance. The openness to multiple, queer, and polyamorous sex and love was perhaps the most discussed and revolutionary aspect of the show and the most obvious presentation of another way of living in the world and in the mind and body of a networked individual. It is telling that the most traditional romantic relationship on the show features a transwoman married to a woman who has four polyamorous parents. As John Lessard notes, "*Sense8* not only problematizes a metaphysics of subjectivity and the correlative logics of containment, intentionality, and self-identity, but also espouses the possibility and desirability of remaining open, 'exposed,' to the distractions of alterity, which is to say, the opening, rupture, or interruption posed by manifold singularities" (11). What feels religious about the whole show is that seeing these eight strangers fighting, partying, thinking, and fucking as a linked consciousness, becomes a metaphor for an infinite number of people breaking through the borders of their limited worlds toward a new kind of freedom, connection, and transcendent love. We might see this religious framing in the sense of a queer theology as developed by thinkers like Marcella Althaus-Reid who writes that "if theology has its own cowardice and fears, the horror of uncontrolled bodies and especially of the orgy made up of unrestricted bodies may be the stronger" (*Queer God* 47). For Althaus-Reid, queer theology "introduced the body into theology, bodies in love, bodies entangled in ethics of passion—and transgressive bodies at that" (Althaus-Reid 48). This religious sense is captured in three central expressions of the radically linked and plural identities in *Sense8*: the fight, the orgy, and the dance club.

Several of the most memorable scenes in the show feature one of the sensates, Riley, a DJ, on stage doing a show, as the music and lighting effects bring characters and plotlines in and out of the club, bending reality and putting her center stage in a communal psychic experience of ecstasy and memory. The opening episode of season two, the "Christmas Episode," later officially renamed "Happy F*cking New Year," features a scene with the eight characters in eight different locations each celebrating their shared birthday. From prison cells to the Amalfi coast, each sensate is celebrating with a best friend, partner, or lover. The soundtrack to this scene is a sonic example of intersecting alternative consciousness. The music begins with American DJ Steve Aoki's remix of "Home We'll Go." As the music changes to the Cuban "Chan," the sensates

226 *Beyond time*

begin dancing together moving from one location to another through their psychic connections. At this point, Riley walks on stage to play with the DJs at a party. Her innocent question "can I play?" is followed by the dance tune "Huff/Puff" from the Kenyan house/funk/disco group Just a Band. As the sensates now seem to physically share the same stage, the music and dance kick into high gear with the EDM remix "Knockdown" from Swiss DJs Dave202 and Gino G—the party then moves from dance to sex and then sex with partners turns into an international psychic orgy, their naked bodies intertwined from San Francisco to Africa. The music here is electronic producer Matstubs's remix of "I'd Love to Change the World" sung by Jetta, a cover and remix of the 1971 blues song by the band Ten Years After. The idea of a DJ and the metaphor of sampling and remixing is powerful here as a way of musically representing a psychically and even spiritually linked communal experience— and a type of radical religious experience. Musical samples from the past fifty years and from around the world are remixed into a new soundscape—one that acknowledges its past and destroys it at the same time—clearing the sonic landscape for something new.

A DJ—playing the role of author, composer, editor, and collage artist—stands over a library of sonic reality and mixes and matches a new world out of previous ones. As Bernard Attias writes, "the DJ set has the potential to communicate new ways of being, of feeling, producing musical discourses that are nevertheless embedded in real-world, material, politics" (7). The DJ, in other words, materially and sonically connects to the world outside of the music in ways beyond what other composers and musicians do—these connections are not just perceived but are actual in very real ways. A DJ cuts, pastes, and reworks slices of history that are not quoted or remembered, but are literally lifted directly out of their original contexts. As Paul D. Miller, aka DJ Spooky, writes in his experimental book *Rhythm Culture*, the "basic idea" of DJing "is to try to make a bridge between the interior and exterior" and is "almost exactly a social approximation of the way web culture collapses distinctions between geography and expression." We can find these intersecting cultural collapses, these blurring of interior and exterior, in the very juxtapositions of lived religion, fan practices, and textual plurality I have been tracing across television. What we see and hear in this scene—an energetic celebration of sexuality, bodies, and community woven together as radically collaborative art that offers another form of interaction—are intersections of images, media, music, sex, and religion that look both forward to a posthuman future and back to pagan animistic traditions. Many major religions along with many marginalized new religious movements share a belief in the world that *might* be, but is not *yet*, and an optimistic speculative fiction like *Sense8* offers a similar perspective. For Miller, the act of DJing a party is also a story of "embarking on the first steps toward transforming the species" where "myth and code are just two sides of the same coin... what holds them together is the machinery of culture as an organizing system."

While the sensates' connections are sometimes described as a higher, more evolved way of being human, and while the metaphor of a more technologically

The future nothing   227

connected world is obvious, when a sensate from a previous generation attempts to describe what they are, he frames it as natural.

> Watch a flock of birds or a shoal of fish move as one…and you glimpse where we came from. Ask how aspen trees feel trauma hundreds of miles apart, or how a mushroom can understand the needs of a forest… you'd begin to grasp what we are ("What is Human?").

This is a different model of a networked identity, in that it is just as ancient and biological as it is technological and posthuman. I also argue that it offers us a more useful definition of what it means to be "religious." In a complicated, but often-quoted passage, Mark C. Taylor defines "religion" as:

> an emergent complex adaptive network of symbols, myths, and rituals that, on the one hand, figure schemata of feeling, thinking, and acting in ways that lend life meaning and purpose and, on the other, disrupt, dislocate, and disfigure every stabilizing structure. (*After God* 250–251 and elsewhere)

This is the religion that *Sense8* communicates and celebrates, and perhaps one best expressed in the sonic collage of a DJ. Across music to ecstasy (both kinds) to sex, parties, queer and polyamorous identities, martial arts, and national holidays, *Sense8* builds an alternative way of being, one that looks back to the forest and forward to the digital future. It is a way of being and imagining that builds a complex fluid network of interrelated natural, social, cultural, religious, sacramental, artistic, and sexual systems to form a new fabric of life that is both singular and plural. Throughout the series—American fireworks and Hindu festivals, European dance clubs and multiple galleries and museums—*Sense8* builds on layers of color and sound and images to claim that our storytelling or our rituals, and our imagination must change from singular to plural. The world of the sensates creates a new kind of religion based on what Thomas Augst calls "mechanisms of circulation and communication." For Augst, these "bring otherwise distant people close de-center the prescriptive authority not only of the church but of literal modes of reading, attachments to particular words, on which it depends" (176). Shows like *Sense8*, *Orphan Black*, and *Mr. Robot* offer a model of storytelling and character and fan interaction that connects digital and DJ culture and electronica with social media and public art in ways that create new modes of processing practices of relating and communicating. At their most speculative, these new modes of communicating re-imagine human ritual. We might think here of anthropologists such as McKim Marriot who have critiqued Western-centric models of the self by using the word "dividual" as opposed to "individual." By using the word "dividual," they point to a concept of the self that takes form through comparisons between not just the West and non-West, but also between two or more non-Western areas. This model suggests a less egocentric sense of self—more of a network of relationships than a centered grid.[4] *Sense8* suggests that the future human may be more porous, connected to

228   *Beyond time*

influences, voices, and identities that are "outside" what we now think of as the human experience.

A theology of the death of God

In the sixth season episode, "The God Complex," the Eleventh Doctor and his companions Amy and her husband Rory mysteriously find themselves trapped in what appears to be a 1980s hotel with changing corridors. They meet other humans and an alien who are also in the hotel without any idea how they arrived. They learn that each hotel room contains the greatest fear of someone who is a guest in the hotel, and that a Minotaur-like creature seems to be feeding off their fear and possessing them. As their fear grows, guests of the hotel can feel this possession growing and they begin to repeat the phrase "praise him" before they are eventually killed. The title comes from a character who rightfully accuses the Doctor of having a God Complex, of seeing himself as a messianic figure of universal salvation, but the word "complex" can be read in other ways as well. The "hotel" is certainly a sort of "God complex," or structure, built on faith, fear, and advanced digital technology, three of the elements that make up a modern god. A third meaning could see the idea of "God" itself as complex, as in God is never simple or singular, but necessarily contains multitudes and the kind of contradictions that the episode reveals in the end.

The themes of faith and religion are established early in the episode as Amy uses religious language to describe how the Doctor has "never let me down" and how he "came back" and "saved me." The plot twist is when Doctor realizes that "it's not fear, it's faith" that the creature feeds off; each person's primal fear leads them to a fundamental faith, whether that is luck, conspiracy theory, or traditional religion, and this faith provides the energy the creature needs. In the episode, as Tim Jones points out, a character's faith in Islam is implicitly equated with secular alternative such as faith in the "power of surrender" or, most obviously, Amy's faith in the Eleventh Doctor—which, as Jones also notes, is contrasted with her husband Rory's rational skepticism (45). Although Jones claims that ultimately "The God Complex" makes a case for the danger of any kind of unconditional faith, secular or sacred, his point can be complicated both philosophically and theologically through this very episode. It is easier to make definitive interpretations if we assume a clear separation between sacred and secular, religious and "non-religious," and between the failings of the Doctor and an omnipotent God. These lines, however, as we have seen throughout this book, are complicated and blurry in popular texts and within scripture and religious practice. The God of any religious faith is constantly disappointing people, and within radical theology, the "weakness of God," or God's doubt in himself, is very much like the Doctor in this episode. Jones finds "The God Complex" as a demonstration of faith as "dangerous" or "mistaken," the Doctor as "unworthy of an unconditional or all-compassing belief" (50–51), and ultimately sees the episode as expressing "obvious and extreme skepticism" (59). I argue that his essay and the episode both present a too narrow definition of religion, and that we can

The future nothing   229

more usefully explore other ways a weak or flawed God is actually an opening to a more active human engagement in religious practice—one where humans do not wait for divine saving, but work out their sacred and ethical practices.

The Doctor's saving realization is when he realizes that the only way he can help Amy is to upset her faith in him—a moment that we can read against the grain as a truly "religious" epiphany. It is this moment when Doctor both admits his God complex and must let it go. Within the Christian tradition, we can compare this realization to two examples of radical divine weakness: the first when God the Father admits he is not enough and therefore must rely upon another divinity (Christ), and the second when that very divinity must die on the cross. Both moments can be seen as Father and Son relenting their God complex and as an abdication of omnipotent divinity—but also perhaps as ethical acts. Like Amy, humanity is now released from obligation and faith—they are on their own now, just like Amy can be—a loss of faith that may ultimately be the only true kind of salvation. The Doctor convinces Amy not to have faith in him:

> Forget your faith in me. I took you with me because I was vain. Because I wanted to be adored…I'm not a hero. I really am just a mad man in a box. And it's time we saw each other as we really are.

What is complicated here is determining just how genuine the Doctor is being. When he concludes by telling Amy that it is time to "stop waiting," it is a moment where he seems to abandon his messianic role—a role that only exists if someone is waiting, and only through absence. As Amy loses faith, the Minotaur collapses, the lights flicker, and the hotel dissolves into a holographic grid. The Doctor goes to and comforts the dying alien creature: "I gave you the space to die. Shush, shush." As the creature dies, its last words are translated out loud by the Doctor:

> An ancient creature, drenched in the blood of the innocent, drifting in space through an endless, shifting maze. For such a creature, death would be a gift. Then accept it, and sleep well. [pause] I wasn't talking about myself.

"I wasn't talking about myself." It's not quite clear whose words these are, but the implication is that the Minotaur's words here actually refer to the Doctor. Our charming, beloved Doctor is also an "ancient creature, drenched in the blood of the innocent, drifting in space through an endless, shifting maze." This Doctor—in a crucifixion moment—is perhaps the one seeking death, the one whose existence is interminable, and one whose death could be a form of salvation for others.

* * *

Every branch of Abrahamic religion has developed ways to answer a fundamental question: How do we represent a dead, invisible, or absent deity? Or, more abstractly, how do we recreate a real sense of the sacred in the absence of a material

230 *Beyond time*

divinity? The answer has been in objects: books, icons, wine, holy water; it has been in actions: reading out loud, consecrating a wafer, kissing an icon, repeating a traditional prayer, or tracing the letters of a word. But objects decay, words are forgotten, and practices lose their magic. Furthermore, as these practices and objects enter our current digital world, every written word and image also points to an absence or something not really there. But even in the pre-digital mid-twentieth century, the ideas of absence, emptiness, and of nothing developed alongside modern ideas of atheism, nuclear annihilation, and biological extinction. From existential literature to abstract painting, from atonal or silent music to emptiness in installation art, and from discoveries of the inner workings of an atom to black holes and dark energy repeatedly, these various "nothings" play a role in understanding modernity and in imagining the human future. Much art, science, philosophy, theology, and, as we have seen, speculative television, accepts the idea of nothing, the absolute absence of being, but not necessarily only as nihilistic expressions of godlessness and despair.

Ancient, medieval, and modern theologians have grappled with how to frame this absent/present God. When mid-twentieth-century theologians such as Paul Tillich say, "God does not exist" or refer to a "God beyond God," they mean a divinity beyond our ability to perceive. God is "ineffable," as the angel Aziraphale from *Good Omens* repeatedly says. More radical theologians have embraced a truer absence by pointing to the "death of God" as the *only* path forward for any kind of religious faith. Thomas Altizer insisted on the necessity of perceiving nothing for any kind of true belief. From him, it is only through the nothing or death of a God that we can experience something close to the divine. This kind of theology of absence has many forms and definitions, but, as Jeffrey Robbins defines radical theology, it is "neither theistic nor atheistic but still recognizes God as a formulation of extremity that gets *at the root* of thought and opens up pathways for thinking" (6). In William Hamilton's 1966 introduction to the Influential *Radical Theology and the Death of God*, he wrote, "I do not see how preaching, worship, prayer, ordination, the sacraments can be taken seriously by the radical theologian" (7). The answer to Hamilton's challenge has been to turn to the "secular" arts, most often literature, but also visual art, and more recently film, music, and television as a way to illustrate the complexities of doubt and belief that are at the core of much radical theological thought.

* * *

Season one of *Good Omens* was a 2019 six-episode miniseries based on a 1990 novel by Terry Pratchett and Neil Gaiman. The main premise of the series is that the demon Crowley and the angel Aziraphale, over their centuries living on Earth, have gradually become best friends and must now work together to prevent the coming of the Antichrist and the end of the world. The third episode ("Hard Times") opens with a twenty-minute sequence not based on material from the book in which we see our two main characters interacting at key points in history from the Garden of Eden to Shakespeare's London to World War II.

The future nothing 231

Opening briefly in the Garden of Eden, where Aziraphale has mistakenly given Adam a flaming sword, the sequence then shifts to Mesopotamia in 3004 BCE where our two heroes join a skeptical crowd watching Noah prepare his ark. The angel Aziraphale remarks on God's bad mood—"God's a bit techy"—but Crowley challenges him to think more critically. "Wiping out the human race?" he asks, "*All* of them?" Aziraphale nods, but then acknowledges it is "Just the locals. I don't believe the Almighty's upset with the Chinese." Crowley won't let God off the hook, though: "They're drowning everyone else?" he asks, and, as the view pans over families and animals, he says "Kids, you can't kill kids…" Although Aziraphale looks troubled, he tries to soften this thought by mentioning that after the flood, God will "put up a new thing, called a 'rain bow,' as a promise to not drown everyone again." "How kind," Crowley remarks sarcastically, as the rain starts to fall.

This scene and the theme of the lack of God's kindness sets up the next scene as we jump ahead 3,000 years, cutting to a close up of the face of Jesus as we hear the sound of the nails being driven into his body. Aziraphale and Crowley are part of a small crowd watching the crucifixion. When asked if he had ever met him, Crowley answers, "I showed him all the kingdoms of the world… He's a carpenter from Galilee, his travel options were limited." The scene then cuts immediately to a graphic close up of a Roman soldier loudly hammering a spike into Jesus' wrist. As they wince, Crowley asks, "What was it he said that got everyone so upset?" Aziraphale answers, "'Be kind to each other.'" The scene ends with swelling dramatic string music and a long shot of the cross being raised as Jesus moans in pain, an uncompromising image presented without irony. So, while the flood—even as it frames the event as a type of genocide—ends on a note of humor ("Oy, Shem, that unicorn's going to make a run for it…") the humor fades out from the crucifixion scene. The final shot shows the three dying men on crosses at sunset, in a desert as the scene fades to black (Images 9.2 and 9.3).

In part because this scene is not in the books and departs from the television show's sense of humor, there is a sense of unreality about this seemingly Christian

Image 9.2 Crucifixion in *Good Omens* ("Hard Times").

Image 9.3 Aziraphale and Crowley watch the crucifixion (*Good Omens*, "Hard Times").

image of goodness and sacrifice. Although the Almighty and his angels are presented as an often humorous and bureaucratic force for the rest of the series, the role of Jesus is never again addressed. This makes sense from a dramatic and artistic viewpoint, but it also leaves this one-minute scene of torture and crucifixion resting uneasily within the arc of the show. Although the cross and crucifixion scenes may have lost their shock value, as Altizer writes, the "cross is the most offensive symbol in the history of religions, one wholly unique to Christianity, and yet profoundly resisted by Christianity itself" (*Living the Death of God* 106). As Altizer reminds us, the cross or crucifixion did not fully appear in Christian art until 1,000 years after Christianity. Its presence here, in an essentially comic series, restores some of that offensiveness.

This explicitly physical depiction of the crucifixion—seen in hundreds of Renaissance paintings—points to the contested spaces between flesh and spirit, human and god, body and mind. Christ's disputed humanity, the transubstantiation of the eucharist, and the ontology of the Quran can all be seen inhabiting versions of this tension between transcendence and immanence. This same tension between transcendence and immanence continues to emerge through the many shows mentioned in this book—"Nothing" and "solid" in *Buffy*, digital "stacks" and physical "sleeves" in *Altered Carbon*—and is another way of framing the search for the "real" found across human religion. In the Bible, the word "covenant," or an agreement between God and humans, is a Latin version of the Hebrew word meaning to "cut" and refers to the cutting of animal flesh; the word literally enacts the lines between the spiritual and the material, between God and flesh, and between the meaning of a word and the animal skin it is written on. As we see presented in much current television, our modern rapid digitalization is also challenging our culture built on covenants, handshakes, books, documents, and signatures.

The death of Jesus in *Good Omens* seems to suggest a kindness outside of a genocidal God the Father; a transcendent kindness that disappears at the moment

The future nothing 233

of crucifixion. It suggests a level of divine purity and goodness that humans and our religions and our gods cannot match. We have gods and prophecies and demons, and a morally ambiguous "ineffable" Almighty, but not the pure goodness represented by this dying man. The power of Jesus in this scene may be that the Christ never existed, or that he briefly flared across history only to disappear. A radical Christian theology might just acknowledge this possibility, but would say that we need to constantly be reminded of this prospect to create a more just world ourselves. The weak or absent God of radical theology leaves the burden of goodness in the realm of flawed humans.

Notes

1 For a much more complete, and different, definition, read the excellent "Introduction" to *The Palgrave Handbook of Radical Theology* by the editors Christopher D. Rodkey and Jordan E. Miller.
2 In season three of *Buffy*, we see Angel reading Sartre's *Nausea* shortly after returning from a hell dimension.
3 The number 828 in *Manifest* is a reference to the show's frequent reference to Romans 8:28: "And we know that in all things God works for the good of those who love him, who have been called according to his purpose."
4 At the end of *Midnight Mass*, as a main character lays dying, bitten by a villager turned vampire, she thinks back and revises her earlier belief in a traditional Christian afterlife: "Myself. My self. That's the problem. That's the whole problem with the whole thing. That word: self" ("Book VII: Revelation").

10 Endings and re-enchanted time

What comes after

With a contribution by Colleigh Stein

As I thought about the chapter and the themes that would conclude this book, I turned to questions of beginnings, endings, and of time. How long have I been writing this book? How have I and the world changed since I started? How do I know when I am done? All of these questions are imbued within Western religious traditions that are built upon a belief in bound sacred books, divine creations, and prophesied endings. Although an orthodox Christian position believes in one God, one holy book, and a promised end, I would hope my more heretical writing questions these singularities. But where then does one locate a sense of the sacred? Perhaps we look for it in a kind of plural pantheistic god, the "crossed boundaries and queer mixtures" (148), as Mary Jane Rubenstein describes it. Her pantheism—a form of incarnated God who is everywhere—is a way of thinking that refutes the

> traditional Western metaphysical divisions of theism and atheism, God and world, spirit and matter, and indeed science and religion— divisions that manage… consistently to privilege light over darkness, male over female, and a carefully circumscribed 'humanity' over everything else" (149).

As we saw in the previous chapter, divine absence in speculative television often turns attention back onto the idea of a privileged humanity. Paola Marrati, writing about religion and cinema, proposes that "our problem is not the absence of a God but instead *our* absence from *this* world. What we lack is belief in the possibility of creating new forms of existence, of experimenting with new forms of life. Such a belief is a matter neither of knowledge nor of representation but rather of a conversion of thought" (227–228). In other words, we must learn to live in and create through absence. This thinking and writing takes place in the absence of absolute endings. Some of my biggest points have been that thinking about religious questions through speculative television encourages us to interrogate the nature of the book, linear narrative, origins and endings, point of view, free will, and the individual, autonomous person—questions that undermine not only many traditional religious perspectives, but even the asking of these questions themselves. All of these chapters certainly undermine any

DOI: 10.4324/9781003227045-14

Endings and re-enchanted time 235

absolute ending of a book. So how do you end a book that doesn't believe in endings?

Endings

All of the shows in this book resist the inbuilt "apocalyptic structure" that literary critic Frank Kermode famously applied to all narrative. Kermode's model sees a full narrative determined by its inevitable conclusion, a narrative model that is Christian but does not apply to the speculative serial dramas of television. *Doctor Who*, with its multiple actors, genres, styles, and time-bending storylines, is, not surprisingly, a good example of incompletion, even if it has shown us the end of the universe several times. The Doctor says, "I always rip out the last page of a book. Then it doesn't have to end. I hate endings." Fans of the show will remember that this "last page" returns at the end of this episode as an afterword from his beloved companion, Amy Pond, telling him that she has been taken into the past and has lived out her life, and is now long gone ("The Angels Take Manhattan"). As Andrew Crome notes, when the "Eleventh Doctor rips out the final pages of a novel so that 'it doesn't have to end,' his actions are perhaps representative of the televisual form as a whole" ("*Doctor Who* and the Apocalypse" 191). Crome finds in the various open-ended and deferred "endings" and apocalyptic narratives of *Doctor Who* a text that matches Jacques Derrida's definition of apocalyptic narratives: texts that "proclaim the possibility of closure while constantly deferring their own ends" (*Doctor Who* and the Apocalypse" 191). Crome cites Derrida's example of the Book of Revelations, the concluding book of the Bible, which repeatedly calls for Christ to "come," which, in the end, of course, he does not (or at least has not). A messiah is an absolute and promised ending that is always deferred, always in the future.

Instead of endings, television serial dramas are often characterized by what Jason Mittell calls their "potentially eternal narrative middles" (13). This potential eternity adds a new and previously contradictory element to narrative, which, in book form, has traditionally been defined by its ending and by its finitude and non-eternal character. Although shows are often judged by their endings, especially those endings deemed inadequate (*Game of Thrones, Lost, True Blood*), it is in their undefined and complex middles where they offer the material for reworking our received ideas about subjects such as free will, the human soul and time and history. Thinking about ending through speculative serial television invites new understandings of narrative. In this first section, I look at the endings of two Joss Whedon television dramas. In both cases, the ending is complicated and subverted by "outside" forces: a change in network, unaired episodes, unanticipated cancellations or renewals, and post-finale graphic novels. Fans and viewers became involved in all of these collisions of diegetic and non-diegetic forces in creative ways—challenging the results, creating their own narratives, or engaging in organized campaigns to change them. Adding another layer of interpretive complexity is the fact that each show presented plots and themes that challenge

236 *Beyond time*

the idea of endings. Like the Doctor's last page, endings are both optional and already written—endlessly deferred and yet in our past.

"I don't know": chaos as possibility in **Buffy**

The first five seasons of *Buffy the Vampire Slayer* were organized around certain assumed ideas: the metaphor of adolescence as hell, the battle of good-versus-evil, and season-long arcs ending with the definitive defeat of a different "big bad." In the final two seasons of the show—the "dark" seasons, the UPN years, after Buffy's death—these defining elements were twisted, even abandoned, as "good" and "bad" characters traded places, evil became a fluid concept, metaphors dissolved and shifted, and faithful and thoughtful viewers were forced to react to what many saw as boring, confusing, offensive, and inconsistent structuring elements and plot developments. *Buffy* had always been subtly subversive; the final two seasons, however, were constantly disruptive, upsetting the progress of storyline and character while drawing attention to these disruptions, forcing viewers to reconsider the narrative consistency of the show.

New formal elements included a musical episode, unreliable narrators, intentionally boring speeches, and the possibility that Buffy was hospitalized and just imagining the whole world.[1] The final seasons challenge metaphysical assumptions about time, continuity, and narrative and cut to the heart of our contemporary anxieties about the stability of those long-held assumptions, creating tension between a desire for coherence and an unsettling awareness of destabilizing figures of rupture. Elements of inconsistency, insanity, and violation serve as subversive structuring devices and push us to question received ideas of structure and reception—questions which may have been part of the thematic structure of the first five seasons, but which now became part of the viewing experience. Season seven, especially, abounds in statements of uncertainty.

Throughout season seven, it is stressed that although we may desire order, a sense of self, and a definition of good and evil, these things are ultimately denied to us. The episode "The Storyteller" is framed as a documentary narrated by a minor character (Andrew) who imagines that he is situated in an old library, dressed in a smoking jacket and holding a pipe. This parody of that symbol of literary television narrative, *Masterpiece Theater*, opens with a close-up of the spines of two leather-bound books labeled "Nietzsche" and "Shakespeare," probably intended to signify a common paring of the two and representing the Western masterpieces of literature and philosophy. But while Shakespeare characterizes a paradigm of the five-act narrative, for Nietzsche "unity, identity, permanence, substance, cause, being" are to be seen as only man-made "fictions" (*Twilight of the Idols*). Therefore, there is a sense in which Nietzsche and Shakespeare do not represent two great fundamental traditions, but opposing kinds of "storytellers" that cancel each other out and clear the playing field for new participants and a new type of story. To appropriate Altizer, if we see Shakespeare as helping us discover "the subject or a center of consciousness," and we see Nietzsche as discovering the "dissolution of that subject" then, for Altizer, it is in this very opposition

Endings and re-enchanted time   237

where "philosophical and theological thinking are truly united" (*Living the Death of God* 7). Although, like Andrew, our host in this episode, we want life to make sense as an organized coherent narrative, for us, like Buffy and her friends in the final season, there is no going back to a simpler, more linear world. Buffy tells Andrew that "life isn't a story," and her character's arc in seasons six and seven involves a gradual realization of the necessity of disorder and uncertainty.

While season six had been defined by questions such as "Where did I go?" and "Is this Hell?" the most important and often repeated answer to questions like these in season seven is "I don't know."

DAWN: What does it mean that Spike is all soul-having?
BUFFY: I don't know.

SPIKE: Why is it [the first Evil] doing this to me?
BUFFY: I don't know.

POTENTIAL SLAYER: Are you, like, back?
BUFFY: I don't know.

SPIKE: What does this mean?
BUFFY: I don't know. Does it have to mean something?

This repeated response to questions of the importance of a soul, structure, plot, and meaning (and also the unstated answer to the final words of the series: "What do we do now?") push the season into a questioning, non-positivistic space of fragmentation and chaos, but also possibility. As Masterpasqua and Perna point out in *The Psychological Meaning of Chaos* "a system in chaos takes the stance 'I don't know.' It is thus open to any number of evolutionary paths" (91). The study of chaos challenges "both the assumption that there is an objective verifiable universe and that there is a self-contained, individual self who can know the one truth" (Demastes 10). Influential theorists of religion, such as Mircea Eliade, have stressed the role of religion in overcoming chaos and establishing order. Both myth and ritual in this formulation retell and reenact and through these repetitions order rules of chaos. But other religious scholars, such as J.Z. Smith and Tyler Roberts, claim that ultimately myths never overcome chaos, but that it persists through religious tricksters, shamans, and prophets (Roberts 26). From this point of view, humans and their religions are "always constructing, always applying, always adapting" (Roberts 34).

To use chaos as a tool for understanding is to develop new ways of processing complex information, and it is what allows Buffy to visualize her plan to defeat The First. As we looked at in the previous chapter, Buffy and Willow's final act together—a ritual that destroys the line of power passed on from one Slayer's body to another, therefore giving every potential Slayer the power of the chosen one—defies the rule of a "bunch of men who died thousands of years ago" ("Chosen"). Western ideas of order, of power against chaos, of a traditional

238 *Beyond time*

religion of stability, all come from the rules of long-dead men: Aristotle, Moses, Paul, Aquinas, Luther, and Newton. Buffy and Willow's act can be seen as an act of anti-myth and as a dismissal of traditional metaphysical order, a releasing of chaos upon cosmic rules to create a new world. If the many potential Slayers in season seven were confusing for viewers, then the final shift to a world of thousands of active Slayers was incomprehensible (or at least until the "season eight" comics). In this final act, Buffy attacks the socially constructed roots and apostolic succession of her own mythology and religion and rids her power of any sense of absolute essence. The body of the Slayer, the space of conflict and magic, is now disseminated to a point of unintelligibility—a type of radical network, like we saw in the previous chapter. The conclusion of season seven, and of the series, becomes, in this context, a metaphorical exploration of what it means to signify the end of a narrative, of the unity of the individual, of teleology, and of history—in short, it questions the ideas of origin, narrative, and continuity on which episodic television (and Western metaphysical traditions) have conventionally been based.

Dollhouse's "Unpredictable Remainders": two pilots, two paths, many truths

Like the final seasons of *Buffy*, *Dollhouse* links formalist challenges of narrative to questions of identity by subverting assumptions about the continuity of self and narrative. The narrative of the show stretches and challenges its own boundaries. It seems to change direction; characters behave inconsistently, and elements such as the unaired pilot "Echo" and "Epitaph One" suggest various and alternative plot directions, almost creating parallel worlds. Depending on whether they had seen the unaired "Epitaph One" at the end of the first season, viewers were essentially watching a different second season. Much of the early critical work on *Dollhouse* focused on the relationship of the fragmented narrative of the show itself to the fragmented selves that make up each Active. Lisa Perdigao describes *Dollhouse* as an "unorthodox television series that seems disordered, like the multiple personality disordered Alpha and Echo" (par. 11). For Julie Hawk, "Echo's subjectivization process... is wrapped up in narrative considerations... the subject is the story and the story is the subject" (par. 2). In other words, the radical "constructedness" of Echo's posthuman psyche "resembles the constructedness of narrative" (par. 6). The show resists efforts at totalization and definitive interpretations; it leaves, as Topher says of his wiping process, "unpredictable remainders" ("The Target"). Like its central premise, the show *Dollhouse* itself challenges ideas of an essential core, a coherent object, or a single linear narrative. Even the characters that run the cooperation—Adelle, Paul, Boyd, and Topher—like the Dolls that they manipulate, shift in ways that do not make sense. For example, on a second viewing of the series, it is hard to accept that Boyd was always a cofounder of Rossum or that DeWitt was acting throughout most of season two to bring the Dollhouse down. Like *Lost*, *Dollhouse* was accused of making it up as it went along. Fans of both critiqued these inconsistencies and found creative ways

Endings and re-enchanted time   239

to justify them: maybe Boyd's original self was wiped and was then imprinted as a co-founder? But the decision is up to the viewer. There is no single truth. It is a form of participatory art.

The function of art, an empty and innocent Echo is told in "Gray Hour," is to show us "who we are." Perdigao points to how the description of a Picasso-esque painting in "Gray Hour" is a "reflection of our world and our fragmentation in the narrative medium of television... illustrating how the broken Dolls of *Dollhouse* and the broken narrative of the series can be put together to make meaning" (par. 4). In the episode, Echo is imprinted to be a master art thief in a classic heist plot. During the engagement, Echo has her imprinted personality myste-riously "wiped," and she is locked into the art vault. The wiped Echo's innocent obsession with the cubist painting—"This one's broken"—is a clear allusion to her existential crisis. But although the point of Picasso's cubist paintings may be the perceiver's reconstruction, art can also demonstrate the impossibility of a coherent whole. A Picasso painting is still framed, contained as a single unit, separate from its surroundings. But the frames around *Dollhouse* (an unaired pilot, "Epitaph One," and "Epitaph Two: Return") fit awkwardly in that they violate rules of traditional narrative and commercial television. It is more like concep-tual or installation art than a modernist painting. The art of *Dollhouse* forces us to consider whether Echo ultimately learns to cohere as a single subject or if she accepts an essential fragmentation. The plot of *Dollhouse* blocks closure and fram-ing. Like Echo, we must hold on to multiplicities.

What is true in the TARDIS?

By Colleigh Stein

To portray a cohesive narrative, the Doctor operates under a set of rules about what moments in time they can and cannot return to, with some events becoming "fixed points," or immutable within the narrative. The reason for scriptwriters to create these rules was, in part, to:

> provide solid reference points for character and narrative development; oth-erwise the Doctor could go back in time and alter events in order to change character psychologies. And he might seek to alter the tragedies of his own past, such as the Time War, which he believes is "timelocked" in "Journey's End." This language of timelocking does suggest that, unlike the notion of specific events being naturally unchangeable, that the Time War has been frozen through some decision or agency. (Hills, *Triumph* 94)

The Doctor assumes the authority of telling their companion (and the viewer) when these immutable moments within the narrative occur. In season four, he pontificates how "Some things are fixed, some things are in flux ... that's how I see the universe. Every waking second, I can see what is, what was, what could be, what must not. That's the burden of the Time Lord" ("The Fires of Pompeii").

240　*Beyond time*

This implies that the Doctor possesses some sort of omnipotent view of the past, present, and future. The implication then becomes that

> Time Lords are in some way time-proof, set apart from normal causality or… immune to the course of history. Time doesn't affect them the way it affects ordinary mortals, even ordinary mortal time-travellers. Due to his unique sense of time seemingly only the Doctor has genuine free will' only he knows when time can be changed. (Hills, *Triumph* 96)

And yet, although the Doctor can jump to different points along the time stream, we follow their journey linearly, one regeneration at a time, moving from single point in time to single point in time, rather than stretching omnipotently across the time continuum. The justification of fixed points and paradoxes serve to stop the Doctor from interfering in events that ought to be immutable facts of history.

However, the internal logic of a narrative can never match its need for drama. Davies' use of fixed points as an "attempt to police and avoid temporal paradoxes… does not set out any narrative rules for determining when history is fixed and when it is in flux at 'fateful moments'" (Hills *Triumph* 96). As a result, instances that are meant to be immutable facts of the show always have the potential to be undone for the sake of development. Continuity, which focuses on the archiving of the past in service of the canon, is thus superseded by narrative advancement that concerns itself with creating the future. This marketing mindset means that "the regular appearance of time paradoxes at the end of series' runs suggests that the confusion of ordinary cause and effect is linked to the need to produce moments of massive narrative shock or revelation" (Hills *Triumph* 97). With this in mind, the previous conception of fixed points exists entirely to be broken; the rules of time in *Doctor Who* can never truly be "fixed." Instead, time becomes a "constantly renegotiated series of permeable and porous 'laws,' bent in service of plot development, character arc, and mythic reconfiguration" (Moss 49). This flexibility is both created by and engenders the space for multiplicity of authorship and canonicity within the Whoniverse. By having fixed points around which to structure a narrative while simultaneously allowing for other voices to enter and shift the narrative, *Doctor Who* employs time travel to destabilize the canon and allow for the mutability of text.

The writing process for a television series is inherently collaborative, featuring writers' rooms, script editors, showrunners, network notes, directors, and numerous other moving parts that affect what ultimately makes it to screen. In this new era of *Doctor Who*, where showrunners have claimed auteur status in the overseeing of their seasons, this open and collaborative model becomes reconstituted to often *appear* more individual, and, as a result, fans often pay closer attention to the styles and signatures of particular writers. Time travel's inherent instability allows for a perfect playing field for the contestation of authorship. The regular series writers serve, in a sense, as disciples. The popular Moffat episodes no doubt played a role in his taking over the showrunner position from Davies. Likewise,

Endings and re-enchanted time   241

Chris Chibnall's successful *Torchwood* spin-off lent him the credence to become the showrunner once Moffat departed. In the September 2021 BBC announcement that Russell T. Davies will take over as showrunner in 2023, Chibnall remarked, "*Doctor Who*'s 60th anniversary will see one of Britain's screenwriting diamonds return home. Russell built the baton that is about to be handed back to him." Hearing this news can feel like its own form of time travel to the fan. The show's viewership has trended downward over the years, as each new writer imparted their own stylistic changes, and the return of Davies brings with him a sense of a return to the old (new) *Doctor Who* of the mid-aughts—that the show might "feel like" *Doctor Who* again.

While time travel in *Doctor Who* lends credence to any author operating under the show's branded BBC mantle, it also allows fans to freely examine, interpret, and challenge "official" events. When Davies brought the show back on air, he was able to decide the rules of the universe, even change them. Speak the words "Time War," and there's no more Gallifreyan history to cloud viewers' perspective, no more High Council of Time Lords to get in the way of the Doctor's decisions. Once Davies passed the helm on to Steven Moffat, the rules could change again. After taking up the reins in 2010, Moffat was in charge of crafting a story for the show's 50th anniversary in 2013. As a result of the episode, Moffat created a new resolution to the Time War, one where Gallifrey is simply lost in space rather than destroyed, where everyone the Doctor has ever known had the potential to return, where he is no longer plagued by guilt or scarred from war. The canon that persisted for eight years of the wandering, genocidal, guilt-ridden loner was eradicated in the face of the wild card Twelfth Doctor who had no such burden to bear. Moffat was thus able to use this opportunity as a reset button to undo a lasting plot device and allow for further introspection into the Time Lord's history and backstory. Two completely different versions of events, two completely different implications for the plot and the characters, a changed past that suggests that any events that happened pre-reset have the potential to be undone. As discussed in Chapter Seven, both are completely canonical. Neither is truer than the other, post-50th is not an adaptation or reboot of pre-50th, the rules of chronology do not apply here. Fans must instead accept two contrasting versions of events concurrently as canon, simply because they were both set in motion by the man literally running the show. Suddenly, although the stories were different, the outcomes were the same. A show about time travel teaches the audience how to reconcile these dissonant canons into a cohesive whole by allowing *both* to be true due to the paradoxical nature of non-linear narratives. The multiplicity of authorship and coexisting canons of *Doctor Who* can allow audiences to reevaluate their understandings of more traditional canonical structures, such as adaptations, and internalize the notion that a singular point of authority or "true" version of a story can never exist. With its multiplicity of authorship and constant reworking of fixed points and paradoxes, *Doctor Who* forces its fans to conceive of the canon as an ever-changing, mutable device that can best be described as: "a Wibbly Wobbly, Timey Wimey ball of… stuff" ("Blink").

242 *Beyond time*

Re-enchanted time

Other than *Doctor Who*, the most popular time travel drama on television since *Lost* has been *Outlander* (2014–present), which is based on an ongoing novel series by Diana Gabaldon and developed for television by Ronald D. Moore of *Battlestar Galactica*. *Outlander* is a romance time travel historical drama about a World War II nurse (Claire Randall) who travels though magic stones back to eighteenth-century Scotland where she falls in love and marries, then returns to the twentieth century where she lives for 20 years with her original husband. She eventually becomes a doctor and chooses to go back to the past when she learns that she can still be with her Scottish husband. Claire survives in the past in large part because of her skills and education acquired in the twentieth century. Despite the mystical time travel, the show rarely touches on religion in practice or historically, but for one episode, after five seasons of time travel, sex, moral difficulties, and violence, the show turns, for the first time, to religion ("Perpetual Adoration"). The episode opens with Claire—during her time in late-twentieth-century Boston before returning to Jamie in the eighteenth—sitting in a church alone. This scene is the first in season five where Claire is seen in the modern world—the effect is one of a "flashback" to the present. The cantor sings the concluding doxology of the mass:

> All glory and honor is yours
> For ever and ever...

The irony is obvious. Claire is a time traveler so what does "forever" mean to her? As Claire kneels at the altar, her voiceover talks of putting herself in the hands of a "being she can't hear, can't see, can't even feel." The show has rarely shown Claire put her faith in a Christian God, and we immediately wonder just who or what she is referring to. When she asks, "how many times have my prayers been answered?" we don't know what this question means until the scene cuts to Claire in the eighteenth century growing penicillin, well over a century before its time, an intervention that will enable her to save lives, but one that will also make her wonder about the morality of changing the future. The obvious connection here—is Claire playing God?—is made for us when we return to her voiceover from the twentieth century. As we see a montage of scenes from different points in her life, we hear again her thoughts:

> Time is a lot of things that people say God is
> There's the preexisting and having no end
> There's the notion of being all powerful
> Because nothing can stand against time

Claire may be in a church, but are these Christian thoughts? The Christian Saint Augustine asks similar questions: "For what is time? ...How is it that there are the two times, past and future, when even the past is now no longer and the future is

Endings and re-enchanted time   243

not yet?" (*Confessions* 11.14.17). Yet for Augustine, God always comes before time: "what was God doing before he made heaven and earth... how can there be a true eternity in which an act of will occurs that was not there before?" (11.10.12). Augustine's answer comes right out of modern physics: "There was no time, therefore, when you had not made anything, because you had made time itself" (11.14.17). Augustine realizes the difficulty in the seeming fact that God could decree eternally that there should be a finite creation of a few thousand years. Since creation had a beginning with time, it also will have a dramatic end with time. But for Augustine, while time may be a mystery, time is a creation, and therefore is *of* God. God is the cause of time. In agreement with Einstein, Augustine would say that time came into being at the moment of creation. The Christian alchemist Isaac Newton, whose theories of time survived until Einstein, also equated time with the God. For Newton, space was the "sensorium of God," and it was Absolute, true, and divinely existed in and of itself and of its own nature, without reference to anything external. If therefore time has no significance for God, how can God eternally determine a finite period of creation? While the experience of being outside this frame, may be only open to God, it may also be open to humans who through science, art, or religion imagine universes or existence outside of space and time—an experience that exists in the multiverse but that also exists in everyday lived experience.

* * *

While Colleigh writes from the point of view of someone who became a *Doctor Who* fan in the twenty-first century, my *Doctor Who* fandom dates back to when it aired in the United States in the 1980s. I watched it pretty regularly, often with friends, knit a Tom Baker scarf, and went to a fan convention in Minneapolis, but I lost track of the show when I graduated college and was barely aware that it had gone off the air. Although post-graduate school, I had started to research and write about television, I was a late convert to the New Who, only starting to watch it around 2013, when I dutifully started with the 2005 season one episodes and progressed through episodes in linear order. The second season episode, "School Reunion," features the return of one of the Doctor's beloved companions from the 70s, Sarah Jane Smith played in both decades by Elisabeth Sladen. In "School Reunion," Sarah Jane encounters the Tenth Doctor while they are both investigating mysterious goings on at a school. The episode reveals that, having waited years for the Doctor to return to her, Sarah assumed he had died and went on with her life. On meeting Sarah Jane, the Doctor's current companion, the young Rose, reflects on what her future will be after the Doctor, and ponders the question every companion must face. How can one go back to the everyday middle of your life after having seen the beginning and end of the universe? How can Moses descend the mountain after having seen God himself?

At first, I barely remembered Sarah Jane, but she became gradually more nostalgically familiar. What I learned on Wikipedia, even before the episode ended was that while she had just been unceremoniously left on Earth back in a 1976

244 *Beyond time*

episode (I would have seen it in American reruns somewhere around 1982), she had returned to become one of the Doctor's longest-serving companions, also appearing on the 1981 television pilot, in the twentieth anniversary in 1983 and the thirtieth anniversary in 1993. During the inter-testimonial period between Old Who and New Who, she co-starred in two BBC radio serials with the Third Doctor and starred in a series of spin-off audio dramas entitled *Sarah Jane Smith*. What I also soon realized, was that following her reemergence in New Who (in several important episodes), she had also gone on to star of her own spin-off series *The Sarah Jane Adventures* from 2007 to 2011, a show that had been canceled following Sladen's death. What I find interesting here, other than how my own appreciation was completely outside of linear time, was that my fan experience echoed the themes of aging, memory, regret, and mortality that were introduced in the very "School Reunion" episode itself, as the now middle-aged Sarah Jane meets the ageless Doctor and his new young companion. In the process of less than an hour, I had revisited my own teenage years, my middle-aged fears of mortality, thought about forgotten friends, and about 30 years of television history: the episode made me ponder how television had changed, how I had changed, how humans now think differently, and about the fluidity of time itself.

When I began writing the *Doctor Who* sections for this book, I engaged in my own "re-watch" of sorts, going back to some early seasons of the New Who. At the same time, I was also enthusiastically keeping up with the new Jodi Whitaker episodes that began airing in the fall of 2018. Furthermore, in an attempt to bring in more non-academic voices, I was following several *Doctor Who* podcasts, each of which were involved in their own "re-watches" and each of which I followed, but not keeping up with their production schedule. The point is, that I was able—and, I would argue that this is not at all unusual—to keep all these different timelines straight. (It is even more complicated than this, as several of the podcasters would discuss their own individual re-watch practices as well.) I was able to appreciate the arc of the show simultaneously from at least half a dozen separate places, and more or less successfully remember what had been revealed at each place on the timeline. As the Doctor says at the end of "Blink": "Things don't always happen to me in quite the right order."

This brings us back to the religious aspects of new practices of thinking about time. For sociologist Max Weber, the "disenchantment" of the Western world—the process that led to what he saw as modern secularism—begins as far back as ancient Hebrew thought, with prophets such as Isaiah proclaiming "idols" as merely powerless stones and statues. For Charles Taylor, a philosopher who has influentially defined for many scholars and readers what our "Secular Age" is, time is an important component in the move from an "enchanted" age (in which a belief in supernatural interaction with daily life is generally accepted) to our current "disenchanted" age. Building on ideas of early-twentieth-century thinkers like Weber, Taylor sees time in the premodern enchanted age as being organized from above, a type of "higher time" rooted in ideas of eternity and the sacred. Time, in our secular and more ordinary age of disenchantment, is stable when one thing happens after the other. Higher time, in the words of Taylor, "gather

Endings and re-enchanted time   245

and reorder" secular time, they "introduce warps" and "inconsistencies." The point here is that the time of *Doctor Who*, and the way that fans experience the show—viewing parties, fan fiction and fan art, comic con cosplay, themed restaurants and bars, and trivia contests—counters what Taylor thinks of a secular or modern. What we see in these ways of experiencing *Doctor Who* might be part of what has been called "re-enchantment." We can see that the human is capable of religious, artistic, and technological self-creation in radically new ways—as an open work that denies closure. These works engage in what Thomas Carlson calls the "endless multiplication of images and forms and ways of being human, within a dynamic that can never exhaust the indeterminate, or infinite, possibility that very need opens and sustains" (23). In other words, it is the human desire for the infinite that creates the experiences of the sacred.

What makes television depictions of time travel particularly significant is that the viewing practices of fans also resist linear structures and narrative. Fan sites, streaming services, re-watches, and podcasts all challenge the traditional organization of serialized drama as fans experience episodes out of order and randomly. Past and present episodes exist at the same time. New practices of thinking about time—at the intersection of science fiction, magic, television, fan culture, and speculative physics—offer new, imaginative possibilities for thinking about possibilities and the (post)human future. The manipulation of time is of course a common aesthetic in television narratives. Jason Mittell points to a specific moment on *Battlestar Galactica* where the show—which through its first two seasons had progressed slowly over 300 hundred days and 27 hours of screen time—suddenly moved ahead one year over the span of a single 30-second close-up of Gaius Baltar's hair (44). While these devices or "narrative special effects" force viewers to "think about how the storytelling might proceed [and] raise questions about what might have occurred during the yearlong ellipsis" (44–45), they have a deeper effect of calling into question the constructed nature of time altogether.

The Doctor steps inside a British police box, *Outlander*'s Claire touches Neolithic stones, *Lost*'s Ben pulls the levers under the island, and in *Dark*, Mikkel explores the caves under a nuclear power site; in each case, a character causes a type of time travel. The Netflix science fiction thriller *Dark* (2017–2020) opens with a quote from Albert Einstein: "The distinction between the past, present and future is only a stubbornly persistent illusion." Unlike many time travel dramas, *Dark*'s main focus is on the psychological and existential results of a whole community learning to accept Einstein's concept of time as a lived experience. What Einstein prefaced his comment with, however, was that this knowledge was held by people "who believe in physics." The word *believe* is significant. Einstein was near the end of his life and was consoling a bereaved sister and son, in other words, not speaking as a scientist. Like Amy's afterword to the Doctor, where she asks him to remember her story to her future child self, Einstein, near the end of his life, reminds his friends that death is not an absolute end to a narrative, but only a moment like any other. Einstein's twentieth-century discoveries built upon nineteenth-century speculative thought that was beginning to imagine time and reality differently—beginning to theorize about a fourth dimension.

246 *Beyond time*

Time has once again circled back around to challenge the secular; it is closer to the "higher" reality found in spiritual theories of Christian theologians like Augustine and Christian scientists like Newton. Time travel can be a plot device, a philosophical thought experiment, or social speculation, but what if time travel is real? What if, as David Lewis writes, "The paradoxes of time travel are oddities, not impossibilities. They prove only... that a possible world where time travel took place would be a most strange world, different in fundamental ways from the world we think is ours" (Lewis 145). In the same way that millions of people in the 1990s claimed to have been abducted by aliens, the new trend of paranormal experiences may very well involve time. A *New York Times* article in November of 2021 described a phenomenon of "ordinary people" experiencing and describing "time slips" (Elvan). These time slips, are the experience of a "global community of believers building an archive of temporals dislocation from the present." The article intentionally uses religious language, calling them "believers" or "congregants" who "testify" to their experiences in time slippage. Like Einstein, they *believe*.

What does it even mean to say, "I believe?" How does belief relate to knowledge? The characteristically American phrase, "I know that God exists," can be read to imply just the opposite. In a dialectical reversal, we can say that if one *knows*, then God becomes part of the material world, an entity that can be perceived empirically, and therefore is not, by most definitions, God, but rather part of our natural existence. The statement I believe in God, or I believe in vampires or ghosts is an ambiguous and subversive statement that admits of simultaneous possibilities and impossibilities, of presence and absence. "God exists," said Jacques Derrida, "because religion exists," and for Freud, there was no important difference between historical fact and psychic fantasy. The point is that time travel and ghosts and demons *do* exist for those who believe in them, people who have no interest in the logic or science that says they do not exist.

* * *

How should I end this book? As I draft this conclusion, it is January 2022. The COVID virus is still a global danger and the United States is still reeling from a President that told us falsely and repeatedly that everything was under control, and who continues to lie about losing the 2020 election. Many churches across the country met only virtually for over a year and some churches that opened earlier are known to have caused sickness and death. From the windows of my apartment, I saw empty Manhattan streets, burning cars, and clouds of tear gas. Walls built around the White House and in Seattle and Portland to contain protesters looked like scenes in *iZombie* and *The Handmaid's Tale*, and the season ten finale of *The Walking Dead* was postponed because of a global pandemic—a meta-irony almost too heavy-handed to mention. And in June of 2021, Pentagon released a statement on UFO sightings (Image 10.1).

Science fiction has often used the trope of an alien invasion being the impetus for humanity putting aside their differences and coming together. If we have

Endings and re-enchanted time 247

Image 10.1 "Church Cancelled" due to COVID.

learned nothing else from the global pandemic and the growing threat of climate change, it is that this optimistic scenario is extremely unlikely. Yet, as Mark Taylor poses as the guiding question of his book *About Religion*, "Can inevitable loss be embraced in a way that leads to creative engagement rather than the endless melancholy of interminable mourning?" (*About Religion* 6). Can our reaction to COVID-19 be seen as another kind of death of God that could perhaps lead to the building of a new future? Or will our theological nihilism take on the form of the Whisperers on *The Walking Dead*, whose hopelessness turns them into monsters?

The questions that have been driving this chapter—What comes after the end?—seem like they will take on new meaning in the coming years, although it is impossible to know how. The year 2020, according to *The New York Times* television critic James Poniewozik, was the "year everything became TV" (December 9, 2020). Throughout the first year of the global pandemic, Poniewozik writes, "screens became our main conduits to let the outside in." In the rapidly blurring world of real and virtual, interior and exterior, these circumstances would "teach us what the kids already knew—that those interactions were as real as anything that takes place between people." A virtual classroom,

248 *Beyond time*

an episode of *Game of Thrones*, or saying goodbye to a dying relative, all took place on the same screen.

This book has not been written in any kind of linear fashion. Viewing, talking, writing, conferencing, re-watching, drafting, workshopping, and revising have until the very end been processes without a beginning, middle, or end. As I draft this paragraph, however—perhaps to be deleted at some point—I have almost ten complete chapters and I am writing the introduction and conclusion to this final one. It is a book that, as of yet, does not exist, although if you are reading it, there is, in your time, a "book" existing in some sense of time and space.

My goal in writing this book was to create a theory of television and religion that brings together ideas I have developed from years of television-watching and my studies of modernist literature, lived religion, radical theology, and queer theory as well as fan studies. In combining these models of thinking, my project has been to both use television as a space where these ideas can create something new, and also to point to something television is doing that has not been fully understood. J. Jack Halberstam suggests that a "worthy project restores the chaos, creates a new sexual, social, political, and religious democracy a radical democracy based on breaking down the structures, styles, borders that we have inherited." In my most optimistic moments, I hope this book does a little of that kind of work. Halberstam's description of productive, radical, democratic chaos is also a style of writing, and I have tried to structure the book to show that. The network, the breaking down, the radicalness, the queerness is not *in* the shows, but in the intersections, the conversations, the juxtapositions that make up part of how we as a community reimagine who we might be tomorrow, what we call sacred, what stories we will tell.

* * *

Supposedly the ninth-century Chinese Buddhist monk Linji Yixuan told his disciples, "If you meet the Buddha on the road, kill him." While this statement has been interpreted in multiple ways, we can see it as way of learning to live in the real world without the expectation of divine presence. From this point of view, enlightenment, transcendence, and salvation are ongoing experiences that you cannot find walking on the road, in sacramental bread, prayer beads, or a temple or cathedral. From a Buddhist perspective, and from a radical Christian or atheist perspective, one must find a way to take away the experience of divine presence—a form of the death of God. Thomas Altizer taught that the teachings of both Jesus and the Buddha suspend "the quest for religious ontology and mystical knowledge" (*Oriental Mysticism* 166). The sacred is not found in an object or a moment, it is not in an historical event, but across time and space, a time experience that reaches both into the past and the future, that is both impossible and eternal. Or perhaps the time traveling Doctor says it best: "The universe is big. It's vast and complicated and ridiculous. And sometimes, very rarely, impossible things just happen and we call them miracles" ("The Pandorica Opens").

Endings and re-enchanted time 249

Note

1 If we are unable to comprehend or fully accept the radical non-being that constituted Buffy in heaven, we are equally unsettled when we witness her, and the show's narrative itself, unraveling in "Normal Again," where Buffy's hallucination that she is in an asylum offers another means of escape. These associations are later conflated by Willow, who, in her most memorable speech, tells Buffy that insane asylums were her "comfy alternative" to the real world and that she was happiest when she was "in the ground" ("Two to Go," 6. 21). Willow's cruel but honest speech links the escapist fantasy of negation with the alternate world of both death and an imagined asylum. In "Normal Again," the psychiatrist treating Buffy remarks that "last summer when you had a momentary awakening," which suggests that Buffy's death and "Heaven" had been just another visit to an asylum when her mom and dad were still together and where monsters never existed. Buffy's heaven and her asylum influence how we read the entire season, yet both are unstable and self-effacing spaces.

Bibliography

Abbott, Stacey. *Undead Apocalypse: Vampires and Zombies in the 21st Century*. Edinburgh University Press, 2016.

Altizer, Thomas. J.J. *The Gospel of Christian Atheism*. Westminster Press, 1966.

Altizer, Thomas. J.J. *History as Apocalypse*. State University of New York Press, 1985.

Altizer, Thomas. J.J. *Living the Death of God: A Theological Memoir*. State University of New York Press, 2006.

Altizer, Thomas J.J. *Oriental Mysticism and Biblical Eschatology*. The Westminster Press, 1961.

Altizer, Thomas J.J. and William Hamilton, *Radical Theology and the Death of God*. Bobbs-Merrill, 1966.

Anderson, Wendy L. "Prophecy Girl and the Powers That Be." *Buffy the Vampire Slayer and Philosophy: Fear and Trembling in Sunnydale*, edited by South, James B. Open Court Editions, 2003, pp. 212–226.

Attias, Bernardo et al. *DJ Culture in the Mix: Power, Technology, and Social Change in Electronic Dance Music*. Bloomsbury, 2013.

Augustine. *Confessions*. Translated by Rex Warner. Penguin, 1963.

Augustine. *Soliloquies: St. Augustine's Cassiciacum Dialogues*. Translated by Michael P. Foley. Yale University Press, 2020.

Augst, Thomas and Kenneth E. Carpenter, eds. *Institutions of Reading: The Social Life of Libraries in the United States*. University of Massachusetts Press, 2007.

Badiou, Alan. *Being and Event*. Translated by Oliver Feltham. Continuum, 2005.

Baudrillard, Jean. *Simulacra and Simulation*. Translated by Sheila Faria Glaser. University of Michigan Press, 1994.

BBC Doctor Who. "Russell T Davies to return as Doctor Who showrunner." www.doctorwho.tv/new

Beal, Timothy K. *Religion and its Monsters*. Routledge, 2002.

Bennett, Jane. *Vibrant Matter: A Political Ecology of Things*. Duke University Press, 2010.

Berger, James. *After the End: Representations of Post-Apocalypse*. University of Minnesota Press, 1999.

Berger, Peter, ed. *The Desecularization of the World: Resurgent Religion and World Politics*. Eerdmans Publishing, 1999.

Berger, Peter. *The Sacred Canopy: Elements of a Sociological Theory of Religion*. Anchor Books, [1967] 1990.

Bersanti, Sam. "*Westworld* Isn't the Next *Game of Thrones*, But It Could Be the Anti-*Game of Thrones*." *AV Club*, 16 March 2020.

Bianculli, David. "Super Yet Natural: Tonight's *Buffy* is a Gem of Realism." *New York Daily News*, 27 February 2001.

252   Bibliography

Birnbaum, Debra. "'Game of Thrones' Creators: We Know How It's Going to End." *Variety*, 2015.

Boorstin, Daniel. "Television." *Life*, 10 September 1971, 36–39.

Borges, Jorge Luis. *Ficciones*. Edited by Anthony Kerrigan. Grove Press, 1962.

Bostrom, Nick. "Are You Living in a Computer Simulation?" *Philosophical Quarterly*, vol. 53, no. 211, 2003, pp. 243–255.

Brison, Susan J. *Aftermath: Violence and the Remaking of the Self*. Princeton UP, 2002.

Brown, Callum B. *The Death of Christian Britain: Understanding Secularisation, 1800–2000*. Routledge, 2009.

Burnett, Colin. "Hidden Hands at Work." *A Companion to Media Authorship*, edited by Jonathan Gray and Derek Johnson. Wiley-Blackwell, 2013, pp. 112–134.

Buse, Peter and Andrew Stott, eds. *Ghosts: Deconstruction, Psychoanalysis, History*. Palgrave Macmillan, 1999.

Busse, Kristina. "The Return of the Author." *A Companion to Media Authorship*, edited by Jonathan Gray and Derek Johnson. Wiley-Blackwell, 2013, pp. 48–68.

Butler, Rose. "The Watchers on the Wall: *Game of Thrones* and Online Fan Speculation." *Fan Phenomena: Game of Thrones*, edited by Kavita Mudan Finn. Intellect Ltd, 2017, pp. 58–69.

Caputo, John D. *Prayers and Tears of Jacques Derrida: Religion without Religion*. Indiana University Press, 1997.

Caputo, John and Gianni Vattimo. *After the Death of God*, edited by Jeffrey Robbins. Columbia, 2009.

Carbone, Gina. "*Walking Dead* Season 3 Spoilers: Who Will Die Next?" *Wetpaint*, 29 March 2013.

Carpenter, Charisma [@AllCharisma]. "My Truth." *Twitter*, 10 February 2021, 11: 20 AM.

Carson, Thomas A. *The Indiscrete Image: Infinitude and Creation of the Human*. University of Chicago Press, 2008.

Cavell, Stanley. *The Claim of Reason*. Oxford University Press, 1979.

Clark, Lynn Schofield. *From Angels to Aliens: Teenagers, the Media, and the Supernatural*. Oxford University Press, 2003.

Cohen, Jeffrey Jerome. "Monster Culture (Seven Theses)." *Monster Theory: Reading Culture*. University of Minnesota Press, 1996.

Coppa, Francesca. "Introduction." *The Fanfiction Reader: Folk Tales for the Digital Age*, edited by Francesca Coppa. University of Michigan Press, 2017, pp. 1–18.

Copson, Andrew. "The Humanistic Values of *Star Trek*." *New Statesman America*, 26 February 2008.

Cox, J. Renée. "Got Myself a Soul? The Puzzling Treatment of the Soul in Buffy." *The Truth of Buffy: Essays on Fiction Illuminating Reality*, Sally Emmons et al. McFarland, 2008, pp. 24–37.

Cramer, Maria. "For 'Buffy' Fans, Another Reckoning with the Show's Creator." *The New York Times*, 15 February 2021.

Crome, Andrew. "Heaven Sent? The Afterlife, Immortality and Controversy in the Steven Moffat/Peter Capaldi Era." *Doctor Who: Twelfth Night: Adventures in Time and Space*, edited by Andrew O'Day. I.B. Taurus, 2019, pp. 111–128.

Crome, Andrew. "Implicit Religion in Popular Culture: The Case of *Doctor Who*." *Journal of Implicit Religion*, vol. 18 no. 4, 2014, pp. 439–455.

Crome, Andrew. "'There Never Was a Golden Age': *Doctor Who* and the Apocalypse." *Religion and Doctor Who: Time and Relative Dimensions in Faith*, edited by Andrew Crome and James McGrath. Cascade, 2013, pp. 189–204.

Bibliography 253

Croskery, Patrick. "Sorry, Human, the Maze is not for You." *Westworld and Philosophy: Mind Equals Blown*, edited by Richard Greene and Joshua Heter. Carus, 2019, 59–69.

Cusack, Carole. *Invented Religions: Imagination, Fiction and Faith*. Routledge, 2010.

Davies, Owen. *The Haunted: A Social History of Ghosts*. Palgrave Macmillan, 2007.

DeCou, Jessica. "The Living Christ and *The Walking Dead*: Karl Barth and the Theological Zombie." *The Undead and Theology*, edited by Kim Paffenroth and John W. Morehead. Pickwick, 2012, pp. 79–100.

Demastes, William W. *Theatre of Chaos*. Cambridge University Press, 2005.

Derrida, Jacques. "Faith and Knowledge: The Two Sources of 'Religion' at the Limits of Reason Alone." *Religion*, edited by Jacques Derrida and Gianni Vattimo. Stanford University Press, 1996, pp. 1–78.

Derrida, Jacques. *Of Grammatology*. Translated by G. C. Spivak. Hopkins University Press, 1976.

Derrida, Jacques. *Writing and Difference*. Translated by Alan Bass. University of Chicago Press, 1978.

Donadio, Rachel. "A Pope's Beatification Stirs Excitement and Dissension." *The New York Times*, 29 April 2009.

Eberl, Jason T., ed. *Battlestar Galactica and Philosophy: Knowledge Here Begins Out There*. John Wiley & Sons, 2008.

Eliade, Mircea. *The Sacred and the Profane: The Nature of Religion*. Translated by W. R. Trask. Harcourt, Inc, 1959.

Elvan, Lucie. "How I became Obsessed with Accidental Time Travel." *The New York Times*, 16 November 2021.

Embry, Stacy. "*Doctor Who* and the Iconographic Search for an Ecstatic Human Religious Experience," *Journal of Implicit Religion*, vol. 18, no. 4, 2015, pp. 517–525.

Engstrom, Erika and Joseph Valenzano. "Religion and the Representative Anecdote: Replacement and Revenge in AMC's *The Walking Dead*." *Journal of Media and Religion*, vol. 13, no. 3, 2016, pp. 123–135.

Espenson, Jane, ed. *Inside Joss' Dollhouse: From Alpha to Rossum*. Benbella Books, 2010.

Farrell, Kirby. *Post-traumatic Culture: Injury and Interpretation in the Nineties*. John Hopkins University Press, 1998.

Fathallah, Judith May. *Fanfiction and the Author: How Fanfic Changes Popular Cultural Texts*. Amsterdam University Press, 2017.

Feuer: "The Concept of Live Television: Ontology as Ideology" in *Regarding Television: Critical Approaches*, edited by Ann Kaplan. University Publications of America, 1983, pp. 12–22.

Finn, Kavita Mudan. "Elio García and Linda Antonsson." *Fan Phenomena: Game of Thrones*, edited by Kavita Mudan Finn. Intellect Ltd, 2017, pp. 52–56.

Finn, Kavita Mudan. *Fan Phenomena: Game of Thrones*. Intellect Ltd, 2017.

Fleming, Mike. "Emmy Q&A With 'Game of Thrones' David Benioff And D.B. Weiss." *Deadline*. 28 June 2013.

Foucault, Michel. *Abnormal: Lectures at the Collège De France, 1974– 1975*, edited by Valerio Marchetti and Antonella Salomoni, translated by Graham Burchell. Picador, 2004.

Foucault, Michel. "What Is an Author?" *Modern Criticism and Theory: A Reader*, edited by David Lodge and Nigel Wood. Routledge, 1988, pp. 280–293.

Frei, Hans. *Eclipse of Biblical Narrative: A Study in Eighteenth and Nineteenth Century Hermeneutics*. Yale University Press, 1980.

Freud, Sigmund. "The Uncanny." *The Standard Edition of the Complete Psychological Works of Sigmund Freud*. Hogarth Press, 1955.

Giles, David. *Illusions of Immortality: A Psychology of Fame and Celebrity*. Palgrave, 2000.

254 *Bibliography*

Gilmore, David D. *Monsters: Evil Beings, Mythical Beasts, and All Manner of Imaginary Terrors*, University of Pennsylvania Press, 2009.

Gilmour, Michael J. "The Living World Among the Living Dead: Hunting for Zombies in the Pages of the Bible." *Zombies Are Us: Essays on the Humanity of the Walking Dead*, edited by Christopher M. Moreman and Cory Rushton. McFarland, 2011, pp. 87–99.

Gittinger, Juli L. *Personhood in Science Fiction: Religious and Philosophical Considerations*. Palgrave, 2019.

Gordon, Avery F. *Ghostly Matters: Haunting and the Sociological Imagination*, University of Minnesota Press, 2008.

Graham, Elaine. *Representations of the Post/Human: Monsters, Aliens and Others in Popular Culture*. Rutgers University Press, 2002.

Gray, Jonathan et al., eds. *Fandom: Identities and Communities in a Mediated World*, 2nd edition. New York University Press, 2017.

Greenblatt, Stephen. *Hamlet in Purgatory*. Princeton University Press, 2001.

Gryboski, Michael. "Texas Church Has Sermon Series Featuring Zombies, Easter." *The Christian Post*, 30 March 2013.

Guerrasio, Jason. "'Justice League' Writer Joss Whedon Is Facing a Slew of Allegations from A-List Actors. Here's a Timeline of the Controversy." *Insider*, 10 April 2021.

Hale, Mike. "Consigning Reality to Ghosts." *The New York Times*, 10 December 2009.

Halfyard, Janet K. (Steve), Linda Jenscon, James Rocha, Alia R. Tyner-Mullings, and Ananya Mukherjea. "Where Do We Go from Here? A Roundtable Discussion of *Buffy*+ Studies and Whether, How, or Why to Forge a Path Forward." *Slayage*, vol. 19, no. 1/2, 2001, pp. 266–305.

Hartman, Geoffrey. *Saving the Text: Literature/Derrida/Philosophy*. Baltimore: Johns Hopkins University Press, 1981.

Harvey, Graham. *Food, Sex and Strangers: Understanding Religion as Everyday Life*. Taylor & Francis Group, 2014.

Hawk, Julie. "Hacking the Read-Only File: Collaborative Narrative as Ontological Construction in *Dollhouse*." *Slayage: The International Journal of Buffy* +, vol 8, no. 2/3, 2010.

Hayles, N. Katherine. *How We Became Posthuman: Virtual Bodies in Cybernetics, Literature, and Informatics*. University of Chicago Press, 1999.

Hayles, N. Katherine. *How We Think: Digital Media and Contemporary Technogenesis*. University of Chicago Press, 2012.

Hedrick, Charles W. "Be There Dragons in the Bible?" *The Fourth R*, vol. 34, no. 3, 2021, pp. 7–8.

Heidegger, Martin. *Basic Writings*, edited by David Farrell Krell. Modern Thought, 2008.

Herbert, Christopher. "Vampire Religion." *Representations* vol. 79, no. 1, 2002, pp. 100–121.

Hill, Annette. *Audiences, Sprits, and Magic in Popular Culture*. Taylor & Francis, 2010.

Hill, Annette. *Paranormal Media: Audiences, Spirits and Magic in Popular Culture*. Routledge, 2010.

Hills, Matt. "Afterword: The Hope of the Doctor," *Journal of Implicit Religion*, vol. 18, no. 4, 2015, pp. 575–578.

Hills, Matt. *Triumph of a Time Lord: Regenerating Doctor Who in the Twenty-First Century*, I. B. Tauris, 2010.

Introvigne, Massimo. "God, New Religious Movements and Buffy the Vampire Slayer." Templeton Lecture (http://www.cesnur.org/2001/buffy_march01.htm)

Jacoby, Henry, ed. *Game of Thrones and Philosophy: Logic Cuts Deeper Than Swords*. John Wiley & Sons, Inc., 2012 @jamesunderscore, 9 July 2013, 10:40 https://www.thedoctorwhoforum.com

Bibliography   255

Jameson, Fredric. *Archaeologies of the Future: The Desire Called Utopia and Other Science Fictions.* Verso, 2005.

Jameson, Fredric. "Marx's Purloined Letter." *Ghostly Demarcations: A Symposium on Jacques Derrida's Specter of Marx.* Verso, 2008, pp. 26–67.

Jameson, Fredric. "Radical Fantasy." *Historical Materialism*, vol. 10, no. 4, 2002, pp. 273–280.

Jenkins, Henry. "Confessions of an ACA-FAN." henryjenkins.org/blog. 10 September 2018.

Jenkins, Henry. *Convergence Culture: Where Old and New Media Collide.* New York University Press, 2008.

Jenkins, Henry. *Fans, Bloggers, Gamers: Exploring Participatory Culture.* Ney York University Press, 2006.

Jenkins, Philip. *The Great and Holy War: How World War I Became a Religious Crusade.* Harper One, 2014.

Jindra, Michael. "Star Trek Fandom as a Religious Phenomenon." *Sociology of Religion*, vol. 55, no. 1. Oxford University Press, 1994, pp. 27–51

Johnson, Chandra. "What 'Star Trek' Teaches Us About Faith 50 Years Later." Shelby-star.com, 25 September 2016.

Johnson, Derek. "Participation Is Magic: Collaboration, Authorial Legitimacy, and the Audience Function." *A Companion to Media Authorship. A Companion to Media Authorship*, edited by Jonathan Gray and Derek Johnson. Wiley-Blackwell, 2013, pp. 135–157.

Johnson, Steven *Everything Bad Is Good for You: How Today's Popular Culture Is Actually Making Us Smarter.* Penguin, 2005.

Jones, Tim. "Breaking the Faiths in 'The Curse of Fenric' and 'The God Complex.'" *Religion and Doctor Who: Time and Relative Dimensions in Faith*, edited by Andrew Crome and James McGrath. Cascade, 2013, pp. 45–59.

Jowett, Lorna. *Sex and the Slayer: A Gender Studies Primer for the Buffy Fan.* Wesleyan University Press, 2005.

Kagan, Shelly. *Death.* Yale University Press, 2012.

Kambhampaty, Anna P. "Many Americans Say They Believe in Ghosts. Do You?" *The New York Times*, 28 October 2021.

Kaveney, Roz and Jennifer Stoy, eds. *Battlestar Galactica: Investigating Flesh, Spirit and Steel.* I.B. Tauris, 2010.

Kearney, Richard. *The God Who May Be: A Hermeneutics of Religion.* Indiana University Press, 2001.

Kearney, Richard. *Imagination Now: A Richard Kearney Reader.* Rowman & Littlefield, 2020.

Kearney, Richard. *Strangers, Gods, and Monsters.* Routledge, 2002.

Kearney, Richard and Brian Treanor. "Introduction: Carnal Hermeneutics: From Head to Foot." *Carnal Hermeneutics*, edited by Richard Kearney and Brian Treanor. Fordham University Press, 2015, pp. 1–15.

Keetley, Dawn. *"We're All Infected": Essays on AMC's The Walking Dead and the Fate of the Human.* McFarland, 2014.

Ketcham, Christopher. "Who or What Is the God of *Westworld*?" *Westworld and Philosophy: Mind Equals Blown*, edited by Richard Greene and Joshua Heter. Carus, 2019, 269–280.

Kiyani, Raphael. "Doctor Who: How New Series Opening Episode Rose Made Me a Fan." *Fansided.*

Kurzweil, Ray. *The Age of Spiritual Machines: When Computers Exceed Human Intelligence.* Viking, 1999.

Kustritz, Anne. "Transmedia Serial Narration: Crossroads of Media, Story, and Time." *M/C Journal: A Journey of Media and Culture*, vol. 21, no. 1, 2018.

256 *Bibliography*

Latour, Bruno. "'Thou Shall Not Freeze-Frame' or How Not to Misunderstand the Science and Religion Debate." *Science Religion and the Human Experience*, edited by Proctor James. Oxford University Press, 2005, pp. 27–48.

Lessard, John. "A Sense of the World: Sense8, Transmedia Storytelling, and the Erotics of Distraction." Paper presented at the UC Berkeley Interdisciplinary German Studies Conference, February 2016.

Levi-Strauss, Claude. *The Savage Mind.* University of Chicago Press, 1962.

Liao, Shannon. "This Season of Game of Thrones Feels Like Fan Fiction." *The Verge*, 20 Augus 2017.

Liedl, Janice. "The Battle for History in Battlestar Galactica." *Space and Time: Essays on Visions of History in Science Fiction and Fantasy*, edited by David C. Wright, Jr. and Allan W. Austin. McFarland, 2010, pp. 189–208.

Linder, Kristin. "A Stark by Any Other Name: A Comparative Analysis of *A Song of Ice and Fire* and *Game of Thrones* Folksonomies." *Fan Phenomena: Game of Thrones*, edited Kavita Mudan Finn. Intellect Ltd, 2017, pp. 100–113.

Lippy, Charles H. *Being Religious, American Style: A History of Popular Religiosity in the United States.* Greenwood Press, 1994.

Livingston, Ira. *Magic Science Religion.* Brill, 2018.

MacFarquhar, Larissa. "How to Be Good." *The New Yorker*, 5 September 2011.

Mangan, Lucy. "Dracula Review – A Blood-Sucking Delight That Leaves You Thirsty for More." *The Guardian*, 1, 1 January 2020.

Marrati, Paola. "The Catholicism of Cinema": Gilles Deleuze on Image and belief." *Religion and Media*, edited by de Vries, Hent and Samuel Weber, 2001, pp. 227–240.

Martin, George R. R. "Someone Is Angry on the Internet." *LiveJournal*, 7 May 2010.

Masterpasqua, Frank and Perna A. Phyllis. *The Psychological Meaning of Chaos.* Amer Psychological Assn, 1997.

McCutcheon, Mark "Buffy the Vampire Slayer and Research as a Public Good." *Academicalism*, 1 October 2012.

McCutcheon, Russell T. *Manufacturing Religion: The Discourse on Sui Generis Religion and the Politics of Nostalgia*, Oxford University Press, 1997.

McGrath, James F. "Explicit and Implicit Religion in *Doctor Who* and *Star Trek*." *Implicit Religion*, vol. 18, no. 4, 2015, p. 471.

McGrath, James F., ed. *Religion and Science Fiction*. Lutterworth Press, 2012.

McLaren, Scott. "The Evolution of Joss Whedon's Vampire Mythology and the Ontology of the Soul." *Slayage: The International Journal of Buffy* +, vol. 5, no. 2, 2005.

McLaughlin, Thomas. *Street Smarts and Critical Theory: Listening to the Vernacular.* University of Wisconsin Press, 1996.

McLevy, Alex. "The Final *Game of Thrones* Brings a Pensive But Simple Mediation About Stories." *AV Club*, 19 March 2019.

McNutt, Myles. *Game of Thrones: A Viewer's Guide to the World of Westeros and Beyond: A Guide to Westeros and Beyond: The Complete Series.* Chronicle Books LLC, 2019.

Mellor, David and Hills, Matt, eds. *New Dimensions of Doctor Who: Adventures in Space, Time and Television.* I. B. Tauris, 2013.

Mendelsohn, Farah. *The Cambridge Companion to Fantasy Literature.* Cambridge University Press, 2012.

Merrett, Jonathan. "Is AI a threat to Christianity?" *The Atlantic*, 3 February 2017.

Metaxis, Eric. *Martin Luther: The Man Who Rediscovered God and Changed the World.* Viking, 2017.

Miller, Paul D. [AKA D.J. Spooky]. *Rhythm Science.* MIT Press, 2004.

Miller, Liz Shannon. "*Westworld* Review: 'The Well-Tempered Clavier' Goes Down the Rabbit Hole for Answers." *Indie Wire*, 27 November 2016.

Mills, C. Wright. *The Sociological Imagination*. Oxford University Press, 1959.

Mincheva, Dilyana. "*Sense8* and the Praxis of Utopia," *Cinephile* vol. 12, no. 1, 2018, pp. 32–40.

Mittell, Jason. *Complex TV: The Poetics of Contemporary Television Storytelling*. New York University Press, 2015.

Moreman, Christopher M. and Cory James Rushton, eds. *Zombies Are Us: Essays on the Humanity of the Walking Dead*. McFarland, 2011.

Morrow, James. "James Morrow on *A Case of Conscience*. Egtverchi's Wake: An Atheist Revisits *a Case of Conscience*." https://sciencefiction.loa.org/appreciation/morrow.php

Moskowitz, Clara. "Are We Living in a Computer Simulation?" *Scientific America*, 7 April 2016.

Moss, Joshua Louis. "Transmedial Time Traveler." In *Ruminations, Peregrinations, and Regenerations: A Critical Approach to Doctor Who*, edited by Christopher Hansen. Cambridge Scholars Publishing, 2010, pp. 47–67.

Mulhall, Stephen. *On Film*. Routledge, 2008.

Mulhall, Stephen. "Theology and Narrative: The Self, the Novel, the Bible." *International Journal for Philosophy of Religion*, vol. 69, no. 1, 2011, pp. 29–43.

Murray, Leah A. "When They Aren't Eating Us, They Bring Us Together: Zombies and the American Social Contract." *The Undead and Philosophy: Chicken Soup for the Soulless*, edited by Richard Greene and K. Silem Mohammad. Open Court, 2006, pp. 211–20.

Murray, Noel. "The First Episode of *The Walking Dead* May Still Be the Show's Finest Hour." *AV Club*, 6 February 2017.

Mutter, Matthew. *Restless Secularism: Modernism and the Religious Inheritance*, Yale University Press, 2017.

Nancy, Jean-Luc. "The Deconstruction of Christianity." *Religion and Media*, edited by de Vries, Hent and Samuel Weber. Stanford University Press, 2002, pp. 112–130.

Ní, Fhlainn, Sorcha. *Postmodern Vampires: Film, Fiction, and Popular Culture*, Palgrave, 2019.

Nightmare Child, 28 May 2011. http://forums.drwho-online.co.uk

Noble, David. *The Religion of Technology: The Divinity of Man and the Spirit of Invention*. Knopf Doubleday, 2013.

Nussbaum, Emily "Must-See Metaphysics." *The New York Times*, 22 September 2019.

Ochse, Weston. "The End of Books: The Bemis Condition." *Storytellers Unplugged*, 19 March 2006.

O'Day, Andrew, ed. *Doctor Who - Twelfth Night: Adventures in Time and Space with Peter Capaldi*. I. B. Tauris, 2018.

Opam, Kofi. "True Blood: Theme Music, Editing and Entrails." Unpublished seminar paper, 2009.

O'Reilly, Bill. "Zombies versus Jesus: Guess Who Was the Big Winner?" *Sun Sentinel*, 6 Apr. 2013.

Orsi, Robert. *Madonna of 115th Street: Faith and Community in Italian Harlem, 1880–1950*, 3rd ed. Yale University Press, 2010.

Orsi, Robert. *History and Presence*. Harvard University Press, 2016.

Paffenroth, Kim and John W. Morehead. *The Undead and Theology*. Wipf and Stock Publishers, 2012.

Pagels, Elaine. *The Gnostic Gospels*. Random House. 1979.

Parfit, Derek. *Reasons and Persons*. Oxford University Press, 1984.

Parsemain, Ava Laure. *The Pedagogy of Queer TV*. Palgrave Macmillan US, 2019.

258 *Bibliography*

Peaty, Gwyneth. "Zombie Time: Temporality and Living Death." *We're All Infected: Essays on AMC's 'The Walking Dead' and the Fate of the Human*, edited by Dawn Keetley. McFarland & Company Inc., 2014, pp. 186–199.

Perdigao, Lisa K. "'This One's Broken': Rebuilding Whedonbots and Reprogramming the Whedonverse." *Slayage: The International Journal of Buffy* +, vol. 8, no. 2–3, 2010.

Phipps, Keith. "*Doctor Who*: 'The Rebel Flesh'." *AV Club*, 21 March 2001.

Picart, Caroline Joan S. and John Edgar Browning. *Speaking of Monsters: A Teratological Anthology*. Palgrave Macmillan, 2012.

Primiano, Leonard Norman. "'I Wanna Do Bad Things With You': Fantasia on Themes of American Religion from the Title Sequence of HBO's *True Blood*." *God in the Details: American Religion in Popular Culture*, edited by Eric Michael Mazur and Kate McCarthy. Routledge, 2011, pp. 41–61.

Prisco, Giulio. *Tales of the Turing Church: Hacking Religion, Enlightening Science, Awakening Technology*, 2nd ed. Independent Publisher, 2020.

Proctor, James D. *Science, Religion, and the Human Experience*. Oxford University Press, 2005.

Rambo, Elizabeth. "'Lessons' for Season Seven of Buffy the Vampire Slayer." *Slayage The International Journal of Buffy* +, vol. 3, no. 3–4, 2004, pp. 11–12.

Rambo, Shelly. "Refiguring Wounds in the Afterlife (of Trauma)." *Carnal Hermeneutics*, edited by Richard Kearney and Brian Treanor. Fordham University Press, 2015, pp. 263–278.

Rastogi, Nina Shen. "Why Does the Night King Want to Destroy 'Memory' on *Game of Thrones*?" *Close Reads*, 23 April 2019.

Reitter, James. "Religion, Blasphemy, and Tradition in the Films of Lucio Fulci." *Zombies Are Us: Essays on the Humanity of the Walking Dead*, edited by Christopher M. Moreman and Cory James Rushion. McFarland, 2011, pp. 100–111.

Rich, Sarah C. "The Deerstalker: Where Sherlock Holmes' Popular Image Came From." *Smithsonian Magazine*, 2012.

Ricketts, Jeremy R. "Varieties of Conversion: Spiritual Transformation in the Buffyverse." *Joss Whedon and Religion: Essays on an Angry Atheist's Explorations of the Sacred*, edited by Anthony R. Mills, John W. Morehead, & J. Ryan Parker. McFarland, 2013, pp. 11–27.

Robbins, Jeffrey W. *Radical Theology: A Vision for Change*. Indiana University Press, 2016.

Roberts, Tyler. *Encountering Religion: Responsibility and Criticism after Secularism*. Columbia University Press, 2017.

Rodkey, Christopher D. and Jordan E. Miller, eds. *The Palgrave Handbook of Radical Theology*, Palgrave, 2018.

Romano, Aja. "A Petition to Remake Game of Thrones' 8th Season Offers a Revealing Glimpse of Wider Fandom Backlash." *Vox*, 2019.

Rothman, Joshua. "Sympathetic Sci-Fi." *The New Yorker*, 14 July 2011.

Rubenstein, Mary-Jane. *Pantheologies: Gods, Worlds, Monsters*. Columbia University Press, 2018.

Rubenstein, Mary-Jane. *Worlds without End: The Many Lives of the Multiverse*, Columbia University Press, 2014.

Sakal, Gregory J. "No Big Win: Themes of Sacrifice, Salvation, and Redemption." *Buffy the Vampire Slayer and Philosophy: Fear and Trembling in Sunnydale*, edited by James B. South. Open Court, 2003, pp. 239–253.

Sanchez, Gabrielle. "A Complete Timeline of Every Joss Whedon Allegation Controversy." *Vulture*, 12 May, 2021.

Santana, Richard and Gregory Erickson. *Religion and Popular Culture: Rescripting the Sacred*, 2nd ed. McFarland, 2016.

Bibliography 259

Saraiya, Sonia. "*Battlestar Galactica*: 'Flesh and Bone' / 'Tigh Me Up, Tigh Me Down.' *The AV Club*, 2 October 2014.

Saraiya, Sonia. "The Leftovers: Pilot." *The AV Club*, 29 June 2014.

Sartre, Jean Paul. *Being and Nothingness: A Phenomenological Essay on Ontology*. Translated by Hazel E. Barnes. Philosophical Library, 1956.

Sartre, Jean Paul. *No Exit and Three Other Plays*. Translated by Stuart Gilbert. Vintage, 1989.

Schneidau, Herbert N. *Sacred Discontent: The Bible and Western Tradition*. Louisiana State University Press, 1976.

Sconce, Jeffrey. *Haunted Media: Electronic Presence from Telegraphy to Television*. Duke University Press, 2000.

Scott, Suzanne. "Dawn of the Undead Author." *A Companion to Media Authorship*, edited by Jonathan Gray and Derek Johnson. Wiley-Blackwell, 2013, pp. 440–464.

Sexton, Max and Dominic Lees. *Seeing It on Television: Televisuality in the Contemporary US 'High-End' Series*. Bloomsbury Academic, 2021.

Sherwood, Harriet. "Robot Priest Unveiled in Germany to Mark 500 Years Since Reformation." *The Guardian*, 30 May 2017.

Simkin, Stephen. "'You Hold Your Gun Like a Sissy Girl': Firearms and Anxious Masculinity in Buffy the Vampire Slayer." *Slayage: The Online International Journal of Buffy* +, vol. 3, no. 3–4, 2004.

Singh, Julietta. *Unthinking Mastery: Dehumanism and Decolonial Entanglements*. Duke University Press, 2017.

Singler, Beth. "An Introduction to Artificial Intelligence and Religion for the Religious Studies Scholar." *Implicit Religion: Journal for the Critical Study of Religion*, vol. 20, no. 3, 2017, pp. 215–231.

Smith, Barbara Herrnstein. *Natural Reflections: Human Cognition at the Nexus of Science and Religion*. Yale University Press, 2009.

Smith, Christian. *What Is a Person?: Rethinking Humanity, Social Life, and the Moral Good from the Person Up*. University of Chicago Press, 2010.

Smith, J.Z. "The New Liberal Arts." 1986.

South, James. *Buffy the Vampire Slayer and Philosophy: Fear and Trembling in Sunnydale*, edited by South, James B. Open Court Editions, 2003.

South, James. "On the Philosophical Consistency of Season Seven: Or, 'It's Not About Right, Not About Wrong…'" *Slayage: The International Journal of Buffy* +, vol. 13–14, 2004.

South, James B. and Kimberly S. Engels, eds. *Westworld and Philosophy: If You Go Looking for the Truth, Get the Whole Thing*. John Wiley & Sons, 2018.

Spier, Fred. *Big History and the Future of Humanity*. Wiley-Blackwell, 2011.

Spivak, Gayatri. C. "Translator's Preface," *Of Grammatology* by Jacques Derrida. Translated by G. C. Spivak, Johns Hopkins University Press, 1976, pp. ix–lxxxvi.

Stafford, Nikki. *Bite Me! An Unofficial Guide to the World of Buffy the Vampire Slayer*. ECW, 2002.

Stephens, Martha. "Fandom Weddings Doctor Who as Religion, Ritual, and, Capital." Unpublished seminar paper. 2018.

Stoker, Bram. *The New Annotated Dracula*, edited by Leslie S. Klinger. W.W. Norton & Company, 2008.

Stoy, Jennifer. "Or Great Zeitgeist and Bad Faith: An Introduction to *Battlestar Galactica*." *Investigating Battlestar Galactica: Flesh, Spirit, and Steel*, edited by Jennifer Stoy. I.B. Tauris, 2010, pp. 1–36.

260 *Bibliography*

Stoy, Jennifer and Roz Kaveney, eds. *Investigating Battlestar Galactica: Flesh, Spirit, and Steel.* I.B. Tauris, 2010.

Styers, Randall. *Making Magic: Religion, Magic, and Science in the Modern World.* Oxford University Press, 2004.

Suvin, Darko. *Positions and Presuppositions in Science Fiction,* Palgrave, 1988.

Taylor, Mark C. *After God.* University of Chicago Press, 2009.

Taylor, Mark C. *Deconstructing Theology.* Crossroad Pub, 1982.

Taylor, Mark C. *Erring: A Postmodern A/theology.* University of Chicago Press, 1984.

Taylor, Mark C. *The Moment of Complexity: Emerging Network Culture.* University of Chicago Press, 2001.

Taylor, Mark C. *Nots (Religion and Postmodernism.* University of Chicago Press, 1993.

Thompson, Hamish. ""She's Not Your Mother Anymore, She's a Zombie!": Zombies, Values, and Personal Identity." *The Undead and Philosophy: Chicken Soup for the Soulless,* edited by Richard Greene and K. Silem Mohammad. Open Court, 2006, pp. 27–37.

Thweatt-Bates, Jeanine. *Cyborg Selves: A Theological Anthropology of the Posthuman.* Routledge, 2016.

Tillich, Paul. [1957] *Dynamics of Faith.* Perennial Classics, 2001.

Tobias, Scott. "*Westworld* Season 3 is Here." *The New York Times,* 13 March 2020.

Todorov, Tzvetan. *The Fantastic: A Structural Approach to a Literary Genre.* Cornell University Press, 1975.

Toswell, M. J. "The Tropes of Medievalism." *Studies in Medievalism XVII: Defining Medievalism(s),* edited by Karl Fugelso. Boydell & Brewer, 2009, pp. 68–76.

Tranter, Kieran. "Her Brain Was Full of Superstitious Nonsense': Modernism and the Failure of the Divine in *Doctor Who.*" *Religion and Doctor Who: Time and Relative Dimensions in Faith,* edited by Andrew Crome and James McGrath. Cascade, 2013, pp. 131–144.

Umstead, R. Thomas. "Paranormal Programming: It Lives." *Multichannel News,* 9 September, 2019.

Vries, Hent de and Samuel Weber, eds. *Religion and Media.* Stanford University, 2002.

Wagner, C. Peter. *Warfare Prayer: How to Seek God's Power and Protection in the Battle to Build His Kingdom.* Regal Books, 1992.

Wagner, Rachel. *Godwired: Religion, Ritual, and Virtual Reality.* Routledge, 2011.

Wardly, K. Jason. "Divine and *Human Nature*: Incarnation and Kenosis in *Doctor Who.*" *Religion and Doctor Who: Time and Relative Dimensions in Faith,* edited by Andrew Crome and James McGrath. Cascade, 2013, pp. 32–44.

Wilcox, Rhonda. *Why Buffy Matters: The Art of Buffy the Vampire Slayer.* I. B. Tauris, 2005.

Wilcox, Rhonda and David Lavery. *Fighting the Forces: What's at Stake in Buffy the Vampire Slayer.* Rowman and Littlefield, 2002.

Wilcox, Rhonda V., Tanya R. Cochran, Cynthea Masson, and David Lavery. *Reading Joss Whedon.* Syracuse University Press, 2014.

Williams, Raymond. *Television: Technology and Cultural Form.* Routledge, 2003.

Wilson, Jonathon. "Warrior Nun review – This Is a Lot Better Than You Think It'll Be." Readysteadycut.com, 1 July 2020.

Winquist, Charles. *Desiring Theology.* University of Chicago Press, 1995.

Winslade, Jason Lawton. "'Oh…My…Goddess': Witchcraft, Magick and Theology in *Buffy the Vampire Slayer.*" *Joss Whedon and Religion: Essays on an Angry Atheist's Explorations of the Sacred,* edited by Anthony R. Mills, John W. Morehead, & J. Ryan Parker. McFarland, 2013, pp. 51–66.

Winston, Diana. *Small Screen, Big Picture: Television and Lived Religion.* Baylor University Press, 2009.

Bibliography 261

Wright, David C. Jr. and Allan W. Austin, eds. *Space and Time: Essays on Visions of History in Science Fiction and Fantasy Television*. McFarland, 2010.

Žižek, Slavoj. "Return of the Living Dead." *iai news*, 28 Oct. 2019, https://iai.tv/articles/return-of-the-living-dead-slavoj-zizek-auid-1261.

Žižek, Slavoj. *The Fragile Absolute or Why Is the Christian Legacy Worth Fighting For?* Verso, 2000.

Žižek, Slavoj and John Milbank. *The Monstrosity of Christ: Paradox or Dialectic?* MIT Press, 2009.

Index

Note: Page numbers followed by "n" denote endnotes.

Abbott, Stacey 76–78, 80
Ahmed, Sara 199
aliens 19–20, 28, 29, 30, 45, 49, 92, 98–99, 154, 166n1
Altered Carbon (television series) 98, 122, 123, 125, 178, 232
Althaus-Reid, Marcella 225
Altizer, Thomas J.J. xiv, 73, 144, 218, 224, 230, 232, 236–237, 248
Andriano, Joseph 153
Angel (television series) 75n7, 134, 135
Antonsson, Linda 207–208
apocalypse 78–79, 113, 235
Asay, Paul 29
atheism 10, 25, 37, 38, 47, 60, 61, 73, 90, 172, 216, 230
Attias, Bernard 225
Auerbach, Nina 74
Augst, Thomas 190–191, 227
Augustine 133–134, 161, 242–243
Aune, Kristine 75n5

Badiou, Alaine 162–163
Baudrillard, Jean 141–142
Battlestar Galactica (television series) 4, 19–20, 21, 25, 30–31, 35, 51, 80; Cylons 30, 31–32, 32–34, 36–37, 116, 125, 148n6; Gaius Baltar 25; Number Six 25, 33, 36; President Roslin 36; S4E01: "Razor" 171–172; Sharon "Boomer" Valerii 36; William Adama 34, 35–37
Beal, Timothy 150, 156
Berger, James 78–79
Berger, Peter 8–9, 10–11, 165
Bersanti, Sam 119
Bible, the 39, 42–43, 44, 154, 165, 169–170, 171, 183–184, 217; Genesis 176, 197; Exodus 55, 56; Isaiah 60;

Mark 103; John 56; Romans 233n3; Revelation 150, 154, 235; Vampire 192n1
Big History 51
Black Mirror (television series) 125, 141
body 66, 76–77, 98, 106–111, 115–117, 121–122, 123, 127, 130, 133–134, 137–141, 147n1, 163
books 15, 21, 41, 111; adaptation 184–186, 205, 212; canon 183–189, 208–211, 241; identity 169–172; preservation and immorality 178–180, 190–192
Boorstin, Daniel 7
Borges, Jorge Luis 176–177
Bostrom, Nick 141
Buddhism 248
Buffy the Vampire Slayer (television series) 4, 13, 20–21, 57–58, 108, 134, 236; Angel 57, 59, 61–62, 74n4, 75n5, 135; Anya 59, 115, 218; Cordelia Chase 202–203; Dawn Summers 59, 109–110, 135; Dracula 61–64; Drusilla 60–61; First, the 74n4, 155–156, 217, 237; Master, the 59, 60; Razor 109–110; Rupert Giles 57, 58, 63–64, 175; S1E01: "Welcome to the Hellmouth" 58–59; S1E02: "The Harvest" 176; S1E12: "Prophecy Girl" 60, 200; S2E01: "When She Was Bad" 200–202; S2E10: "What's my line, Part 2" 60–61; S2E15: "School Hard" 60; S2E22: "Becoming, Part 2" 61; S3E10: "Amends" 74n4; S5E01: "Buffy vs. Dracula" 62–64; S5E12: "Checkpoint" 59; S5E14: "Crush" 135; S5E16: "The Body 115; S5E22: "The Gift" 59–60, 63, 75n5, 106; S6E01 & 2: "Bargaining" Parts 1&2 108–110; S6E13: "Dead Things" 121; S6E17: "Normal Again"

264 *Index*

249n1; S7E01: "Lessons" 59; S7E05: "Selfless" 219; S7E07: "Conversations with Dead People" 216–217; S7E16: "The Storyteller" 236; S7E22: "Chosen" 217–218, 237–238; Spike 57, 60–61, 106, 109, 134–135, 219; Willow Rosenberg 57, 60, 108, 212; Xander Harris 57

Buse, Peter 97

Butler, Matt 104

Butler, Rose 206

Caputo, John 42, 52, 144

Carlson, Thomas A. 125–126, 145, 221, 245

Carpenter, Charisma 203–204

Carroll, Noah 153

Cavell, Stanley 154

chaos 41, 87, 145–146, 150, 221, 237–238, 248

Chibnall, Chris 241

Christianity: baptism 66, 82; cathedral 76–77; church 246–247; crucifixion 18, 60, 73–74, 82, 87, 111, 114, 128–129, 142–143, 231–233; devil 156–157, 159; eucharist 67, 106–108, 111, 114, 232; God 55–56, 163; idols 244; interpretation of 32, 69–70; myth 106; principals 28, 46, 66–68; Reformation 92–93; relics 101; religious signifiers 37–38, 56, 59–60, 68–69, 71–74, 84, 135, 230

Clarke, Arthur C. 102

Cohen, Jeffrey Jerome 53, 56–57, 78, 152–153, 159, 161

Copson, Andrew 28

COVID xvi, 7, 90, 200–201, 204–205, 246–248

Cox, J. Renée 134

Crome, Andrew 46, 47, 235

Croskery, Patrick 120

Crucifixion *see* Christianity

cyborg 20, 25, 119–122, 125, 127–128, 137

Davies, Russell T. 18, 42, 47, 209–210, 240–241

Death of God 10, 36, 43, 70, 73–74, 144, 230, 247, 248

DeCou, Jessica 86

Derrida, Jacques 41, 42, 111, 235, 246

Djawadi, Ramin 213

Doctor Who (television series) 4, 19–21, 31, 44–46, 51–52, 102, 209, 239, 243–244;

Amy Pond 130, 131, 228–229, 245; Cassandra 91; Clara Oswald 110–111, 127–128; Clive Finch 48–49; Daleks 50; "The Day of the Doctor" 213; Doctor, the 47, 48, 49, 52, 91, 116–117, 223; Face of Boe 17, 18; Gangers 130, 131, 133; Jo Grant 45; Martha Jones 17, 18, 46; Master, the 46–47; Moffat, Steven 47, 210–211, 240; Novice Hame 17; Rose Tyler 47–48, 49, 50–51, 91, 92, 99; S1E01: "Rose" 47–48, 49–50; S1E02: "The End of the World" 81, 91, 222–223; S1E03: "The Unquiet Dead" 98–99, 101; S1E12: "Bad Wolf" 50; S1E13: "The Parting of the Ways" 50, 51; S2E01: "New Earth" 91–92; S2E02: "Tooth and Claw" 52; S2E03: "School Reunion" 243–234; S2E08: "Impossible Planet" 157; S2E09: "Satan Pit" 156–159; S3E02: "The Shakespeare Code" 103; S3E03: "Gridlock" 17–18, 91, 114; S3E08: "Human Nature" 116; S3E09: "The Family of Blood" 116; S3E10: "Blink" 241, 244; S4E02: "The Fires of Pompeii" 239; S4E08: "Silence in the Library" 177–179; S4E09: "Forest of the Dead" 177; S5E12: "The Pandorica Opens" 248; S6E04: "The Doctor's Wife" 128–129; S6E05: "Rebel Flesh" 130; S6E06: "The Almost People" 130, 131; S6E07: "A Good Man Goes to War" 131–132, 147n2; S6E11: "The God Complex" 228–229; S7E05: "The Angels Take Manhattan" 235; S7E07: "Rings of Akhaten" 223; S7E13: "The Name of the Doctor" 110–112; S8E01: "Deep Breath" 127; S10E06: "Extremis" 141; Sarah Jane Smith 243–244; TARDIS 48, 50, 81, 110–111, 129, 198–199; Time War 18, 50, 209, 241; Vashta Nerada 177–179

Dollhouse (television series) 20, 21, 136, 137, 238–239; Actives 135, 136; Alpha 138–140; Boyd Langton 136; Echo 136, 137–139, 238–239; S1E01: "Ghost" 123; S1E02: "Target" 137, 138, 238; S1E03: "Stage Fright" 138; S1E04: "Gray Hour" 141, 239; S1E05: "True Believer" 138; S1E06: "Man on the Street" 140; S1E12: "Omega" 138–140; S2E08: "A Love Supreme" 137; S2E13: "Epitaph Two" 140–141; Topher Brink 136, 139, 238

doubles 122–123, 130, 131

Dracula (novel) 20, 53, 55–57, 58
Dracula (television miniseries) 70; S1E01: "The Rules of the Beast" 70–71, 72; S1E02: "Blood Vessel" 71; S1E03: "The Dark Compass" 71–72
dragons 149–152, 164–165
During, Simon 7

Easter 84–85, 87, 88–90
Einstein, Albert 243, 245
Eliade, Mircea 10, 144, 145–146, 237
Engstrom, Erika 82–83, 93n1
Epiphany Award 18
Eucharist *see* Christianity

fan studies 12–15, 45, 185–190, 194–199, 205–214
fantasy 149, 151, 170
Firefly (television series) 19–20, 30–31, 37–38, 136; Espenson, Jane 38; Jayne Cobb 42–44, 161; Malcolm Reynolds 39–40, 41, 43, 160–161; Mudders 42–43; Reavers 159–161; River Tam 42, 44, 221–222; S1E02: "The Train Job" 39–40, 41; S1E03: "Bushwhacked" 159–162; S1E04: "Jaynestown" 42; S1E14: "Objects in Space" 40–41; *Serenity* (film) 38; "Serenity" (pilot episode) 38; Shepherd Book 39–40, 41, 42–44, 160–161; Zoe Washburne 40, 161
Foucault, Michel 4, 14, 150, 187
Frankenstein (novel) 26, 32
free will 63, 120–121, 125, 133, 173, 220
Frei, Hans 171
Freud, Sigmund 122–123, 130, 153–154, 165, 246

Game of Thrones (television series) 4, 20–21, 149, 151, 182, 184–185, 205–209, 213; Bran Stark 183, 186; Citadel Library 180–182, 187; Jon Snow 186; S6E10: "Winds of Winter" 180–182; S7E07: "The Dragon and the Wolf" 150; S8E01: "Winterfell" 182; S8E02:" A Knight of the Seven Kingdoms" 182–183, 208; Samwell Tarly 180–182, 183, 186–187; Three-Eyed Raven 182
García, Elio 207–208
ghosts 20, 97–106
Giles, David 197–198
Gilmore, David D. 153
Gilmour, Michael J. 76
Good Omens (television series) 230; S1E03: "Hard Times" 230–232

Gordon, Avery 97
Graham, Elaine 2, 5, 26, 53, 64, 99, 159
Gray, Jonathan 195, 207
Greenblatt, Stephen 101, 103

Halberstam, J. Jack 248
Hamilton, William 230
Hartman, Geoffrey 170
Harvey, Graham 9, 68, 214
Hawk, Julie 140, 238
Hayles, Katherine N. 126
Hedrick, Charles 150
Hegel, Georg 162
Heidegger, Martin 41, 104, 162, 219–220
Hell 58, 62, 81, 110, 142, 145, 157, 236–237
heresy 132; Gnosticism 98, 103, 138
Hill, Annette 105
Hills, Matt 196–197, 199, 209–210, 239–240
Hollinger, Veronica 57–58

implicit religion 68, 147n3
Islam 52, 124, 137, 171, 228

Jabès, Edmond 111
Jameson, Fredric 26, 35, 102–103, 149
Jenkins, Henry 14, 196, 214
Jindra, Michael 198
Jones, Tim 228

Kagan, Shelly 116–117
Kass, Leon 125
Kearney, Richard 53, 111, 125, 155, 165
Keetley, Dawn 79–81
Kermode, Frank 235
Kieckhefer, Richard 198–199
Kierkegaard, Soren 75n6
Kiyani, Raphael 48–49
Kull, Anne 122
Kurzweil, Ray 123
Kustritz, Anne 126–127

Latour, Bruno 158–159
Lees, Dominic 113
Leftovers, The (television series) 21, 112–113, 156; Book of Kevin 192–193n1; Nora Durst 113–114; S1E06: "Guest" 113–114; S1E10: 'The Prodigal Son Returns" 114
Liedl, Janice 31
Lessard, John 225
Levinas, Emmanuel 73, 220
Levi-Strauss, Claude 152

266   *Index*

libraries 173–183, 187, 190–192, 193n4
Livingston, Ira 102
Lucretius 115
Luther, Martin 93, 124, 170

MacCulloch, Diarmaid 86
magic 16, 45–47, 101–102, 149, 151–152, 158, 159
Mangan, Lucy 70
Manifest (television series) 100, 102, 175, 233n3
Marrati, Paola 234
Marriot, McKim 227
Masterpasqua, Frank 237
McCutcheon, Mark A. 175
McCutcheon, Russell T. 9, 199
McGrath, James 28, 45–46
McLaren, Scott 136
McLaughlin, Thomas 196
McLevy, Alex 182, 183
Mendelsohn, Farah 26–27
Metaxas, Eric 93
Midnight Mass (television miniseries) 53, 74n4, 166n2, 166n3, 233n4
Miller, Liz Shannon 143
Miller, Paul D. (aka DJ Spooky) 226
Mills, C. Wright 8
Mincheva, Dilyana 224–225
Mittell, Jason 2, 5, 12, 235, 245
monsters 20–21, 64, 80, 97, 130, 150, 152, 159, 165; as gods 155, 162; as humans 160–161
monster theory 152–154
Moravec, Hans 139–140
Morrow, James 30
Mowen, Thomas 105
Mulhall, Stephen 170
Murray, Noel 80, 87

Nancy, Jean-Luc 172–173
Newton, Isaac 243
Nietzsche, Friedrich 80, 90, 138, 144, 218, 236–237
Night of the Living Dead (film) 53, 78
nothingness 21, 38, 104, 155–156, 161–162, 183, 218, 219–222, 223–224, 230

Ochse, Weston 192
Once Upon a Time (television series) 172–173; S4E08: "Smash the Mirror" 173
Opam, Kofi 65–66
O'Reilly, Bill 87
Orphan Black 147n2
Orsi, Robert 9, 101–102, 106

Outlander (television series) 242; S5E05: "Perpetual Adoration" 242

Paradise Lost 121
Parfit, Derek 127–128, 131
Perdigao, Lisa 238–239
Perna, A. Phyllis 237
Phipps, Keith 130
Plato 133, 156, 171
Poniewozik, James 31, 247–248
posthuman 4–7, 11, 20, 92, 122–123, 126–127, 136, 140, 145, 227, 238
Primiano, Leonard 66, 69–70, 107, 218

queer 74, 224, 225

radical theology 10, 18, 36, 90, 137, 144, 145, 164, 199, 215–216, 220; Christian Atheism 142–143; divine absence 216–218, 229–230, 233, 234; divine failure 51–52; weakness of God 228–229
Rastogi, Nina Shen 183
Reality television 104–105
Reitter, James 76, 78, 86
resurrection 59–61, 82, 85–88, 90, 100, 103, 116, 131, 163
ritual 30, 68, 76–77, 109, 158, 160, 230
Robbins, Jeffrey 36, 230
Roberts, Tyler 237
Rothman, Joshua 224
Rubenstein, Mary Jane 234

Sakal, Gregory 60
Saraiya, Sonia 113
Sartre, Jean-Paul 161, 218, 220
Savitsky, Amy 104–105
Schneidau, Herbert 165, 217
Scholem, Gershom 218
science fiction (SF) 26–27, 30, 51, 122, 125, 132, 170, 246–247
Sconce, Jeffrey 104
secularization theory 8–9, 26, 45
Sense8 (television series) 224–225; S1E10: "What is Human" 227; S2E01: "Happy F*cking New Year" 225–226
Serres, Michel 145
Sexton, Max 113
Shakespeare, William 103, 121, 236–237; *Hamlet* 103–104
Singler, Beth 124
Sloterdijk, Peter 199–200
Smith, Barbara Herrnstein 100
Smith, Christian 126
Smith, J.Z. 2, 145–146, 237

Socrates 171
South, James 119, 217
Spivak, Gayatri 134
Star Trek (television franchise) 19, 28–29, 38, 197–198; James T. Kirk 28; Jean-Luc Picard 28; S3E23: "All Our Yesterdays" 174; Spock 29–30
Star Wars (films) 27–28
Stein, Colleigh 21, 131, 182, 195, 197, 200
Stevens, Martha 7–8
Stoker, Bram *see Dracula*
Stott, Andrew 97
Stoy, Jennifer 35
Styers, Randall 16, 152, 159
Suvin, Darko 26

Taylor, Charles 244–245
Taylor, Mark C. 44, 101, 126, 170, 193n2, 227, 247
Thomas, Keith 103
Thweatt-Bates, Janine 122, 137
Tilich, Paul 90, 230
time 21, 34, 143, 222–223, 239–240, 242–243
Time Machine, The (novel) 26, 51
time travel 21, 48, 49–51, 110–111, 170, 240–241, 242–246
Todorov, Tzvetan 105–106
Toswell, M.J. 151
Tranter, Kieran 36, 51–52
True Blood (television series) 4, 20, 64, 68, 106–107, 162–163; Ball, Alan 65; Bill Compton 19, 68–70, 107, 162; Godric 163–164; Reverend Steve Newlin 66, 67; S1E01: "Strange Love" 65–66; S1E06: "Cold Ground" 19, 68–69, 106–107; S2E09: "I Will Rise Up" 163; S2E11: "Frenzy" 218; Sookie Stackhouse 19, 66–67, 87–88, 106–107, 163; Tara Thornton 66–67, 107; Vampire Bible 192n1
Tyson, Neil Degrasse 141
Twilight Zone, The (television series): S1E08: "Time Enough to Last" 191–192

Valenzano, Joseph 82–83, 93–94n1
vampires 20, 53–55, 55–75, 76, 79, 106–108, 162–164, 218–219
Vydrin, Eugene 178–179

Wagner, Rachel 14, 190
Walking Dead, The (television series) 4, 14–15, 20, 79–81; Andrea 85–87, 94n3; Carl Grimes 81, 86, 89–90; Carol Peletier 84; Dog 94n2; Jesus 88; Michonne 86, 89; Milton 85–86; Morgan 82; Rick Grimes 80–82, 84, 89; S1E01: "Days Gone Bye" 81–82; S2E01: "What Lies Ahead" 82–84, 124–125; S3E16: "Welcome to the Tombs" 84–88; S6E15: "East" 88; S8E14: "Still Gotta Mean Something" 88–89; S10E04: "The Whisperers" 90; Saviors 88
Wardley, K. Jason 116
Warfare Prayer 154
Warrior Nun 164–165
Waterhouse, Ruth 153
Weber, Max 244
Westworld (television series) 4, 11, 20, 21, 98, 119–120, 128; Arnold 143–144; Bernard 118, 142–144; church 143–146; Dolores 118–119, 122, 143–144; Forge, the 179–180; Hosts 125, 135, 142–143; Rehoboam 147; Robert Ford 121; S1E01: "The Original" 118–119; S1E08: "Trace Decay" 142; S1E09: "The Well-Tempered Clavier" 142–145; S1E10: "The Bicameral Mind" 121; S3E01: "Parce Domine" 146–147; S3E05: "Genre" 147; William (the Man in Black) 121
Whedon, Joss 38, 39, 42, 75n4, 134, 203–204, 235
Wicca 75n5
Williams, Raymond 7
Wilson, Jonathan 164
Winslade, Jason 60, 75n5
Winquist, Charles 136
Winston, Diana 6

The X-Files (television series) 98

Yixuan, Linji 248

Žižek, Slavoj 53, 70, 114, 137, 141, 162, 224
zombies 20, 53, 76–94

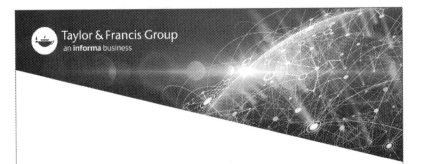

Printed in the United States
by Baker & Taylor Publisher Services